Master of Magic™

The Official Strategy Guide

NOW AVAILABLE FROM PRIMA

Computer Game Books

The 7th Guest:
    The Official Strategy Guide
Aces Over Europe:
    The Official Strategy   Guide
Aegis: Guardian of the Fleet—
    The Official Strategy Guide
Betrayal at Krondor:
    The Official Strategy Guide
CD-ROM Games Secrets, Volume 1
Computer Adventure Games Secrets
DOOM Battlebook
DOOM II: The Official Strategy Guide
Dracula Unleashed:
    The Official Strategy Guide & Novel
Front Page Sports Baseball '94:
    The Official Playbook
Harpoon II: The Official Strategy Guide
Lemmings:
    The Official Companion (with disk)
Master of Orion: The Official Strategy Guide
Microsoft Flight Simulator:
    The Official Strategy Guide
Microsoft Golf: The Official Strategy Guide
Microsoft Space Simulator:
    The Official Strategy Guide
Might and Magic Compendium:
    The Authorized Strategy Guide
    for Games I, II, III, and IV
Myst: The Official Strategy Guide
Outpost: The Official Strategy Guide
Pagan: Ultima VIII—
    The Ultimate Strategy Guide
Panzer General: The Official Strategy Guide
Prince of Persia: The Official Strategy Guide
Quest for Glory:
    The Authorized Strategy Guide
Rebel Assault: The Official Insider's Guide
Return to Zork Adventurer's Guide
Shadow of the Comet:
    The Official Strategy Guide
Sherlock Holmes, Consulting Detective:
    The Unauthorized Strategy Guide

Sid Meier's Civilization,
    or Rome on 640K a Day
Sid Meier's Colonization:
    The Official Strategy Guide
SimCity 2000: Power, Politics, and Planning
SimEarth: The Official Strategy Guide
SimFarm Almanac:
    The Official Guide to SimFarm
SimLife: The Official Strategy Guide
SSN-21 Seawolf:
    The Official Strategy Guide
Strike Commander:
    The Official Strategy Guide and
    Flight School
Stunt Island: The Official Strategy Guide
SubWar 2050: The Official Strategy Guide
TIE Fighter: The Official Strategy Guide
Ultima: The Avatar Adventures
Ultima VII and Underworld:
    More Avatar Adventures
Under a Killing Moon:
    The Official Strategy Guide
Wing Commander I and II:
    The Ultimate Strategy Guide
X-COM UFO Defense:
    The Official Strategy Guide
X-Wing: The Official Strategy Guide

How to Order:

For information on quantity discounts contact the publisher: Prima Publishing, P.O. Box 1260BK, Rocklin, CA 95677-1260; (916) 632-4400. On your letterhead include information concerning the intended use of the books and the number of books you wish to purchase. For individual orders, turn to the back of the book for more information.

Master of Magic™

The Official Strategy Guide

Alan Emrich,
Petra Schlunk,
and
Tom E. Hughes, Jr.

Prima Publishing™

Secrets of the Games is an imprint of Prima Publishing, Rocklin, California 95677.

Publisher, Entertainment: Roger Stewart
Managing Editor: Paula Munier Lee
Acquisitions Editor: Hartley Lesser / Ed Dille
Creative Director, Secrets of the Games: Rusel DeMaria
Project Editor: Brett Skogen
Cover Production Coordinator: Anne Flemke
Copy Editor: Kelley Mitchell
Technical Reviewer: Ray Pfeifer
Book Design and Layout: Stewart A. Williams
Cover Design Adaptation: Page Design, Inc.

ISBN: 1-55958-722-9
Library of Congress Catalog Card Number: 94-69111
Printed in the United States of America
95 96 97 98 BB 10 9 8 7 6 5 4 3 2

Table of Contents

Section II:
The Duel-It-Yourself Ruling Wizard Kit...17

What Makes You So Special?...19

A Leader of Men (or Trolls or Klackons)...33

Table of Contents

Spell Books: The Write Stuff...55

Section III:
Spell Binding...63

Gray Matters...65

White On...73

9

Black Off, Jack!...91

10

Red Hots...109

11

Green Genes...127

Table of Contents

12
The Blues...145

13
Seeing Rainbows...165

16

Urban Planning...221

Section V:
Who Goes There?...239

17

Vast, Unending Armies...241

18

Heroes...257

19

Magic Items...273

Section VI: Magic & Might...279

20

Normal Combat: A Drop of Blood, A Load of Dead and Thou...281

21

Magic In Combat...321

Table of Contents

22

Putting It All Together: Forming Armies...335

23

Post Combat...343

Section VII:
Global Considerations...347

24

Large Scale Spell Casting...349

25

Diplomacy or "Mirror, Mirror on the Wall..."...359

26

Random Events...381

27

Early Strategies...387

Table of Contents

28

Odds & Ends...395

Appendices...403

A
The Next Turn Sequence of Play...405

B
The Making of a Computer Player Wizard...407

C
Monsters & Treasure...415

D
Translating the Runes...423

E
Neutral Cities...425

F
Combat Tables...427

G
Dispelling in Combat...443

List of Tables

List of Tables

Acknowledgments

As we complete this book circa Christmas 1994, there is no shortage of people to thank. Primarily, thanks belong to *Computer Gaming World* magazine, where Alan Emrich labors. While Alan is in "book mode," the number of articles he can manage for that prestigious publication is limited. So, too, thanks are due to the new Interchange network developed by Ziff-Davis, Alan's new employer. They took him knowing that this book remained to be written.

Naturally, we must thank SimTex's terrific people. Steve Barcia and his wife, Grissel, to whom the word "gracious" simply isn't big enough. Also generous with their time and advice were the Barcia's fellow programmers, Ken Burd and Jim Cowlishaw. This is the team that wrote the code that made the game that MicroProse published that you bought that we wrote this book about that Prima published that lives in the house that Jack built.

While we must also thank the many gamers who've discussed *Master of Magic* over the various bulletin boards online (they helped keep this tome focused on what players were asking about), it was our proofreading team that always earns special kudos. Drew Fundenberg, in particular, deserves a campaign ribbon for his efforts here. He was the only reader to cross the finish line and make it through every chapter. This Harvard educator might teach probability and game theory, but he's pretty good in practice as well

as in theory. If you see Piemax online, say "Hi" to Drew for us!

Otmar Schlunk, too, deserves to be singled out. Sure, he's Petra's brother, but he's also a devoted game analyst, designer, and programmer. Even while laboring on an original role-playing game with his sister, he found the time to play *Master of Magic* and critique chapters hot off our word processors. That kind of flash feedback is invaluable.

Other vaunted proofreaders include Mark "skulker" Carroll (who has been working with Alan on several books, now), Michael Hinde ("our man in Sweden," who has also helped Alan with several previous strategy guides for Prima), and Leanne Pike (a friend of Tom Hughes' and avid gamer).

Besides the authors' extensive labors, the reason this book was not rushed and was given the time it needed to include the level of quality material presented herein is that those at Prima defend the ideal of quality over speed. God bless Ben Dominitz, Roger Stuart, Paula Munier Lee, Ed Dille, and our editor Brett Skogen, all from Prima, who stood by our triumvirate of writers. If we thought we were crazy taking on such a large book project, they were equally crazy being so supportive and backing us up all the way. Their devotion to quality in this make-a-fast-buck world is why we enjoy writing for Prima so much.

Alan Emrich, Petra Schlunk,
and Tom E. Hughes, Jr.

Section 1

In a Mana of Speaking

How To Use This Book

Most people do not read computer game strategy guides for their health. However, the exercise you'll get lifting this one up and down while you pore over what is, arguably, one of the finest computer strategy games yet devised, might increase your health and hit points while you learn. As this guide's girth suggests, the authors have spared no effort to be as thorough as possible.

Is This Book Really Necessary?

You might think, after reading the approximately 200 pages included in the *Master of Magic* instruction manual and spell book, that there is little left to say about the game. How wrong that assumption is! Due to the nature of computer game manual production, which is often severely limited by space and deadlines, much information simply could not be included in the *Master of Magic* game package—in particular, the detailed formulas and analyses that constitute the bulk of this tome. In addition, this book was kept current with the myriad of changes made to *Master of Magic* during its final weeks of playtesting and development (which occurred *after* the manual was sent to the printer) and in the game's subsequent upgrades and patches.

Authors' Assumptions

The authors expect the reader to be adequately familiar with the instruction manual and spell book that accompany the game. It is imperative that you have a working knowledge of the game's documentation, as it is the foundation for the many advanced strategies you'll discover in this guide.

Organization

We have tried to organize this strategy guide in roughly the same manner as the instruction manual. We've broken the information into seven sections: ground work, getting started, spells, the worlds, units, combat, and global considerations.

Die Rolls

Often in this guide, we explain how something occurs in the game based upon probability. We will remark that the computer decides a matter by *rolling a die* (our figurative expression that means the computer simply generates a random number). We abbreviate this probability by using the letter "d" followed by a number indicating the number of *sides* on that die. For example, when the computer generates a random number from 1 to 6, it rolls a d6. When there is a certain percentage chance of an occurrence, the computer rolls a d100, etc.

Terminology

We have used the following terms interchangeably for both descriptive and literary reasons:

Arcane = gray magic
Chaos = red magic
Death = black magic
Life = white magic
Nature = green magic
Sorcery = blue magic
Attack Strength = swords
Defense Strength = shields
Archery Ranged Attack = bows
Heavy Ranged Attack = rocks
Magic Ranged Attack = fireballs
Resistance Strength = crosses
Hits Per Figure = hearts
Fantastic unit = summoned unit
Dispel = used as a noun to signify any of the Dispel Magic, Disenchant or Disjunction spells

Onward!

In the words of Yogi Berra, "It's *déjà vu* all over again."

Many of you reading this guide will be familiar with similar MicroProse strategy game offerings including, no doubt, *Master of Orion*

and *Civilization* and may have read Alan Emrich's books from Prima on these games. Well, here we go again! Prepare yourself, worthy apprentice, for we are about to unlock the secrets that will make you, truly, the Master of Magic!

The Ultimate READ.ME File

"A life spent making mistakes is not only more honorable but more useful than a life spent doing nothing."—George Bernard Shaw

A week after he was assigned the task of writing America's Declaration of Independence, the homesick Thomas Jefferson had made little progress. The story is told that John Adams and Benjamin Franklin dropped by to see how the document was coming along, and learned that not only was the Declaration not finished, it was not yet begun! After Adams, upset by this delay, remarked that the whole Earth was created in only a week, Jefferson sarcastically replied "One day, you must tell me how you did it."

So it was with the writing of the *Master of Magic* manual. Generally, computer game manuals are written at the worst possible time in a game's production cycle: about six weeks before the game is expected to be shipped to stores. Often, this leaves too little time to write, check, rewrite, edit, correct, lay out, proof, correct the page proofs, and lay out the corrections before the manual has to go to the printer (usually about three to four weeks before the game is scheduled to be shipped). While the manual is being created, the game is usually in a state of flux as playtesters provide designers with information they need to make last minute tweaks to the program to improve the play or balance of the game. Even as the manual is being printed, changes to a computer game happen right up until the moment the disks are "mastered" for duplication.

Now, picture such a frenzied writing schedule for creating the epic 200-page manual included with *Master of Magic*. Consider the extra effort it took to cram the composition of those 60,000 words (roughly the size of a typical book!), complete with many tables, into a period of two weeks. So, considering the speed in which the manual was written, the amount of material it covers, the last minute changes that were made to the game, and in response to queries from *Master of Magic* players, we decided to composed a special chapter of errata to make the game's manual as up-to-date and air tight as possible.

Master of Magic

And then, reality set in... We started to note change after change in *Master of Magic*: hundreds more than those printed in the first edition of the game manual. After a while, we were swamped. This chapter became huge in an already too large book, and we couldn't even be sure we had caught everything. (The designers had made so many small changes during pre-release playtesting and over the course of the game's several major patches that even *they* couldn't remember them all! To that end, this book might have an odd mistake or two in it because we could not playtest every conceivable combination or because we trusted the programmers to fix bugs from earlier versions that have remained in the game.)

So we, the authors, decided to incorporate into the text of this book every change we could find. Think of these 400-plus pages as a new manual, pumped up with plenty of extra strategy tips and tabular information. It's not how we wanted to present all of the changes to you, but it is a compromise we simply had to make.

From Here to Victory

From here, we take a bit of literary license and begin with an ending. Allow us to quickly go over your ultimate objective when playing *Master of Magic*: to win (and in this game, there's more than one way to kick staffs and take planes).

3
What You Wand—
To Be The Master of Magic

oe Kennedy, patriarch of the American Kennedy dynasty, is quoted by his famous political offspring as telling them: "You show me a good loser, and I'll show you a loser." Unfortunately, at the outset of a game of *Master of Magic*, you are not born into the same position of privilege as the Kennedys were, so buying a victory is out of the question. Instead, you must prevail in the realms of Arcanus and Myrror the old fashioned way: You have to *earn* it.

Here, we discuss the important pre-game and general strategies for winning *Master of Magic*. While the manual defines the conditions for victory, it is important to begin each game by deciding which of the two victory conditions you will pursue. This is because, as enjoyable as it is to follow the many diverse paths available in the exploration and conquest portion of the game, the best way to ensure victory over the other wizards in the game is by staying focused on the victory condition you're striving for and following our suggestions for obtaining it as rapidly as possible.

Die, Charlatan!

The most direct way of winning the game is through brute force. Eliminating all the other wizards in the game by storming their En-

Figure 3-1. *There's nothing like banishing another wizard.*

chanted Fortresses and banishing them from the game is truly satisfying.

To smooth the path for a military victory, choose your set-up from the options listed below. These will help you generate the strongest possible forces and give you the best possible combat spells.

Wizard Skills

At the beginning of the game you have the option to choose, as some of your spell picks, special wizard skills. Choosing the right skills can enhance your armies and your spell-casting skills in combat. With an eye towards victory through combat, you will find some of the following skills particularly useful:

Alchemy gives all of your normal units magic weapons and a +1 To Hit in combat. It functions as if your cities all have alchemist's guilds, even when they don't. The improved accuracy and the ability to damage creatures with weapon immunity will make your early fighting units far more powerful than they would otherwise be. Since several of the more militaristic races (Gnolls, Klackons, Lizardmen, and Trolls) can't even build alchemist's guilds, this wizard skill is the perfect complement to a militarily oriented game played with such races.

Finally, large armies can be expensive to maintain; having the Alchemy skill also allows you to directly convert your excess mana into gold, without a loss, to support your armies. Once your income is sufficient, you can even lower your mana wand to zero and concentrate all your mana income on research and spell-casting skill, adding mana to your reserve by converting surplus gold instead.

Channeler halves all of your mana upkeep costs and allows you to cast spells in combat without paying the distance penalty (see Chapter 4). This spell is an ideal adjunct for militaristic wizards with a tight mana budget. It's great even if you have a lot of mana since it allows you low maintenance costs on all your summoned creatures and devastating enchantments.

🐲 Chaos Mastery should not be overlooked by militaristic wizards. Since Chaos magic is the most destructive and combat-oriented form of magic, excelling at researching and casting Chaos spells can make your goals much easier to attain. On top of reducing the research and casting costs of Chaos spells, this skill will make any of your brutal enchantments (Great Wasting, Armageddon, Chaos Rift, etc.) twice as difficult to dispel. It also doubles the mana received from Chaos nodes. See Chapter 4 for more details on Chaos Mastery.

🐲 If mana won't be a problem for you, consider the Conjurer skill. This skill makes researching and casting summoning spells 25 percent cheaper percent *and* reduces the upkeep costs of summoned creatures by 25 percent. Conjurer makes it easy for you to create and maintain huge armies of fantastic units. Consider combining this skill with Chaos Mastery (since their discounts are additive).

🐲 Famous: First, this option gets you more, better, and cheaper heroes, mercenaries, and magic items to fight with. Second, the +10 Fame points translate directly to a savings in that amount of gold per turn that would otherwise have gone to *troop* maintenance costs. Early in the game, when money is tight and large armies are impractical to maintain, this skill can be a tremendous edge.

🐲 Myrran is an expensive skill to get, but starting on Myrror means that you can start with one of the special races—Beastmen, Dark Elves, Draconians, Dwarves, or Trolls—and with few (if any) neighbors to impede your early growth. These races tend to have pow-

erful units that are great for building strong armies. Furthermore, Myrror is the only place you can find adamantium, the mineral that, in combination with an alchemist's guild, can make your normal units virtually unstoppable (see Chapter 14 and 16). The biggest caveat to starting on Myrror is that to beat other wizards, you have to find them—and most of your opponents will be on Arcanus. Get to that lower plane as fast as you can; they start off pretty weak down there.

🐲 Warlord gives all of your normal units an extra experience level and allows them to reach ultra-elite status. Experienced units are significantly better than new ones, and having all your troops start at one level higher than they otherwise would is a tremendous advantage, especially at the beginning of the game.

Spell Books

Certain colors of magic lend themselves better to winning battles and, hence, vanquishing other wizards during the ultimate encounter—the one fought at their Enchanted Fortress!

🐲 Red, or Chaos, magic is the strongest combat magic color. This magic type has more destructive and powerful combat spells (Doom Bolt, Disintegrate, Call Chaos, Flame Strike, etc.) than any other. Further, red magic offers an enormous number and variety of fantastic units and devastating global and city enchantments. If it's blood you're seeking, see red.

🐲 Black, or Death, magic also has many strong combat spells (Wrack, Word of Death, Death Spell, Animate Dead, etc.) and wicked overland enchantments (Cursed Lands, Famine, Zombie Mastery, etc.). Death magic units tend to be cheaper to maintain because most cannot heal. This magic type is also the only one that lets you create undead units from fallen opponents.

While the remaining magic colors have combat spells and powerful unit enhancements, their strengths tend to lie in areas not directly related to or supportive of an aggressive military approach.

Races

While no race (save, perhaps, the Halflings) is particularly bad in combat, some races are better for those seeking to wage war offensively. Our philosophy is that the units you obtain early will greatly influence your expansion capabilities. However, it is a race's special units, the production end-line "heavy hitters," who decide if a race can truly wage war offensively.

The races we have found best for conducting wars of annihilation are listed below. See Chapter 5 for our reasons why they are the most militarily useful.

Good Military Races:

Beastmen, Dark Elves, Dwarves, Gnolls, High Men, Klackons, Lizardmen, and Trolls

Spell This!

The more peaceful option for winning is to play *Master of Magic* as a race game. Here, you are striving to learn and cast the Spell of Mastery before any other player does and then to hang on to your empire while waiting for the spell to take effect. After all, once you begin casting the Spell of Mastery, everyone will declare war on you promptly in an effort to prevent you from winning. At that time, batten down the hatches and full steam ahead!

To help ensure that you can win this race while building and maintaining an empire large enough to support your efforts, choose your set-up from the options listed below. They are designed to help you keep your nose clean

Figure 3-2. *There is nothing penultimate about casting the Spell of Mastery.*

vis-à-vis other wizards and get the most bang for your buck when researching magic spells.

Wizard Skills

Some wizard skills can help you cast your Spell of Mastery faster than others or at least give you more breathing room to do so.

⚒ Archmage is a skill that lets you cast the Spell of Mastery quickly, once you've learned it. Adding 10 to your spell-casting skill through this option will gain you early magic support in combat and help you win some early battles. It will also help you in later combat by allowing you to cast more powerful spells more often.

⚒ Being Charismatic improves your relations with other wizards. This is important for avoiding protracted wars. You need to concentrate on rapid spell research, so having other wizards off your back is a tremendous boon.

⚒ Divine Power and Infernal Power make your religious buildings more productive. The higher levels of mana you earn with one of these skills will help you research and cast the Spell of Mastery sooner.

Mana Focusing applies five mana to your mana reserves for every four mana you "bank" there. This will ensure that you have plenty of mana to spend on spells and upkeep throughout the game. Plus, when you've got to pump hundreds, nay *thousands*, of mana points into casting the Spell of Mastery before you are overwhelmed by other wizards, this bonus can spell the difference between victory and defeat.

Myrran lets you start your game on Myrror, and this is likely to give you some breathing room (away from enemy wizards) during the early stages of the game. In addition, Myrran nodes average twice the mana of those on Arcanus, and Myrror has many more special minerals (crysx, mithril, and adamantium) from which to generate even more mana.

Node Mastery doubles the mana you receive from all nodes in addition to letting you cast all spells at nodes without risk of a fizzle. You must have lots of mana to pour into learning and casting the Spell of Mastery. This skill is particularly useful in that regard. Remember, nodes tend to be the richest mana sources, particularly if you are playing at a medium or powerful magic setting.

Runemaster gives you a 25 percent discount on researching and casting Arcane magic spells, including the Spell of Mastery. If there was ever a direct line for helping you cast this spell, this skill is it. To greatly speed your spell book progress, combine Runemaster with other skills that give research and casting discounts.

Sage Master gives a 25 percent bonus toward all your research efforts. Since research is most of the battle in the race to acquire Spell of Mastery, Sage Master provides a considerable advantage. Also, because it lets you research everything more quickly, other spells will be available to you earlier in the game, which is always helpful.

Of course, there are other skills that will help you learn and cast the Spell of Mastery quickly, if you use them well. Here, we've listed just the ones with the greatest or most direct impact on such an effort.

Spell Books

Certain colors of magic are better for the type of siege mentality that a wizard needs if he is determined to win by casting the Spell of Mastery. Good defensive magic is found in the colors listed below.

White, or Life, magic is loaded with protective or enhancing spells. Furthermore, white magic confers an intrinsic positive diplomatic effect, giving a wizard some respite from endless declarations of war by other wizards.

Green, or Nature, magic is also very strong in protective and enhancement spells. It is a bit more balanced than white because it has stronger combat, summoning, and destructive spells, but Nature magic gets no inherent diplomatic bonus.

Blue, or Sorcery, magic has a few special features that are valuable to a wizard trying to win through spell casting. It has the Aura of Majesty spell, which gives a constant, low-level improvement in diplomatic status with opponents. It also has various ways to stop other wizards' spell-casting efforts. So even if you fall behind in the spell race, you can prevent others from moving too far ahead.

Races

As far as choosing a good race for winning by casting the Spell of Mastery, you are probably best off with either a race that inherently produces mana (Beastmen, Dark Elves,

Draconians, or High Elves) or one that can build cathedrals (Beastmen, Draconians, Halflings, High Men, Nomads, Orcs, or Trolls). For either kind of race, you should expect to build as many cities as you can (for more mana-producers and more cathedrals). To this end, the races that also grow relatively quickly are helpful: Beastmen, Halflings, High Men, and Orcs.

Heroes

Heroes with their own spell-casting skill can help you *cast* (not research) overland (i.e., non-combat) spells when stationed at your Enchanted Fortress. When the time comes for you to cast the Spell of Mastery, recall these heroes to your Enchanted Fortress. A coven of these cooks, when using all of your per turn mana income, will hasten casting the Spell of Mastery considerably.

Through The Looking Glass

That, dear apprentice, is what winning in *Master of Magic* is all about. Planning your path to glory before a new game even begins is an essential aspect for obtaining victory. No less important is staying focused on your approach, either militaristic or scholarly, as the fastest route to the finish line.

Elimination of a Wizard

On your path to victory, you will probably destroy a wizard or two by capturing their Enchanted Fortress and conquering their remaining cities.

After you have captured an opponent's Enchanted Fortress, the losing wizard is banished and must cast Spell of Return to come back to Myrror or Arcanus. The only mana sources for Spell of Return must come from the wizard's mana or gold (via alchemy) reserves. While the wizard is banished, he or she may not cast combat spells or move units, although their production in cities continues. Upon returning, the wizard chooses a new site

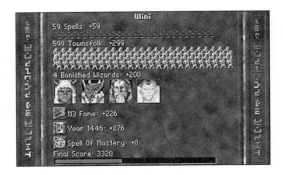

Figure 3-3. *Accounting for victory.*

for the Enchanted Fortress in one of his or her remaining cities.

If you wish to completely eliminate another wizard through combat, you must conquer all of his or her towns. Of course, casting the Spell of Mastery automatically banishes everyone else without your ever having to lift a finger.

Victory Screen Information

After winning, you will see the victory screen. Your score is a measure of how well you played and is recorded in the Hall of Fame screen. The quality of your victory is measured according to the formula below:

Victory Point Formula

+1 Point per number of spells in your spell book

+1/2 Point per citizen (rounding the odd citizen down)

+100 Points per banished wizard

+2 points per fame

+500 points for casting the Spell of Mastery

+2,000 points for the winner (in a "pool" that is reduced by the next modifier)

-2 points per game turn played (so the faster you win, the better)

The total points accumulated are then multiplied by either 3, 2, 1, 0.75, or 0.5 if the difficulty level of the game was impossible, hard, average, easy, or simple, respectively. That value is then divided by 8,000 to get the percent score of your victory.

Note from this formula the things that will improve future scores. Trading spells with wizards before you finish them always helps, as does building, conquering, and developing many cities. Improving your fame through battles by having legendary heroes and by being Famous, also helps. Speed, however, is a decisive factor, especially when you're trying to get a high score at the harder difficulty levels.

Hint: Rather than kill off the last enemy wizard, cast the Spell of Mastery to maximize your score.

Setting The Path

The key, therefore, is setting things up correctly before the game ever begins. Have a victory goal in mind—from creating your wizard to playing each game turn—and stay focused on it.

Creating the right wizard, with the right abilities, and the right number of the right colored spell books, and then leading the right race, is crucial. The next three chapters cover these pre-game elements in detail. The next chapter begins by taking you, a mighty wizard, through the looking glass and applying the old adage, "Know thyself."

Section 2

The Duel-It-Yourself Ruling Wizard Kit

What Makes You So Special?

Remember, you, personally, are a wiz–ard in *Master of Magic*. As such, you will have certain attributes, such as skills, fame, and spell knowledge, that you must use to forge victory. The good news is that there are a wide variety of ways to define yourself as a wizard in *Master of Magic*. The bad news is that creating an effective wizard can be a little overwhelming, especially when learning the game.

This chapter is the mirror to your character's soul. Here we will note every trade-off you make when creating your wizard and even consider what race to pick after putting on your war paint.

Spell Pick Primer

When you opt not to use the pre-fabricated wizards and, instead, "roll your own," you have eleven *picks* to divide between spell ranks and wizard abilities. You must consider two major issues when allocating your picks.

The first is whether to concentrate on one or two colors of magic (i.e., *going deep* in each one by choosing four or more spell books in that color) or to acquire a few spell books in three or four magic realms (i.e., *going wide*). Going deep has the advantage of providing more starting spells at the beginning of the game and more powerful spells at the end. Going wide offers a variety of every color's common and uncommon spells and provides a lot of flexibility when trading spells with other wizards. (See Chapter 6 for a discussion of the different colors of magic.)

The second major issue concerns how many picks to spend on *retorts*, which we refer to as *wizard skills*, as opposed to spell ranks. While it takes time to fully reap the rewards of spell ranks, wizard skills are effective from the first turn, often jump-starting your abilities during the early stages of the game. Note that you are limited to 6 wizard skills and 13 spell books, including the ones you might find later

Figure 4-1. *Designing your own wizard.*

in the game through node and lair exploration (see Chapter 14).

A slightly slower start results if you choose more spell ranks. However, you *will* start with several spells to cast and a higher initial spell-casting skill level with which to cast them (see Chapter 6). Also, with more spell ranks, you will have more spells, and spells with greater power, at your disposal later in the game.

Before the philosophy lesson, though, some knowledge is needed. Let us begin with a quick examination of the benefits of each wizard skill.

The Three-Pick Ability: Myrran

While the cost of three spell picks is high, the advantages of starting as a Myrran are many:

🐍 You start with Myrror as your playground and have, at most, two other wizards there to directly oppose you. Fewer neighbors means fewer early conflicts and, thus, potentially easier empire-building during the early stages of the game.

🐍 Myrror is a richer world than Arcanus, with almost twice as many mineral sites, including adamantium, crysx crystals, and magic nodes that are twice as powerful as those on Arcanus. Even Enchanted Fortresses produce five more mana than they do on Arcanus.

🐸 Although the nodes are tougher, the rewards are also better on Myrror. New retorts (that is, wizard skills), spell books, magic spells, prisoners, and magic items, along with greater amounts of gold and mana crystals, are more readily found on Myrror.

🐸 You can choose from among *all* the races to start with, including the five Myrran races: Beastmen, Dark Elves, Draconians, Dwarves, and Trolls. See Chapter 5 for a detailed discussion of the various races in *Master of Magic*.

🐸 Conquering neighboring cities often means adding another of these five powerful and exotic Myrran races to your empire.

Those Myrran advantages sound great, right? Well, there are some disadvantages, too:

🐸 Fewer neighbors means less chance for diplomacy and spell trades early on.

🐸 Those tougher nodes and lairs on Myrror can impede your early growth until you muster an army powerful enough to clean them out.

🐸 Neighboring neutral cities, while offering other exotic races upon their capture, are usually difficult to take for that very reason. Dark Elves (with each unit's magic ranged attack) and Dwarves (with their mega-hit points) have particularly tough nuts to crack.

🐸 To make matters worse, interracial tension—and the rebels created by it—is particularly bad between the races populating Myrror (see Chapter 15).

🐸 These tougher nodes and neutral cities will go unconquered longer, meaning they will spew out more (and more powerful) raiders to be dealt with over the course of a game.

The ultimate question to ask of the Myrran ability is whether it's worth paying 3 of your 11 spell picks for it. This is a debatable point, thanks to Myrror's higher risks and rewards. With these pros and cons in mind, however, you can make an informed decision. If you choose to start as a Myrran, what happens to you during the early stages of the game will be far more interesting and significant than it would have been on Arcanus.

The Two-Pick Abilities

The abilities that cost two spell picks, covered in this section, provide a significant jump start to your early empire development.

Don't Change That Channeler!

Channeler is extremely useful. Not only does it eliminate all of the extra costs of casting combat spells to support your distant armies, it also cuts your mana maintenance costs in half (the total is computed, then halved and rounded down). Thus, you can maintain many more enchantments and fantastic creatures on the map before feeling the strain on your per turn mana income.

Being a Channeler is particularly useful when you have a lot of Chaos (and, to a slightly lesser extent, Death) magic because these colors offer a plethora of important combat spells. Keeping their casting cost down is especially beneficial.

Finally, always consider Channeler when you go deep into one magic color. When you concentrate your efforts on one magic color, you eventually learn a myriad of expensive and powerful spells that you *will* want to cast. Without the Channeler ability, it is easy to burn through your mana reserves quickly, especially when engaged in multi-front wars.

Divine or Infernal Power

Divine Power and Infernal Power are Life and Death magic counterparts, each improving all your cities' religious institutions. Both their mana production and unrest-calming effects are increased by 50 percent (adding these building's values together in a city before dropping any fraction).

The net effect of this retort is that, in cities where you have built all of the four available religious centers, you will produce an extra five mana per turn and calm two additional rebels. To make the most of Divine or Infernal Power, start with a race that can build the highest level of religious buildings, cathedrals (Beastmen, Draconians, Halflings, High Men, Nomads, Orcs, or Trolls). If you do pick one of the other races, however, be certain *not* to pick the Klackons, since this race cannot use these skills at all! Note that since Death magic also has the Dark Rituals spell, the mana production from your cities, if you have Infernal Power, can be tremendous.

The Price of Fame

Famous improves your fame by +10 right from the start and has a number of other effects. Fame saves you gold for troop maintenance and attracts more and better heroes, plus more merchants (with items) and mercenaries, doubling the chance of opportunity knocking for you (see the Fame section toward the end of this chapter). Consider combining Famous with Life magic spell books to further enhance your fame by casting the spell Just Cause.

Warlord: The Sword Can Be Mightier Than The Wand

The Warlord skill gives all your normal troops and heroes a free, extra level of experience. It also allows normal troops to achieve one rank beyond what they otherwise could.

This bonus is considerable, particularly at the beginning of the game. Troops such as basic spearmen, for instance, with the extra (+1) sword provided by a free experience level, are suddenly twice as strong. This makes a huge improvement in their fighting ability.

Later in the game, fully developed units can reach an ultra-elite status. They can even reach their highest level, champions, if a Warlord also casts the Life spell Crusade.

Because Warlord affects all your normal units and heroes, this skill has tremendous consequences on your conquests. Warlord also enables you to restructure your armies and garrisons to some extent, knowing that fewer or cheaper units can well do the job. When combined with Alchemy and a race of soldier builders like the Gnolls, Klackons, Lizardmen, or Trolls, Warlords rule!

The One-Pick Abilities

Because every wizard skill is a straight trade-off in spell books, abilities that "cost" only one spell rank may have more appeal than those worth two or three. Now, to determine which skill provides the best tools for your playing style, read on.

Alchemy: Or Magic Meets The Golden Rule

Alchemy has simple effects. First, it allows transmutation of gold into mana, or vice versa, on an equitable one-for-one basis (as opposed to the one-for-two premium otherwise charged). The problem is, how often do you *really* to use alchemy? Now, there are some approaches to playing *Master of Magic* that might profit from your using a lot of alchemy: in particular, approaches where you plan on diverting the bulk of your mana income to research or spell-casting skill. In such a case, you'll want to use alchemy to obtain the mana you need for spell casting from your gold reserves. If you have enough gold to keep your mana reserves well stocked, this approach can speed your research and spell-casting skill development significantly.

Alchemy's second function is that, throughout the game, it will give magic weapons to all of your newly built units, just as though they were forged at an alchemist's guild. In other words, they can ignore an enemy's Weapons Immunity and receive a +1 To Hit modifier (for melee and ranged attacks). For races that can't otherwise build alchemist's guilds (Gnolls, Klackons, Lizardmen, and Trolls), this aspect of Alchemy is particularly useful. Even for other races, never needing to rush to make and maintain alchemist's guilds is nice. (With this wizard skill, the main reasons for building alchemist's guilds are to get the three mana they generate per turn and to get the attack strength and defense bonuses that mithril and adamantium mines provide.)

The Golden Arches: Archmages, That Is

The Archmage skill gives you an initial +10 spell-casting skill. In addition, for every two mana you allot to improving your spell-casting skill, three mana points are registered on your Skill ratio wand on the Magic Summary screen. In other words, you receive a 50 percent bonus for improving your spell-casting skill. As an added advantage, this wizard skill makes your enchantments twice as difficult to dispel.

Your spell-casting skill dictates how much mana you can spend during a battle. It also limits the amount of mana that can be funneled into casting an overland spell each turn. Starting the game with a higher spell skill means that you will be able to cast more powerful spells earlier (assuming that you also have the mana reserves for casting them, of course).

The Archmage ability is fairly flexible. You can decrease the amount of mana you place into your skill wand, increasing the mana used for research or mana reserves, while still preserving a fairly rapid spell skill development.

For a single spell pick, this skill is a bargain in terms of the power you can potentially wield with it, particularly during the early part of a game when you need every boost you can get. The ability to cast a vicious combat spell,

or global enchantment earlier, etc., is not to be taken lightly.

Art and Artifice

Artificer allows you to construct magical artifacts at a 50 percent cost reduction. Now, think about that for a minute. You get to make cheaper items for your heroes, or you can break them and get all of the mana you put into them back out. When combined with Runemaster, you'll get a 75 percent price break on new items, which you can actually break and show a *profit* in mana!

While artifacts are critical for improving your heroes, the question is, do you want to spend a lot of your time and mana casting artifact creation spells instead of casting other spells? Because the spell picks you'll spend on wizard skills are so precious, you have none to waste on frivolities. Artificer, in our opinion, is a somewhat frivolous skill. It is best used when you're just playing *Master of Magic* for fun at the easier levels.

Picking Your Nodes: Chaos, Nature and Sorcery Mastery

Chaos, Nature, and Sorcery Mastery have equivalent effects. These skills double the mana obtained from the corresponding nodes under your control and, in addition, reduce the research *and casting* costs of Chaos, Nature and Sorcery spells, respectively, by 15 percent. These skills also make all your enchantments from their corresponding magic realm twice as difficult to dispel.

The only reason for choosing Chaos, Nature, or Sorcery Mastery would be if you were focusing exclusively on the corresponding magic type and, thus, could really benefit from the research savings. Even in this case, you'll always have Arcane spells to research, including Spell of Mastery. Besides, it is unlikely that you would make a point of systematically conquering *only* the nodes that will pay you double mana, although such nodes *will* be easier for you to conquer because you will have spells of the corresponding magic type. Note that there are more Sorcery nodes than Chaos or Nature nodes (see Chapter 14), so Sorcery Mastery may be more valuable in the long run than Chaos and Nature Mastery.

Sage Mastery Made Easy

Generally, it is better to pick Sage Master than the above colors of Node Mastery. This is because Sage Master reduces *all* your research costs, including those for Arcane spells like the Spell of Mastery, by 25 percent.

Sage Master also helps make up for racial deficiencies in production of buildings that yield research benefits. In particular, Barbarians, Dwarves, Gnolls, Halflings, Klackons, Lizardmen, and Trolls can produce nothing higher than a sage's guild (or, in some cases, nothing higher than a library!). Obviously, these races are poor choices if you plan to play a research/magic oriented game. The Sage Master skill can help offset this weakness.

In combination with skills that increase your research speed in specific areas, or skills that otherwise enhance your magic abilities, Sage Master promises to make you a powerful wizard much earlier than you could otherwise be.

Node Mastery, The Mana Maker

Node Mastery doubles the mana production from all nodes under your control, which gives you a leg up on the single magic realm mastery skills above. (Having both Node Mastery and Nature Mastery, though, would produce *four times* the mana from Nature nodes! The same holds true for the other Mastery skills) Furthermore, it allows you to cast spells of any type at nodes without them ever fizzling.

Node Mastery is quite valuable as it can quickly and dramatically increase your mana income. Taking and holding nodes is a far easier task, too, when your spells never fizzle!

Consider this wizard skill under any circumstance, no matter your strategy for winning.

Although this wizard skill particularly benefits races that don't have a high rate of mana production from urban sources (the Klackons, Lizardmen, Gnolls, or Dwarves), it works well for everyone. When used in combination with Sage Master, you'll have a the complement of magic skills that often prove decisive.

Oozing Charisma

Having Charisma gives you a diplomatic boost, doubling the effects of your positive actions and halving the penalties of any of your negative actions (see Chapter 25). Often, this can delay or abate aggressive maneuvers by your opponents, thus affording you time to develop your empire and your magic skills to a level where you're ready to assert yourself as a world power.

Additionally, Charisma gives you a 50 percent discount on opportunities that come your way (i.e., all mercenaries, heroes, and artifacts offered). Not that you'll see *better* opportunities come along nor more often; they'll just be cheaper to grab.

A Charismatic wizard has a real advantage in a long, slowly developing game (such as those where it takes a long time for *all* wizards to develop; i.e., with starting parameters set to small land masses and weak mana) where there is more time for diplomacy. In games where you take only one spell color, or start with a slow growing race that requires extensive urban development to reach its military zenith, you might consider adding Charismatic to your wizard skills. In games where you start with large land masses and quickly encounter other wizards, Charisma will also aid you.

Because of the diplomatic benefits of Charisma, this skill may be good to combine with Death magic spell books to help offset the automatic diplomatic penalty of these books. You may also wish to combine Charisma with white magic to get a further diplomatic boost, or with Sorcery magic because of the positive diplomatic effects from the Aura of Majesty spell.

Conjurer: Never Being Alone

The Conjurer skill grants a 25 percent discount on the cost of researching, casting, and maintaining fantastic creatures. This skill makes it much easier to bring out and maintain more powerful fantastic creatures earlier in the game. If you are playing with a race that doesn't have many spectacular military units — Barbarians, Draconians, Gnolls, Halflings, Nomads, or Orcs — building large armies of fantastic units is a sound approach. In particular, if you combine red or green magic, both of which have many summoning spells, (black is good, too) with Conjurer, you can build strong armies comprised solely of summoned creatures.

Stay Focused on Mana Focusing

With Mana Focusing, for every four mana income you generate for your mana reserves (from which the mana for upkeep and casting spells is drawn), an additional mana point appears in the reserves. Hence, you get a 25 percent *interest bonus* on such income. For example, if 20 of the mana you earn from your combined urban and node sources (i.e., your per turn mana income, see Chapter 15) is allotted to your reserves, 25 mana will actually appear there. When you adjust the Mana wand on your Mana Summary screen, this bonus *is automatically reflected in the value beneath that wand.*

In effect, everything that costs mana from your reserve receives a 20 percent discount; every spell you cast, in combat or out, and every creature or enchantment you maintain enjoys this benefit. For example, casting a spell that costs 100 mana still draws that much from your reserve. However, with Mana Focusing, you only needed to add 80 reserve mana to receive that 100. Thus, every 100 mana in costs only requires 80 mana in income.

For one spell pick, Mana Focusing delivers a great benefit. The only drawback is that it does not directly hasten spell casting, research, or your casting skill level. The only way this skill can affect research speed and spell-casting skill is if you decrease the proportion of mana income that goes to your reserves (because of the bonus reserve mana you get from this skill).

Runemaster or: Hooked on Runics

Runemaster gives you a 25 percent discount in both research and casting costs of Arcane spells. Since Arcane magic is utilitarian and easy to trade, this wizard skill has its uses. Note that the reduced research and casting costs of the Arcane magic *include* the Spell of Mastery (and, when necessary, the Spell of Return). Thus, this skill allows you to learn and cast the game-winning spell faster than normal. Although this is not a great wizard skill for normal, turn-to-turn play, it has its uses, particularly when making items or summoning heroes.

Another big plus for Runemasters is the ability to punch another wizard's spells out. What this means is that the strength of all dispelling spells cast by Runemasters is *doubled*. For example, if you pumped 350 mana into a Disjunction spell, the chance of it succeeding would be based on it having a value of 700 mana. Dispel Magic True, Disenchant True, and Disjunction True spells cast by a Runemaster would be valued at *six times* the mana put into them! This may be a good skill to combine with Sorcery spell books and possibly with Sorcery Mastery.

Note that this skill combines with Artificer to give a 75 percent discount on casting items; with Sage Master to give a 50 percent discount for researching Arcane spells; and with Conjurer to give a 50 percent discount on sum-

Table 4.1 *Wizard Skills' Subjective Ranking by Author*

Wizard Rank

	Skill	Total	Alan	Petra	Tom
1	Warlord	94	32	29	33
2	Myrran	89	24	32	33
3	Channeler	80	30	30	20
4	Node Mastery	72	27	25	20
5	Alchemy	71	21	30	20
6	Famous	69	26	23	20
7	Infernal Power	60	22	13	25
8	Divine Power	59	21	13	25
9	Charismatic	57	23	24	10
10	Runemaster	53	19	19	15
11	Archmage	50	19	16	15
11	Sorcery Mastery	50	17	13	20
13	Sage Master	49	18	21	10
14	Chaos Mastery	48	16	12	20
14	Nature Mastery	48	16	12	20
16	Conjurer	40	15	15	10
17	Artificer	36	13	8	15
18	Mana Focusing	35	19	11	5

moning magic and guardian spirits, plus a 50 percent discount on researching and casting Summon Hero and Summon Champion.

Color Me Thoughtful

So, in the cosmic scheme of things, it should be clear that certain skills are inherently better than others. Here is our overall ranking of the wizard skills. We've each assigned every wizard skill a value ranging from 0 (completely useless) to 33 (supremely useful under every circumstance). Then we totaled these values and ranked them in order.

Wizard Skills and Magic Colors

Naturally, some wizard skills combine better with certain colors of magic. For example, a wizard specializing in Death magic is going to have a real popularity problem with the other wizards (see Chapter 25). Therefore, being Charismatic will help make up this glaring deficiency. Again, we present the authors' subjective evaluation of wizard skills based on the predominant type of magic that wizard will use. (Chapter 6 offers more information on choosing magic colors at the beginning of a game.)

Table 4.2 *Wizard Skills and Magic Colors Reference*

Wizard Skill	Spell Books				
	Life	Death	Chaos	Nature	Sorcery
Myrran	•	•	•	•	•
Divine Power	Req	Can't	•	•	•
Infernal Power	Can't	Req	•	•	•
Famous	Help	•	•	•	•
Warlord	Help	•	•	•	Help
Alchemy	Help	•	•	•	Help
Archmage	•	•	•	•	•
Artificer	•	•	•	•	•
Channeler	•	•	•	•	•
Chaos Mastery	•	•	Req	•	•
Nature Mastery	•	•	•	Req	•
Sorcery Mastery	•	•	•	•	Req
Node Mastery	•	•	Req	Req	Req
Charismatic	•	Help	•	•	•
Conjurer	•	Help	Help	Help	•
Mana Focusing	•	Help	Help	•	Help
Runemaster	•	•	•	•	Help
Sage Master	•	•	•	•	•

• = Helps that color of magic about average.
Can't = Can't be selected with this color magic.
Help = This skill supplements wizards who emphasize this color of magic,
either offsetting a particular weakness or enhancing a particular strength.
Req = Required to select this Wizard Skill.

Wizard Skills and Race

Finally, there is the matter of what race a wizard wants to lead to victory. Since certain wizard skills benefit certain races more by helping them make up a deficiency or fully exploit a skill's usefulness, we have prepared a table of the authors' opinions on the matter.

(Chapter 5 has helpful information on choosing your beginning race.)

Fame

With all the wizard skills, magic colors, and races swirling in your mind as you ponder which combinations might be best (don't

Table 4.3 *Wizard Skills and Race Reference*

Wizard Skill	Barb	Gnoll	Half	HiMen	H-Elf	Klack	Lizard	Nomad	Orc	Beast	Dk-Elf	Drac	Dwarf	Troll
Myrran	•	•	•	•	•	•	•	•	•	Req	Req	Req	Req	Req
Divine Power	•	•	Max.	Max.	•	Don't	•	Max.	Max.	Max.	•	Max.	•	Max.
Infernal Power	•	•	Max.	Max.	•	Don't	•	Max.	Max.	Max.	•	Max.	•	Max.
Famous	•	•	•	•	•	•	•	•	•	•	•	•	•	•
Warlord	•	•	•	•	•	•	•	•	•	•	•	•	•	•
Alchemy	•	Help	•	•	•	Help	Help	•	•	•	•	•	•	Help
Archmage	•	•	•	•	•	•	•	•	•	•	•	•	•	•
Artificer	•	•	•	•	•	•	•	•	•	•	•	•	•	•
Channeler	•	Help	•	•	•	Help	Help	•	•	•	•	•	Help	•
Chaos Mastery	•	Help	•	•	•	Help	Help	•	•	•	•	•	Help	•
Nature Mastery	•	Help	•	•	•	Help	Help	•	•	•	•	•	Help	•
Sorcery Mastery	•	Help	•	•	•	Help	Help	•	•	•	•	•	Help	•
Node Mastery	•	Help	•	•	•	Help	Help	•	•	•	•	•	Help	•
Charismatic	•	•	•	•	•	•	•	•	•	•	•	•	•	•
Conjurer	•	Help	Help	•	•	Help	•	•	•	•	•	Help	•	•
Mana Focusing	•	Help	•	•	•	Help	Help	•	•	•	•	•	Help	•
Rune Master	•	•	•	•	•	•	•	•	•	•	•	•	•	•
Sage Master	Help	Help	Help	•	•	Help	Help	•	•	•	•	•	Help	Help

Don't = Don't bother. You'll gain no benefit from this skill with this race.
Help = This skill helps this race offset one of its particular weaknesses (see Chapter 5).
Max. = You can derive the maximum benefit from this skill combined with this race.
Req = Required to select this race.

Table 4.4 *Acquiring Fame*

Fame Gained	Action
+1	Defeating 4+ enemy units in a single battle
+1	Winning a battle where the enemy lost a very rare creature
+1	Conquering a town (9 to 12 Population points)*
+2	Conquering a city (13 to 16 Population points)*
+3	Conquering a capital (17+ Population points)*
+5	Banishing (not killing) a computer player
+10	Casting and maintaining the Life spell Just Cause
+10	Having the wizard skill Famous
+#	Having a Legendary hero rating

* = These awards are voided if the captured city is razed.

Table 4.5 *Losing Fame*

Fame Lost	Action
-1	Losing 4+ units in a single battle (only if you have more than 20 fame)
-1	Razing or losing through enemy conquest a hamlet (1 to 4 Population points)
-2	Razing or losing through enemy conquest a village (5 to 8 Population points)
-3	Razing or losing through enemy conquest a town (9 to 12 Population points)
-4	Razing or losing through enemy conquest a city (13 to 16 Population points)
-5	Razing or losing through enemy conquest a capital (17+ Population points)
-#	Losing a hero in battle (the fame lost equals half of the hero's level*)

* = Totaled for the levels of all heroes lost in a single battle, halved, and then rounded down.

worry, we'll have more discussion on the matter in later chapters), we'll now examine two more attributes that set you apart from other wizards: fame and spell-casting skill. Let us broach the former subject first.

How Fame is Earned

Fame can be earned (and your Fame Points increased) in a number of ways, as shown in Table 4.4.

How Fame is Lost

Unfortunately, fame can also be lost. Table 4.5 shows the circumstances that will dim your rising star. Note that a player's fame can never go below 0.

Note that if 50 battle turns are completed and both sides retire exhausted, the defending player in that battle is deemed to have won. All adjustments in fame for both players are made accordingly.

The Effects of Fame

Each Fame Point reduces the *total* maintenance cost of army units and heroes by one gold per turn. Thus, if you have a fame of 20, you will save 20 gold per turn in troop/hero maintenance costs. Fame also influences the quality of heroes who approach you for hire (see Chapter 18).

The frequency in which opportunity knocks for players (to offer them a new hero, mercenary, or item) also increases with their fame, as shown in Table 4.6. Note that to get an opportunity to purchase an item or to hire someone, however, you must have enough gold. If opportunity knocks but you don't have the money to pay for the mercenaries, hero, or item, you forfeit that opportunity and are not even notified that you missed your chance!

When mercenaries appear (see Table 4.6), fame affects both their quantity and quality. The computer rolls a *separate* d100, adding that wizard's fame to it, for the *quality* and *quantity* of the mercenary unit(s). Results lower than 60 provide a single unit or regular troop quality. Results between 61 and 90 offer two units or veteran troop quality. Results of 91 or more provide three units or elite troop quality. Table 4.7 extrapolates this a bit.

Table 4.6 *Opportunity Knocks*

Chance that a Hero will offer services =
((3% + Fame/25) x2 if Famous) / **Heroes Variable**

The Heroes Variable depends on how many heroes you already have. This number is one if you have no heroes; two if you have one or two heroes; three if you have three or four heroes; and four if you already have five heroes.

Chance that a Mercenary will come by =
(1% + Fame/20) x2 if Famous

Chance that a Merchant will come by =
(2% + Fame/25) x2 if Famous

Merchants will only offer you an item if you have three times the purchasing price in your gold reserves. If you are Charismatic, you only need half of this amount available.

The *maximum* probability that a mercenary, hero, or item appears at your doorstep is always 10 percent, even for Famous wizards.

The chance that any of these appears in a game turn, depending on your fame, is shown below (double the percentages shown, up to a maximum of 10 percent, when that wizard possesses the skill Famous):

Condition*	0	20	25	40	50	60	75	80	100
Wizard Fame Point Level									
Hero (0)	3%		4%		5%		6%		7%
Hero (1-2)	1%		2%			3%			
Hero (3-4)	1%					2%			
Hero (5)	0%		1%						
Mercenary	1%	2%		3%		4%		5%	6%
Merchant	2%		3%		4%		5%		6%

* = The chance that a hero appears depends on how many heroes you already have (shown in parentheses in this column).

Table 4.7 *Mercenary Quantity and Quality*

Wizard's Fame	1 Unit or Regulars	2 Units or Veterans	3 Units or Elite
0	60	30	10
10	50	30	20
20	40	30	30
30	30	30	40
40	20	30	50
50	10	30	60
60	0	30	70
70	0	20	80
80	0	10	90
90+	0	0	100

Numbers show the percent chance of receiving that quantity or quality of mercenaries at various fame levels.

Spell Skill

A wizard's spell skill is also a defining characteristic. Spell skill is, essentially, a speed limit. Its value is the amount of mana that you, personally, can spend casting spells at a single battle (provided that you have sufficient mana reserves to pay for the spells and the additional mana required for conducting combat at great distances from your Enchanted Fortress [see Chapter 21]). Your skill level is also measured by the amount of mana that you can pour into overland (i.e., non-combat) spell casting, each turn, from your mana reserve.

Improving Your Spell Skill

No practice is necessary; your spell casting skill improves as you divert mana income (*a.k.a.* your "magic power") into your Skill wand (as shown on the Magic Summary screen) according to the following formula:

Skill Level Improvement Formula

Amount of mana investment required to raise a wizard's skill level by 1 = (2 x Present Skill Level)

For example, you have a skill level of 12. Investing twice your present level of 12 (which is 24) mana in improving your skill will raise it to level 13. Mana invested beyond the exact amount required to reach a new skill level is applied toward the next level (don't worry; none of it gets wasted).

Therefore, the more mana income you have, and the more of it you allocate to improving your skill level, the faster your wizard's spell-casting skill will increase. In addition to the things that increase your mana income, there are other ways to improve your spell-casting skill:

🐸 The wizard skill Archmage improves your ability to increase your spell casting skill by 50 percent (for every whole two mana applied to your spell skill per turn, three mana points show up beneath your Skill Wand and are applied to improving your spell skill). Archmages also starts with a +10 bonus to their spell skill.

🐸 Each spell book picked at the start of the game increases your starting skill by two.

🐸 Heroes with their own spell-casting skill can artificially increase your wizard's spell-casting skill. Whenever such heroes are stationed at your Enchanted Fortress, half of their spell-casting skill contributes to that of your wizard's for purposes of casting overland spells (not for casting in combat!). Their combined contribution is limited to twice the wizard's spell-casting skill.

If, for example, you have a hero with a spell skill of 35 at your Enchanted Fortress, you can funnel an additional 17 mana per turn into casting overland spells (including the Spell of Mastery).

Death magic also provides a way to improve a wizard's spell casting relative to his or her opponent's. Casting Cruel Unminding permanently destroys 10 percent of the mana that a target wizard has put into improving his or her spell-casting skill (something that could take many turns for that wizard to recover from).

Know Thyself

Dividing spell picks between wizard abilities and spell ranks is not an easy task. Many factors come into consideration.

What race do you want to play with? Is it magically inclined (like the Dark Elves or Beastmen) predominantly militaristic (like the Klackons or Lizardmen) or does it fall somewhere in between? Are you planning to play a quickly developing game, in which choosing many skills rather than spell ranks may be best, or are you thinking of a longer game in which your wizard can develop formidable magic abilities?

You may want to balance more militarily oriented races with a longer, magic-oriented agenda, simply to give yourself the chance to conquer nodes, lairs, and neutral cities early in the game. You may want to balance the more magically oriented races with shorter term, militaristic goals, simply because your magic abilities will develop, even if untended, and eventually magic will make your military units even more powerful.

There is no need, however, to adopt a balanced approach. Skewing things heavily in one direction or another will simply result in a different kind of game. Making the most of what you start with is just as important, ultimately, as the choices you make before you begin.

The Races On

This chapter gave our reflections of what the mirror holds when you create your own wizard. How you design your wizard sets the tone of the entire game.

Another important element that adds pitch to that tone is the race you start with. Here, it is important to discriminate according to your plans and desires. Every race has varying strengths and weaknesses. For now, though, the starting gun has fired and the races begin with the next chapter.

A Leader Of Men
(or Trolls or Klackons)

Each race in *Master of Magic* has its own characteristics, some positive and some negative. While the particular starting race you select isn't necessarily going to make or break you during play, it will influence the speed and ways in which you can develop your empire. In this chapter, we list the pros and cons of each race, along with suggestions for how to compensate for or capitalize on each race's characteristics.

Explanation of Tables

Each of the races in *Master of Magic* is briefly discussed in this chapter. In addition, each race has a table listing its pros and cons, along with comments or suggestions. Each area in the table is evaluated by whether it represents a strength, weakness, or neither for that race. The following categories are examined:

Units: Briefly looks at the military potential of the bulk of that race's units.

End-Stage Units: Evaluates the quality of the best units that race can make.

Unit Statistics: The attack strength, To Hit, special abilities, defense, resistance, hit points, and unit costs of the race's standard units are compared to equivalent units of other races.

Spell Research: Shows the net research point production per city.

Mana Production: Shows the net mana production per city, including citizens.

Gold Production: Examines how easy it is for the race to stay in the black, depending on buildings and units produced.

Food Production: Looks at farmer productivity and net food production in cities that are important for the population growth rate and support of armies.

Population Growth: Describes the inherent growth rate of this race, disregarding city resources, spells, and buildings.

Outpost Growth Rates: Describes the inherent growth rate of this race disregarding city resources and spells.

Road Building: Looks at whether the race can make engineers. This can influence the speed with which you can respond to threats or get your armies together.

Shamans and Priests: Looks at whether the race can make these units. This is important as several events and spells can corrupt land around cities. Without these units or special spells, there is no way to purify corrupted land.

Rebellion-normal: Examines the ability of the race to handle rebellion in its own cities. This depends on the building limitations the race has.

Interracial Unrest: Assesses how friendly or unfriendly a race is when conquering or being conquered by other races.

Use of X: Assesses how well a race can use potential city resources. This will depend on the building limitations of the race.

Seaworthiness: Evaluates the ship types a race can build, which influences the speed of expansion, retaliation, or overseas conquest when you are playing with small or medium land masses.

Note that when a race is ranked as average in an area, that just means the particular area is not necessarily an asset or liability for that race.

The color and skill recommendations following each table are not meant to suggest that other magic colors or wizard skills won't work well. The particular colors and skills were chosen because they compensate for a racial weakness or enhance a particular strength. Depending on how you want to play the game, a myriad of other options are available.

Barbarians

The Barbarians have two outstanding features. First, they grow quickly, so expanding by planting a lot of outposts with this race is a good idea. Second, some of the Barbarian units have first strike, thrown weapons, allowing them to initiate attacks on flying units and do damage before an enemy counterattacks.

Their end-stage unit, the berserkers, are not particularly great; without being super-enchanted, this unit isn't going to score any spectacular wins for you. On the other hand, it is a solid unit that can form the core of most of your important garrisons and armies.

Table 5.1 lists more pros and cons of the Barbarian race.

Suggested Colors and Wizard Skills when playing Barbarians:

🐾 Chaos, Death, Life, Nature magic

🐾 Alchemy, Conjurer, Node Mastery, Sage Mastery, Warlord

Beastmen

Beastmen are one of the most versatile races. All standard Beastmen units start with an extra sword and heart, making this race's early units fairly powerful and useful for early expansion through conquest. In addition, this race offers the powerful minotaurs and can build strong ranged attack units.

Beyond providing superior military units at all stages of the game, Beastmen are very productive in terms of mana and spell research, making them just as useful for a balanced or magic-oriented game as for a military game.

Finally, for being a Myrran race, Beastmen grow exceptionally quickly and, therefore, lend themselves as well to expansion by colonization as to expansion through conquest.

Table 5.2 provides more Beastmen details.

Suggested Colors and Wizard Skills when playing Beastmen:

🐾 Death, Life, Nature, Sorcery magic

🐾 Divine Power, Infernal Power, Myrran (required)

Dark Elves

Dark Elves all have a special magic-ranged attack, giving their early units an impressive weapon to wield during their expansion efforts. In addition, the extra mana that Dark Elves generate can decrease the need to look for nodes as mana sources, allowing this race to strike sooner at neutral and enemy cities. Eventually, Dark Elves can build strong unit types, in particular the flying nightmares and Doom Bolt casting warlocks.

The biggest drawback of the Dark Elves is the snail-speed growth of their outposts and cities. Start outposts for this race as fast as you can. If you wish to expand more by conquering neutral and enemy cities, bear in mind that the fire power wielded by the Dark Elf units is best capitalized on as quickly as possible, before others' garrisons are well stocked with strong units.

Table 5.1 *Barbarians Information*

Area of Consideration	Strength	Average	Weakness	Notes and Suggestions
Units		yes		green, red, or black magic for summoning strong units; Conjurer to reduce costs
End-stage unit(s)		yes		Berserkers
Attack Strength		yes		average; use unit enchantments
To Hit		yes		average
Special Features	yes			thrown attacks (cavalry, spearmen, swordsmen); can attack flyers and have first strike; Life magic has spells that improve thrown attacks (Chapter 17)
Defense		yes		average
Resistance		yes		+1 for normal units
Hearts		yes		average
Unit Costs			yes	slightly higher costs for units with thrown weapons
Spell Research			yes	no universities or wizard's guilds; focus on collecting nodes; pick skills that lower research costs (Sage Mastery) or that increase mana (Node Mastery)
Mana Production		yes		can't build cathedrals
Production rates		yes		can build up to miner's guilds
Gold Production			yes	as for most races, gold can sometimes be a problem; limit production of expensive structures; use more fantastic units; consider starting with Alchemy
Food Production			yes	cannot build animist's guilds
Population Growth	yes			focus on quick expansion
Outpost growth rates	yes			good for early expansion
Road Building			yes	no engineers
Shamans or Priests		yes		shamans
Rebellion-normal		yes		can't build oracles, animist's guilds or cathedrals
Interracial Unrest	yes			generates low levels of tension; good for conquering or being conquered
Use of Gold, Silver, Gems			yes	no banks or merchant's guilds
Use of Adamantium and Mithril		yes		can build alchemist's guilds
Use of Coal and Iron		yes		
Use of Crysx and Quork		yes		
Seaworthiness	yes			can build warships

Table 5.2 *Beastmen Information*

Area of Consideration	Strength	Average	Weakness	Notes and Suggestions
Units	yes			use this race for early military expansion
End-stage unit(s)	yes			Minotaurs
Attack Strength	yes			+1 swords; strong for military use
To Hit		yes		average
Special Features		yes		none
Defense		yes		average
Resistance		yes		+1 for normal units
Hearts	yes			+1 heart; strong for military use
Unit Costs			yes	units are expensive
Spell Research	yes			build universities and wizard's guilds
Mana Production	yes			each person makes 1/2 mana per game turn; consider Death magic for Dark Rituals (because this race can build cathedrals)
Production rates	yes			can build mechanician's guilds
Gold Production			yes	excess unit production can quickly over-burden system; limit produc tion of expensive structures; convert some cities to trade goods as early as possible
Food Production		yes		can build animist's guilds
Population Growth		yes		
Outpost growth rates		yes		
Road Building	yes			engineers
Shaman or Priests	yes			priests
Rebellion-normal	yes			build oracles and cathedrals
Interracial Unrest			yes	generate considerable unrest; build large garrisons or religious buildings early; white magic (Just Cause) or green (Gaia's Blessing) may help
Use of Gold, Silver, Gems		yes		no merchant's guilds
Use of Adamantium and Mithril		yes		build alchemist's guilds
Use of Coal and Iron		yes		
Use of Crysx and Quork		yes		
Seaworthiness			yes	cannot build galleys or warships; Sorcery magic for floating islands or flight

Table 5.3 offers more information on the Dark Elves.

Suggested Colors and Wizard Skills when playing Dark Elves:

🐉 Death, Life, Nature Magic

🐉 Myrran (required)

Draconians

Draconians have a couple of definite advantages over all other races: they fly, and they fly *fast*! This makes Draconians superb for early exploration and rapid expansion. Picking small land masses should give you a strong start with this race, since flying is more of an advantage when other players desperately need ships.

Draconian military credentials are not impressive, although the fast-flying, rock-throwing air ships are good. The Draconians' flying ability *does* allow them to take advantage of their fiery breath attacks and lets them hang back in battles, keeping them safe from most normal melee attacks and, therefore, providing you more opportunities to cast spells. This works particularly well because Draconians are also one of the strongest mana producers.

Table 5.4 provides more information on Draconians.

Colors and Wizard Skills when playing Draconians:

🐉 Chaos, Death, Life, Nature magic (OK, OK, so they're all good)

🐉 Conjurer, Divine Power, Infernal Power, Myrran (required)

Dwarves

Dwarves are a rich and powerful race. They offer several distinct advantages for military oriented game play. First, all of their normal units come with +2 hearts and +4 resistance, making Dwarves hard to kill. Second, Dwarves produce hammerhands and golems, both exceptionally strong end-stage units. Finally, Dwarves make more money than any other race, giving them the wherewithal to produce and maintain enormous armies.

To balance their physical and financial power, the Dwarves lag behind in growth, spell research, and mana production. Still, early Dwarf units are strong enough to aggressively conquer nearby neutral cities at the beginning of the game. Because of their weaknesses, when playing the Dwarves, you should establish outposts early and acquire nodes as fast as you can.

Table 5.5 has more information on Dwarves.

Suggested Colors and Wizard Skills when playing Dwarves:

🐉 Life, Nature, Sorcery magic

🐉 Myrran (required), Node Mastery, Sage Master

Gnolls

Gnolls are in most ways a limited race, but they have some distinct advantages for a military game. All of their units get an additional two swords, making them tough fighters and giving Gnolls an early advantage when used properly. The Gnolls' biggest problem is that their end-stage unit, the wolf riders, are not particularly strong. Wolf riders, however, move quickly and can be used effectively on the

Table 5.3 Dark Elves Information

Area of Consideration	Strength	Average	Weakness	Notes and Suggestions
Units	yes			magic ranged attacks make early units deadly; use for early expansion
End-stage unit(s)	yes			Nightmares and Warlocks
Attack Strength		yes		average
To Hit		yes		average
Special Features	yes			ranged magic attacks
Defense		yes		average
Resistance	yes			+3 for normal units
Hearts		yes		average
Unit Costs			yes	units are expensive
Spell Research	yes			build universities and wizard's guilds;
Mana Production	yes			cannot build cathedrals, but each person generates one mana per turn; high city mana production (parthenons) can be exploited by casting the Death magic spell, Dark Rituals
Production rates	yes			can build mechanician's guilds
Gold Production		yes		economic situation is easily strained; moderate unit and building production to prevent economic difficulties
Food Production		yes		can build animist's guilds
Population Growth			yes	Nature or Life magic for Gaia's Blessing or Stream of Life will improve growth
Outpost growth rates			yes	get an early start growing Dark Elf cities and try to place them in places with high future populations to get maximum growth
Road Building			yes	no engineers
Shamans or Priests	yes			priests
Rebellion-normal		yes		cannot build cathedrals; some difficulty dealing with high levels of unrest
Interracial Unrest			yes	generate the highest levels of unrest; build large garrisons or religious buildings early; Life magic (Just Cause, Stream of Life) or Nature (Gaia's Blessing)
Use of Gold, Silver, Gems	yes			build merchant's guilds
Use of Adamantium and Mithril		yes		build alchemist's guilds
Use of Coal and Iron		yes		
Use of Crysx and Quork		yes		
Seaworthiness		yes		cannot build warships

Table 5.4 *Draconians Information*

Area of Consideration	Strength	Average	Weakness	Notes and Suggestions
Units	yes			flying at two moves per turn makes units ideal for early exploration and "combat from a distance" if you have appropriate combat spells.
End-stage unit(s)		yes		Doom Drakes; Air Ships; neither is a heavy hitter; these units work best against weak enemies or if you have strong spells
Attack Strength		yes		average; supplement armies with fantastic units; Conjurer and green, red, or black magic
To Hit		yes		average
Special Features	yes			flying and fiery breath attacks; flight makes rapid expansion over multiple continents possible
Defense	yes			+1 defense
Resistance	yes			+2 for normal units
Hearts		yes		average
Unit Costs			yes	units are expensive
Spell Research	yes			build universities and wizard's guilds;
Mana Production	yes			build cathedral and each draconian generates 1/2 mana per turn; consider Death magic for Dark Rituals
Production rates		yes		cannot build mechanician's guilds
Gold Production		yes		economic situation is fairly stable, but can be overburdened; moderate unit and building production to avoid problems
Food Production		yes		can build animist's guilds
Population Growth		yes		
Outpost growth rates		yes		
Road Building			yes	no engineers
Shaman or Priests		yes		shaman
Rebellion-normal	yes			build all unrest-quelling institutions; eventually able to tolerate high unrest
Interracial Unrest			yes	can generate much unrest; build large garrisons or religious buildings early; white magic (Just Cause) or green (Gaia's Blessing) may help
Use of Gold, Silver, Gems	yes			can build merchant's guilds
Use of Adamantium and Mithril		yes		can build alchemist's guilds
Use of Coal and Iron		yes		
Use of Crysx and Quork		yes		
Seaworthiness		yes		cannot build warships (airships carry no cargo, but then, all units fly)

Table 5.5 *Dwarves Information*

Area of Consideration	Strength	Average	Weakness	Notes and Suggestions
Units	yes			strong units help early (and late) expansion through conquest
End-stage unit(s)	yes			Hammerhands and Golems: powerful units capable of tackling almost everything
Attack Strength		yes		average
To Hit		yes		average
Special Features		yes		none
Defense		yes		average
Resistance	yes			+4 for normal units
Hearts	yes			+2 hearts
Unit Costs			yes	units are expensive
Spell Research			yes	build no universities and wizard's guilds; collect nodes; pick skills that lower research costs (Sage Master) or that increase mana (Node Mastery)
Mana Production			yes	cannot build parthenons, cathedrals
Production rates	yes			high worker productivity levels (+3 production points per worker)
Gold Production	yes			richest race; use to develop several massive armies since you can afford the upkeep
Food Production			yes	cannot build animist's guilds
Population Growth			yes	green magic for Gaia's Blessing or white magic for Stream of Life will help
Outpost growth rates		yes		
Road Building	yes			engineers
Shamans or Priests			yes	no shamans or priests; hang on to any mercenaries or heroes who can purify corrupted land; white or green magic for anti-corruption spells
Rebellion-normal			yes	may eventually need huge garrisons or white magic (Just Cause, Stream of Life)
Interracial Unrest			yes	can generate high unrest; construct large garrisons or religious buildings early; white magic (Just Cause) or green (Gaia's Blessing) may help
Use of Gold, Silver, Gems		yes		cannot build banks or merchant's guilds, but get double bonuses from deposits
Use of Adamantium and Mithril		yes		can build alchemist's guilds and get double mana bonus from these deposits
Use of Coal and Iron		yes		double production bonus from coal and iron
Use of Crysx and Quork		yes		double mana bonus from these deposits
Seaworthiness			yes	only build triremes; Sorcery magic for floating islands

battlefield to destroy the weaker units in an enemy army's rear.

Since Gnolls don't have much else in the way of particular advantages, use them aggressively at the beginning of the game to conquer nearby towns, nodes and lairs. Prioritize conquering other races and exploiting their units' capabilities. To help with this, Gnolls get along pretty well with most other races, so unrest levels should not be a major concern in your conquered cities.

Table 5.6 contains illumination on the subject of Gnolls.

Suggested Colors and Wizard Skills when playing Gnolls:

🐍 Life, Nature magic

🐍 Alchemy, Node Mastery, Sage Master, Warlord

Halflings

Halflings are a friendly race of fast-growing farmers. These attributes make them excellent for supporting large armies, growing and expanding quickly, and getting along well as either a conquering or subjugated race. Because of the extra food made by Halfling farmers, it is completely feasible to build a settler unit from the first moment you begin a game with this race. This gives the Halflings a big head start in expansion.

Although Halflings tend to be on the weak side militarily, their slinger units, when built near mithril or adamantium mines, can hold their own against almost anything. Halflings work best in a balanced game of peaceful and aggressive expansion (you need to capitalize on how well these little guys get along with everyone).

Table 5.7 has our short notes on Halflings.

Suggested Colors and Wizard Skills when playing Halflings:

🐍 Chaos, Death, Nature, Sorcery magic

🐍 Alchemy, Conjurer, Infernal Power, Node Mastery, Sage Mastery, Warlord

High Elves

All High Elves come with a +1 To Hit, giving their attacks a deadly accuracy. They also have many good unit types. Their early longbowmen are particularly good at killing enemy units at long range. Their strongest unit, the elven lords, enjoy armor-piercing, first strike attacks that can wreak devastation on enemy units.

High Elves are also the only Arcanian race to naturally produce mana and can build most available structures. They suffer a few drawbacks, the worst of which are slow growth (so start their outposts early) and lack of means for dealing with corruption on their land. If you've dealt with maniacal Chaos-wielding enemies before, you'll realize that this can become a huge problem.

High Elves are good at almost everything and lend themselves well to any style of *Master of Magic* game play. More details on High Elves can be found in Table 5.8.

Suggested Colors and Wizard Skills when playing High Elves:

🐍 Life, Nature magic

🐍 No specific recommendations for wizard skills

Table 5.6 Gnolls Information

Area of Consideration	Strength	Average	Weakness	Notes and Suggestions
Units		yes		unit strengths are best exploited early in game, when relative advantage is highest; focus on early, rapid conquest; consider Warlord skill
End-stage unit(s)			yes	Wolf Riders: only advantage is speed
Attack Strength	yes			+2 swords
To Hit		yes		average
Special Features		yes		none
Defense		yes		average
Resistance		yes		average
Hearts		yes		average
Unit Costs		yes		
Spell Research			yes	can build no sages guilds, universities, or wizard's guilds; collect nodes and pick skills that reduce research costs (Sage Master) or that increase mana (Node Mastery)
Mana Production			yes	cannot build parthenons, cathedrals
Production rates		yes		cannot build mechanician's guilds
Gold Production		yes		gold can become a problem; limit unit and building production
Food Production			yes	cannot build animist's guilds
Population Growth		yes		
Outpost growth rates		yes		
Road Building			yes	no engineers
Shamans or Priests			yes	no shamans or priests; hang on to any mercenaries or heroes who can purify corrupted land; white or green magic for anti-corruption spells
Rebellion-normal			yes	may eventually need huge garrisons, white magic (Just Cause, Stream of Life) or green magic (Gaia's Blessing)
Interracial Unrest	yes			fairly easy-going race; good for conquering other Arcanian races
Use of Gold, Silver, Gems			yes	cannot build banks or merchant's guilds
Use of Adamantium and Mithril			yes	cannot build alchemist's guilds; consider Alchemy skill or white magic (Holy Weapon)
Use of Coal and Iron		yes		
Use of Crysx and Quork		yes		
Seaworthiness		yes		cannot build warships

Table 5.7 *Halflings Information*

Area of Consideration	Strength	Average	Weakness	Notes and Suggestions
Units		yes		on the weak side; consider green, red, or black magic and Conjurer for summoning; consider Alchemy or Warlord for improving units
End-stage unit(s)	yes			Slingers can become very strong missile units
Attack Strength			yes	-1 swords
To Hit	yes			+1 To Hit
Special Features	yes			Lucky
Defense	yes			+1 To Defend
Resistance		yes		+1 crosses
Hearts		yes		average
Unit Costs			yes	
Spell Research			yes	can build no universities or wizard's guilds; collect nodes and pick skills that lower research costs (Sage Master) or that increase mana (Node Mastery)
Mana Production		yes		can build cathedrals
Production rates	yes			cannot build mechanician's guilds, but efficient farming increases number of workers
Gold Production		yes		gold can become a problem; limit unit and building production
Food Production	yes			each farmer can harvest three food
Population Growth		yes		
Outpost growth rates	yes			exceptional for early expansion especially with high early food production rates
Road Building			yes	no engineers
Shamans or Priests		yes		
Rebellion-normal		yes		can build cathedrals
Interracial Unrest	yes			friendliest race; makes expansion through conquest feasible
Use of Gold, Silver, Gems			yes	cannot build banks or merchant's guilds
Use of Adamantium and Mithril			yes	can build alchemist's guilds
Use of Coal and Iron		yes		
Use of Crysx and Quork		yes		
Seaworthiness			yes	cannot build galleys or warships; Sorcery magic for floating islands

Table 5.8 *High Elves Information*

Area of Consideration	Strength	Average	Weakness	Notes and Suggestions
Units		yes		
End-stage unit(s)	yes			Elven Lords, Pegasi, and the earlier Longbowmen are all excellent units
Attack Strength		yes		average
To Hit	yes			+1 To Hit
Special Features		yes		none
Defense		yes		average
Resistance	yes			+2 crosses
Hearts		yes		average
Unit Costs			yes	moderately high unit costs
Spell Research	yes			can build universities and wizard's guilds
Mana Production		yes		cannot build parthenons, cathedrals, but each elf generates 1/2 mana per turn
Production rates	yes			can build mechanician's guilds
Gold Production		yes		gold can become a problem; limit unit and expensive building production
Food Production		yes		can build animist's guilds
Population Growth			yes	white or green magic (Stream of Life or Gaia's Blessing) to increase growth rates
Outpost growth rates		yes		
Road Building			yes	no engineers
Shamans or Priests			yes	no ability to purify corrupted squares: keep mercenaries or heroes capable of this around; white and green magic for spells that decrease corruption
Rebellion-normal		yes		cannot build parthenons, but can erect animist's guilds; unrest will become a problem at higher tax rates
Interracial Unrest			yes	an unfriendly race; use large garrisons or build religious institutions quickly; White magic for Just Cause or green magic for Gaia's Blessing will help
Use of Gold, Silver, Gems	yes			can build banks and merchant's guilds
Use of Adamantium and Mithril			yes	can build alchemist's guilds
Use of Coal and Iron		yes		
Use of Crysx and Quork		yes		
Seaworthiness		yes		cannot build warships

Table 5.9 *High Men Information*

Area of Consideration	Strength	Average	Weakness	Notes and Suggestions
Units		yes		
End-stage unit(s)	yes			Paladins are one of the best units
Attack Strength		yes		average
To Hit		yes		average
Special Features		yes		none
Defense		yes		average
Resistance		yes		average
Hearts		yes		average
Unit Costs		yes		
Spell Research	yes			can build universities and wizard's guilds
Mana Production		yes		have all mana-producing buildings
Production rates	yes			can build mechanician's guilds
Gold Production		yes		gold can become a problem; limit unit and expensive building production
Food Production		yes		can build animist's guilds
Population Growth		yes		
Outpost growth rates		yes		
Road Building	yes			engineers
Shamans or Priests	yes			priests
Rebellion-normal	yes			can build all unrest-quelling institutions
Interracial Unrest	yes			fairly friendly race
Use of Gold, Silver, Gems	yes			can build banks and merchant's guilds
Use of Adamantium and Mithril			yes	can build alchemist's guilds
Use of Coal and Iron		yes		
Use of Crysx and Quork		yes		
Seaworthiness	yes			can build warships

High Men

High Men are slow to develop economically. If you can hang on long enough, though, their big end-stage unit, the paladin, is probably the strongest normal unit type in the game. Armies of paladins can destroy all but the toughest nodes, lairs, and garrisons. Keep a low profile when playing High Men until you can make paladins; then build a bunch of them and let loose!

On a more sedate note, High Men are average at just about everything. They make almost every building and get along with most other races. Remember, it takes a long time to get them on a solid military footing, so be prepared to wait things out, or hurry things along a bit by opting for one of the straight military wizard skills, like Alchemy or Warlord.

Table 5.9 predicts the High Men's future.

Suggested Colors and Wizard Skills when playing High Men:

🐸 Any magic color

🐸 Alchemy, Warlord

Table 5.10 Klackons Information

Area of Consideration	Strength	Average	Weakness	Notes and Suggestions
Units	yes			good units for early conquest
End-stage unit(s)		yes		Stag Beetles are good because you can get them early in the game; play aggressively
Attack Strength		yes		average
To Hit		yes		average
Special Features		yes		none
Defense	yes			+2 shields
Resistance		yes		+1 resistance
Hearts		yes		average
Unit Costs			yes	high unit costs
Spell Research			yes	cannot build sage's guilds, universities, or wizard's guilds; consider Sage Master for accelerated research or Node Mastery and node conquering for extra mana
Mana Production			yes	concentrate on conquest, node collection; consider skills like Node Mastery
Production rates	yes			all workers are extra productive (three prod. points each)
Gold Production		yes		gold situation generally stable due to few buildings to maintain and good return from Trade Goods setting
Food Production			yes	cannot build animist's guilds
Population Growth		yes		
Outpost growth rates		yes		
Road Building	yes			engineers
Shamans or Priests			yes	cannot purify corrupted land; white or green magic for spells that purify; hang on to heroes/mercenaries with this skill
Rebellion-normal		yes		if left alone, "hive" mentality will keep unrest down; otherwise large garrisons
Interracial Unrest			yes	one of the unfriendliest races; large garrisons; white magic for Just Cause or green magic for Gaia's Blessing
Use of Gold, Silver, Gems			yes	cannot build banks or merchant's guilds
Use of Adamantium and Mithril			yes	cannot build alchemist's guilds; consider Alchemy skill; white magic (Holy Weapon)
Use of Coal and Iron		yes		
Use of Crysx and Quork		yes		
Seaworthiness			yes	cannot build galleys or warships; Sorcery magic for floating islands

Klackons

Klackons, like Gnolls, are best played in a quick, expansionist game. Their normal units all get +2 shields, greatly increasing their longevity in battle. The Klackon's high productivity level means that their stag beetles can be made fairly early in the game, at a point where your enemies are still building units like halberdiers. Play the Klackons on big continents so that you can easily send their stag beetles everywhere. Correctly played, the Klackons can quickly take over nearby neutral and enemy cities, giving them a strong power base during the crucial early stages of the game.

Similarly, try to make a point of capturing nodes as early as you can if you are playing with the Klackons, since they lag significantly behind all other races in mana production and spell research.

More information about the Klackons is provided in Table 5.10.

Suggested Colors and Wizard Skills when playing Klackons:

🐸 Life, Sorcery magic

🐸 Alchemy, Node Mastery, Sage Master

Lizardmen

Lizardmen are a lot like Klackons. They're not the greatest race, but they build their cities quickly (through a decided lack of building options). Their normal units get an extra shield and hit point, helping them last longer in combat. Their dragon turtles are nice units that can be built early and, since they swim, can be sent across oceans to conquer cities on other continents.

The swimming ability of the Lizardmen and their settlers is particularly helpful in early exploration and rapid transcontinental colonization efforts (especially since the Lizardmen grow fast too). Make sure you start the game on small land masses to get the maximum benefit from the Lizardmen's swimming ability. Like the Klackons, Lizardmen are best played with an aggressive start.

The low base productivity of Lizardmen cities is both a boon and a curse. The low production is due to the paucity of buildings this race can erect, but the lack of building options allows Lizardmen to pay low maintenance costs for cities and to convert their production to units and trade goods at an early point in the game. Table 5.11 sheds light (and skin) on Lizardmen.

Suggested Colors and Wizard Skills when playing Lizardmen:

🐸 Life, Nature magic

🐸 Alchemy, Node Mastery, Sage Mastery

Nomads

Nomads are neither militaristically mighty combatants nor superior spell researchers and mana producers, they are simply a balanced race. Their basic units are completely all right, though they could use a bit of enhancing. The Nomads' end-stage unit, the griffin, is a solid, but not a killer, unit.

Nomads do have a trade bonus for their gold production, which makes them more economically stable than many other races in the early stages of the game. Since that's also when your financial worries often start, Nomads can be a good race with which to begin a game.

What Nomads lack is spice. Think about picking spell books that give you interesting unit enchantments or fantastic units to excite things a bit. Alternately, perk up your troops' abilities by starting with Alchemy or Warlord

Table 5.11 *Lizardmen Information*

Area of Consideration	Strength	Average	Weakness	Notes and Suggestions
Units	yes			good units for early conquest
End-stage unit(s)		yes		Dragon Turtles are good since you can get them early in the game; play aggressively
Attack Strength		yes		average
To Hit		yes		average
Special Features	yes			swimming; excellent for rapid exploration and expansion
Defense		yes		+1 shields
Resistance		yes		average
Hearts	yes			+1 hearts
Unit Costs			yes	high unit costs
Spell Research			yes	cannot build sage's guilds, universi-ties, or wizard's guilds; consider Sage Master for accelerated research or Node Mastery and node conquering for extra mana
Mana Production			yes	concentrate on conquest, node collection; consider skills like Node Mastery
Production rates			yes	cannot even make a sawmill; white magic for Inspirations or green, Gaia's Blessing, for increased men and production
Gold Production		yes		gold situation generally stable due to few buildings to maintain
Food Production			yes	cannot build animist's guilds
Population Growth	yes			early expansion is a good idea
Outpost growth rates		yes		
Road Building			yes	no engineers
Shamans or Priests		yes		shamans
Rebellion-normal			yes	can only make shrines and temples to deal with unrest; consider white magic for Just Cause and Stream of Life or green magic for Gaia's Blessing
Interracial Unrest		yes		
Use of Gold, Silver, Gems			yes	cannot build banks, merchant's guilds or miner's guilds
Use of Adamantium and Mithril			yes	cannot build alchemist's guilds; consider Alchemy skill; Life magic (Holy Weapon)
Use of Coal and Iron			yes	no miner's guilds
Use of Crysx and Quork			yes	no miner's guilds
Seaworthiness			yes	cannot build any ships (but they swim, so who cares)

Table 5.12 *Nomads Information*

Area of Consideration	Strength	Average	Weakness	Notes and Suggestions
Units		yes		unspectacular units; consider red, green, or black magic and Conjurer for summoning
End-stage unit(s)		yes		Griffins, Horsebowmen
Attack Strength		yes		average
To Hit		yes		average
Special Features		yes		none
Defense		yes		average
Resistance		yes		average
Hearts		yes		average
Unit Costs		yes		
Spell Research		yes		can build universities, but not wizard's guilds
Mana Production		yes		have all mana-producing buildings; capitalize on this with Death magic (Dark Rituals) and Infernal Power
Production rates	yes			can build mechanician's guilds
Gold Production	yes			if, on occasion, gold becomes a concern, limit unit and expensive building production
Food Production		yes		can build animist's guilds
Population Growth		yes		
Outpost growth rates		yes		
Road Building			yes	no engineers
Shamans or Priests	yes			priests
Rebellion-normal	yes			can build all unrest-quelling institutions
Interracial Unrest	yes			friendly race
Use of Gold, Silver, Gems	yes			can build banks and merchant's guilds
Use of Adamantium and Mithril			yes	can build alchemist's guilds
Use of Coal and Iron		yes		
Use of Crysx and Quork		yes		
Seaworthiness		yes		cannot build warships

skills. Otherwise prepare yourself for a slowly developing, balanced game.

Nomad details are wandering around in Table 5.12.

Suggested Colors and Wizard Skills when playing Nomads:

 Chaos, Death, Nature magic

 Alchemy, Conjurer, Infernal Power, Warlord

Orcs

What can be said about the Nomads, goes double for the Orcs, except the Orcs don't even get a trade bonus! On the positive side, Orcs can build everything and, so, are capable of quelling high levels of unrest, traveling the seas in solid warships, and producing large quantities of mana and spell research. Conversely, Orcs can take a long time to reach their potential.

Orcish units are unremarkable. In fact, their end-stage units, the wyvern riders, have as their greatest asset the fact that they fly

Table 5.13 *Orcs Information*

Area of Consideration	Strength	Average	Weakness	Notes and Suggestions
Units		yes		unspectacular units; consider red, green, or black magic and Conjurer for summoning
End-stage unit(s)	yes			Wyvern Riders fly quickly
Attack Strength		yes		average
To Hit		yes		average
Special Features		yes		none
Defense		yes		average
Resistance		yes		average
Hearts		yes		average
Unit Costs		yes		
Spell Research	yes			can build universities and wizard's guilds
Mana Production		yes		have all mana-producing buildings; capitalize on this with Death magic (Dark Rituals) and Infernal Power
Production rates	yes			can build mechanician's guilds
Gold Production			yes	gold can be serious problem at times; try not to overdevelop cities
Food Production		yes		can build animist's guilds
Population Growth		yes		
Outpost growth rates		yes		
Road Building	yes			engineers
Shamans or Priests		yes		shamans
Rebellion-normal	yes			can build all unrest-quelling institutions
Interracial Unrest		yes		
Use of Gold, Silver, Gems	yes			can build banks and merchant's guilds
Use of Adamantium and Mithril			yes	can build alchemist's guilds
Use of Coal and Iron		yes		
Use of Crysx and Quork		yes		
Seaworthiness	yes			can build warships

quickly. Regardless, the Orcs have a lot of versatility and scads of potential. As for the Nomads, you may want to spice these guys up with enchantments or fantastic units, or by taking full advantage of their mana production (by using Death magic, Infernal Power and Dark Rituals). For a slightly more powerful team, opt for Alchemy or Warlord to keep the early parts of the game from moving too slowly.

Table 5.13 provides an Orcish horde of information.

Suggested Colors and Wizard Skills when playing Orcs:

Chaos, Death, Nature magic

Alchemy, Conjurer, Infernal Power, Warlord

Table 5.14 *Trolls Information*

Area of Consideration	Strength	Average	Weakness	Notes and Suggestions
Units	yes			strong regenerating units excellent for early conquests; make phenom–enal garrisons
End-stage unit(s)	yes			War Trolls and War Mammoths
Attack Strength	yes			+2 swords
To Hit		yes		average
Special Features	yes			regeneration; fewer figures per unit; Death magic since units can still regenerate when enchanted by black magic
Defense		yes		average
Resistance	yes			+3 crosses
Hearts	yes			+3 hearts
Unit Costs			yes	most expensive units in the game
Spell Research			yes	cannot build sage's guild, university or wizard's guilds; consider Sage Master or Node Mastery and focus on conquering nodes
Mana Production		yes		have all mana-producing buildings except alchemist's guilds; consider Divine Power or Infernal Power
Production rates			yes	cannot build miner's or mechanician's guilds; white magic (Inspirations)
Gold Production		yes		gold is generally not a serious concern; apply the usual care in decisions on what to build
Food Production		yes		can build animist's guilds
Population Growth			yes	increase growth rates with Gaia's Blessing or Stream of Life (green or white magic)
Outpost growth rates			yes	start expanding as early as you can to make up for low outpost growth rates
Road Building			yes	no engineers
Shamans or Priests		yes		shaman
Rebellion-normal		yes		cannot build oracles
Interracial Unrest			yes	unrest levels can get quite high; use big garrisons and build religious structures quickly; white magic (Just Cause) or green magic (Gaia's Blessing)
Use of Gold, Silver, Gems			yes	cannot build banks, merchant's guilds, or miner's guilds
Use of Adamantium and Mithril			yes	no alchemist's or miner's guilds; consider Alchemy skill; white magic (Holy Weapon)
Use of Coal and Iron			yes	cannot build miner's guilds
Use of Crysx and Quork			yes	cannot build miner's guilds
Seaworthiness			yes	cannot build galleys or warships; Sorcery magic for floating islands

Trolls

Trolls build strong, ultra-hardy units. They all start with two extra swords, extra resistance, and three extra hit points. Also, all Troll units (except war mammoths), regenerate. Trolls are clearly meant to stick around once they arrive at a battlefield. Their strength and regenerative powers make them doubly deadly.

Trolls grow very slowly, however, as you might expect from a race with regenerating units. Therefore, get their outposts established early. On the other hand, because of their physical strength, they are ideal for early conquering of neutral and enemy cities.

Starting with Trolls will cause you to lag behind in spell research. Try to offset this through judicious wizard skill picks at the beginning of the game, or make a point of early node-conquering, and emphasize the building of shrines, temples, etc.

Troll information has been regenerated in Table 5.14.

Suggested Colors and Wizard Skills when playing Trolls:

🐸 Life, Death, Nature, Sorcery magic

🐸 Alchemy, Divine Power, Infernal Power

Race to the End

Thus, the races ended. This overview of the varying races in *Master of Magic* should help you see the advantages and disadvantages inherent in each and steer you on a steadier course to victory.

All that remains to be considered when creating your wizard, then, is magic—and there is a lot to consider there! The next chapter paints the general overview of how magic works in this game. It is followed by chapters detailing the spells in each of the five dominant colors, plus Arcane magic. Poof!

6
Spell Books:
The Write Stuff

Before analyzing all of the spells in *Master of Magic*, let's take a look at the different colors of magic. Here, we'll explore the basic things you should know when allocating spell picks before the game commences.

Weighty Decisions

When you create your own wizard, you get eleven spell picks to divide between wizard skills and spell books. The choices you make at this early stage are going to greatly affect many aspects of the game.

Wizard Skills: The Last Retort

First, how you divide spell picks between wizard skills and spell ranks is going to influence how quickly your game can or should develop. Wizard skills are effective from the beginning of the game and, if you choose several wizard skills, you can usually get off to a strong start. However, if you only have a few spell books, you will eventually lag far behind your opponents in spell-casting options.

With fewer spell books, you'll have fewer spells to research. Consequently, you will quickly reach the stage of researching Spell of Mastery (which can take eons).

To increase your spell-casting options, therefore, play aggressively. Capitalize on whatever skills you got from your initial spell picks and grab nodes and lairs as fast as you can—you'll need their spells and spell books to upgrade your abilities.

Remember, the game limits each player to 6 retorts and 13 spell books. Some retorts also cost more than one spell pick. You can acquire a greater value in terms of *net spell picks* by grabbing retorts from nodes and lairs instead of choosing them from your spell picks. It is the *number* of retorts that is the limiting factor, not their value in picks. The *value* of the retorts in picks limits how many you can choose at the beginning of the game. See

Chapter 4 for more information on specific wizard skills.

Spelling Lessons

Your game will develop more slowly when you choose more spell books instead of more wizard skills to start the game. However, at the start of the game, you will know more spells and have a higher spell-casting skill. Also, your later spell-casting abilities, assuming you hang in there, will be quite powerful when you have more spell books.

The second major decision you have to make is how to divide your spell books over colors. Will you focus your efforts solely or predominantly on one magic color, to reap the benefits of reduced research and casting costs and to enjoy that color's more powerful spells later in the game? Or, will you spread your color selection out a bit, opting for more, broader, but less powerful spells and more spell trading possibilities with other wizards?

Let's take a look at what happens when you decide to grab more spell books than wizard skills. Keep these advantages in mind:

You get to pick one common spell with which to start the game for every spell book after the first one chosen in a specific color. For example, choosing one Chaos spell book doesn't net you any spells with which to start the game. But, choosing two Chaos spell books means that you get to pick one common Chaos spell that you'll know from the first turn of the game (i.e., no research is required). If you choose eleven spell books in one color, you automatically start the game with all of that magic color's common spells, as well as your choice of two uncommon spells and one rare spell.

You get two points of spell-casting skill for every spell book you start with. For example, if you choose four Chaos books, four Life books and Myrran as your eleven spell picks,

Table 6.1 Research and Casting Cost Discounts for Spell Books

Number of Spell Books	Research Bonus and in One Magic Realm Casting Cost Discount
8	10%
9	20%
10	30%
11	40%

you will get a starting spell-casting skill of 16 (two for each of your eight spell books). Remember that your spell-casting skill determines the amount of mana you can pour into spell casting each game turn and per combat.

🐸 Your Enchanted Fortress generates one mana per game turn for each spell book you own (plus five more if you start on Myrror).

🐸 If you choose eight or more spell books in one magic color, you get research bonuses and casting cost discounts for spells of that color. Table 6.1 shows the discounts for having large numbers of spell books in a single magic realm.

For example, if you choose nine Life magic spell books, you will have to pay 20 percent less for researching and casting Life magic spells. Note that your research and casting costs for Arcane magic spells, or for spells from other magic realms, will be unaffected.

🐸 You can only learn, acquire through trade, or, while conquering nodes and lairs, find *rare* and *very rare* spells of a particular magic realm if you have at least *two* or *three* (respectively) spell books of that magic color. Therefore, if you want a chance to find or trade for very rare Chaos magic spells, pick at least three Chaos spell books when you begin the game.

🐸 The only way you can guarantee that you will get all the spells of a particular color is to pick 10 spell books of that type.

🐸 If you choose eleven spell picks in one color, 3,000 research points are deducted from the cost of learning the Spell of Mastery (Chapter 7).

🐸 The only way you can guarantee that you will get all the uncommon spells from a magic realm is to choose at least eight spell books of that type.

🐸 Trading can only be initiated when you and the other wizard have spell books of the same color. If you don't share any spell book colors, the other wizard won't even trade Arcane magic with you!

Consequently, your trading potential improves if you have more magic realms represented in your spell picks. For example, picking eight spell books, two each in Chaos, Nature, Sorcery, and Life magic, will enable you to trade with all wizards except those who know only Death magic. Remember, your casting options and final score (Chapter 3) improve with the number of spells you know. In addition, each spell you know, regardless of how you learned it, contributes half of its base research value toward researching the Spell of Mastery (Chapter 7).

Swimming in a Sea of Color

Besides choosing how many spell books to take, you'll have to choose their colors. Do you choose one color and go for the big research and casting bonuses (not to mention the very rare spells)? Or do you spread out, go for variety with a batch of uncommon and common spells, trading options, etc.? And then what colors do you choose? Here, experience will be your best teacher. Once you've decided to either specialize or generalize your magic colors, we have some thoughts on how each different color affects your play.

White Magic

Life magic focuses heavily on unit, constructive city, and global enchantments. It basically makes things better. As such, it offers you a slow starting game and, eventually, the tools to make your starting race immensely powerful. It features tons of ways to rectify urban problems (gold, growth, productivity, unrest) and to defend against destructive Chaos and Death magic spells.

On top of all this, Life is *the* friendly magic type, giving all other wizards, except those with the antithetical black magic, the tendency to like you more. You'll benefit from this edge, too, since in a slow game you'll need the other players to like you or, at least, leave you alone.

White magic is most deficient in destructive and summoning spells. If you plan to start with Life magic, choose a stronger, faster playing race, such as the Dwarves, Klackons, Lizardmen, or Trolls. White plays well with any race, however, depending on your patience.

Some wizard skills are particularly beneficial if you choose Life magic:

🐸 Divine Power requires you have Life magic before you can pick it. It boosts the mana production from your cities' religious buildings and reduces unrest in your cities.

🐸 Warlord or Alchemy will give you a military boost while you wait for your magic research to catch up.

🐸 Famous will further enhance Just Cause's effects and provide you with more material for strong armies.

🐸 Charisma will accentuate the positive diplomatic effects that specializing in white magic already gives you.

Finally, there are certain outstanding heroes, including Torin the Chosen, that you can only obtain if you have Life magic (see Chapter 18).

Black Magic

Death magic offers many ways to undercut your enemies, while giving you a fantastic host of units to summon. Although black has few constructive spells, it does have Dark Rituals, a spell that increases the mana production from shrines, temples, parthenons, and cathedrals. Death magic can be a fast-playing color since even its early combat spells are nasty and effective. Death's common spell, Dark Rituals, can quickly raise your mana income and speed your research and spell-casting skill development.

Black magic has several drawbacks. Everyone hates students of Death magic, even other practitioners. Further, this magic color has few positive spells of any kind. Creatures of Death don't heal, although their casting and upkeep costs are commensurately lower.

Of the races that play well with Death magic, Halflings and Barbarians are good choices. They have rapid growth rates and building options that allow them to make reasonable use of the power-boosting Dark Rituals. Also, they are a little weak militarily and can benefit from the creature infusion that black magic offers. Trolls are a good complementary race, too, since the Death's enchantments that turn normal units into non-healing undeads do not eliminate the regenerative powers of this race.

Wizard skills that go well with Death magic include:

🐸 Infernal Power requires you to have Death magic spell books; this skill increases the mana production from your religious buildings and decreases unrest in your cities. Combined with Dark Rituals, the mana production bonus from your religious buildings climbs to three times normal!

🐸 Channeler or Conjurer will give you discounts on your spell maintenance costs, making the already cheap Death magic creatures even easier to support. Conjurer will also make these loathsome monsters less expensive to summon and maintain.

🐸 Mana Focusing will give you even more mana to augment what you get from casting Dark Rituals, for summoning monsters or casting your negative combat spells, and city or global enchantments.

🐸 Charismatic will help you partially compensate for the negative public image caused by owning Death magic books.

Note that some of the heroes in *Master of Magic* can only be summoned or acquired if you own Death magic books (see Chapter 18).

Red Magic

Chaos magic is brutal. It's loaded with destructive combat spells, global enchantments, and multitudes of fantastic creatures to summon. While many early Chaos magic spells are not great, a fast-playing game is definitely possible with red magic. By the time you start learning rare and very rare red combat spells (Doom Bolt, Disintegration, etc.) you can usually just charge ahead and win the game.

Red magic does not have many protective spells or unit enchantments; however, its combat spells are so powerful that it doesn't require them. As a result, Chaos magic is a good color to complement races with relatively weak or uninteresting units, such as the Barbarians, Gnolls, Halflings, Nomads, and Orcs. It's especially good for complementing these races

because Chaos has so many cool fantastic units to summon.

The biggest drawback for red magic, aside from its lack of protective spells, is that its combat spells are so good that it is disgustingly easy to run out of mana as you run around the worlds conquering cities! In fact, many of our wizard skill recommendations are based on compensating for this drawback:

🐸 Channeler will let you cast all those awesome Chaos spells in combat without paying the distance penalty for them. It also lets you maintain all of your nasty global and city enchantments at half price.

🐸 Chaos Mastery gives you a discount on researching and casting Chaos spells (which is additive to any other discounts you get), doubles the mana you get from conquered Chaos nodes, and makes your Chaos enchantments a lot more difficult to dispel. Note that you must have Chaos books to pick this skill at the beginning of the game.

🐸 Conjurer will lower the casting and upkeep costs of all those fun Chaos creatures.

🐸 Mana Focusing will decrease the amount of mana you need to cast spells.

Green Magic

Nature magic is a philosophical blend of Chaos and Life magic. It has a lot of constructive and positive unit, city, and global enchantments (like Life magic). However, it also offers a slew of fantastic units and some very powerful combat spells (like Chaos magic). Best of all, it has the only spells that alter terrain and mineral types in a positive way. Because green is a balanced color with its priority placed on positive spells, it tends to make your game play faster than Life magic, but slower than Chaos magic.

Nature magic can compensate for a lot of racial deficiencies, both urban-related (population growth, food production, productivity) and unit-related (enchantments for weak units and many summoning options). While we recommend this magic color for all races, it may be particularly helpful for races with poor food production capabilities (cast Gaia's Blessing) that limit army development: Barbarians, Gnolls, Dwarves, Klackons, and Lizardmen; or those with largely weak or uninteresting unit types, such as the Halflings, Nomads, and Orcs.

Wizard skills that may go well with Nature magic are:

 Nature Mastery, of course, is the skill of choice when you have a high concentration of green spell books. It gives you a 15 percent lower cost on researching and casting Nature spells, double the mana from nature nodes, and it will make all your Nature enchantments twice as hard to dispel.

 Conjurer will reduce the cost for summoning and maintaining the myriad of Nature creatures available to you.

 Anything else (except for Divine and Infernal Power, which you can't choose unless you also have white or black magic, respectively) will work well with Nature magic. You may wish to guide your choices for additional skills by the race you want to play or how you want to win (through casting the Spell of Mastery or through combat).

Blue Magic

Sorcery magic is more on the defensive side of things, although its primary means for being defensive is to pull fast ones and upset other wizards' plans. Nonetheless, its strength isn't aggressive in nature, so blue games are often slow ones. Fortunately, Sorcery offers the common spell, Aura of Majesty, to keep things running smoothly with other wizards as you develop your empire.

Among the cool things blue magic can do are 1) summon floating islands that can transport huge stacks just about anywhere; 2) cast the Flight enchantment to make units faster, more mobile, and less accessible to enemies in battle; and 3) provide powerful creatures to summon during combat (the phantom units and air elementals). Finally, Sorcery has some of the strongest rare and very rare spells in the game (Suppress Magic, Mass Invisibility, Disjunction True, Spell Binding, etc.)

Blue is a color that can strengthen races that have poor naval options, such as Beastmen, Halflings, Klackons, and Trolls, through its floating islands and Flight spells. However, it can do wonderful things for any race, since its effects are not so much compensatory in nature (as the other colors often are) as they are unique and useful in their own right.

Since Sorcery magic begets a slow game, use a physically strong race to help you survive until you're ready to win. Good choices include the Dwarves, Klackons, Lizardmen, and Trolls (although Beastmen, Dark Elves, Gnolls, and even High Men aren't too bad in this regard).

Helpful wizard skills include:

 Sorcery Mastery, of course. This skill will save you 15 percent on the casting and researching costs of all your Sorcery spells, while making any blue nodes you own twice as productive and your blue enchantments twice as hard to dispel. Be aware that blue nodes tend to appear more than any other color (see Chapter 14), making Sorcery Mastery particularly useful if you are specializing in this color.

 Alchemy and Warlord will help get your race's units in shape as you prepare to dig in and hang on until you are powerful enough to take over the worlds.

Charismatic will keep other wizards off your back until you are ready to move. Also, this skill works very well in conjunction with Aura of Majesty.

Mana Focusing or Channeler will help keep up your supply of mana as you cast expensive Sorcery combat spells (like Mass Invisibility and summoning phantom beasts), overland spells (like Spell Blast), or as you try to maintain nasty global enchantments (like Suppress Magic).

Pre-Fab Wizards

The brief descriptions of colors in this chapter and of the wizard skills in Chapter 4 should give you a pretty good idea of what you will net, in terms of game play possibilities, when you choose one of the pre-made wizards. It should also give you a basic idea of how your opponents' games will develop (see Chapter 28 for more information on enemy wizards).

Of course, we happen to think it's much more fun to make your own wizards. Regardless of whether you create your own or choose one off the rack (ahem), the wizard whose identity you play is removed from your pool of potential opponents.

Authors' Killer Combos

So, what combinations of skills, magic colors, and races work best together and why? Well, each of the authors has his or her own preferences.

Alan tends to be a militaristic, Machiavellian empire builder. He likes the Warlord, Fame, and Charismatic skills a lot. While he prefers the High Men and Orcs because of their considerable options for urban development and diverse troop types (see Chapter 16), Alan also likes to start with the Halflings on Myrror. That combination allows him to conquer the exotic Myrran races with a minimum of resentment (everyone likes the Halflings — see Chapter 15). When it comes to magic, Alan is partial to red (for combat spells) and green (to help with his empire building).

Petra is an exploration-oriented expansionist. She spends most of her games looking for new lairs and nodes to clean out and dislikes races that require too much development before they can build their best units. She loves Dwarves because of their extra gold and production, in addition to their hardy units. She also likes the Halflings, because of their slingers, and Trolls, because they regenerate. Her favorite magic color is green (versatile, protective magic and, specifically, for the Web and Gaia's Blessing spells) and there are few games in which a green spell book doesn't make it into her wizard's picks. Mixing magic types is her favorite way to set up a game, since almost all of Petra's favorite spells are cheap (i.e., either common or uncommon). She likes playing with Channeler and Warlord skills since her favorite form of expansion is conquering other cities.

Tom plays the Dark Elves when he starts on Myrror and either the High Elves or High Men (he *loves* paladins!) when he begins on Arcanus. He prefers to take at least a couple of spell books in each of four different colors in order to maximize his trading potential with other wizards. Since Tom is a grow-like-a-weed empire builder, he pushes settlers out fast, finding the most efficient ways to settle every square of land on the map. Tom is also great at using alchemy to convert gold to mana so that he can concentrate his per turn mana income on research and spell-casting skill.

Finally, we asked designer Steve Barcia what his favorite starting options were. Ruthless player that he is, Steve opts to start on Myrror with the Dark Elves. He'll take the Warlord wizard skill (the extra sword makes a big difference for the Dark Elves) and put the rest of his picks into Death magic. Steve uses Dark Rituals liberally under these circumstances to make a ton of urban mana and then goes around stomping others with ruthless, gleeful abandon.

Looking Ahead

The following chapters are each devoted to a particular magic color, giving you in depth descriptions and suggestions for using all the spells in *Master of Magic*. After we exhaustively illustrate the possibilities, Chapter 13 closes the circle by analyzing how to mix and match the colors.

Section 3

Spell Binding

7

Gray Matters

Because it has no specific color, Arcane magic is often referred to as "gray." Every wizard begins each game with all of the Arcane magic spells in his or her spell book. This means that every wizard is capable of learning, casting, and trading every Arcane magic spell in every game. The following sections break down all Arcane spells by spell type. Within each type, the spells are arranged by rarity, from common to very rare.

Summoning Spells

These are spells that summon a new, *fantastic* unit into existence at the owner's Summoning Circle (if that square is already filled to capacity, it will appear in an adjacent square). Instead of requiring food and gold for upkeep, summoned creatures consume mana every turn to maintain their existence.

Magic Spirit

Every wizard knows this spell from the first turn of the game. Magic spirits are pretty reasonable fighters for their casting cost. Most of the time, however, these creatures are primarily summoned to do their work melding with nodes. This allows the spirit's caster to reap the mana that node provides.

One player's magic spirit can freely replace another's on a node by simply melding with it. The controller of the last spirit to successfully meld with a node gets its mana. The former spirit melded with that node is simply removed from the game without effect.

Note that you have only a 25 percent chance of successfully replacing a node that

has a guardian spirit melded to it. Failure results in the loss of the spirit attempting to replace the guardian spirit.

Getting a magic spirit to a newly conquered node isn't much of a problem. Since they are non-corporeal, they pay half of a movement point for all terrain types, including oceans. Thus, they'll make good time marching directly to any waiting node. If your Summoning Circle is a long distance from a newly won node, casting the white spell of Endurance will increase your spirit's speed (see Chapter 8).

Hint: Use magic spirits for early exploration. They're cheap, move two squares per turn (even across water) because they are non-corporeal, and can peek into lairs quickly in hopes of finding empty ones before the other players do. At the beginning of the game, a band of magic spirits of the game is also strong enough to conquer some weakly garrisoned neutral cities, a move that can tremendously boost your development.

Combat Spells

These spells are thrown by both players and heroes with spell-casting abilities while engaged in battle. Chapter 21 has all of the details on using magic in combat.

Dispel Magic

All negative spells cast by an opponent that affect one of your combat units (such as Weakness, Black Sleep, Confusion, etc.) might be removed by casting this spell. The formula for successfully casting Dispel Magic can be found on page 107 of the game manual.

Statistically, it is better never to put extra mana into dispel spells (like Dispel Magic). Your odds are a bit better when casting such spells

Magic Spirit Summary Information

Spell Rarity	Research Point Cost	Combat Casting Cost	Overland Casting Cost	Upkeep Cost Per Turn	Notes
Common	N/A	N/A	30	1	N/A

multiple times (if the first one doesn't work) rather than casting one spell with multiple times its base strength.

Recall Hero

For those who do not save the game just prior to a battle (or have forgotten to!) this spell can rescue a hero from a desperate situation. This a good spell to use when it appears that you will win a battle but no longer need a hero there who is badly beaten up and being picked on by enemy troops. Get the hero out of danger and let the rest of your army finish the battle.

This spell is also a clever way to reinforce the city with your Summoning Circle. This is handy only if you see that the enemy is about to attack in the *next* turn and you have the ability to charge your hero blindly into battle in *this* turn so that (s)he can be recalled.

Global Enchantments

We affectionately call these spells "world busters." They affect everything applicable to that spell in both worlds. We're talking big league magic here.

Spell of Mastery

When researching this, the ultimate spell, don't plan on learning any other new spells for a while. Usually, this

Dispel Magic Summary Information

Spell Rarity	Research Point Cost	Combat Casting Cost	Overland Casting Cost	Upkeep Cost Per Turn	Notes
Uncommon	100	10 to 50	N/A	N/A	N/A

Recall Hero Summary Information

Spell Rarity	Research Point Cost	Combat Casting Cost	Overland Casting Cost	Upkeep Cost Per Turn	Notes
Uncommon	350	20	N/A	N/A	N/A

one will take many, many turns to research. To that end, you might want to increase the amount of mana going toward research because a little extra mana per turn, over time, can shave a few turns off the wait.

While casting this spell, look out for a critical drain on your mana reserves. If you have less mana going into your wand (reserve) than your skill level (the rate at which mana is taken from your reserve and applied to spell casting), your reserves could be sucked dry. The worst possible time to run out of mana is while casting this spell since, at this time, all

Spell of Mastery Summary Information

Spell Rarity	Research Point Cost	Combat Casting Cost	Overland Casting Cost	Upkeep Cost Per Turn	Notes
Very Rare	60,000*	N/A	5,000	N/A	Game Winning

* = less half the RP value of all spells previously learned or acquired by that wizard; wizards who have 11 spell picks in one color get another 3,000 Research Points off the cost

Summoning Circle Summary Information

Spell Rarity	Research Point Cost	Combat Casting Cost	Overland Casting Cost	Upkeep Cost Per Turn	Notes
Common	150	N/A	50	N/A	N/A

Detect Magic Summary Information

Spell Rarity	Research Point Cost	Combat Casting Cost	Overland Casting Cost	Upkeep Cost Per Turn	Notes
Uncommon	400	N/A	200	3	N/A

Detect Magic

This spell is your wizard spy. It displays what spell is currently being cast by each wizard you've contacted. The name of the spell appears above their gem on your Magic Summary display. Knowing what everyone is doing helps you decide when to start bribing them into a better attitude towards you and, if you have Sorcery magic, deciding when to cast Spell Blast.

of the others declare war (usually attacking relentlessly) against the caster.

Therefore, plan your mana usage wisely, both while researching and casting the Spell of Mastery. If you can hang on and finish casting this one, there will be a big reward in terms of victory points at the end of the game (see Chapter 3).

Special Spells

These are unique spells that do not fit neatly in the other categories.

Summoning Circle

Quite simply, this spell allows you to move your Summoning Circle to any other friendly city. Here you want to position the Summoning Circle strategically so that newly summoned creatures are brought in at the most advantageous spot. Presumably, this means a city well connected by roads with embattled areas and not on a distant continent from which the troops must be ferried over in ships. Also, placing your Summoning Circle on the *plane* where reinforcements are most needed (or, at the very least, near a controlled Tower of Wizardry) is an important consideration.

When you have cast Detect Magic, make sure you get your mana's worth by vigilantly monitoring your Magic Summary screen every turn. You're paying a lot in upkeep, so make the most out of the knowledge you gain. In particular, pay attention to how long it takes each wizard to cast the spells he or she is working on (this will give you an idea how high the wizard's spell-casting skill and mana income are).

Figure 7-1. *Detect Magic*

Disenchant Area

All negative spells cast by an opponent affecting all of your units on one square of the map (or the entire battlefield, if cast in combat) might be removed by casting this spell. This includes unwanted enchantments on your units, cities, nodes, and land. The formula for successfully casting Disenchant Area

Disenchant Area Summary Information

Spell Rarity	Research Point Cost	Combat Casting Cost	Overland Casting Cost	Upkeep Cost Per Turn	Notes
Uncommon	300	50 to 250	50 to 250	N/A	N/A

Enchant Item Summary Information

Spell Rarity	Research Point Cost	Combat Casting Cost	Overland Casting Cost	Upkeep Cost Per Turn	Notes
Uncommon	450	N/A	Varies	N/A	N/A

can be found on page 107 of the game manual.

Statistically, it is better never to put extra mana into dispel spells (like Disenchant Area). Your odds are a bit better when casting such spells multiple times (if the first one doesn't work) rather than casting one spell with multiple times its base strength. A way to maximize the strength of this spell (and others like it), while not sacrificing game time, is to put extra mana into casting the spell so that the casting cost is equal to your spell-casting skill (i.e., the amount of mana you can pump into casting non-combat spells every game turn) or some multiple of this if your skill is less than the base casting cost of the spell.

Enchant Item

This is a low-level, do-it-yourself magic item creation spell. These items are given to your heroes to enhance their abilities. With this spell, no special powers can be added from your spell book to the item if the power's RP value exceeds 200 (double this if you're placing the enchantment into a miscellaneous item). Thus, only lower level spells and bonuses are available for items created with an Enchant Item spell.

The trick here is not to get greedy when creating new items. Maxing out every category you can will mean creating an item that could take you several turns to conjure, especially during the early stages of the game. These could be turns where an emergency crops up requiring a rapid creature summoning, or your plans could be delayed while you are waiting to cast another spell. (On the up side, you can always think of the mana spent on new magic items as "banked," because breaking them on your anvil will give you half your mana investment in them back.)

Finally, remember each item has inherent restrictions on its maximum abilities. While these are shown in Table L of the manual, all of those maximums are lower when casting an Enchant Item spell. Their full values apply when using the Create Artifact spell listed below.

More information on creating items can be found in Chapter 19.

Summon Hero Summary Information

Spell Rarity	Research Point Cost	Combat Casting Cost	Overland Casting Cost	Upkeep Cost Per Turn	Notes
Uncommon	500	N/A	300	Varies	N/A

Awareness Summary Information

Spell Rarity	Research Point Cost	Combat Casting Cost	Overland Casting Cost	Upkeep Cost Per Turn	Notes
Rare	700	N/A	500	3	N/A

Summon Hero

Although heroes appear from time to time at no cost in mana to you, occasionally your need will be pressing. If you feel it is worth the time and mana required to cast this spell (less if you are a Runemaster, see Chapter 4), when completed you will be rewarded with a hero—sort of.

This hero will not be one of the best 10 on the hero list (see Summon Champion, below), nor will he be a dead hero back to life (see Chapter 8, Resurrection). You will still need to pay that hero's normal maintenance cost every turn, as well. So what do you really get for your 300 mana?

The big advantage of casting this spell is that all non-champions are in the lottery to be summoned, each with an equal chance. This is true regardless of the summoning wizard's fame, which might be lower than the minimum required to summon a particular hero. For the details on champions and minimum fame requirements for attracting heroes, see Chapter 18.

Generally, it is best to wait and see what heroes turn up for free. The time and mana spent summoning heroes is pretty much wasted unless your need is acute.

Awareness

When you're still in the exploratory stages of the game, this spell can help focus the direction of your military campaigns. This spell reveals every city and outpost on the map (plus the terrain in each square adjacent to them) *on both planes*, plus any new cities developed while this spell remains in effect. Armed with this information, you can shoot your armies toward them like a rifle, cutting through darkened squares as they march toward these objectives. If you want to know where to find an enemy's Enchanted Fortress or where to pick up an elven city, to add to your empire, for example, casting Awareness is the quickest way to find out.

Create Artifact

This is the high-powered version of Enchant Item. The primary difference is that the sky is the limit in terms of how much mana you can pump into the artifact created. This means top-notch enhancements and spells can be added to create artifacts of tremendous power—at a cost, of course.

Again, don't get greedy. It's all too tempting to begin creating the ultimate item, only to see that it will take fifty or more turns and bleed your mana reserves dry. Keep your wits about you and try to create specific artifacts for specific heroes. Don't combine a spell-casting bonus with an attack-strength bonus, for instance, unless that hero is really going to do both. See Chapter 19 for more details on artifact creation.

Disjunction

"When in danger, when in doubt, run in circles, scream and shout." While that is most people's first reaction to being splattered by some vicious enemy global enchantment (like Suppress Magic, Planar Seal, Meteor Storms, etc.), it is better to fight magic with magic. In this case, to shut off their global and city enchantments, you want to cast Disjunction. Consequently, getting this spell researched and in your spell book as quickly as possible should be a priority, particularly at the more difficult game levels (where enemy wizards will start casting these nasty spells much sooner).

The formula for the success of casting dispels can be found on page 107 of the game manual. Statistically, it is better never to put extra mana into dispel spells (like Disjunction). Your odds are a bit better when casting such spells multiple times (if the first one doesn't work) rather than casting one spell with multiple times its base strength.

Sometimes, you simply can't wait and need that enemy spell eliminated as soon as possible. In that case, carefully consider how much extra mana to put into Disjunction. Every turn it takes to cast drains more of your mana reserves and adds more time that you'll be suffering the enemy's enchantment. However, you can generally put a little extra oomph into these spells without increasing the time it takes to cast them if you pump enough extra mana into the spell so that the total casting cost is equal to a multiple of your spell-casting skill (i.e., the amount of mana you can funnel into casting non-combat spells every turn).

Summon Champion

Summon Champion works similarly to the Summon Hero spell but costs considerably more to cast. The important difference is that you will always get one of your 10 best heroes, except for Torin the Chosen, collectively known as champions (Aerie the Illusionist, Deathstryke the Swordsman, Elana the Priest-

Create Artifact Summary Information

Spell Rarity	Research Point Cost	Combat Casting Cost	Overland Casting Cost	Upkeep Cost Per Turn	Notes
Rare	1,000	N/A	Varies	N/A	N/A

Disjunction Summary Information

Spell Rarity	Research Point Cost	Combat Casting Cost	Overland Casting Cost	Upkeep Cost Per Turn	Notes
Uncommon	750	N/A	200 to 1,000	N/A	N/A

Summon Champion Summary Information

Spell Rarity	Research Point Cost	Combat Casting Cost	Overland Casting Cost	Upkeep Cost Per Turn	Notes
Rare	1,250	N/A	750	Varies	N/A

Spell of Return Summary Information

Spell Rarity	Research Point Cost	Combat Casting Cost	Overland Casting Cost	Upkeep Cost Per Turn	Notes
N/A	N/A	N/A	1,000	N/A	starts being cast as soon as you are banished

Spell of Return

Spell of Return is automatically in every wizard's spell book. When a wizard's Enchanted Fortress is captured, he or she is banished. If, however, the wizard has enough gold or mana, they start casting this spell. The only source of mana that can be used to cast Spell of Return is that in the wizard's mana or gold (through alchemy) reserves. When the spell is finally cast, the wizard gets to choose one of his or her remaining cities in which to establish a new Enchanted Fortress. See Chapter 3 for more information on what happens when a wizard is banished.

ess, Roland the Paladin, Mortu the Black Knight, Alorra the Elven Archer, Sir Harold the Knight, Ravashack the Necromancer, or Warrax the Chaos Warrior). Note that Roland and Elana can only be summoned by a wizard with some Life spell books, while Mortu and Ravashack can only be summoned by a wizard with some Death spell books (see Chapter 18).

Unlike Summon Hero, the Summon Champion spell is a good way to fill a vacancy in one of your six hero slots if you can afford the time and mana. The quality of these particular heroes is so great that the trade-off in mana to summon them is worth the time saved in getting them.

White Wash

So much for a trip to the Penny Arcane, those common gray spells that every wizard shares. While these general utility spells are necessary for rounding out every wizard's spell book, it is the magic found in the five colors that makes *Master of Magic* such an interesting game. From here, we're adding bleach, getting the gray out, and moving on to white magic, pure and not-so-simple.

Figure 7-2. *Spell of Return*

White On

ife magic is weak in summoning and special spells, but strong in city and creature enhancements. White magic is, arguably, the weakest color to play by itself, although if you can stick around long enough, its powerful rare and very rare enchantments will make your cities and units almost unbeatable. White makes an excellent supporting color with its good selection of common and uncommon combat spells and creature enhancements.

White magic tends to be protective and healing in nature. Generally, it is used offensively to beef up unit strengths and defenses to help insure their victory on the battlefield. White magic also increases a wizard's popularity among other players (at least those who do not opt to take many black spell books, see Chapter 25).

Because white magic is the opposite of black and, to a lesser degree, red magic, there are several potent spells that specifically counter these colors' units and enchantments. This added insurance against those two powerful offensive magic colors also makes white magic a good secondary spell book color to choose.

Summoning Spells

These are spells that summon a new, *fantastic* class unit into existence at the owner's Summoning Circle (if that square is already filled to capacity, it will appear in an adjacent square). Instead of requiring food and gold for upkeep, summoned creatures consume mana every turn.

Sadly, white magic is really weak in the critter department. Players planning to go with all white magic will want to choose a strong military starting race such as the Lizardmen, Klackons, Dwarfs, or Trolls. These races develop

Figure 8-1. *Guardian Spirit*

rapidly and can produce powerful units fairly quickly. You'll need this when playing with pure white magic because white creature summoning simply won't help your military plans.

Guardian Spirit

Guardian spirits are adequate fighters for their casting cost. Their non-corporeal aspect gives them immunity to webbing, and when they are enhanced with an Endurance spell to speed their movement (see below), they can rush and attack through enemy city walls. Guardian spirits can be effective in groups when you have enchantments such as True Light that pump up the ratings of all Life creatures in battle.

Usually, though, guardian spirits are summoned to meld with nodes and reap the mana there. In this regard, their advantage over magic spirits (see Chapter 7) is that a guardian is not freely replaced like a magic spirit is. Rather, any spirit (magic *or guardian*) trying

Guardian Spirit *Summary Information*

Spell Rarity	Research Point Cost	Combat Casting Cost	Overland Casting Cost	Upkeep Cost Per Turn	Notes
Common	220	N/A	80	1	None

to evict a melded guardian spirit only has a 25 percent chance to do so. Otherwise, the already melded guardian spirit stays in possession of the node while the spirit failing to meld with that node is removed from the game without effect.

Like magic spirits, getting a guardian spirit to a newly conquered node isn't much of a problem. Their non-corporeal nature means that they pay only one-half a movement point for all terrain types, including oceans. This means they'll make good time marching directly to any waiting node. When it is a long way from your Summoning Circle to a newly won node, cast an Endurance spell to increase your spirit's speed (see below).

Unicorns

Unicorns are on the pricy side to cast and maintain, so their role in combat is better as a supporting unit (especially because they give +2 resistance to all friendly units), rather than as the bulwark of a force. Unicorns, for their part, make excellent *snipers*, if you will. This is because their teleport ability can take them adjacent to an enemy's weaker rear units, where the unicorns can inflict damage upon them in melee combat. Unfortunately, unicorns are only good, not great, fighters. However, as a tool for attacking weak spell-casting and missile units, unicorns can often take a few down with them.

Angel

Angels are an even better form of supporting unit for an army than unicorns

because they provide a +1 holy bonus for all the friendly units in their square (or in the same battle with them). This gives all the units with them (including the angel) one additional sword, shield, and cross for every figure on their side in battle. This holy bonus makes angels (and arch angels, for that matter) a great *supporting* combat unit when used in conjunction with other unit types in a stack.

For their part, angels deliver some considerable punch and can reach an enemy's weaker units fairly quickly with their flying rate of three squares per turn. Their +2 bonus To Hit means that each of the 13 sword icons they wield has a 50 percent chance of hitting (see Chapter 20), so angels can slice and dice pretty well, too. Angels also have a special advantage over red and black creatures because of their Dispel Evil attack (see Chapter 20).

Arch Angel

Basically, the arch angel is an angel on steroids. It functions just like an angel in all respects, but   it bestows a +2 holy bonus to its side and has a killer 60 percent chance of hitting with each of its 15 swords. Before charging into battle, though, you might want

| | Research | Combat | Overland | Upkeep | |
| Spell | Point | Casting | Casting | Cost | |
Rarity	Cost	Cost	Cost	Per Turn	Notes
Uncommon	560	N/A	250	5	None

Unicorns *Summary Information*

| | Research | Combat | Overland | Upkeep | |
| Spell | Point | Casting | Casting | Cost | |
Rarity	Cost	Cost	Cost	Per Turn	Notes
Rare	1,400	N/A	550	15	None

Angels *Summary Information*

Arch Angel *Summary Information*

Spell Rarity	Research Point Cost	Combat Casting Cost	Overland Casting Cost	Upkeep Cost Per Turn	Notes
Very Rare	5,000	N/A	950	20	None

Bless *Summary Information*

Spell Rarity	Research Point Cost	Combat Casting Cost	Overland Casting Cost	Upkeep Cost Per Turn	Notes
Common	20	5	25	1	vs. red or black only

to take advantage of the 40 mana in white magic (any white magic combat spell that costs less than or equal to 40 mana is fair game, whether you know the spell or not) it can throw in combat. Thus, with an arch angel, you can get a few additional creature enhancements and combat spells cast to help you arrange your battlefield dispositions just right.

Creature Enchantments

These spells allow you to customize your troops through magical enhancements. When cast overland, these spells will become a permanent part of the unit's abilities for as long as its maintenance costs are paid. When cast in combat, its effects usually end with the battle.

As a rule, creature enchantments should be thought of as tools in the tool box. Each has a specific function, and many provide en-

hancements that address only very specific problems.

Bless

The thing to remember about a unit that is blessed is that its +3 shields and +3 crosses are only good against breath attacks and attacks from red and black fantastic (i.e., summoned) creatures. Thus, this is a handy spell to throw on your front line fighters when attacking a red node, but its usefulness is more problematic in other battles.

Note, because these enhancements are only good against certain creature types, they will not appear on a blessed unit's statistics.

Endurance

This is a *wonderful* spell that increases a unit's movement allowance by one. You should consider casting it on units in the following circumstances:

- When a spirit is on its way to a distant node
- When a settler is on its way to a distant city site
- When one or two units in a terrific army stack are slowing it down

Endurance *Summary Information*

Spell Rarity	Research Point Cost	Combat Casting Cost	Overland Casting Cost	Upkeep Cost Per Turn	Notes
Common	60	N/A	30	1	None

Holy Weapon *Summary Information*

Spell Rarity	Research Point Cost	Combat Casting Cost	Overland Casting Cost	Upkeep Cost Per Turn	Notes
Common	80	10	50	1	normal units only

 Before entering battle, if you're planning on engineers breaching enemy wall during combat

 When you're really using cargo carriers, such as slow moving triremes

 When conducting a battle with slow-moving units that deliver strong, up-close attacks (i.e., a golem, minotaur, chaos spawn, earth elemental, and hydra)

Holy Weapon

This spell is most useful for units that were not built at a city with an alchemist's guild. It provides units the same kind of weapons that an alchemist's guild does, weapons that can damage creatures with weapons immunity. Such weapons also have a +1 To Hit. Carefully consider casting this on units that already have weapons forged at an alchemist's guild; the only benefit they'll reap is another +1 To Hit.

Heroes often benefit greatly by being permanently en-chanted with a Holy Weapon (provided they're not used exclusively for casting magic in battle).

If you plan to start out with any Gnolls, Klackons, Lizardmen, or Trolls, which can't build alchemist's guilds, you'd better have a little white magic in hopes of getting this spell. Permanently enchanting good units (that weren't made with the help of an alchemist's guild) is effective because of the spell's reasonable upkeep cost.

Holy Armor

Holy armor increases a unit's shields by +2. In combat, it costs 18 mana to cast, making it a fair value. When cast as an overland spell to permanently enchant a unit, it's a good deal, despite the upkeep cost, because a bonus in

Holy Armor *Summary Information*

Spell Rarity	Research Point Cost	Combat Casting Cost	Overland Casting Cost	Upkeep Cost Per Turn	Notes
Common	130	18	90	2	normal units only

Heroism *Summary Information*

Spell Rarity	Research Point Cost	Combat Casting Cost	Overland Casting Cost	Upkeep Cost Per Turn	Notes
Common	250	20	100	2	normal units only

True Sight *Summary Information*

Spell Rarity	Research Point Cost	Combat Casting Cost	Overland Casting Cost	Upkeep Cost Per Turn	Notes
Uncommon	300	20	100	2	None

Planar Travel *Summary Information*

Spell Rarity	Research Point Cost	Combat Casting Cost	Overland Casting Cost	Upkeep Cost Per Turn	Notes
Uncommon	680	N/A	150	5	None

shields is worth considerably more to a unit than a bonus in swords.

Heroism

This spell gives units elite status, meaning a net increase to a unit's lowest level (recruit) statistics of: +2 swords, +1 To Hit, +1 shield, +3 crosses, and +1 heart *per figure*. The beauty of this spell is that you can't inadvertently cast it on a unit that has already obtained elite status (or higher). Furthermore, when cast as a permanent enchantment on a unit, it automatically shuts itself off once that unit reaches elite status through the normal experience accumulation process (see Chapter 17).

True Sight

Unless you're on a crusade to wipe out several well developed Dark Elf cities where hordes of night stalkers might be lurking, or on a campaign over a blue node's rich landscape where phantom warriors and beasts abound, there is no need to use this spell as a permanent enchantment on a unit (particularly in light of its upkeep cost).

Instead, just use it as needed to help your ranged units see invisible units at a distance so they don't have to move adjacent to them to shoot them and, thus, can avoid an invisible unit's direct wrath. This spell also negates another unit's advantage of illusionary attacks (which phantom warriors and beasts use), which ignore all of the defender's shields when applying damage.

True Sight will also have some value for your ranged units when you are fighting battles against wizards whose cities are encased in Walls of Darkness. True Sight will allow your troops to fire on such a city's garrison with ease.

Planar Travel

Because of its high casting and upkeep cost, this spell is not practical to maintain on too many units. As the *Master of Magic* spell book suggests, transports (ships and floating islands) are probably the most efficient units to keep this spell on. Draconian air ships, in fact,

Lion Heart *Summary Information*

Spell Rarity	Research Point Cost	Combat Casting Cost	Overland Casting Cost	Upkeep Cost Per Turn	Notes
Rare	880	40	200	4	None

are particularly well suited to the benefits of this spell because there is no "illegal" square they could appear in on the opposite plane! Planar Travel is also the only way (besides Plane Shift) to get ordinary ships between Arcanus and Myrror, so if your predominant mode of transporting armies is by sea, this spell will be helpful for your transplanar wars.

Lion Heart

You can get this spell early enough for it to make a big difference in your battles. Lion Heart is a fine spell that works well in conjunction with Heroism to make tough hombres out of raw recruits. It offers substantial benefits when cast on fragile units like magicians or bowmen. Additionally, Lion Heart can be thrown on a fantastic creature. While the casting and upkeep costs   aren't cheap, the benefits are worth it: +3 swords (plus thrown and missile attacks), +3 crosses, and +3 hearts *per figure*. Impressive...most impressive.

Invulnerability

This is a darn good spell, even in light of its high upkeep cost. The double benefits of receiving weapon immunity and negating the first two hits scored against each figure in the enchanted unit from any attack are truly awesome.

Righteousness

Righteousness confers immunity to all red and black magic spells, breath attacks, and red and black magic ranged attacks (see Chapter 20) but seldom seems to get used. Because of its high casting cost in combat, it will rarely be cast there (usually in favor of more offensive spells that directly take out the red and black magic threats).

Overland, padding units with Righteousness may be reasonable. However, unless you are campaigning against Rjak (Mr. Death), Tauron (Mr. Chaos), or Sharee (Ms. Chaos/Death combo), or crusading against red nodes and special terrain features (lairs, ruins, etc., each of which has a high probability of featuring Chaos or Death fantastic creatures, see Appendix C), this spell just isn't that helpful.

Combat Spells

These spells are thrown by both players and heroes with spell-casting abilities while engaged in battle. Chapter 21 has all of the details on using magic in combat.

Note that white combat magic is primarily defensive. What offensive punch it does have is aimed at Death and Chaos creatures.

Invulnerability Summary Information

Spell Rarity	Research Point Cost	Combat Casting Cost	Overland Casting Cost	Upkeep Cost Per Turn	Notes
Rare	1,040	40	200	5	None

Righteousness Summary Information

Spell Rarity	Research Point Cost	Combat Casting Cost	Overland Casting Cost	Upkeep Cost Per Turn	Notes
Rare	1,120	40	200	2	vs. red or black only

Star Fires *Summary Information*

Spell Rarity	Research Point Cost	Combat Casting Cost	Overland Casting Cost	Upkeep Cost Per Turn	Notes
Common	40	5	N/A	N/A	vs. red or black only

Star Fires

Although this reasonably priced spell only affects Death and Chaos creatures, hitting them with a 15 magical attack sounds pretty impressive. The results, however, are often less impressive. For some reason, Star Fires just doesn't seem to cut deep into the ranks or hearts of these creatures. While a nice spell, Star Fires isn't particularly potent, but, then, what did you expect for that price?

Healing

This is, arguably, the most important white spell of all and the single best reason to have a Life spell book or two. Healing is a common spell that is relatively inexpensive to learn. Although it costs 15 mana to cast this spell, doing so can often be the difference between winning and losing a battle, especially early in the game. Returning five hit points to a unit can completely revive some of the least expensive troops, such as spearmen, or return a figure or two in hardier units, such as halberdiers. Often, Healing can turn a battle around through the judicious replacement of five hearts on any unit, replenishing its ranks and keeping it alive for one more round while a key enemy threat is eliminated. A handy Healing spell is also a great way to save an important unit (such as a hero or magicians) from immanent destruction in combat.

True Light

This spell is useful when combating the fantastic forces of Death. By enchanting the entire battlefield, each black magic unit suffers a -1 sword, -1 shield, and -1 cross. Although Life creatures gain +1 in each of these categories, that advantage is seldom a major con-

Healing *Summary Information*

Spell Rarity	Research Point Cost	Combat Casting Cost	Overland Casting Cost	Upkeep Cost Per Turn	Notes
Common	100	15	N/A	N/A	Death creatures do not heal

True Light *Summary Information*

Spell Rarity	Research Point Cost	Combat Casting Cost	Overland Casting Cost	Upkeep Cost Per Turn	Notes
Common	190	20	N/A	N/A	affects white and black only

cern since there are only four types of white units (guardian spirits, unicorns, angels, and arch angels).

Occasionally, a host of guardian spirits, perhaps, might want to party in battle together. Such a case would make this spell valuable for supporting an army of white creatures. Primarily, though, this spell is for degrading a black host. Note that the effects of this spell are canceled if its evil opposite, Darkness, is cast (see Chapter 9).

Dispel Evil

Although the Dispel Evil spell is pricy to cast in combat, you can really get your nickel's worth with it. All Chaos and Death units must make a saving roll, at -4 to their resistance (see Chapter 20), or perish instantly. Units that have been raised from the dead have an even greater penalty to their saving throw of -9. No doubt about it, this is an effective kill-o-zap spell to toss on nasty creatures of Death.

Raise Dead

This is an expensive, last ditch spell to right a problem that you shouldn't encounter in the first place—raising an important unit that was killed in a previous battle turn. Raised units reappear with only half their hit points and no enchantments; but the question is, why are you raising a dead unit in the first place? Okay, enough on the lecturing.

This spell can really save you during a "last stand" battle. If you had the foresight to husband a spell caster's 35 mana, raising a particularly strong unit back so that you can continue a close battle might mean the difference between victory and defeat. It's also a good way to bring back a fragile unit (or a hero) that you would prefer not to make, summon, or buy again. In this regard, Raise Dead is a better Healing spell, but at more than twice the price.

Note, units that have been *destroyed* by Cracks Call, stoning, Petrify, or Disintegrate or stolen by Possession may not be raised from the dead.

Dispel Evil Summary Information

Spell Rarity	Research Point Cost	Combat Casting Cost	Overland Casting Cost	Upkeep Cost Per Turn	Notes
Uncommon	450	25	N/A	N/A	vs. red or black only; targets resist at -4 or -9

Raise Dead Summary Information

Spell Rarity	Research Point Cost	Combat Casting Cost	Overland Casting Cost	Upkeep Cost Per Turn	Notes
Uncommon	620	35	N/A	N/A	cannot raise fantastic units

Prayer

This extremely useful spell improves all units on the caster's side by +1 cross, +1 To Hit, and +1 To Defend (i.e., each shield has a 40 percent chance of stopping a hit, rather than a 30 percent

Prayer *Summary Information*

Spell Rarity	Research Point Cost	Combat Casting Cost	Overland Casting Cost	Upkeep Cost Per Turn	Notes
Uncommon	800	30	N/A	N/A	None

Mass Healing *Summary Information*

Spell Rarity	Research Point Cost	Combat Casting Cost	Overland Casting Cost	Upkeep Cost Per Turn	Notes
Rare	1,600	50	N/A	N/A	None

chance; see Chapter 20 for details). If you've got the 30 mana to spare and a large army in a battle, don't hesitate to use this spell.

Mass Healing

Don't let the name confuse you. A Mass Healing has nothing to do with a religious revival. Instead, it is a Healing spell that restores up to five hearts to every unit on your side of a battle.

The trouble is, usually, that your losses tend to get concentrated in only one or two units until those units die. Notable exceptions, however, occur when an enemy casts Wrack (see Chapter 9), Flame Strike, Call Chaos (see Chapter 10), or Call Lightning (see Chapter 11).

Unless you have at least four units concurrently injured to some serious degree, the casting cost of 50 mana is going to be too steep to pay. It is usually better to simply cast in-

dividual Healing spells on an as-needed basis.

However, cunning players (like you) will usually withdraw a unit that's in immediate danger of being killed by melee attacks and continue to fight the enemy with fresher units in less danger of dying. This preserves the endangered units so they can fight another day, (i.e., they can efficiently heal up after the battle or, with Mass Healing, *during* the battle).

Holy Word

Weigh your decision to cast this pricy *pièce de résistance* very carefully. This white tornado can clean up all of an enemy's summoned creatures, particularly the undead ones, who must resist at -7. Since each figure resists separately, this spell can cut through an enemy's fantastic and undead units like a scythe, but for a price...60 mana! It may be a *long* time before you'll have that level of skill handy for a battle and can even *consider* casting this "fantastic enema."

Holy Word *Summary Information*

Spell Rarity	Research Point Cost	Combat Casting Cost	Overland Casting Cost	Upkeep Cost Per Turn	Notes
Rare	1,700	60	N/A	N/A	most targets resist at -2; undeads resist at -7

High Prayer

When you want to go all out and really beef up a large army in battle, the casting cost for this spell isn't bad, considering the bennies. Check this out: All your units get +2 swords, +1 To Hit, +2 shields, +1 To Defend (see Chapter 20), and +3 crosses. The bigger your army, the better the benefit, so stack 'em tall or, at the very least, get your summoned creatures on the battlefield before casting High Prayer. Note that the effects of Prayer and High Prayer are not additive.

High Prayer Summary Information

Spell Rarity	Research Point Cost	Combat Casting Cost	Overland Casting Cost	Upkeep Cost Per Turn	Notes
Very Rare	1,850	60	N/A	N/A	None

Heavenly Light Summary Information

Spell Rarity	Research Point Cost	Combat Casting Cost	Overland Casting Cost	Upkeep Cost Per Turn	Notes
Uncommon	740	N/A	150	2	affects white and black only

City Enchantments

Spells that enchant cities come in two flavors: help and hinder. Help spells are cast on your own cities, while hinder spells are reserved for casting on opponents.

In the case of white magic, we're talking seriously helpful city enhancements, and plenty of them. If empire building is your thing, you're going to love tapping into the rare and very rare white city enchantments.

Heavenly Light

Think of this spell as a permanent True Light spell, cast overland. Like a long-life bulb, as long as you pay the upkeep, the city is protected for all combat there as if a True Light spell were in effect (see above). If you're in a rumble with Rjak or some of the other wizards (Sharee, Kali, or Tlaloc) who weave that old black magic, leaving the Heavenly Lights on along your border cities can be a wise precautionary measure.

Prosperity

Prosperity tacks on gold to a city's income in a manner identical to a merchant's guild (i.e., it's a straight addition of cash to the bottom line city income equal to 100 percent of the city's normal tax income). For a lousy two mana per turn, this can translate into a lot of gold. So, what are you waiting for?

Any city that produces 5 or more gold per

Prosperity Summary Information

Spell Rarity	Research Point Cost	Combat Casting Cost	Overland Casting Cost	Upkeep Cost Per Turn	Notes
Rare	1,200	N/A	250	2	None

turn should have this spell on it (at that point, you can use alchemy to transmute four of those gold back into your two mana spent for upkeep and still have one gold left over for profit). Scouting out mineral deposits that yield a lot of gold, or even choosing races that can produce large quantities of money, becomes less of a consideration if you choose enough spell books in Life magic to obtain this spell.

Altar of Battle

This spell is akin to conjuring up a "super" war college in that city. While a normal war college makes *veterans* of all new units built there, the Altar of Battle does them one better and makes the units *elite* (see Chapter 20). Elite status provides every figure in a unit a combined bonus of: +2 swords, +1 To Hit, +1 shield, +3 crosses, and +1 heart.

This spell is particularly useful for militaristic races that cannot build war colleges (Gnolls, Klackons, Lizardmen, and Trolls). Even less militaristic races that can't build war colleges (Barbarians, Dwarfs, and Halflings) might want to consider using this spell. Even

races that *have* war colleges operating in a city still receive the difference between veteran and elite units that are built where they have an Altar of Battle, which is not inconsiderable (+1 sword, +1 To Hit, +1 cross, and +1 heart).

However, consider the price. Oh, the 300 mana to cast the spell, while steep, isn't so terrible. But paying five mana per turn for upkeep (when a war college is only five gold) means that maintaining this spell is not a very good value for cities that are not really "soldier factories." Try to be conservative when using this enchantment.

Stream of Life

Although the casting cost is about right, the high upkeep cost means you must judiciously and carefully parcel out your use of this spell. Since it doubles population growth, allows all units in that city to heal completely at the end of every turn, and eliminates all rebellion there, what might be the best circumstances under which to cast this spell?

Well, any of the slow-growing races (see Table 15.5), namely the Dark Elves, Dwarves, High Elves, and Trolls will want to cast this spell to help an important city site grow quickly and avoid unrest. Interestingly, these races, along with the Klackons, Beastmen, and Draconians, are also among the most hated by their conquered subjects (and hateful of their conquerors), as shown later in Table 15.2. When playing these races, a Stream of Life spell can be of

Altar of Battle *Summary Information*

Spell Rarity	Research Point Cost	Combat Casting Cost	Overland Casting Cost	Upkeep Cost Per Turn	Notes
Rare	1,300	N/A	300	5	normal units only

Stream of Life *Summary Information*

Spell Rarity	Research Point Cost	Combat Casting Cost	Overland Casting Cost	Upkeep Cost Per Turn	Notes
Rare	1,500	N/A	300	8	None

considerable assistance in quelling unrest, particularly during the early growth of the cities, when unrest due to conquest constitutes an inordinately high proportion of a city's population.

Its ability to heal units completely at the end of each turn is a less consequential benefit unless there is one particular city that you're staging a war from. If a certain city site, however, becomes a primary place of healing for you during some protracted war, then casting a Stream of Life spell at that site might be worthwhile.

For the Dark Elves, Dwarves, High Elves, and Trolls, though, don't leave your Enchanted Fortress without it. Just make sure that you don't overextend yourself with a lot of cities consuming eight mana per turn in Stream of Life upkeep costs!

Inspirations

This is the production point equivalent of Prosperity. For a slightly higher casting cost than Prosperity and the same upkeep cost, Inspiration tacks on more resources to a city's production in a manner identical to two miner's guilds. (It's a straight addition of resources to the bottom line city production equal to 100 percent of the city's base production level. See Chapter 15 for details on production.) For a mere two mana per turn, this can translate into a lot of extra production.

While its not always as good as gold, you can take production to the bank via trade goods (again, see Chapter 15), so

this spell, too, becomes profitable once your resource production is 5 or more. This one's a "no brainer." Cast it particularly where you will be building your normal troop units—you'll be turning them out at an amazing rate indeed (particularly with some races, like the Klackons or Dwarves). The major downside to this spell is that, because it is very rare, it is likely to influence only the end game, when its effects are probably less significant.

Astral Gate

This spell creates a limited Tower of Wizardry at the city it is cast upon. Provided there are no cities or enemy troops on its square on the other plane, units can shift between planes where a city has an Astral Gate. While neither the casting cost nor the upkeep cost is outrageous, by the time you discover this spell you will control a couple of Towers of Wizardry already. At that point, the value of this spell decreases considerably except, perhaps, if you're conducting an inter-planar war and need as many "holes" into the enemy's territory as you can find.

Inspirations *Summary Information*

Spell Rarity	Research Point Cost	Combat Casting Cost	Overland Casting Cost	Upkeep Cost Per Turn	Notes
Very Rare	2,000	N/A	350	2	None

Astral Gate *Summary Information*

Spell Rarity	Research Point Cost	Combat Casting Cost	Overland Casting Cost	Upkeep Cost Per Turn	Notes
Very Rare	2,250	N/A	350	5	None

Consecration Summary Information

Spell Rarity	Research Point Cost	Combat Casting Cost	Overland Casting Cost	Upkeep Cost Per Turn	Notes
Very Rare	3,000	N/A	400	8	None

Planar Seal Summary Information

Spell Rarity	Research Point Cost	Combat Casting Cost	Overland Casting Cost	Upkeep Cost Per Turn	Notes
Uncommon	500	N/A	500	5	None

Consecration

This is an expensive spell with a high upkeep cost, but may be cheaper in the long run for protecting your cities from negative enchantments than casting Disjunction repeatedly. For your investment, *all* negative enchantments on that city are dispelled instantly, and future negative effects from Death and Chaos spells cannot occur there. Because of the high price tag, this spell is probably best used on your capital cities (particularly the one where your Enchanted Fortress is located), should they be threatened.

Global Enchantments

These spells affect everything applicable on both worlds. We're talking big league magic here. Note, spells that adversely affect other players are likely to have long term diplomatic repercussions (see Chapter 25).

Planar Seal

This is one terrific spell. The ability to prevent players who are entirely (or even primarily) on one plane from projecting their forces on the other is strategically awesome. Note that it shuts the door on the caster's units, too,

and works on every method of inter-planer travel (Towers of Wizardry, Astral Gate, Plane Shift, etc.).

Because it is not the most expensive global enchantment, though, it is more vulnerable to other player's Disjunction spells. Its reasonable upkeep cost means that computer players who cast this spell will keep it going for a long, long time (see Chapter 28). However, if you cast this spell, choosing the right time to shut it off can give you an important military advantage. By massing up your troops for a transplanar strike at the time of your choice, you can really get the drop on another player's forces.

There is a "cheat" that gets forces through a Planar Seal. Your Summoning Circle can be moved between planes while a Planar Seal is in effect. Spells that teleport units to your

Figure 8-2. *Planar Seal*

Summoning Circle (Recall Hero, Word of Recall) still work and will bring those units to the Summoning Circle even through a Planar Seal.

Holy Arms

When you examine it closely, Holy Arms is just a global Holy Weapon spell. This means that, when it is cast, all friendly normal units that don't already have Holy Weapons will receive its bonus of +1 To Hit and the ability to attack creatures that have weapon immunity.

Holy Arms *Summary Information*

Spell Rarity	Research Point Cost	Combat Casting Cost	Overland Casting Cost	Upkeep Cost Per Turn	Notes
Very Rare	2,500	N/A	900	30	normal units only

Life Force *Summary Information*

Spell Rarity	Research Point Cost	Combat Casting Cost	Overland Casting Cost	Upkeep Cost Per Turn	Notes
Very Rare	3,500	N/A	1,000	10	500 dispel vs. Death magic

Frankly, though, for 30 mana per turn in upkeep, this is not a great boon. First, this spell's bonus is not cumulative with Holy Weapon. Second, with most races, you can easily produce units with weapons that circumvent others' weapon immunity through alchemist's guilds. Third, all fantastic creatures ignore weapon immunity anyway.

So what's the big deal? Unless you have a host of Gnolls, Klackons, Lizardmen, or Trolls (because their cities can't produce alchemist guilds), there really isn't one. By the time you can afford to cast this spell, all of the other races should be producing units with magic weapons anyway. Besides, that 30 mana per turn maintenance cost only makes this spell remotely practical for the four specific races listed.

Life Force

Think of this as a black magic pre-nuking spell. For only 1,000 mana down and 10 mana per turn, all other wizards trying to cast *any* form of Death magic, outside of combat, might have it dispelled (fizzle). The dispelling strength of Life Force is calculated at 500 mana (see page 107 of the manual for the formula).

Actually, if Rjak (or even Sharee, Kali or Tlaloc) has you up against the wall, casting this spell is a good insurance policy. While it is no panacea, it can be an effective thorn in their side and one that might decide the outcome of any wars between you.

Tranquility

This is the anti-Chaos magic counterpart to Life Force. Although it costs 100 more mana to cast (1,100 mana), the upkeep is still only 10 mana per turn. Like Life Force, its dispelling strength is 500 mana. You will want to consider casting this insurance spell when locked in mortal combat with the likes of Tauron (in particular), or even Lo Pan, Oberic, or Sharee.

Tranquility *Summary Information*

Spell Rarity	Research Point Cost	Combat Casting Cost	Overland Casting Cost	Upkeep Cost Per Turn	Notes
Very Rare	4,000	N/A	1,100	10 500	dispel vs. Chaos magic

Crusade *Summary Information*

Spell Rarity	Research Point Cost	Combat Casting Cost	Overland Casting Cost	Upkeep Cost Per Turn	Notes
Very Rare	4,500	N/A	1,100	10	normal units only

Crusade

Like Stream of Life, Crusade is another no brainer. It has a similarly expensive casting cost, but the maintenance is very reasonable. Crusade raises all of your normal units' (that includes heroes, remember) status by one experience level. Thus, every recruit receives the stats of a regular, veterans get elite unit stats, etc. (see page 130 of the *Master of Magic* manual for the specific benefits of increasing experience levels).

This is one way (besides being a Warlord, see Chapter 4) for units to receive ultra-elite status and the *only* way (if the spell caster is also a Warlord) for them to obtain the status of champions. With this spell on, it is time to emphasize normal troop production. Go forth and conquer!

Charm of Life

Certainly one of the best spells in the game for an empire's self-improvement,

Charm of Life is one of the most expensive spells in the entire game to cast, but only costs 10 mana per turn to maintain. Its benefit, having the number of hearts of every single figure in every single unit on your side increased by 25 percent (with a minimum of +1 heart per figure), is just awesome—even for its price. This extra staying power is usually achieved only by units that reach elite status, so receiving it as a global benefit on both planes is just great. If you have the time and mana, you can't go wrong casting Charm of Life.

Special Spells

These are unique spells that do not fit neatly in the other categories.

Just Cause

Here is a handy little spell. For a casting cost of a mere 150 mana, plus a reasonable three mana per turn for upkeep, Just Cause increases the caster's fame by 10 (see Chapter 4). Since each point of fame decreases troop maintenance costs by one gold per turn, sav-

Charm of Life *Summary Information*

Spell Rarity	Research Point Cost	Combat Casting Cost	Overland Casting Cost	Upkeep Cost Per Turn	Notes
Very Rare	6,000	N/A	1,250	10	None

ing up to 10 gold per turn for a cost of three mana per turn makes Just Cause a good deal right from the start. As a bonus, the increased fame will improve the frequency that mercenaries, magic items, and heroes will appear (and can bring higher quality heroes, too).

Just Cause Summary Information

Spell Rarity	Research Point Cost	Combat Casting Cost	Overland Casting Cost	Upkeep Cost Per Turn	Notes
Common	160	N/A	150	3	None

Plane Shift Summary Information

Spell Rarity	Research Point Cost	Combat Casting Cost	Overland Casting Cost	Upkeep Cost Per Turn	Notes
Uncommon	350	N/A	125	N/A	None

While the boost in fame is reason enough to cast Just Cause, this spell has an added bonus: it calms one rebel in each of your cities! Each calmed rebel is one more person working and paying taxes.

Just Cause is a winner. Cast it, live it, love it.

Plane Shift

This spell allows you to move a stack from the square it's in to its opposite square on the other plane, provided that unit could normally move onto that square. Therefore, some planning is needed before this spell is cast. Units without the ability to move over water will not make it to an ocean square, and ships can't Plane Shift onto a land square.

This spell really requires you to look before you leap. It might be unwise to use this spell to "break into" another plane for the first time, unless you can explore it magically in advance (see Chapter 14). Casting this spell is a good way to get a killer stack to surprise an enemy on a different plane or, early on, to conquer a foothold there. It is also a good way for units facing an enemy's wrath to make a strategic retreat to safety.

Resurrection

MacArthur might have said that old soldiers never die, but this spell really means it. When the paltry 250 mana is spent to cast this spell, a list of your dead heroes appears for you to choose from (assuming all six of your hero slots are not already filled). The hero will return to your Summoning Circle in normal health and at the same experience level as when (s)he died, but *sans* any magic items or unit enchantments possessed when that hero died.

This is a great spell. It's much cheaper than either of the Arcane spells Summon Hero (which costs 300 mana) or Summon Champion (at 750 mana). In

Resurrection Summary Information

Spell Rarity	Research Point Cost	Combat Casting Cost	Overland Casting Cost	Upkeep Cost Per Turn	Notes
Uncommon	400	N/A	250	N/A	None

Incarnation *Summary Information*

Spell Rarity	Research Point Cost	Combat Casting Cost	Overland Casting Cost	Upkeep Cost Per Turn	Notes
Rare	960	N/A	500	none	None

addition, it gives you a choice from among all your dead heroes, rather than assigning you a random one. In this way, you can choose from among your casualties a hero who is more specifically tailored to your immediate needs.

Incarnation

This is, arguably, the ultimate white spell (and it's not even *very* rare!). At a cost of 500 mana, this spell summons Torin the Chosen, the ultimate hero (see Chapter 18). Don't let his 12 swords, 8 shields, 12 crosses, and 12 hearts make you think he's less than great. This dude also boasts super might, constitution, immunity to magic, super leadership, prayer master, and spell caster 15 with True Light, Healing, Holy Armor, and Lion Heart (plus a couple of other random abilities). Can you say "one-man wrecking crew?" We thought so...

Torin can be resummoned or resurrected if he dies. In either case, he'll come back at whatever experience level he died at, less any items or unit enchantments he might have had.

Here's To Death

With our summary analysis of Life magic thus complete, we flip the coin over to consider Death magic. The next chapter continues our spell discussion with our bright observations on the dark subject of black magic. Hold onto your black cats, folks, we're in for a bumpy ride.

Black Off, Jack!

Apart from its use as a song title, that old black magic packs a lot of punch in *Master of Magic*. With a good dose of all kinds of spells, black is arguably the most self-sufficient single color in the game.

The good news about Death magic is that its summoned creatures are cheap (*real* cheap) and get the innate benefits of being creatures of Death (as listed below). Death magic also offers strong creatures, many of whom have life-stealing attacks and/or the ability to regenerate. As for urban mana production, nothing beats the Infernal Power/Dark Rituals combination.

While it is not as forceful as Chaos magic, black magic is insidious and painful to the enemy. It makes them suffer.

On the downside, black spell books are a tremendous diplomatic bane (see Chapter 25). Also, their units' inability to heal themselves greatly offsets their advantage of relative cheapness.

Summoning Spells

Black magic is very strong in creature production. From the lowliest skeleton unit with its marginal upkeep cost, to the powerful spell Zombie Mastery that turns all normal units that have died during your battles into obedient zombies fighting for you, Death magic means you will never hurt for monsters. However, creatures of Death (which includes undead units and units that have had Black Channels or Animate Dead cast on them) do not heal unless they have regeneration or life-stealing attacks. To offset this regenerative disability, creatures of Death generally have relatively lower upkeep costs than comparable units from other magic realms. Consider combining the Channeler skill with black magic to further lower your summoned creature upkeep costs, as this will allow you to easily maintain hordes of skeletons, ghouls, and other undeads.

Death magic is the only type that produces creatures with life-stealing attacks (see Chapter 20). It is also the major source of creatures with weapon immunity (see Chapter 20). *All* creatures of Death, except for units who become undead through life-stealing or ghoul attacks, are also automatically immune to *all* Death spells, cold attacks, illusions, and poison attacks. Note that units who become undead through life-stealing attacks only gain immunity to Death spells.

Undead Units

Certain spells will either only affect undead units, have more severe effects against undead units, or turn other units into an undead unit type. Allow us to define, exactly, what an undead unit is.

🐍 All creatures summoned by Death magic (*all* of 'em!)

🐍 Any normal unit raised from the dead after being mauled in combat by ghouls

🐍 Any normal unit that was a victim of the life-stealing attacks of wraiths, death knights, demon lords, the Necromancer hero, the spell Life Drain, and artifacts with life-stealing ability (see Chapter 20)

🐍 Any unit raised after a battle via the Animate Dead spell

🐍 Any unit transformed by a Black Channels spell

Note that if you convert a unit to an undead creature, its upkeep cost is increased by 50 percent. Specific undead units, summoned through the practice of death magic are discussed below.

Skeletons

Skeletons are the cheapest Death magic creatures you can summon. Their immunity to normal missiles and three-strength melee attacks at a +1 To Hit makes these little "cheapies" a good investment. This is especially true at the beginning of the game, when your town(s) need to focus on development and expansion more than on troop production.

Skeletons are also the cheapest Death magic spell to research. Thus, you can learn this spell and start summoning these monsters very quickly in the game, when their potential use is greatest.

Skeletons *Summary Information*

Spell Rarity	Research Point Cost	Combat Casting Cost	Overland Casting Cost	Upkeep Cost Per Turn	Notes
Common	20	N/A	25	1	None

Ghouls *Summary Information*

Spell Rarity	Research Point Cost	Combat Casting Cost	Overland Casting Cost	Upkeep Cost Per Turn	Notes
Common	130	N/A	80	1	None

Ghouls

Early in the game, armies of ghouls can do wonders for your wizard. These units have a low upkeep cost, but their casting cost is a little steep. The great thing about ghouls is that they can create undead units. If you gather an army of ghouls together and kill other units, dead enemy normal (not fantastic) units that had more than half their hit points taken by ghouls will rise from the dead to serve you!

This gives you a double bonus. First, you get extra units for free. They rise from the dead, not as zombies, but as undead halberdiers, spearmen, cavalry, etc.—unable to regenerate hit points lost while serving you in their undead state. The only benefit to their present undead status is Death immunity.

Second, undead units are as good as normal units for rear area garrison duties (they're still considered normal units for quelling rebels). That means, if you play your cards right, you can wander around with an army of ghouls, taking over towns and leaving the risen undeads behind as the city's garrison that you would have otherwise had to pay for!

Of course, this isn't quite as easy as it sounds; you will not get more than a total of nine units in any stack, so you will only raise from the dead the number of units for which you have room in your army currently on that square. Nevertheless, their relatively low cost makes ghouls powerful early game units.

Night Stalker

The night stalker is the strongest cheap unit that black magic can summon. Although there is only one figure per unit, a night stalker is invisible and, therefore, can sidle right up to enemy units without being hit by ranged at-

Night Stalker *Summary Information*

Spell Rarity	Research Point Cost	Combat Casting Cost	Overland Casting Cost	Upkeep Cost Per Turn	Notes
Uncommon	560	N/A	250	1	None

Shadow Demons *Summary Information*

Spell Rarity	Research Point Cost	Combat Casting Cost	Overland Casting Cost	Upkeep Cost Per Turn	Notes
Uncommon	800	N/A	325	7	None

Wraiths *Summary Information*

Spell Rarity	Research Point Cost	Combat Casting Cost	Overland Casting Cost	Upkeep Cost Per Turn	Notes
Rare	1,120	N/A	500	5	None

really have it all. Their biggest drawback is their high maintenance costs, but given what they can do and that they regenerate, the maintenance costs are still not too much to pay.

Wraiths

Wraiths are expensive to cast, but you won't need more than a few of them to do a lot of damage. These units, like the shadow demons, are flying and non-corporeal (hence immune to webbing). In addition, they are immune to weapons *and* they have life-stealing attacks.

Life-stealing attacks allow wraiths to suck life points out of their enemies while they, themselves, heal. These attacks also mean that normal units losing more than half their hit points to wraiths will, like those similarly killed by ghouls, rise from the dead to serve you. What more can you ask? These deadly units can replace your ghouls as city conquerors, leaving their newly raised undead garrisons behind to keep peace in newly taken cities.

tacks. Its invisibility makes the unit harder to hit (enemy units have a -1 To Hit penalty against invisible units), and it has a fair melee attack strength of seven swords.

In addition, night stalkers have a death gaze (with a -2 resistance) which has a chance, both when the night stalker is attacking and defending, of taking out enemy figures before melee combat even begins. For its low upkeep, you really can't do much better than a night stalker.

Shadow Demons

Shadow demons have so many advantages it's hard to know where to begin. First, they fly, but the best part is that they can't be webbed because they are non-corporeal! Second, they have a decent magic ranged attack (four fireballs times four figures per unit) with eight shots.

Shadow demons are immune to normal weapons, can regenerate, and freely travel between planes. These guys

Death Knights

The death knights are fast-moving, flying units that deliver a lot for an almost laugh-

Death Knights *Summary Information*

Spell Rarity	Research Point Cost	Combat Casting Cost	Overland Casting Cost	Upkeep Cost Per Turn	Notes
Very Rare	2,250	N/A	600	8	None

ably low upkeep cost. Check out these features: +3 To Hit, first strike, armor-piercing, and life-stealing attacks. This means these guys get their hit points back when they attack,

Demon Lord *Summary Information*

Spell Rarity	Research Point Cost	Combat Casting Cost	Overland Casting Cost	Upkeep Cost Per Turn	Notes
Very Rare	6,000	N/A	1,000	15	None

before their enemies have a chance to hit them! Further, their enemies have a harder time hitting death knights because they also enjoy weapon immunity.

As with all life-stealing attacks, if death knights kill enemy units, those units will rise from the dead (just like they do when killed by ghouls and wraiths). Granted, death knights show up fairly late in a game; perhaps, even, after you complete most of your conquering. However, if you step up your research efforts and get them early enough, they are well worth the cost.

Demon Lord

What's worse than a melee life-stealing attack? A ranged life-stealing attack!

Demon lords have only one figure per unit, but they can launch eight ranged magic at-

Figure 9-1. *Demon Lord*

tacks, each of strength 10 and life-stealing in nature. This is scary stuff.

In addition, these flying demon lords can summon up to three demons to serve them in a battle. Each of these lesser demons flies and has a powerful 14-sword melee attack. Besides these valuable properties, both demon lords and demons are immune to normal weapon attacks.

About the only weakness of demons and demon lords is that they're susceptible to ranged attacks. Therefore, hiding them behind a wall of darkness while inside a city is a good idea. The Demon Lord spell is the most expensive Death magic spell to research. Demon lords are also expensive to cast and maintain. Once you have summoned one or two of these brutes, its worth any extra effort to keep them alive.

Creature Enchantments

Black magic excels at casting negative enchantments upon enemy units. Thus, Death magic is good for softening up enemy units before delivering the killing blow to them the old fashioned way.

Weakness

This is one of those great little gems. Weakness is a very cheap combat creature enchantment that can decrease a target enemy unit's attack strength by 2. Using this spell liberally, early in a battle, can allow mediocre troops to squeak by with victories they should never have had. Note that creatures of Death are immune to this spell, as are phantom war-

Weakness *Summary Information*

Spell Rarity	Research Point Cost	Combat Casting Cost	Overland Casting Cost	Upkeep Cost Per Turn	Notes
Common	40	5	N/A	N/A	targets resist at -2

Cloak of Fear *Summary Information*

Spell Rarity	Research Point Cost	Combat Casting Cost	Overland Casting Cost	Upkeep Cost Per Turn	Notes
Common	80	12	60	1	no resistance modifiers

riors and beasts, golems, heroes that are charmed, and units with magic immunity (sky drakes and paladins).

Cloak of Fear

Cloak of Fear is another great spell in disguise, although it doesn't sound like much until you read the fine print. Every figure in every troop, except for those immune to Death magic, must pass a resistance roll before they will attack *or* counterattack one of your units during melee combat. (Breath and gaze attacks are not subject to this resistance roll.)

This has two important benefits. First, your unit will get hit fewer times by some special attack types, like first strike, that only work when the enemy unit is on the offensive. Second, when you attack with a cloaked unit, your enemies have

less ability to hit you back. In essence, this spell gives you a certain number of "free hits" against other units. This spell is definitely worth using, particularly when you have a good unit up against a lot of cheap ones.

Black Sleep

When this combat spell works, your problems are over. Black Sleep makes an enemy unit fall fast asleep and remain completely defenseless for the remainder of combat. Every attack against a sleeping unit automatically inflicts all possible hits. This is a great combat spell—cheap to cast and fast to research. Used carefully, it can aid inadequate armies at critical junctures in battles.

Possession

Possession is a combat creature enchantment that attempts to give you control of a normal enemy unit during combat. Unfortunately, this spell is expensive to cast in the mere hope that the enemy unit will fail its resistance roll and you'll get control of it. There are better, simi-

Black Sleep *Summary Information*

Spell Rarity	Research Point Cost	Combat Casting Cost	Overland Casting Cost	Upkeep Cost Per Turn	Notes
Common	100	15	N/A	N/A	targets resist at -2

larly priced combat spells that exert more widespread effects on the battlefield. Possession is best attempted as a last ditch effort when you have only a few units against many.

Possession *Summary Information*

Spell Rarity	Research Point Cost	Combat Casting Cost	Overland Casting Cost	Upkeep Cost Per Turn	Notes
Uncommon	350	30	N/A	N/A	normal units only; targets resist at - 1

Lycanthropy

This spell turns any friendly normal (non-hero) unit, including those cheap little spearmen, into vicious, marauding werewolves (with a new werewolf unit icon). Werewolves are immune to normal weapons and are fairly strong (six figures with five swords each). Note that they are not much stronger than ordinary halberdiers with a little experience.

However, werewolves can regenerate, making them more valuable than ordinary halberdier units, if you can afford the steep upkeep cost. On balance, only upgrade your worst normal unit types (spearmen and swordsmen) with Lycanthropy. Even then, you may find better uses for that five mana per turn upkeep cost.

Black Channels

Black Channels is another great little Death spell. It gives a normal unit super strength, defense, and resistance (along with the other benefits and curses of being undead).

Black Channels is good for giving your units some added oomph, but is particularly useful to cast on any hardy Troll units you own. With the Troll's inherent regeneration ability negating the undead's inability to heal, you've got a killer combo on your hands.

Note that Black Channels stops a unit's accrual of experience. However, any attribute bonuses accrued before being converted through Black Channels remain a part of that unit's statistics. For best results, therefore, use Black Channels on very experienced units.

Berserk

Berserk is the ultimate form of dancing with death. Doubling a unit's melee attacks while stripping away its shields, this spell should

Lycanthropy *Summary Information*

Spell Rarity	Research Point Cost	Combat Casting Cost	Overland Casting Cost	Upkeep Cost Per Turn	Notes
Uncommon	400	N/A	180	5	normal units only

Black Channels *Summary Information*

Spell Rarity	Research Point Cost	Combat Casting Cost	Overland Casting Cost	Upkeep Cost Per Turn	Notes
Uncommon	500	N/A	100	1	normal units only

Berserk *Summary Information*

Spell Rarity	Research Point Cost	Combat Casting Cost	Overland Casting Cost	Upkeep Cost Per Turn	Notes
Uncommon	740	30	N/A	N/A	None

Wraithform *Summary Information*

Spell Rarity	Research Point Cost	Combat Casting Cost	Overland Casting Cost	Upkeep Cost Per Turn	Notes
Rare	880	30	150	3	None

not be cast willy-nilly. It's a spell to cast only when you *really* mean it (and at 30 mana a pop, it's too expensive to cast at any other time, anyway).

Consider using this spell with killer units that have a lot of hit points, to absorb enemy hits, or with units that have first strike capabilities, so you can take out the enemies using the double melee strength before they get to you. Also consider using this on units that have few, if any, shields to lose (e.g., phantom warriors, phantom beasts, werewolves, or even bowmen). Don't use this spell on units that can't spare the shields unless it's their last chance to destroy the last enemy unit in a battle.

Wraithform

Wraithform gives the target both weapon immunity and a non-corporeal nature. This is a bit like an advanced Water Walking spell and is probably not worth the effort of casting on a unit, unless you have no other options, especially because of its upkeep cost.

You shouldn't bother using this spell on units that are primarily going after lairs and nodes, since all of the fantastic creatures guarding them will ignore the weapon immunity that Wraithform provides. Stick to taking cities and killing enemy armies with troops using Wraithform.

Animate Dead

The ultimate Death creature enchantment is raising the dead...sort of. Animate Dead lets you return any *one* unit (friend or foe) from the dead *during* battle. The animated creature is an undead, but stays with your army even after combat is over. Note that heroes and enemy units with magic immunity may not be animated. Units that have been *destroyed* by Cracks Call, Disintegrate, stoning or Petrify, or stolen by Possession, may not be animated.

Animate Dead *Summary Information*

Spell Rarity	Research Point Cost	Combat Casting Cost	Overland Casting Cost	Upkeep Cost Per Turn	Notes
Very Rare	3,000	50	N/A	special	upkeep is 50 percent more than usual

Animate Dead is an expensive spell, and the animated unit will have an elevated upkeep cost (50 percent more than usual). However, this is a great way to quickly increase your army size, especially when you find yourself in a panic during the middle of a losing battle.

Combat Spells

As one would expect, Death magic combat spells are generally quite destructive in force. Note that Death magic spells are particularly geared to combat the effects of Life magic.

Life Drain

Life Drain lets you direct a life-stealing attack at a particular unit. What you get in return is a *permanent* spell-casting skill increase of three points for every damage point you cause to the target if your wizard casts this spell, or hit points if a hero casts the spell. Increased amounts of mana pumped into the spell lower the target unit's resistance roll versus that attack. This is a limited, direct attack to be used against certain units (e.g., nonelite troops and others with a low number of crosses). Its primary advantage is that it gives you more undead units to fight with after the battle is over.

Terror

Terror is a selectively helpful spell since it can only prevent enemy attacks, *not counterattacks*. It is most useful early in the game, when your opponents tend to be weak anyway, because enemy units get a resistance *bonus* (+1 cross) when defending themselves from the spell's effects. This spell can be helpful against units that have first strike, thrown, or breath weapons (i.e., ones that exert their effects only when attacking, not counterattacking).

Mana Leak

Mana Leak drains enemy spell casters, wizards, and heroes alike, by five mana per combat turn. More importantly, your enemies will lose one magic ranged attack per combat turn when this enchantment is in effect. This is one of those spells you should cast if your troops are up against armies of sprites or Dark Elves.

If you're looking for a quick way to drain your enemy wizard's mana reserves, black magic offers better options, such as the over-

Life Drain Summary Information

Spell Rarity	Research Point Cost	Combat Casting Cost	Overland Casting Cost	Upkeep Cost Per Turn	Notes
Common	160	10 to 50	N/A	N/A	target resists at -1 per five mana over base cost of 10

Terror Summary Information

Spell Rarity	Research Point Cost	Combat Casting Cost	Overland Casting Cost	Upkeep Cost Per Turn	Notes
Common	190	20	N/A	N/A	targets resist at +1

Mana Leak *Summary Information*

Spell Rarity	Research Point Cost	Combat Casting Cost	Overland Casting Cost	Upkeep Cost Per Turn	Notes
Common	220	· 20	N/A	N/A	None

Darkness *Summary Information*

Spell Rarity	Research Point Cost	Combat Casting Cost	Overland Casting Cost	Upkeep Cost Per Turn	Notes
Common	250	25	N/A	N/A	affects white and black only

land spells, Evil Presence and Drain Power. Enemy hero spell casters are not useful targets for this spell since the computer generally has them drain their mana reserves through casting expensive spells as fast as they can.

Darkness

Darkness is a classic black combat spell, useful under many circumstances. It gives *all* creatures of Death statistical boosts (+1) in their attack strength, defense, and resistance. For that reason alone, it's worth casting in most combat situations, especially if you are fighting with a large corps of undeads.

If you're fighting against creatures of Life, admittedly a rare occurrence, it gives you a double bonus because the Darkness spell curses Life creatures (-1 sword, shield, and cross) as it blesses undeads. Note that the effects of this spell are canceled out by the Life magic spells, True Light and Heavenly Light.

One final, but important, point is that this spell will enhance *all* undead creatures' skills *on both sides*. Therefore, this is not the spell to cast when you're fighting *against* demon lords, death knights, or hordes of ghouls.

Black Prayer

Black Prayer is a great combat spell. At 35 mana, its cost is significant, but it essentially tenderizes all of your opponents by decreasing their swords (-1), shields (-1), and crosses (-2). Cast this spell before other directed spells since the lowered resistance of your enemies will increase your future chances of successfully casting spells against them during that battle.

Wrack

Black magic is full of combat gems; Wrack is another one. If you have enough mana, cast Black Prayer first, then Wrack 'em. This is advantageous because a figure's resistance gets a bonus of +1 in defending itself against the Wrack.

Black Prayer *Summary Information*

Spell Rarity	Research Point Cost	Combat Casting Cost	Overland Casting Cost	Upkeep Cost Per Turn	Notes
Uncommon	450	35	N/A	N/A	None

The Wrack takes one hit point from every enemy figure in every battle turn when the figure fails to resist this spell. This spell is, of course, most useful against normal units who tend to have fairly low numbers of hit points per figure and few crosses to start. It can be a life-saver when your troops are far outnumbered and outclassed by swarms of multi-figure enemy units. Note that this spell will not work against undead or phantom units.

Wrack Summary Information

Spell Rarity	Research Point Cost	Combat Casting Cost	Overland Casting Cost	Upkeep Cost Per Turn	Notes
Rare	960	40	N/A	N/A	targets resist at +1

Word of Death Summary Information

Spell Rarity	Research Point Cost	Combat Casting Cost	Overland Casting Cost	Upkeep Cost Per Turn	Notes
Very Rare	2,000	40	N/A	N/A	targets resist at -5

Word of Death

Have you ever walked into a battle and discovered that you were up against hordes of weak units complemented by a single ferocious one that could single-handedly destroy your entire army? Well, what you needed was Word of Death, an awesome spell that gives each figure in the target unit one chance to defend itself from death (with a -5 penalty to their resistance!). This is an expensive spell, but you probably won't cast it unless you're desperate, anyway (and then who cares about the casting cost). To get the most out of this spell, especially when casting it against powerful units, cast Black Prayer first to reduce your enemies' resistance.

Death Spell

Death Spell is for those occasions when your army is up against a little more than it can handle, or for times when you're just feeling lazy. Attempting to kill outright every figure in every unit (with a -2 resistance), this spell strives to take care of all your problems at once.

Death Spell Summary Information

Spell Rarity	Research Point Cost	Combat Casting Cost	Overland Casting Cost	Upkeep Cost Per Turn	Notes
Very Rare	2,500	50	N/A	N/A	targets resist at -2

Dark Rituals *Summary Information*

Spell Rarity	Research Point Cost	Combat Casting Cost	Overland Casting Cost	Upkeep Cost Per Turn	Notes
Common	60	N/A	30	N/A	None

Wall of Darkness *Summary Information*

Spell Rarity	Research Point Cost	Combat Casting Cost	Overland Casting Cost	Upkeep Cost Per Turn	Notes
Uncommon	680	40	200	5	None

The price you pay for this enchantment is a lower city growth rate and increased unrest, so save this spell for fairly developed, well-garrisoned cities. Remember, not all races can produce every religious building, so the benefits of casting this spell on a particular city will depend on the race inhabiting it (see Chapter 5).

This spell won't help much against some of the more powerful creatures in *Master of Magic*, since they have high innate resistances, but it is useful in most circumstances. It is quite expensive to cast, but what do you expect from a spell that tries to kill all your enemies in one shot?

City Enchantments

Except for a few early city enchantments, many of the Death magic city spells are designed to cripple your enemies' cities. Causing famine, mana shortages, and disease, Death magic city spells give you the means to slowly and thoroughly destroy your opponents.

Dark Rituals

Dark Rituals is a real boon when you are trying to build up armies of fantastic creatures or maintain several global and city enchantments at the same time. This spell doubles the mana produced by a city's religious buildings (i.e., shrines, temples, parthenons, and cathedrals). Dark Rituals even doubles the extra power you get through Infernal Power.

Wall of Darkness

Wall of Darkness completely protects a city's garrison from incoming ranged attacks unless your opponents are enchanted with the Life magic spell True Sight. Wall of Darkness can be cast both outside of and during combat. When you choose to cast it will depend on where your cities are and whether you're at war with another wizard.

This spell is expensive to maintain, so casting it on a city far from your front lines is not prudent. Note, however, that this spell can really save an inadequate garrison from stacks of enemy shamans and bowmen.

Evil Presence

Evil Presence is a great way to pull the magic carpet out from under your opponents. Cast it on one of their cities for the measly cost of 100 mana. This spell stops *all* mana production and calming effects of the target city's religious institutions! When combined with one of the other deadly black city enchantments, such as Famine, Evil Presence can make a given city virtually useless. Note that this spell cannot be cast on a city if the controlling wizard has any Death magic spell books.

Cloud of Shadow

Cloud of Shadow gives a city an ongoing Darkness spell. Since Darkness is at its best when you are commanding undead armies in battle against Life creatures, its long-term version, Cloud of Shadow is best used on cities that are bordering territories controlled by wizards with Life spell books or on cities garrisoned by fantastic Death creatures.

Evil Presence *Summary Information*

Spell Rarity	Research Point Cost	Combat Casting Cost	Overland Casting Cost	Upkeep Cost Per Turn	Notes
Rare	1,040	N/A	100	4	None

Cloud of Shadow *Summary Information*

Spell Rarity	Research Point Cost	Combat Casting Cost	Overland Casting Cost	Upkeep Cost Per Turn	Notes
Rare	1,200	N/A	150	3	affects white and black only

Famine

Famine is truly evil. This spell halves the food harvested by a city's farmers, forcing more of its citizens to work as farmers. This decreases worker productivity while slowly starving the population. On top of this, Famine increases unrest by an additional 25 percent of the city's people. By destroying its food, productivity, and, ultimately, its people, you strike at the economic heart of a wizard's empire and undercut its armies through more subtle means than battle.

Keep famines going as part of your campaign to defeat an enemy. Even at its high maintenance cost, Famine is worth casting against strong opponents.

Note that on the hard and impossible game settings, Famine will be relatively less useful than at other settings because your opponents' cities will be producing excess food (50 percent and 100 percent, respectively), anyway, at these game settings. The only thing you will gain from this spell, then, will be a relative evening of the playing field.

Cursed Lands

Cursed Lands causes a city's gross productivity to fall to half its value while increasing local unrest by one person. Given its casting and upkeep costs, it's not clear that this spell is really worth more than its sister Death spells: Famine, Evil Presence, or Pestilence. Those other spells have more evil consequences: loss

Famine *Summary Information*

Spell Rarity	Research Point Cost	Combat Casting Cost	Overland Casting Cost	Upkeep Cost Per Turn	Notes
Rare	1,600	N/A	200	5	None

Cursed Lands *Summary Information*

Spell Rarity	Research Point Cost	Combat Casting Cost	Overland Casting Cost	Upkeep Cost Per Turn	Notes
Rare	1,700	N/A	150	2	None

Pestilence *Summary Information*

Spell Rarity	Research Point Cost	Combat Casting Cost	Overland Casting Cost	Upkeep Cost Per Turn	Notes
Very Rare	3,500	N/A	350	5	None

of life and mana and significant increases in unrest, than Cursed Lands offers.

Still, Cursed Lands is cheaper to maintain, and halving the speed with which an enemy's major army production center spits out fresh units may be worthwhile during long, grinding wars of attrition.

Note that, as for Famine, Cursed Lands will be relatively useless on the hard and impossible game settings since your opponents' cities have increased production levels (50 percent and 100 percent, respectively) at these settings. At these levels, the best this spell can do is to slow down some key production points in your enemy's empire.

Pestilence

This spell slowly, but surely, destroys the population base of a city. Pestilence can kill up to one Population point per turn. When this spell, or its event analog, Plague, is active in a city, the computer rolls a d10 every game turn. If the town's population is greater than the die roll, one Population point dies. As a result, you can never completely destroy a town with this spell; one person will always remain. You can, however, virtually annihilate a town's food, gold, and production contributions to an enemy's plans (especially since one of the by-products of this spell is an additional two rebels in the target city!)

Global Enchantments

Continuing with its evil ways, Death magic's global enchantments are right up there with the worst malevolence you can imagine. Brace yourself.

Zombie Mastery

Zombie Mastery turns *Master of Magic* into a *Night of the Living Dead* sequel. While it is an expensive spell to maintain, at 40 mana per turn, its benefit is almost priceless.

When normal enemy or friendly units die during battles that you win, they will rise from the dead as zombies to fight for you. (Best of all, zombies have *no* maintenance costs!)

Zombie Mastery *Summary Information*

Spell Rarity	Research Point Cost	Combat Casting Cost	Overland Casting Cost	Upkeep Cost Per Turn	Notes
Rare	1,500	N/A	800	40	None

Casting this spell is a good way to generate huge armies quickly and is especially useful when you're fighting another wizard.

Eternal Night

Eternal Night is a spell that puts both Arcanus and Myrror under a Darkness spell. (Be sure to turn off all those Cloud of Shadow city enchantments if you cast Eternal Night.)

Unless a map square has specifically had True Light or Heavenly Light cast on it, any battles taking place will enhance the attributes of creatures of Death and deplete Life creatures' statistics. Unless your armies are made up primarily of undead units and unless you are fighting in an endless series of battles, this spell is simply too expensive to cast and maintain

Eternal Night Summary Information

Spell Rarity	Research Point Cost	Combat Casting Cost	Overland Casting Cost	Upkeep Cost Per Turn	Notes
Very Rare	4,000	N/A	1,000	15	affects white and black only

Evil Omens Summary Information

Spell Rarity	Research Point Cost	Combat Casting Cost	Overland Casting Cost	Upkeep Cost Per Turn	Notes
Very Rare	4,500	N/A	1,100	10	+50 percent cost for Life and Nature

without reason. Eternal Night is best cast when a final war heats up between you and a Life spell-casting wizard (e.g., Merlin, Ariel, Sss'ra, or Horus).

Evil Omens

Evil Omens is a spell that basically sucks mana out of any Nature or Life spell-casting wizard such as Merlin, Ariel, Oberic, Freya, etc. This spell increases the cost of casting *all* Nature and Life spells, including yours, by 50 percent, forcing these wizards to waste a lot of time and mana to use their magic. Don't bother casting Evil Omens unless you plan to keep this enchantment active for a long time, or you will never get an adequate return on its casting cost.

Death Wish

Have you ever closed your eyes and wished everyone you hated would just *go away*? Death Wish does that. This global spell at-

![Figure 9-2. Eternal Night]

Figure 9-2. *Eternal Night*

Death Wish *Summary Information*

Spell Rarity	Research Point Cost	Combat Casting Cost	Overland Casting Cost	Upkeep Cost Per Turn	Notes
Very Rare	5,000	N/A	500	N/A	no resistance modifiers

tempts to kill *all* enemy normal (i.e., non-fantastic) units in one fell swoop! It is one of those nasty ways to undercut your enemies, by depleting their garrisons and any armies that may be marching towards your cities.

Special Spells

These unique spells do not fit neatly in the other categories. Black magic's specialties in this area are focused on destroying enemy magic abilities.

Drain Power

Drain Power lets you spend 50 mana to drain between 10 and 200 mana from an enemy's mana reserves. As an ordinary spell to cast just for the heck of it, Drain Power lacks pizzazz. However, this spell is useful under very specific circumstances, such as just before launching an attack against an enemy, knowing that draining the enemy's reserves with this spell will cripple his or her spell casting ability during your upcoming battle(s).

Subversion

Subversion is the old cheap trick of pointing your finger at someone else to focus suspicion on them instead of you. When you're in diplomatic difficulties, which you often will encounter when you are playing with Death magic, and when you are straining to divert your enemies' attentions away from you long enough to gather much needed strength, Subversion is the spell to cast. Be aware that you may have to cast this spell multiple times to have a significant effect, especially at the harder difficulty settings, where negative diplomatic effects between computer opponents are buffered.

Subversion is most effective against a wizard who is already somewhat disliked by the others in the game. Then this spell may create the final diplomatic adjustment needed to make your target the nidus for everyone else's hate (see Chapter 25 for this spell's specific diplomatic consequences).

Drain Power *Summary Information*

Spell Rarity	Research Point Cost	Combat Casting Cost	Overland Casting Cost	Upkeep Cost Per Turn	Notes
Uncommon	300	N/A	50	N/A	None

Subversion *Summary Information*

Spell Rarity	Research Point Cost	Combat Casting Cost	Overland Casting Cost	Upkeep Cost Per Turn	Notes
Uncommon	620	N/A	100	N/A	None

Warp Node

Now, if you want to create a long-lasting drain on an enemy's mana reserves and magic abilities, Warp Node is the best way to do it. Cheap, at 75 mana per casting (and *no* upkeep cost!), this spell causes a node to *drain* five mana per turn out of the controlling wizard's reserves, rather than adding any to it.

If you cast this spell on enough of their nodes, something not too difficult to do at only 75 mana per pop, you can make it difficult for an enemy to cast and to maintain spells. This spell should form part of a long-term program designed to bring an enemy to their knees.

Note, if you meld a spirit with a warped node, it will still be warped. You must cast Disenchant Area or Disenchant True to remove this enchantment.

Black Wind

Black Wind is an attempt to kill all figures in all units on a target map square. This is a good spell to use when a stack of enemy units is approaching one of your nodes or cities, but it might take a while to cast it at 200 mana

Warp Node Summary Information

Spell Rarity	Research Point Cost	Combat Casting Cost	Overland Casting Cost	Upkeep Cost Per Turn	Notes
Rare	1,300	N/A	75	N/A	None

Black Wind Summary Information

Spell Rarity	Research Point Cost	Combat Casting Cost	Overland Casting Cost	Upkeep Cost Per Turn	Notes
Rare	1,400	N/A	200	N/A	targets resist at -1

per zephyr. Black Wind is often more useful, therefore, when cast upon an enemy city to deplete its garrison before you attack there.

Cruel Unminding

Cruel Unminding destroys 10 percent of the mana that has been spent on developing a target wizard's spell-casting skill, thus decreasing the wizard's skill level accordingly. Now, this may not seem like much, but at this casting cost, you can generally afford to hit a wizard several times before your mana reserves get too low. By destroying your enemy's spell-casting skill, you destroy much of his or her ability to wield magic effectively.

Seeing Red

Thus, we are turning out the lights on black magic. If evil is as evil does, than you'll be able to do a fun bit of role-playing with enough

Cruel Unminding Summary Information

Spell Rarity	Research Point Cost	Combat Casting Cost	Overland Casting Cost	Upkeep Cost Per Turn	Notes
Very Rare	1,850	N/A	250	N/A	None

Death magic at your command.

From here, we move to the heavy-hitting Chaos magic. When you're seeing red, destruction soon follows.

10

Red Hots

Chaos magic is hard hitting, like a pit bull. Red is the attack dog of magic colors and no other color is nearly as strong, particularly in combat. If you want to wield a big stick, remember its color is red.

Summoning Spells

Chaos magic is the only magic type that can rival Nature magic in terms of creature summoning possibilities. It is through red magic that the fiery great drakes and the nine-headed hydras can be summoned. Many Chaos creatures have fiery breath or similar special attacks (see Chapter 20). In addition, more than half of the chaos creatures can fly, making them invaluable for forming special armies (see Chapter 22).

Hell Hounds

Hell hounds are decent units early in the game. They have fire breath that allows them to attack flying units when necessary. Because they are not too expensive to cast, they can be summoned quickly for help when raiders or rampaging monsters are threatening your cities. Use hell hounds to flesh out your early forces

until better units can be created to replace them.

Fire Elemental

There is nothing quite like having creatures summoned on the battlefield itself. If you are attacked and understaffed, or if you accidentally walked into an overwhelming situation, fire elementals could help you overcome the odds. It's not that fire elementals are such great fighters, but every unit on the field of battle helps.

Although fire elementals are immune to fire, stoning, and poison, don't expect them to last long in battle. That's not what they're there for. What they *can* do is draw fire that might have been aimed at one of your other fighting units and act as physical barriers to keep charging enemies from getting to your rear line bowmen or shamans too quickly. Of course, fire elementals can also get in a few hits to help take down a non-flying foe.

Fire Giant

Fire giants are nice, garden variety, middleweight fantastic units, although they're a tad pricy. Their stats are good, with 10 swords and 15 hearts, but their special gift is their two rock attacks, each of strength 10. Finally, they can be particularly useful for assaulting cities with their two movement and wall crushing ability.

Gargoyles

Gargoyles are interesting. Flying in packs of four, each gargoyle figure has about same defen-

Hell Hounds *Summary Information*

Spell Rarity	Research Point Cost	Combat Casting Cost	Overland Casting Cost	Upkeep Cost Per Turn	Notes
Common	80	N/A	40	1	None

Fire Elemental *Summary Information*

Spell Rarity	Research Point Cost	Combat Casting Cost	Overland Casting Cost	Upkeep Cost Per Turn	Notes
Common	250	20	N/A	N/A	None

sive ability as a death knight and more than an angel, both of which are considerably more expensive and rare.

Luckily (if you're up against them), or unfortunately (if you happen to be using them in your armies), gargoyles don't have a lot of hit points (four hearts per figure). So, if a unit can get past their defenses, gargoyles can be whittled down easily. They are only immune to poison and stoning attacks, so almost any brutal physical or magic attack will put the hurt on gargoyles.

Doom Bat

The doom bat is one of the fastest flying units in *Master of Magic*, at four squares per turn. If you can summon one of these early in the game, you can do a lot of exploring with it. As an army unit, though, you can probably do better.

Doom bats have high upkeep costs of eight mana per turn and, although they have a 10 strength melee attack on top of a fiery touch attack (see Chapter 20), a few strong missile units will easily turn doom bats into ding bats. Doom bats are really best in swarms, and they are simply too expensive for that.

Chimera

Chimeras are hardy, fire-breathing, flying creatures that are expensive to cast and maintain, although they *are* good fighters. Unless you are in desperate need of flying units to get somewhere special, however, you are probably better off with a few solid fighting units instead

Fire Giant Summary Information

Spell Rarity	Research Point Cost	Combat Casting Cost	Overland Casting Cost	Upkeep Cost Per Turn	Notes
Common	350	N/A	150	3	None

Gargoyles Summary Information

Spell Rarity	Research Point Cost	Combat Casting Cost	Overland Casting Cost	Upkeep Cost Per Turn	Notes
Uncommon	500	N/A	200	5	None

Doom Bat Summary Information

Spell Rarity	Research Point Cost	Combat Casting Cost	Overland Casting Cost	Upkeep Cost Per Turn	Notes
Uncommon	620	N/A	300	8	None

Chimera Summary Information

Spell Rarity	Research Point Cost	Combat Casting Cost	Overland Casting Cost	Upkeep Cost Per Turn	Notes
Uncommon	800	N/A	350	10	None

Chaos Spawn *Summary Information*

Spell Rarity	Research Point Cost	Combat Casting Cost	Overland Casting Cost	Upkeep Cost Per Turn	Notes
Rare	1,040	N/A	500	12	None

Efreet *Summary Information*

Spell Rarity	Research Point Cost	Combat Casting Cost	Overland Casting Cost	Upkeep Cost Per Turn	Notes
Rare	1,300	N/A	550	15	None

of the expensive chimeras. As with any corporeal flying unit, one of the best ways to fight against these creatures is to web them, if you can, and then take them out with ground troops.

Chaos Spawn

These bobbing balls of death, doom, and destruction, while cute, are virtually useless. Why? Because they are slow and completely helpless against missile attacks. If they ever got close enough to another unit to attack or counterattack, chaos spawns would be deadly since their gaze attacks are very difficult to resist and, as with all gaze attacks, their effects take place before regular melee combat (see Chapter 20).

However, chaos spawns only have a movement allowance of one square per turn, so they're usually pin cushions before they can ever get close enough to an enemy unit to use their special abilities. At their

high upkeep cost, you may want to give these units a miss.

Efreet

An efreet can be quite useful. These flying units are spell casters who get 20 mana per battle in Chaos magic spells, allowing them to summon a fire elemental or cast Warp Wood spells—or even an Eldritch Weapon spell—in *every* battle. They also have fairly strong magic attacks (nine fireballs) and fire immunity.

However, their casting cost and wickedly high upkeep cost means they're not a bargain. Therefore, efreets are best to use in small numbers to round out the offensive possibilities of a stack of units.

Hydra

The nine-headed hydra is enormously sturdy; each head has nine hit points and four shields. Worse, these guys regenerate. If you can summon hydras to fight for your wizard, you won't need any special tips on how to use them. Just bear in mind that their high upkeep cost is the going price for a regenerating, fire-breathing, solid unit like this.

Hydra *Summary Information*

Spell Rarity	Research Point Cost	Combat Casting Cost	Overland Casting Cost	Upkeep Cost Per Turn	Notes
Very Rare	1,850	N/A	650	14	None

When you're up against a hydra horde, however, you must be acutely aware of their nature. Because hydras regenerate, if you do not kill their entire army, then they will

Great Drake *Summary Information*					
Spell Rarity	Research Point Cost	Combat Casting Cost	Overland Casting Cost	Upkeep Cost Per Turn	Notes
Very Rare	4,500	N/A	900	30	None

all be back in full health (even the ones you thought you killed), immediately after the combat ends. So, prepare well before you wander into lairs or Chaos nodes infested with these creatures. Take plenty of sturdy, long-range missile units with you: slingers are fine, so are longbowmen, and make sure you do the job right the *first* time.

Great Drake

The great drake is arguably the strongest individual unit in *Master of Magic*, certainly on a par with the sky drake and great wyrm. Great drakes are extraordinary fighters with melee attacks of 30 strength, *on top of* a fiery breath attack of 30! Because they can fly, they can pick and choose their opponents unless they have been webbed first. They also have

Figure 10-1. *Summoning a Great Drake*

a high innate resistance to spells and are hard to damage by that means.

Fortunately, if you are facing a few of them, they don't move too fast and you can definitely shoot several down if you have plenty of missile units in your army. Having one of these drakes supporting your own "killer stack" will make you nearly invincible.

One final note: Great drakes have an enormous upkeep cost. However, by the time you can afford to quickly summon a great drake, you should easily be making enough mana per turn to support it.

Creature Enchantments

Chaos magic features few creature enchantments, but most of them are powerful spells designed to enhance the fighting capabilities of your troops. Best of all, these spells are all common or uncommon, so even if you choose only one or two spell ranks in Chaos magic, you stand a good chance of getting one or more of these enchantments in your spell book.

Eldritch Weapon

This useful spell gives the target unit a magic weapon (i.e., one that can hit creatures with weapon immunity). Although this spell does not increase the attack strength or To Hit values of the unit, an Eldritch Weapon penalizes an enemy's shields with a -1 To Defend modifier.

Eldritch Weapon is an *anytime* spell. It never hurts to cast it on one of your units in combat, unless there is an outstanding alternative spell available. It certainly doesn't hurt

113

Eldritch Weapon *Summary Information*

Spell Rarity	Research Point Cost	Combat Casting Cost	Overland Casting Cost	Upkeep Cost Per Turn	Notes
Common	130	15	75	1	normal units only

Warp Creature *Summary Information*

Spell Rarity	Research Point Cost	Combat Casting Cost	Overland Casting Cost	Upkeep Cost Per Turn	Notes
Uncommon	220	18	N/A	N/A	targets resist at -1

to have your main melee units permanently enchanted with this spell, unless you are having trouble producing enough mana to pay the upkeep.

Warp Creature
One of the hallmarks of chaos is that you never know what will happen. A few spells reflect this unpredictability, and Warp Creature is one of them. Designed to just do something bad to an enemy unit (possible effects include halving defense or attack strengths and removing the target's resistance), the problem with Warp Creature is that you cannot count on it to do what you need done. While its casting cost is not outrageous, for a random effect it is still steep. Only use this as a last-ditch spell.

Chaos Channels
Chaos Channels is another random-

effect spell. Chaos Channels permanently alters the basic characteristics of a friendly normal unit, turning it into a creature of Chaos as it does so. All of its effects (flight, +3 shields, or a 2-strength fire-breathing attack) are worthwhile, especially at its casting cost of 50 mana with no maintenance required. The trouble is that this spell can be cast on a unit only *one* time. Still, you can't lose with it.

Note that a unit's experience level will not increase after it has been altered by Chaos Channels.

Flame Blade
Flame Blade enchants a normal unit's weapons so that they are magical, allowing them to hit creatures with weapon immunity (see Chapter 20). The enchanted weapons are also stronger with +2 swords *per figure*.

This is a fine spell to cast, particularly when combat comes down to two similar units fighting things out or when matters are being settled by two units with a slight inequality in

Chaos Channel *Summary Information*

Spell Rarity	Research Point Cost	Combat Casting Cost	Overland Casting Cost	Upkeep Cost Per Turn	Notes
Uncommon	400	N/A	50	N/A	normal units only

attributes. Casting Flame Blade under such circumstances basically gives your unit(s) the added punch they need to win the battle. Even though this spell is pricy to cast, its effects are impressive enough to warrant employing it in the right circumstances.

Fire Blade Summary Information

Spell Rarity	Research Point Cost	Combat Casting Cost	Overland Casting Cost	Upkeep Cost Per Turn	Notes
Uncommon	450	25	125	2	normal units only

Immolation

Immolation gives a target unit a strength four fiery touch attack (equivalent to a strength four fireball) in addition to its normal melee attack. This is not a significant bonus, even for weak units, since this attack is defended separately (all of a unit's shields apply) from its melee attack. It is also expensive to cast under both combat and non-combat situations and affects only units that don't have fire or magic immunity (see Chapter 20).

Combat Spells

Chaos magic's real strength lies in its destructive combat spells. At higher levels, Chaos magic has awesome destructive spells. Some are so powerful (Flame Strike, Disintegration, etc.) that you would be wise to boost the mana going into your spellcasting skill and reserves (see Chapter 15) rather than into research, just so you can make as much use of these spells as possible. If you choose a heavy dose of Chaos magic when you begin the game, the wizard skill Channeler will be most useful in supporting it.

Warp Wood

Warp Wood is a handy spell. For a paltry casting cost, it destroys all bow and sling (not rocks) ammunition in the hands of opposing normal units. Since the defending unit cannot avoid the effects of Warp Wood, this spell

Immolation Summary Information

Spell Rarity	Research Point Cost	Combat Casting Cost	Overland Casting Cost	Upkeep Cost Per Turn	Notes
Uncommon	740	30	150	2	None

Warp Wood Summary Information

Spell Rarity	Research Point Cost	Combat Casting Cost	Overland Casting Cost	Upkeep Cost Per Turn	Notes
Common	20	10	N/A	N/A	normal units only; no resistance possible

Disrupt *Summary Information*

Spell Rarity	Research Point Cost	Combat Casting Cost	Overland Casting Cost	Upkeep Cost Per Turn	Notes
Common	40	15	N/A	N/A	None

Fire Bolt *Summary Information*

Spell Rarity	Research Point Cost	Combat Casting Cost	Overland Casting Cost	Upkeep Cost Per Turn	Notes
Common	60	5 to 25	N/A	N/A	None

is remarkably useful when your troops are up against a stack of enemy bowmen or slingers.

In many battles, things often come down to a few scraggly units left after the missile units have had their day. Reducing your opponent's fire power, therefore, is the key to winning such battles. Note that Warp Wood does not affect magic ranged attacks; it only destroys *normal* ammunitions: arrows, slings, and javelins.

Disrupt

This spell acts like an automatic wall crusher, blowing up bits of stone wall. If you are trying to take a walled city with a stack of bowmen or other missile units, this spell is particularly useful. If you blast away a section of wall with it, your attacks are no longer subject to the +3 shield modifier the defending unit receives when standing behind a wall section.

If you are trying to take the city using troops without missile attack capability, however, there is not much reason to destroy a stone wall. The wall's gateway usually provides adequate room for battle and doesn't hinder spell casting in any way.

Fire Bolt

Fire Bolt is your basic low-level combat spell. For all the mana you can waste pumping this spell up, the killing power just isn't sufficient to make it worthwhile. Also, it does not affect any unit immune to fire (fire elementals, efreets, and fire giants). Its best use is against weakly shielded units in the enemy's rear line (bowmen, slinger, shaman, etc.), and only then when you have no other recourse against them and have nothing better to do with your combat mana.

Shatter

Shatter is a nifty spell that exerts potentially powerful effects for a low price. If successful, and there are no resistance modifiers for this

Shatter *Summary Information*

Spell Rarity	Research Point Cost	Combat Casting Cost	Overland Casting Cost	Upkeep Cost Per Turn	Notes
Common	190	12	N/A	N/A	no resistance modifiers; normal units only

spell, Shatter destroys all of the target unit's melee, thrown, and missile attacks, causing them to fall to a token value of 1.

This spell can only target normal units, but it can, for instance, disarm powerful warship, stag beetle, golem, javelineer, and slinger units. However, powerful units generally have a high resistance value, so if you have any resistance modifying spells like Black Prayer or High Prayer, cast these before you cast Shatter.

Lightning Bolt Summary Information

Spell Rarity	Research Point Cost	Combat Casting Cost	Overland Casting Cost	Upkeep Cost Per Turn	Notes
Common	300	10 to 50	N/A	N/A	None

Fire Ball Summary Information

Spell Rarity	Research Point Cost	Combat Casting Cost	Overland Casting Cost	Upkeep Cost Per Turn	Notes
Uncommon	560	15 to 75	N/A	N/A	None

Lightning Bolt

The Lightning Bolt spell directs armor-piercing damage against an enemy. This spell, because it halves enemy shields, is basically twice as damaging as the lowly Fire Bolt and, consequently, costs twice as much. Fortunately, there is no such thing as lightning immunity, and so a lightning bolt has considerable versatility. Because every additional point of mana spent casting this spell increases the lightning bolt's strength by 1, you can blast enemy units with an armor-piercing attack of up to 45 strength! Very powerful (and expensive).

Fireball

Casting Fireball is the equivalent of sending a Fire Bolt against every figure in an enemy unit individually. Whereas a Fire Bolt hits the first figure and excess damage carries over to the next (like a normal melee attack, see Chapter 20), a Fireball blasts every figure in a unit individually, with its full force (without excess damage carrying over to later units).

It costs three times as much mana to cast a Fireball as it does a Fire Bolt, although it has the potential to be significantly more effective when cast against units with more than three figures. To make a Fireball worthwhile, you need to pump a lot of additional mana into it (gaining one strength for every three additional mana spent casting it). By the time you've pumped this spell up, however, you would be better off with the Disintegrate spell or Doom Bolt.

Of course, you will probably learn Fireball much sooner in the game than Disintegrate or Doom Bolt. When it's all you have, a Fireball works well enough. Use it to take down or cripple strong normal units with multiple figures (halberdiers, pikemen, etc.) when you are outnumbered or outclassed by your opponents. It also works well, even at low strength, against phantom warriors.

Doom Bolt

A Doom Bolt causes 10 damage to its targets, regardless of their defenses. This spell will completely annihilate weaker units during

Doom Bolt *Summary Information*

Spell Rarity	Research Point Cost	Combat Casting Cost	Overland Casting Cost	Upkeep Cost Per Turn	Notes
Rare	1,120	40	N/A	N/A	no resistance possible

Warp Lightning *Summary Information*

Spell Rarity	Research Point Cost	Combat Casting Cost	Overland Casting Cost	Upkeep Cost Per Turn	Notes
Rare	880	35	N/A	N/A	None

combat, cripple powerful units (including heroes), and finish off previously damaged units before they can get to you. It is expensive to cast, but its damage is impressive and *guaranteed*. Note, this spell is ineffective against units with magic immunity (sky drakes, paladins).

Warp Lightning

Warp Lightning directs a series of diminishing strength, armor-piercing attacks through a target unit, hitting the entire unit with up to 45 points of damage. Of course, the figures in the unit get to defend themselves from the attack, but a lot of destructive force is still being sent at a single unit.

If you wish to eliminate a unit with 10 or fewer hit points left, hit it with a sure fire Doom Bolt. If you have a stronger unit to kill, however, you may

want to cast Warp Lightning instead, unless the unit has six or more shields, in which case a Doom Bolt will still do more damage on average than Warp Lightning.

Metal Fires

Metal Fires is a combat enchantment that gives all of your normal units magic weapons with an increased (+1) melee and missile strength *per figure*. This is a great spell to cast when you have a large army of normal unit types. Although an increased attack strength of one may not seem like much, the attack potential is increased tremendously when combined over all the figures of those several normal units,. In combination with missile units, this spell can be devastating to your foes. Note that the effects of Metal Fires and Flame Blade are not additive.

Warp Reality

Have you ever found your lowly spearmen or swordsmen facing imminent death as they confront halberdiers, cavalry units, bowmen, etc.? If you do not have the more destructive

Metal Fires *Summary Information*

Spell Rarity	Research Point Cost	Combat Casting Cost	Overland Casting Cost	Upkeep Cost Per Turn	Notes
Rare	960	40	N/A	N/A	normal units only

Chaos spells ready when you encounter these units, Warp Reality can be extremely helpful if you are fighting with an army of Chaos units (Chaos Channeled units count, too).

By inflicting a -2 To Hit penalty on all non-Chaos units in the battle, this spell renders their attacks up to two-thirds less effective than normal and makes most missile units almost completely ineffective (after factoring in the distance modifiers; see Chapter 20). Combine this spell with Metal Fires when you can (if you have enough normal units in the battle to make it worthwhile), and you'll have roast enemy for dinner.

Warp Reality Summary Information

Spell Rarity	Research Point Cost	Combat Casting Cost	Overland Casting Cost	Upkeep Cost Per Turn	Notes
Rare	1,500	50	N/A	N/A	affects all non-Chaos only

Magic Vortex Summary Information

Spell Rarity	Research Point Cost	Combat Casting Cost	Overland Casting Cost	Upkeep Cost Per Turn	Notes
Rare	1,200	50	N/A	N/A	None

Magic Vortex

Magic Vortex is a fantastic spell to pull out of your wizard's cap but only under special circumstances. This spell creates a mini-tornado that lasts until the end of combat. This vortex has a "mind" of its own; each combat round, it will move three squares, randomly, while you guide its fourth move. Before you cast it, make sure your remaining units can get out of the Vortex's way (a minimum speed of two per unit should be sufficient for this).

There are two situations in particular where a Magic Vortex is quite helpful: against giant wyrms and city garrisons. Giant wyrms can be killed without too much difficulty by sending in a flying unit or two and casting this spell. Don't bother attacking the wyrm, just hang around and direct the Vortex as close to the wyrm as you can. Every time it spins over

a unit it does an *automatic* five points of damage, except to units with magic immunity, such as paladins and sky drakes. It also has a 25 percent probability of sending an eight-strength armor-piercing lightning bolt at units in neighboring squares.

City garrisons can also be reduced easily in this way, without your units ever risking their skins. The big drawback, however, is that the Vortex can destroy buildings, too. The spell may not be worth trying under such circumstances, unless there is a specific reason you want to take that town; such as when you are trying to banish another wizard by destroying his or her Enchanted Fortress.

Flame Strike

This combat spell showers all enemy units with a 15-strength fireball attack. This is an expensive spell to cast, but Flame Strike can virtually annihilate all your enemies. It's got a knack for destroying most figures in any normal troops as well as weaker fantastic creatures. Two Flame Strikes are guaranteed to destroy all but the hardiest opponents. Note

Flame Strike Summary Information

Spell Rarity	Research Point Cost	Combat Casting Cost	Overland Casting Cost	Upkeep Cost Per Turn	Notes
Rare	1,600	60	N/A	N/A	None

Disintergrate Summary Information

Spell Rarity	Research Point Cost	Combat Casting Cost	Overland Casting Cost	Upkeep Cost Per Turn	Notes
Very Rare	2,000	50	N/A	N/A	no resistance possible for most units

that creatures with magic or fire immunity (see Chapter 20) can resist the effects of this spell.

Disintegrate

This spell destroys a target unit with a resistance lower than 10. There is no saving throw; the unit simply disappears and can never be regenerated or brought back from the dead by any other means, period. This is clearly a valuable spell. The certainty of destruction that Disintegrate carries is well worth its casting cost.

Because Disintegrate is expensive, though, you probably cannot cast it often (at least not until very late in the game). However, do cast

it when you are up against stronger opponents who meet the minimal susceptibility requirements of this spell.

Call Chaos

This is the ultimate Chaos combat spell. Call Chaos hits every enemy unit on the battlefield with one of a variety of spells. Featuring a grab bag of effects, including Doom Bolt, Disintegrate, Warp Lightning, and even Chaos Channels, Call Chaos offers a wide range of powerful effects for a relatively low price.

Given the opportunity to specifically target destructive forces with spells like Disintegrate, the random nature of Call Chaos brings its utility into question. On the other hand, for wreaking unbridled destruction on your enemies as an early tenderizing battlefield maneuver, this spell fits the bill. Generally, though, Flame Strike will be more useful.

City Enchantments

Chaos magic is destruction in magic form. It is no surprise, then, that two of its three city spells are purely destructive in nature.

Wall of Fire

Wall of Fire costs more than it is worth, particularly considering its upkeep cost. Fortunately, it can be cast during battle, i.e.,

Call Chaos Summary Information

Spell Rarity	Research Point Cost	Combat Casting Cost	Overland Casting Cost	Upkeep Cost Per Turn	Notes
Very Rare	3,000	75	N/A	N/A	None

specifically when you need it. A Wall of Fire protects units within the city walls by forcing a unit passing *into* the city to take damage from the flames (a five-strength fireball attack). Similarly, outside units, except for flying or teleporting units, which attack across the wall, suffer fire attacks during melee combat. Basically, this spell is another way to give weaker defending units an edge against non-missile wielding attackers.

Chaos Rift

This spell is a way to slowly but surely destroy a city and its inhabitants. The Chaos Rift shoots five lightning bolts randomly at garrisoned troops in the target city every turn. In addition, during every game turn, each building within the city has a five percent chance of being destroyed.

Chaos Rift is useful before you've acquired Call the Void. It is good for reducing garrisons before attacking a city or simply as a way to slowly undercut an opponent's power base of people and productive buildings.

Call the Void

Call the Void is an amazingly powerful spell. It basically destroys half of a city and casts the equivalent of a Doom Bolt on every unit there. Like Chaos Rift, this is the kind of spell

you might cast before trying to conquer a city, although the massive loss of buildings and life (not to mention the vast corruption of neighboring land) makes it somewhat counterproductive for such aims. It is more productive to cast this spell before trying to take over a city you don't mind ruining anyway, such as the one where an enemy's Enchanted Fortress is located.

Global Enchantments

So, you want to be a bastard, eh? You want to take off the gloves and declare war on the whole world? You want to rain on everyone's parade and don't give a hoot what others think? Well, has red got the global enchantments for you...

Wall of Fire Summary Information

Spell Rarity	Research Point Cost	Combat Casting Cost	Overland Casting Cost	Upkeep Cost Per Turn	Notes
Common	160	30	150	2	None

Chaos Rift Summary Information

Spell Rarity	Research Point Cost	Combat Casting Cost	Overland Casting Cost	Upkeep Cost Per Turn	Notes
Rare	1,700	N/A	300	10	None

Call the Void Summary Information

Spell Rarity	Research Point Cost	Combat Casting Cost	Overland Casting Cost	Upkeep Cost Per Turn	Notes
Very Rare	5,000	N/A	500	N/A	None

Meteor Storms *Summary Information*

Spell Rarity	Research Point Cost	Combat Casting Cost	Overland Casting Cost	Upkeep Cost Per Turn	Notes
Very Rare	2,250	N/A	900	10	None

Great Wasting *Summary Information*

Spell Rarity	Research Point Cost	Combat Casting Cost	Overland Casting Cost	Upkeep Cost Per Turn	Notes
Very Rare	2,500	N/A	1,000	20	None

Meteor Storms

Casting Meteor Storms is a good way to cripple your opponents. By dinging away at enemy units (with strength four fireball attacks) and destroying their buildings (each building has a one percent chance of being destroyed every game turn), you can often destroy their stacks of troops before enemies ever reach you.

Go ahead and laugh as their settlers die before they can build outposts. Gloat as their engineers are blasted before roads are finished. Well, you get the picture. Of course there is a minor caveat. All garrisoned troops are protected from Meteor Storms, and *all* ungarrisoned units are subject to the fireball attacks, including yours!

This is destruction on a large scale, but that is its purpose. The biggest problem with Meteor Storms is that, along with its sisters—Great Wasting and Armageddon—there won't be much left for you to conquer afterward.

Great Wasting

Great Wasting causes corruption to blossom like a deadly weed all over Arcanus and Myrror, and corrupted squares yield no food or minerals. Enemy cities each get an additional rebel as well, causing an even greater burden on their increasingly strained economic predicament.

Eventually, with enough of this rotting going on around them, enemies will crumble internally. Great Wasting is the ultimate way to gain the upper hand by putting everyone else down. It is also a good way to keep everyone else distracted while you're off casting the Spell of Mastery.

Chaos Surge

If you are the only wizard wielding significant quantities of Chaos magic, seriously consider casting this spell, especially in support of Doom Mastery. Chaos Surge makes all Chaos creatures, including those altered by Chaos Channels, fight much more effectively throughout the worlds. Units with multiple figures will, as with all such spells, reap the greatest relative reward from the +2 *per figure* benefit to their melee, missile,

Chaos Surge *Summary Information*

Spell Rarity	Research Point Cost	Combat Casting Cost	Overland Casting Cost	Upkeep Cost Per Turn	Notes
Very Rare	3,500	N/A	1,000	40	None

magic, and breath attacks, and the +2 bonus to their shields and crosses.

Doom Mastery

Doom Mastery transforms all of your newly constructed normal units with a Chaos Channels spell. This gives them either an extra +3 shields, the skill of flight, or a +2 strength fire breath attack. This is a great spell to cast later in the game if you wish to win militarily. Your units will be more versatile and powerful as they're produced.

If you have a Chaos Surge spell working simultaneously, *all* of the units you produce will be much stronger, because they will all be, as a result of *this* spell, creatures of Chaos! Combining these two spells is a powerful way to quickly build almost unstoppable armies of basic unit types.

Doom Mastery *Summary Information*

Spell Rarity	Research Point Cost	Combat Casting Cost	Overland Casting Cost	Upkeep Cost Per Turn	Notes
Very Rare	4,000	N/A	1,100	15	normal units only

Armageddon *Summary Information*

Spell Rarity	Research Point Cost	Combat Casting Cost	Overland Casting Cost	Upkeep Cost Per Turn	Notes
Very Rare	6,000	N/A	1,250	40	None

Figure 10-2. *Chaos Surge*

Armageddon

This is the most powerful Chaos spell. Every turn that this spell is in effect, up to six volcanoes appear on Arcanus and Myrror and all enemy cities become afflicted by two of their Population points going rebel. The six possible volcano squares are chosen at random and a volcano appears there, if those squares don't contain an ocean, coast, volcano, or city and if they are not within the city limits of one of the caster's cities.

Volcanoes destroy all production, food, and mineral bonuses on the map squares that they occupy. The beauty of Armageddon is that each new volcano contributes one mana per turn to the income of the casting wizard!

Armageddon is a spell to cast when your frontiers are closed and you don't wish to expand the limits of your empire (for instance, when you're casting Spell of Mastery). In any case, this is the ultimate spell to decimate your enemies' cities and development. The destroyed lands will cause losses of lives over time, while the rebel problem will undercut productivity and gold income. All the while,

Corruption Summary Information

Spell Rarity	Research Point Cost	Combat Casting Cost	Overland Casting Cost	Upkeep Cost Per Turn	Notes
Common	100	N/A	40	N/A	None

Raise Volcano Summary Information

Spell Rarity	Research Point Cost	Combat Casting Cost	Overland Casting Cost	Upkeep Cost Per Turn	Notes
Uncommon	680	N/A	200	N/A	None

you'll be laughing and drawing in more mana to fuel your continued efforts.

Special Spells

Chaos magic excels in destruction, and this ability forms the basis of its special spells.

Corruption

Corruption temporarily destroys all food, mineral, and production provided by the targeted map square. It is a cheap spell to cast and you will notice that angry opponents of yours will cast this spell on your cities with alarming fervor and frequency. Fortunately for you, its messes are easy to clean up with a shaman or priest.

Corruption is a great way to prick an enemy. You can systematically and cheaply put their mines, wild game, and other special squares out of commission. You can even direct your efforts at their Enchanted Fortress. With enough corrupted squares sur-rounding it, you can exert effects similar to a Famine or Cursed Lands, and without the upkeep costs.

Raise Volcano

Raise Volcano is expensive, but its effects are almost permanent; the only spells capable of transforming volcanoes or their burnt out hulks (see Chapter 14) into reasonably useful land are Nature's Change Terrain and Gaia's Blessing. (**Hint**: Tundra squares can be "vulcanized" and then targeted with Change Terrain.) Note that volcanoes may not be raised on rivers, hills, mountains, or nodes.

A volcano destroys all productivity and bonuses on its map square while it pays you a return of one mana per game turn (think of this spell as a mini-Armageddon). In addition, if a volcano is raised directly on a city, every building within the city has a 15 percent chance of being destroyed.

Note that you can systematically and permanently destroy your enemies' special terrain bonuses, and you can completely destroy their favorite cities, their Enchanted Fortresses, surrounding lands, etc., if you cast Raise Volcano on enough of the target cities'

Fire Storm Summary Information

Spell Rarity	Research Point Cost	Combat Casting Cost	Overland Casting Cost	Upkeep Cost Per Turn	Notes
Rare	1,400	N/A	250	N/A	None

nearby map squares. Also note that your computer opponents have no compunction about using this strategy on you.

Fire Storm

A Fire Storm is a great way to diminish the size of a garrison or an approaching army. This spell conducts an eight-strength fire attack against each *figure* on the targeted square. While this is not strong enough to destroy every figure in every unit, it will certainly pare down a unit's size and health. Before invading a city, consider casting this spell on it to soften up the garrison without destroying the city's buildings or inhabitants. (You may as well have something worth taking over when you've defeated what's left of the armies there).

Similarly, if a menacing army is approaching one of your undergarrisoned nodes or cities, casting a Fire Storm on it will help you defend your territory without taking heavy losses.

Naturally

You can take it as red that Chaos magic is powerful. With the greatest amount of brute force in the game, there is little that it cannot bash to bits.

Opposite this magic of destruction, however, is the green magic of Nature with its building ways. In the next chapter, we'll give you a green light and help you to go—naturally.

11
Green Genes

Nature magic is fairly balanced, with a strong emphasis on useful common creature enhancements. Even one or two spell books of green magic are good because, once into their uncommon spell strata, spells like Change Terrain, Cracks Call, and Pathfinding become available. At the higher levels there are several tough monsters that can be summoned, plus the spell Gaia's Blessing offers a myriad of wonders for city building.

Green is the color of building and tapping into nature's power. It is a great supplementary color for its variety of useful common and uncommon spells, but it also proves worthy as a stand alone color for those who like to pursue its very rare spells. Green magic is so useful, in fact, that you really notice when you don't have any!

Summoning Spells

Green magic is pretty good for creature summoning. Militarily weaker races such as the Halflings, Nomads, and Barbarians often benefit by having their forces supplemented with green creatures, particularly the rare and very rare breed. Look out once those Nature creatures start appearing on the map!

War Bears

What did you expect for such a bargain price, dragons? War bears are low-level, down and dirty fighting units whose best feature is their movement allowance of two. Summon them when you want to keep your shock army fleshed out (furred out?) and when you can better afford the mana upkeep of war bears than the gold upkeep of normal units. The usefulness of war bears is fairly short-lived, but they can be summoned quickly when the city with your Summoning Circle is threatened.

Sprites

Since you've probably fought *against* them enough times while clearing nodes and lairs, you have no doubt learned that sprites aren't bad. Sure, they can be killed, but their magic ranged attacks, especially when there are droves of them, can really wreak havoc.

However, they're slightly better on defense than offense because getting in the first shot is pretty important to sprites. For their casting and upkeep costs, sprites are no gift. They'll do in a pinch for an army that lacks the magical supporting firepower of shamans or magicians, but their staying power is just too limited once those units appear. At that point, replace your sprites with the shaman or magician.

War Bears *Summary Information*

Spell Rarity	Research Point Cost	Combat Casting Cost	Overland Casting Cost	Upkeep Cost Per Turn	Notes
Common	130	N/A	70	2	None

Sprites *Summary Information*

Spell Rarity	Research Point Cost	Combat Casting Cost	Overland Casting Cost	Upkeep Cost Per Turn	Notes
Common	220	N/A	100	3	None

Giant Spiders

These paired spiders are especially useful

(or deadly, when confronting them) in battles against fast or flying creatures. While their strength in melee combat is marginal (with only four swords and a four-strength poisonous attack), their Web spell makes them worth their cost. Although each spider unit can only cast a single Web spell per battle, the spell often impacts the outcome.

Consider taking some spider units with you when invading blue or red nodes (where green magic is prone to fizzle), especially the more strongly defended ones on Myrror. These nodes frequently have as their denizens the dreaded great drake or sky drake. A spider's Web spell immobilizes drakes for one combat round and will also prevent them from flying for the remainder of the combat. This combination allows you to do two things. First, you can get in an extra missile attack, which may mean the difference between surviving the battle or not. Second, you're then allowed to attack these creatures with your other, non-flying troops. Attacking is important, because the drake's breath attacks only affect combat when these units are attacking. Also, being able to attack these flyers allows you to concentrate your efforts on one or two drakes, instead of being forced into a defensive position (when the drakes can fly and your troops cannot) where you have no such control.

Giant Spiders *Summary Information*					
Spell Rarity	Research Point Cost	Combat Casting Cost	Overland Casting Cost	Upkeep Cost Per Turn	Notes
Uncommon	450	N/A	200	4	Cool Web spell

Cockatrices

Cockatrices and basilisks are similar, but their differences are important. While both types of creatures move two, cockatrices *fly*. The single basilisk in a unit has 30 hearts, while the four cockatrices in a unit have only three each! Fortunately, cockatrices are slightly better defended with three shields each, and their stoning touch is better (with a -3 resistance, compared with a basilisk's gaze of -1).

Basilisks and cockatrices can be used almost interchangeably when forming an army. An important exception might be when mustering a "flying corps" of units that can cross both land and sea. Such formations necessitate a preference for cockatrices when using one or two to round out a balanced stack of troops.

Basilisk

A basilisk has got verve with plenty of swords, hearts, and stoning gaze for combat. Its weakness is in protective shields and crosses, which makes it relatively easy to kill. Still, if it can close in on an enemy, a basilisk usually wreaks plenty of destruction before going down. They seem pricy for what you get, but a basilisk or two can round out an army of mixed units very nicely.

Cockatrices *Summary Information*					
Spell Rarity	Research Point Cost	Combat Casting Cost	Overland Casting Cost	Upkeep Cost Per Turn	Notes
Uncommon	620	N/A	275	8	None

Basilisk *Summary Information*

Spell Rarity	Research Point Cost	Combat Casting Cost	Overland Casting Cost	Upkeep Cost Per Turn	Notes
Uncommon	800	N/A	325	7	None

Stone Giant *Summary Information*

Spell Rarity	Research Point Cost	Combat Casting Cost	Overland Casting Cost	Upkeep Cost Per Turn	Notes
Rare	1,040	N/A	450	9	None

Stone Giant

These are "budget bad boys." Sure, they can lob off a couple of 15-strength rock attacks, but in general, stone giants have to get in there and swing with the grunts. Their hefty defense of eight shields, plus poison and stoning immunity, can keep them in the fray for quite a while, too. This allows their 12 swords to hurt all but the best defended units. Stone giants offer value for your mana, but they'll need magic support to win the tough fights.

Gorgons

Gorgons are your basic middle-weight fantastic creatures. With plenty of swords, shields and hearts and 2 flying moves (even a nice stoning gaze), they can kill weak units and usually ding up stronger ones before succumbing. Their high mana cost means that you won't have a lot of them, even though you might need three or four of these units to give an army a good, tough backbone.

Earth Elemental

Like the phantom warriors and fire elementals, earth elementals are summoned only for the duration of a battle. Therefore, summon them early to get the maximum benefit from them.

Their high summoning cost means you won't be summoning these babies to your early battles, but they can be quite supportive as the game develops and your casting skill improves. Because of their impressive 25 swords, earth elementals are pretty much capable of pounding the snot out of most ordinary units (and many fantastic ones, for that matter). This spell is like the American Express™ card: Don't leave your Enchanted Fortress without it.

Behemoth

Riddle: Where does a behemoth go?
Answer: Anywhere it wants to.

Okay, so behemoths are pricy. Big deal. When you've got a unit running around with 9 shields, 10 crosses, and 45 hearts that can flick off 25 swords per attack, the other guy had better have some fast, powerful magic,

Earth Elemental *Summary Information*

Spell Rarity	Research Point Cost	Combat Casting Cost	Overland Casting Cost	Upkeep Cost Per Turn	Notes
Rare	1,700	60	N/A	N/A	None

or you'll pound him into dust. It almost seems a waste of effort to melee attack against a behemoth (it only makes them angry). Killing one requires a virtual siege, striking the behemoth hard and repeatedly before it begins to crack.

The weakness of a behemoth is that it has no ranged attack. Thus, fast enemy units can maintain their safety by keeping their distance. Also, they have no special immunities. Casting enchantments on a behemoth to give them magic (or even weapon) immunity is creating a monster, indeed! If some units are fit to be used as one-man armies, count behemoths among them.

Behemoth *Summary Information*

Spell Rarity	Research Point Cost	Combat Casting Cost	Overland Casting Cost	Upkeep Cost Per Turn	Notes
Very Rare	2,000	N/A	700	15	None

Colossus *Summary Information*

Spell Rarity	Research Point Cost	Combat Casting Cost	Overland Casting Cost	Upkeep Cost Per Turn	Notes
Very Rare	3,500	N/A	800	17	None

Colossus

Picture this: A colossus is a behemoth on steroids. It is a bit more expensive to cast, though, and has fewer swords and hearts (20

Figure 11-1. *Summoning a Colossus*

and 30, as compared to a behemoth's 25 and 45, respectively).

However, for your nickel, you get a couple of 20-strength rock attacks and considerably more defense (10 shields, 15 crosses, plus poison and stoning immunity). Top that off with a Colossus' first-strike capability, and you've got another bad boy to rampage through your enemy's territory.

Great Wyrm

There is nothing penultimate about the great wyrm. It makes those sand worms on *Dune* look like fishing bait. The question is, how do you stop something with 12 shields, 12 crosses, and 45 hearts that teleports around the battlefield? After all, its impressive 20 swords and 15-strength poisonous bite can munch just about any non-flying creature in one swipe. (And it had better, for its high price!)

The ground, however, is the wyrm's weakness as well as its strength. Flying units can patiently wait out a battle where a land-bound great wyrm is attacking and can even lob in missiles and magic from the safety of their altitude. Another antidote for a case of wyrms is casting Cracks Call on them. A rupture in

Great Wyrm *Summary Information*

Spell Rarity	Research Point Cost	Combat Casting Cost	Overland Casting Cost	Upkeep Cost Per Turn	Notes
Very Rare	5,000	N/A	1,000	20	None

Resist Elements *Summary Information*

Spell Rarity	Research Point Cost	Combat Casting Cost	Overland Casting Cost	Upkeep Cost Per Turn	Notes
Common	40	5	25	1	vs. red or green only

the ground (or water, when fighting sea battles) swallows a whole unit, be it ship, spearmen, or wyrm. Of course, if you could cast Flight on your great wyrm, what could stop you then?

Creature Enchantments

Nature magic provides the most common, utilitarian creature enhancements.

Resist Elements

Think of Resist Elements as a minimal insurance policy for a unit's safety. It gives +3 crosses when defending against red or green magic spells. Since red is particularly vicious at attacking units, that extra resistance can come in handy when marshaling your forces against another wizard with a lot of Chaos spell books.

The other purpose of this spell is for defending against all regular ranged green or red magical attacks (in this case, improving the unit by +3 shields). This will be particularly useful for units with few shields, such as low-level heroes and rear-line, ranged attack units (for example, bowmen and shamans). Those extra shields come in really handy when you're up against a bunch of sprites or other enemy units with ranged magic attacks.

Note that neither the bonus crosses nor shields from this enchantment will appear on the unit's statistics. This is because they apply only to specific types of attacks. The cost of casting Resist Elements is as cheap as any, making it an attractive value. If you can remember the times when this spell comes in handy, it can serve you well.

Giant Strength

This fairly inexpensive spell simply improves a creature's melee strength by +1 sword *per figure*. Therefore, the more figures a unit has, the more net swords you'll gain by casting this spell on the unit.

Casting Giant Strength on a weaker unit improves its relative attack capability. For example, casting this spell on a bowmen unit

Giant Strength *Summary Information*

Spell Rarity	Research Point Cost	Combat Casting Cost	Overland Casting Cost	Upkeep Cost Per Turn	Notes
Common	80	8	40	1	None

of six figures with one sword each will *double* each figure's attack strength to two swords. This is a net increase of *six* swords, one for each figure in the bowmen unit.

Web Summary Information

Spell Rarity	Research Point Cost	Combat Casting Cost	Overland Casting Cost	Upkeep Cost Per Turn	Notes
Common	100	10	N/A	N/A	only non-corporeal can resist

Web

What a great little spell! Web is especially useful in battles against flying creatures or those that move quickly. Webbing a unit destroys its ability to fly, which lowers it to where your surface-bound units can get their licks in on it (complete with the benefits of their first strike weapons, etc.). Only non-corporeal units cannot be webbed. See the description for giant spiders, above, for more thoughts on the Web spell.

Stone Skin

We're talking about a +1 shield bonus *per figure* for units enchanted with Stone Skin. In terms of getting the most for your mana, the same guidelines apply to Stone Skin as for Giant Strength. Cast this spell on units with a lot of figures, each having few shields. In fact, phantom warriors (see Chapter 12) are ideal candidates, as they are summoned onto the battlefield with no shields and eight figures.

When casting in combat, only cast it on units that will actually be attacked. If your weak bowmen, shamans, or heroes will be subject to enemy ranged attacks, Stone Skin 'em. If your spearmen or swordsmen are going to clash with the enemy first, concentrate this spell on them.

Water Walking

While this overland spell is not particularly expensive, it is easy to get carried away with it and try casting it on every unit in your killer stack. Instead, prioritize your use of Water Walking. Good candidate units include:

- settlers who must cross some ocean squares to get where you want them
- heroes

Stone Skin Summary Information

Spell Rarity	Research Point Cost	Combat Casting Cost	Overland Casting Cost	Upkeep Cost Per Turn	Notes
Common	160	10	50	1	None

Water Walking Summary Information

Spell Rarity	Research Point Cost	Combat Casting Cost	Overland Casting Cost	Upkeep Cost Per Turn	Notes
Common	190	N/A	50	1	None

Pathfinding *Summary Information*

Spell Rarity	Research Point Cost	Combat Casting Cost	Overland Casting Cost	Upkeep Cost Per Turn	Notes
Uncommon	560	N/A	50	1	None

Elemental Armor *Summary Information*

Spell Rarity	Research Point Cost	Combat Casting Cost	Overland Casting Cost	Upkeep Cost Per Turn	Notes
Rare	880	35	175	5	vs. red or green only

🐸 powerful, land-bound normal and fantastic units

Other unit types can generally be built on the other side of the water or brought over the ocean more quickly and cheaply by ships.

Pathfinding

Here is another mindboggling useful spell. A unit with Pathfinding allows every non-flying unit in its stack to enter any square for half a movement point per square (except for magic roads, such as those on Myrror, which still cost no movement points).

You can make good time moving troops around with Pathfinding, particularly in undeveloped regions of the board. Designate one key unit (usually a hero) in each of your hunter/killer stacks as a pathfinder to get where you're going quickly. Note that Pathfinding also works well for stacks of units that can walk on water (ocean walking also becomes half a movement point per square)!

Elemental Armor

Elemental Armor is the Resist Elements spell on steroids. Although it won't show up on the receiving unit's statistics, it receives +10 crosses when defending against red or green magic spells and +10 shields when defending against regular ranged red or green magical attacks (see Chapter 20). The same tips for using Resist Elements apply for Elemental Armor, but beware of the cost. As an overland spell, its high upkeep is seldom worth the price unless you've got a lot of red and green casting enemies you're currently at war with — even then, cast this spell sparingly on your main shock troops.

Iron Skin

Not many units in *Master of Magic* start with a defense of five shields, let alone more. Iron Skin, when cast on one of your units, increases its shields *by* five, at an upkeep cost of five mana per turn. This is an enormous increase in defensive ability, even for creatures with a

Iron Skin *Summary Information*

Spell Rarity	Research Point Cost	Combat Casting Cost	Overland Casting Cost	Upkeep Cost Per Turn	Notes
Rare	1,120	40	200	5	None

strong defense to begin with. Think about casting this spell as a permanent enchantment on some of the weaker units in your main killer army; ranged attack units, such as magicians and bowmen, can really benefit from this additional defense. Furthermore, casting Iron Skin on your tougher fighting units will make them virtually invulnerable to most normal attacks. In a pinch, Iron Skin can be used in combat to help save a valued unit or to enable your last unit to outlast your opponents.

Regeneration

Regeneration is just about the best unit enchantment available. Although it's expensive, both to cast and to maintain, it is well worth the cost. This spell, whether cast during combat or as a unit enchantment, will return one hit point to an injured unit at the end of every combat turn. When combat ends, all injured regenerating units instantly return to full health, as do all friendly units with Regeneration that were killed. Note, there are a few exceptions. If a regenerating unit is killed by life-stealing or ghoul attacks, through banishing or unsummoning spells (such as Dispel Evil), or destroyed by Disintegrate, Cracks Call, Petrify, or stoning attacks, it will *not* regenerate when combat ends.

Regeneration Summary Information

Spell Rarity	Research Point Cost	Combat Casting Cost	Overland Casting Cost	Upkeep Cost Per Turn	Notes
Very Rare	1,850	60	300	10	None

Regeneration has many uses. Cast on fragile but powerful units, such as warlocks and slingers, it enables them to serve their proper function in battle without risking their permanent loss, especially since your opponents will make a beeline for them during combat. Regeneration may be combined with creatures of Death that do not have this ability naturally, since these units cannot heal otherwise. It's also a good spell to cast on an almost dead but valued unit during combat to save it from extinction.

Finally, by casting this on several, or even all depending on your mana situation, of the units in your main army, you can slow or cease unit production in some of your cities, switching those resources to production of trade goods or less expensive units that can follow your main army and garrison the towns and nodes you'll capture.

Combat Spells

All of Nature magic's combat spells look sort of mundane on the surface, but once you use them, you will find that they are nearly as valuable as Chaos and Death magic combat spells, if less spectacular.

Earth to Mud Summary Information

Spell Rarity	Research Point Cost	Combat Casting Cost	Overland Casting Cost	Upkeep Cost Per Turn	Notes
Common	20	15	N/A	N/A	None

Earth to Mud

Earth to Mud is one of the least expensive combat spells to cast, yet it is one of the most useful if you have ranged attack units in your army.

Cracks Call *Summary Information*

Spell Rarity	Research Point Cost	Combat Casting Cost	Overland Casting Cost	Upkeep Cost Per Turn	Notes
Uncommon	300	20	N/A	N/A	only flying and non-corporeal are unaffected

This spell lets you place a 5 by 5 square mud patch on the battlefield (you denote the center square of the patch) that slows all units except for flying, non-corporeal, and teleporting units. Everyone else uses all of their remaining movement points for a combat turn whenever they enter one of the mud squares.

This little spell is good for two reasons. First, it will slow oncoming monsters allowing you to continue firing at them as they approach. Second, enemy units tend to circumnavigate mud, moving around it in counterproductive ways that slow their progress toward your troops even more. A particularly useful and inexpensive casting combination, when facing flying units, is the Web spell (to ground them) followed by the Earth to Mud spell (to slow them down).

Cracks Call

Cracks Call offers a 25 percent chance of destroying an entire unit for a casting cost of 20 mana. This chance is unmodified by the unit's resistance, defenses, or anything else. The only units that cannot be destroyed in this way are flying or non-corporeal units. Oh, and check this out: Cracks Call even works at sea, making it great for swallowing up warships and powerful units walking on the water!

This spell offers you a straight shot at getting rid of any undesirable element on the battlefield. You cannot count on it to work when you need it, but it's always worth a try when your forces are outclassed. Don't forget that this is a Nature spell — meaning that it can be cast at Nature nodes against great wyrms, behemoths, basilisks, and other units that can easily kill most of your normal troops.

Note that Cracks Call can also be used to coincidentally destroy city wall sections. When you target a unit that is occupying a wall square, that wall section will break, whether the unit dies or not. If part of your strategy is to destroy walls when you attack a city, Cracks Call may be useful for you.

Ice Bolt

Ice Bolt is the "cold magic" version of the Chaos spell Fire Bolt, although its base cost is slightly higher. This spell gives a you starting, strength five cold attack. The strength of the attack increases by one for each additional mana point pumped into the spell.

Ice Bolts are fairly effective on normal, low quality units like spearmen, swordsmen, and other units with poor defensive abilities. Unfortunately, creatures of Death are completely immune to cold attacks. As is true for many attack spells into which you

Ice Bolt *Summary Information*

Spell Rarity	Research Point Cost	Combat Casting Cost	Overland Casting Cost	Upkeep Cost Per Turn	Notes
Uncommon	400	10 to 50	N/A	N/A	None

can pump mana, the bang just isn't there for your buck. Ice Bolt is okay for chipping away a few hit points, but don't expect it to destroy any but the weakest units.

Petrify

This spell tries to destroy all figures in a unit by turning them to stone. Only units immune to stoning (e.g., all elementals, colossus, gargoyles, and stone giants) and those immune to magic (e.g., sky drakes and paladins) are automatically immune to petrification. Of course, most of the powerful units in *Master of Magic* have high innate resistances, and so your best chance with this spell is when you target weak or medium strength creatures.

Entangle

Entangle is a combat enchantment that slows all enemy units by one movement point. (Note that the enemy units will have to move one square before they can become entangled.) This means units that can ordinarily move only one square per turn may not move, even to attack, although they will still counterattack.

Petrify Summary Information

Spell Rarity	Research Point Cost	Combat Casting Cost	Overland Casting Cost	Upkeep Cost Per Turn	Notes
Rare	960	35	N/A	N/A	no resistance modifiers

Entangle Summary Information

Spell Rarity	Research Point Cost	Combat Casting Cost	Overland Casting Cost	Upkeep Cost Per Turn	Notes
Very Rare	2,250	50	N/A	N/A	None

This spell lets you stop entire armies of slow-moving units. Thus, you can initiate attacks in an order to your liking (see Chapter 20). Slowing or stopping enemy units also gives you a chance to finish firing missiles and magic ranged attacks before being overrun by enemies. When your spell-casting skill gets high enough, combining Entangle with a spell like Call Lightning can be quite a powerful means to destroy your enemies without much risk of damage to your own forces.

Call Lightning

Call Lightning is perfect when you have a few units, preferably very fast or flying units, fighting large armies. This spell lets Mother Nature do the work for you by calling down an electrical storm that lasts for the remainder of combat. Every turn, you will see up to five lightning bolts (strength eight, armor-piercing) strike random enemy

Call Lightning Summary Information

Spell Rarity	Research Point Cost	Combat Casting Cost	Overland Casting Cost	Upkeep Cost Per Turn	Notes
Very Rare	3,000	60	N/A	N/A	None

Wall of Stone *Summary Information*

Spell Rarity	Research Point Cost	Combat Casting Cost	Overland Casting Cost	Upkeep Cost Per Turn	Notes
Common	60	N/A	50	2 gold	None

Nature's Eye *Summary Information*

Spell Rarity	Research Point Cost	Combat Casting Cost	Overland Casting Cost	Upkeep Cost Per Turn	Notes
Uncommon	350	N/A	75	1	None

units. Under such conditions, your enemies won't last for long. The trick here is to keep your own unit(s) out of danger while the lightning kills your enemies, which is why having flying or fast units is the best option.

Note that Call Lightning is often helpful when you are trying to conquer cities (as long as the garrison isn't loaded with shamans, bowmen, and other such units). Flying in with a cockatrice or some other such unit, you can take entire towns without doing a thing.

City Enchantments

Nature has *the* city enchantment, Gaia's Blessing, as well as a number of other, generally positive, city spells.

Wall of Stone

This handy spell lets you "cast" a city wall instead of building it (for the same upkeep of two gold per turn). Your garrisoned troops will get an extra three shields defending against enemy attacks if they are behind a city wall, making Wall of Stone a practical spell when you are attacked by armies loaded with bowmen or other such units.

Nature's Eye

Nature's Eye extends the scouting range of the target city to five squares in all directions. This is farther than any building or city structure can scout. For cities on the border of your territory, this spell can be used as an early warning system that enemy troops are on their way. The upkeep cost is minimal and the benefits, under appropriate circumstances, are well worth it.

Earthquake

Earthquake is Nature's modest answer to certain Chaos and Death spells like Call the Void and Famine. While not an earth-shattering spell for all its name implies, it can still cause some useful destruction to the enemy's city. Buildings stand a 15 percent chance of being destroyed, while all units, except those that are non-corporeal or flying, have a 25 percent chance of dying.

Earthquake is best used when you are trying to wear down a city before attacking it, or

Earthquake *Summary Information*

Spell Rarity	Research Point Cost	Combat Casting Cost	Overland Casting Cost	Upkeep Cost Per Turn	Notes
Rare	1,300	N/A	200	N/A	None

when you are hitting specific enemy production points. If you're going to spend the mana to cast this spell, go for the juiciest targets in an attempt to get the most out of it.

Gaia's Blessing

Gaia's Blessing is one of the best reasons to grab several Nature picks when you make your wizard. It increases the city farmers' food production by 50 percent, increasing the maximum population size and growth rate of a city. The increased food production and growth rates hasten a city's development and improve your gold income (more citizens to tax), production rates, and even mana income if the inhabitants generate mana naturally. The increased food production also means that you can support more troops, if food was the limiting factor. The increased growth rates from casting this spell make Nature magic a good complement to a slow-growing race, such as the Elves, Trolls, or Dwarves.

Aside from this "boom town" effect, Gaia's Blessing can, over time, convert all desert squares within a city into grasslands and volcanoes into hills. Such conversions also increase the maximum city size and will increase the population's growth rate. Even corrupted lands are cleaned by themselves. Not all of these things happen at once, but each of these events has a small chance (10 percent for converting deserts and volcanoes; 20 percent for purifying corruption) of happening every game turn. Gaia's Blessing is the best answer there is to an enemy wizard using Chaos magic spells willy-nilly.

Gaia's Blessing *Summary Information*

Spell Rarity	Research Point Cost	Combat Casting Cost	Overland Casting Cost	Upkeep Cost Per Turn	Notes
Rare	1,600	N/A	300	3	None

Earth Gate *Summary Information*

Spell Rarity	Research Point Cost	Combat Casting Cost	Overland Casting Cost	Upkeep Cost Per Turn	Notes
Very Rare	4,000	N/A	250	5	None

On top of all of this, Gaia's Blessing increases a city's production by doubling the production bonuses from forests (to 6 percent, see Chapter 15) and reduces a city's unrest level by two rebels. All this for a paltry three mana per turn. There is no bad time to cast this spell, unless you are short of mana or have other obvious casting priorities. What you get back for your investment is priceless in *any* game situation.

Earth Gate

Earth Gate lets you place a teleporation device in a city. A unit or stack can travel between any two cities with an Earth Gate. Note that this is limited to cities *on the same plane.*

Because Earth Gates have a relatively high upkeep cost, you may want to use them reactively. For example, you may want to place Earth Gates in a couple of your big production centers. Then, when enemy armies are approaching a city that is too far away to reach with any of your available armies, you can cast an Earth Gate in the vulnerable city and immediately transport a stack of units from your production centers to the city.

Nature's Awareness *Summary Information*

Spell Rarity	Research Point Cost	Combat Casting Cost	Overland Casting Cost	Upkeep Cost Per Turn	Notes
Very Rare	2,500	N/A	800	7	None

Herb Mastery *Summary Information*

Spell Rarity	Research Point Cost	Combat Casting Cost	Overland Casting Cost	Upkeep Cost Per Turn	Notes
Very Rare	4,500	N/A	1,000	10	None

Global Enchantments

Nature magic's global enchantments take a subtler form than the bludgeoning spells of Death or Chaos. Less annoying than Sorcery, but on par with Life's quality magic, Nature has very few global enchantments. However, those it has could redefine the word "useful."

You can set up other temporary Earth Gates in cities near places you wish to conquer, such as nodes and Towers of Wizardry, decreasing the length of time it takes for you to transport your new troops there. Also, you may simply wish to have an Earth Gate on every continent in which you have a city, allowing you to travel between them without boats or special skills.

Figure 11-2. *Mother Nature keeps an eye on things for you with Nature's Awareness.*

Nature's Awareness

This is such a cheap spell to maintain for its benefits that it should be cast right away. Nature's Awareness reveals all cities, land, and non-invisible units on both Arcanus and Myrror. (Once you have cast Nature's Awareness, you may want to undo your Nature's Eye spells, as they're redundant at that point.) This spell also places you in direct contact with all wizards you have not met yet.

Being aware of your enemies' activities is the first step in dealing with them effectively. This watchful spell is the perfect security system, giving you a chance to build garrisons before enemies get too close or to take the offense before they do.

Herb Mastery

Herb Mastery is a great spell. For 10 mana per turn, all of your units heal *completely* at the end of every game turn. This allows your troops protecting cities or nodes (those that form the major target points of enemy efforts) to recover instantly after unsuccessful take-over attempts. Once you've angered a wizard or two, you'll really appreciate the effects of this spell. Your marching armies that travel from one lair or node to the next can also completely recover, without wasting time, before tackling their next venture.

Nature's Wrath

It's not nice to fool Mother Nature.

Nature's Wrath causes earthquakes (slightly milder than those caused by the Earthquake spell) that will shake *all the cities of anyone, anytime* they cast an overland (non-combat) Chaos or Death magic spell! Thankfully, that doesn't include you, should you cast such spells.

These tremors cause buildings to crumble (at a 5 percent chance per building) and garrisoned units to die (at a 15 percent chance per unit, except for flying and non-corporeal creatures). Clearly, this is the spell to cast when you're duking it out with Chaos or Death wizards, such as Rjak, Tauron, Sss'ra, etc. The upkeep cost is steep, but, given the insurance of its effects, well worth it.

Special Spells

Nature magic has several spells that relate to transforming or revealing land. In addition, this magic realm has the one spell that will allow you to change your "starting race," Move Fortress. This can be very useful as a tool to readjust your rebel populace (see Chapter 15).

Nature's Wrath Summary Information

Spell Rarity	Research Point Cost	Combat Casting Cost	Overland Casting Cost	Upkeep Cost Per Turn	Notes
Very Rare	6,000	N/A	1,250	20	affects Chaos and Death only

Earth Lore Summary Information

Spell Rarity	Research Point Cost	Combat Casting Cost	Overland Casting Cost	Upkeep Cost Per Turn	Notes
Common	250	N/A	30	N/A	None

Earth Lore

If the last thing you want to do is hunt around with units looking for what's out there (and risk offending your touchy neighbors while you do it), Earth Lore is the spell for you. This is a *cheap* spell to cast and well worth it, as long as you can afford the casting cost.

Change Terrain

Nature magic has the ideal way for you to turn a lousy bit of land it into something useful. Change Terrain lets you alter your cities' surrounding lands. Unfortunately the worst type of terrain, tundra, (have you ever noticed how tons of those poor neutral cities are surrounded by tundra?) cannot be altered by this spell,

Change Terrain Summary Information

Spell Rarity	Research Point Cost	Combat Casting Cost	Overland Casting Cost	Upkeep Cost Per Turn	Notes
Uncommon	500	N/A	50	N/A	None

Transmute *Summary Information*

Spell Rarity	Research Point Cost	Combat Casting Cost	Overland Casting Cost	Upkeep Cost Per Turn	Notes
Uncommon	680	N/A	60	N/A	None

although tundra *can* be altered by Raise Volcano (see Chapter 10).

By carefully converting a city's lands, you can create a larger, more productive city. Note that special minerals and other features remain after you change the underlying terrain type (i.e., you can still keep the nightshade even though you convert the swamp it is on to grassland). Most terrain types become grasslands, grasslands become forests and volcanoes, and mountains are changed into hills when this spell is cast.

While most of the listed conversions are good, note that some have the potential to be extremely beneficial. For example, a city situated over lands in which there are no forest squares cannot build a sawmill, forester's guild, shipyard, or their derivative buildings! Similarly, a city with no grasslands can't build any stables or animist's guilds. Aha! Now here's great use for this spell. Convert a relatively worthless bit of land into something that increases your building options, and you'll really be making the most of this spell. (Note that you will *not* lose such buildings, once erected, if you later zap away all of the surrounding forests or grasslands that enabled them to be built in the first place.)

Since this is an uncommon spell, you stand a good chance of getting it (especially through exploring lairs and green nodes) even if you just pick one Nature spell rank when you create your wizard. Since Change Terrain helps you convert poor cities into rich ones and gives you a valuable means to fight the Chaos spells Raise Volcano and Armageddon, this spell is one of the best values available for a minimal spell book investment.

A powerful spell, Change Terrain lets you focus your city building efforts on areas that provide the best minerals instead of those offering the best growth potential. You can, after all, always recreate the land to increase your city's size.

Transmute

For your avarice, Transmute allows you to change the mundane minerals of coal and iron to the gold producers, gems and gold. More importantly, it also allows you to convert silver into the mithril. (Note, this spell also lets you transmute gems, gold, and mithril into coal, iron, and silver!)

Whether this spell is worth casting on your coal or iron deposits depends entirely on your gold situation. If you are chronically struggling to make ends meet, these changes may be worth your effort. After all, while coal and iron offer you a decrease in unit production costs in relevant cities, units still require upkeep. Therefore, making the units more slowly and then having the money to support them later may be quite reasonable. On the other hand, if you're swimming in bucks, there's not much point to destroying your coal or iron deposits, is there?

The conversion of silver to mithril, though, is worthwhile, particularly if the city's race can make an alchemist's guild (see Chapter 5). Not only does the mithril provide a modicum of magic power (one per turn prior to a miner's guild construction), it also strengthens the units built (+1 sword *per figure*) if there is an alchemist's guild in the city.

Nature's Cures

Nature's Cures allows you to completely heal an entire stack of units (exception: creatures of Death cannot be healed). The casting cost is expensive, but this spell is very useful under certain specific circumstances. In particular, if you have a stack of armies defending a node or a city, you will notice that your opponents frequently send in wave after wave of armies to wear you down. Nature's Cures gives you a chance to return each of your garrisoned units to working order before the next turn's assaults against them begin. This is certainly the most economical use of this spell.

Nature's Cures can also be used, somewhat frivolously, to heal stacks of armies as they go from battle to battle, conquering nodes, cities, lairs, and Towers of Wizardry as they come upon them. Nature's Cures will ensure that these armies are always in peak condition before their next combat.

Ice Storm

Ice Storm rains a strength six cold attack onto every figure in every unit in the target map square (including hostile cities). This spell costs 200 mana to cast and, so, will probably take a turn or two to cast. However, it can be used repeatedly and effectively to wear down the garrison at your next target or to ding up an army that is descending on one of *your* cities, although stronger units in a target army will remain relatively untouched by such attacks. In either case, the enemy stack should be sufficiently tenderized so that it is easier to defeat once it arrives. Note that creatures of Death are immune to cold attacks and, therefore, will suffer no damage from this spell.

Move Fortress

Move Fortress lets you do just that for a mere cost of 200 mana. Wow! Consider the possibilities....

You can alter your primary (i.e., "starting") race (since that is defined by the inhabitants of your Enchanted Fortress city), thus altering the amount of rebellion in conquered cities. For example, if you started with the Dark

Nature's Cures Summary Information

Spell Rarity	Research Point Cost	Combat Casting Cost	Overland Casting Cost	Upkeep Cost Per Turn	Notes
Uncommon	740	N/A	75	N/A	None

Ice Storm Summary Information

Spell Rarity	Research Point Cost	Combat Casting Cost	Overland Casting Cost	Upkeep Cost Per Turn	Notes
Rare	1,200	N/A	200	N/A	None

Move Fortress Summary Information

Spell Rarity	Research Point Cost	Combat Casting Cost	Overland Casting Cost	Upkeep Cost Per Turn	Notes
Rare	1,500	N/A	200	N/A	None

Elves, whom everyone hates, but eventually took over a city owned by the well-loved Halflings, you could move your Enchanted Fortress to the Halfling city and immediately decrease the level of unrest in many of your conquered cities (of course the Dark Elves would object, but who cares? Muhuhahaha!).

Moving your fortress can enable you to tuck this valuable building deep into the center of your territory, making it more difficult for enemy armies to reach. You can move it at the last minute from a city that is about to be swarmed by an army too powerful for your garrison and magic spells to handle. You can also place your Enchanted Fortress closer to your current war zone, decreasing the casting costs of your spells during battles (if you are not a Channeler) and, thereby, saving you considerable amounts of mana. That three-fold increase in casting costs for combat far from your Enchanted Fortress can quickly break your mana banks later in the game, otherwise.

Am I Blue?

Some wizards are green because it's in their Nature. Others get the blues. We close this chapter on green magic with a reminder that it's a fun color for empire builders and anal-retentive types who like to have their cities "just so."

Blue magic, on the other hand, is the anti-magic color. Sorcery excels at undercutting other players' magic abilities and is the subject of the next chapter.

The Blues

Sorcery magic is largely defensive in nature. Its primary purpose is to take the wind out of other player's sails. With its ability to undercut and foil enemy plans, it is the spell-casting equivalent of "Oh, yeah? Well, you take *that!*"

Blue is a color that you should either go into lightly (with only one to three spell books) or all the way (with at least seven or eight spell books). That is because Sorcery's most useful spells can be found at the extreme ends of common and very rare.

Summoning Spells

Sorcery magic has an interesting array of summoned creatures; almost half of these creatures can only be summoned during combat, while one is not really a creature, but more like a ship! Because Sorcery magic has so many creatures that can be summoned during combat, wizards specializing in this color can wander around with fewer units than other wizards, knowing they can easily supplement their forces on the battlefield.

Floating Island

Floating islands can carry up to eight units and, unlike other ships, they provide a floating platform that allows the units they are transporting to participate in their "naval" battles. The result is that the floating island never engages in combat directly (forget its stats, they're completely moot). Instead, the units it's carrying will do all the fighting. Putting your killer stack on a floating island means that you can make it the scourge of *both* the land and sea! Think about it....

Floating islands cost a fair amount to summon but can be placed on *any* known water square. Their maintenance costs are prohibitive, though, at five mana per island. Obviously, these units were designed for immediate use and prompt dismissal.

Phantom Warriors

Phantom warriors can only be summoned during combat, and then only if you have fewer than nine units there. These units are not great fighters, but they have their uses.

First, phantom warriors can be enchanted to make them harder to kill or to make their illusionary attacks more devastating. Second, phantom warriors can be used as simple blocking devices to protect your bowmen and other missile units so that they can use up all of their ammunition before being forced to engage in melee combat.

Blocking the enemy with phantom warriors works for two reasons. Either the computer opponent will single-mindedly go after your missile units, refusing to swat at the lowly phantom warriors blocking them, or when they do take

Floating Island *Summary Information*

Spell Rarity	Research Point Cost	Combat Casting Cost	Overland Casting Cost	Upkeep Cost Per Turn	Notes
Common	60	N/A	50	5	None

Phantom Warriors *Summary Information*

Spell Rarity	Research Point Cost	Combat Casting Cost	Overland Casting Cost	Upkeep Cost Per Turn	Notes
Common	100	10	N/A	N/A	None

the time to deal with the phantom warriors, you will still have delayed the enemy's progress. Note that phantom warriors are non-corporeal and are immune to Death magic. (Thus, the Wrack spell will have no effect on these guys).

Nagas *Summary Information*

Spell Rarity	Research Point Cost	Combat Casting Cost	Overland Casting Cost	Upkeep Cost Per Turn	Notes
Common	220	N/A	100	2	None

Having phantom warriors or other creatures that can be summoned during combat is a great way to minimize your costs. These summoned units can flesh (and we use the word loosely) out meager armies in an instant on an as-needed basis, allowing you to understaff your city garrisons and free your money, food, or troops for other things.

Nagas

At the beginning of the game, balancing gold and mana production while trying to build settlers and some sort of army can be tricky. Being able to summon creatures that can fight but that cost mana in upkeep instead of in gold and food is a good way to help alleviate a cash flow crisis or a food shortage.

To that end, you can summon Nagas. They are not much better fighters than ordinary units, although their poison spittle attack is nominally useful. What they are is *an option*— not a great one, not even a very good one really, but a troop type option you can summon to supplement the normal forces you can build.

Phantom Beast

These creatures can only be summoned during combat. They are powerful units with an illusionary attack. With a bit of enchantment during combat, they can be made very powerful indeed.

Phantom beasts can easily hold their own against scores of weaker monsters. Even without shields, they have enough hit points (20 hearts) to take them far in most combat situations. Note that these units are non-corporeal and immune to Death magic. They are quite capable of destroying flocks of ghouls, zombies, and skeletons.

Finally, once you can summon phantom beasts, you can readjust your garrison sizes to suit your economic and expansionist aims. Phantom beasts can easily replace most garrison unit types during battles, and they cost nothing in upkeep.

Storm Giant

Chances are, you've fought against these guys at blue nodes. If so, you know about their devastating lightning bolt attacks. Each storm giant has four strength 10 armor-piercing attacks, and their hand-to-hand attacks are also armor-piercing. On top of that, they have a lot of hit points (20 hearts). Storm giants are definitely worth adding to your armies.

If you are facing one or more storm gi-

Phantom Beast *Summary Information*

Spell Rarity	Research Point Cost	Combat Casting Cost	Overland Casting Cost	Upkeep Cost Per Turn	Notes
Uncommon	800	35	N/A	N/A	None

Storm Giant *Summary Information*

Spell Rarity	Research Point Cost	Combat Casting Cost	Overland Casting Cost	Upkeep Cost Per Turn	Notes
Rare	1,200	N/A	500	10	None

Air Elemental *Summary Information*

Spell Rarity	Research Point Cost	Combat Casting Cost	Overland Casting Cost	Upkeep Cost Per Turn	Notes
Rare	1,300	50	N/A	N/A	None

ants, only attack them with units sturdy enough that some of them will outlast the storm giants' vicious ranged attacks. Large groups of longbowmen or other strong missile units can be useful, as well. Two Sorcery spells, Invisibility and Magic Immunity, are particularly useful for protecting your units from the storm giants' wrath.

Air Elemental

Air elementals are incredible creatures that can

Figure 12-1. *Summoning a Storm Giant*

only be summoned during combat. These units are invisible, so they cannot be targeted at range by either missile weapons or spells (unless they are targeted by a unit with immunity to illusions). They also fly at a speed of five squares per turn! Even better, they are immune to almost everything: weapons, stoning, and poison.

This combination produces a forceful monster that can rip through weaker units with no difficulty. Ranged-attack-only armies and many basic units stand no chance against air elementals. They can be defeated by strong units, units with immunity to illusions, or those with True Sight, since none of these will suffer the -1 To Hit penalty when fighting invisible monsters.

Djinn

Djinns, like the Chaos magic efreets, are effective fighters. They can launch magic ranged attacks, teleport, fly, and wind walk. Beyond that, they can cast up to 20 mana in Sorcery spells during every combat, allowing them to cast quality spells like Confusion or enchant units and summon phantom warriors when needed.

Their biggest drawback is that they're extremely expensive to maintain for a unit that can be killed quickly by a few good missile units. Killing a djinn is not much of a problem. They tend to cast their spells immediately, usually summoning phantom warriors or casting spells like Guardian Wind on other units. This often gives you a chance to get in a few good ranged shots at them in the following combat round and, often, you can kill them quickly this way.

Sky Drake

Sky drakes are great when they're on your side (and worth every bit of their upkeep cost). But fighting against them is another matter altogether.

Sky drakes tend to stay in packs of two to six. Worse, they fly fast and have magic immunity (making them immune to magic ranged attacks and spells). They are born killers, too, with a strong lightning breath attack *in addition to* their strong melee attack.

They *can* be killed, however. Armies solidly packed with missile units, such as slingers and longbowmen, that have been enchanted or produced in cities with alchemist's guilds can usually take down a sky drake or two before being cut down. Hardy units like hammerhands, golems, minotaurs, and paladins also stand up very well to sky drakes. While you may not be able to capture a node guarded by these creatures on your first attempt, whittling down their numbers by one or two per battle will allow you to take such nodes after the second or third try.

Djinn Summary Information

Spell Rarity	Research Point Cost	Combat Casting Cost	Overland Casting Cost	Upkeep Cost Per Turn	Notes
Very Rare	1,850	N/A	650	17	None

Sky Drake Summary Information

Spell Rarity	Research Point Cost	Combat Casting Cost	Overland Casting Cost	Upkeep Cost Per Turn	Notes
Very Rare	4,500	N/A	1000	25	None

Creature Enchantments

Sorcery magic has some of the most useful creature enchantments in *Master of Magic*. Ranging from the inexpensive, but highly useful Confusion spell, to the protective Invisibility and Magic Immunity spells, most of blue's creature enchantments are valuable. We feel they're the best argument for including a Sorcery book or two among your wizard's spell picks.

Resist Magic

Resist Magic is an inexpensive spell that increases a target unit's resistance by five, which can be helpful when you're fighting units with special attacks (gaze, poison, and stoning are all defended by resistance, not shields). This spell will also help your units defend against destructive combat enchantments, like the Death magic spell Wrack.

Confusion

Confusion is a great little spell. It has a reasonable chance of

Resist Magic Summary Information

Spell Rarity	Research Point Cost	Combat Casting Cost	Overland Casting Cost	Upkeep Cost Per Turn	Notes
Common	20	5	25	1	None

149

Confusion *Summary Information*

Spell Rarity	Research Point Cost	Combat Casting Cost	Overland Casting Cost	Upkeep Cost Per Turn	Notes
Common	130	15	N/A	N/A	targets resist at -4

Guardian Wind *Summary Information*

Spell Rarity	Research Point Cost	Combat Casting Cost	Overland Casting Cost	Upkeep Cost Per Turn	Notes
Common	80	10	50	2	None

success on units with a resistance of 10 or less. (Note that this spell has a chance on any unit with a resistance less than 14.) Confused units become time bombs. Eventually, they will start attacking their allies, doing your job for you. This spell is a great way to equalize a battle in which you are the underdog. It is especially helpful when you are trying to capture a walled city, where the garrison placidly sits, waiting to kill your forces as they approach. A confused unit in the midst of a city's defenders often becomes the traitor needed to make a city fall.

Note that creatures taken over through spells like Confusion (e.g., Creature Binding, Possession, etc.) need not be killed in order to end a battle. For the purposes of declaring a winner, they are considered dead to their previous owner.

Guardian Wind

Guardian Wind gives the target unit immunity to all bow and sling attacks (i.e., the unit's defenses are raised to 50 shields when defending against such attacks). This spell is invaluable when you are being attacked by whole stacks of missile units. It is also helpful to cast this on some of *your* missile units or priests before invading an opponent's cities. This prevents these units from being targeted by your enemies' missiles, giving you more of an opportunity to use them. At an upkeep cost of two mana per turn, this spell is most worthwhile during the later stages of the game, when mana isn't a problem and when wars against wizards escalate.

Spell Lock

Spell Lock is Sorcery magic's answer to Dispel Magic. This spell locks the caster's positive enchantments onto the target unit, requiring the lock to be dispelled before any other enchantments can be removed. If you've just spent a fortune in mana souping up a particular unit, the last thing you need is to have its enchantments dispelled. For an additional one mana per turn in upkeep, Spell Lock will prevent this from happening. You can also cast

Spell Lock *Summary Information*

Spell Rarity	Research Point Cost	Combat Casting Cost	Overland Casting Cost	Upkeep Cost Per Turn	Notes
Uncommon	450	20	100	1	None

the spell during combat, in case you forgot beforehand. Note, this spell also protects against Banish and Dispel Evil.

Flight

Flight is a tremendous enchantment at fair cost. This spell not only allows the enchanted unit to go anywhere, but it enables the unit to travel there at a speed of three squares per turn, making Flight significantly more valuable than white magic's Endurance spell and green's Water Walking spell combined. Flying units can attack over walls; they can pick and choose whom they will attack when fighting ground troops who don't have ranged weapons of any type.

Flying units can also wait out a disadvantageous combat situation. By casting Flight on a unit, you can keep it out of the way of many attackers (both through its ability to fly and by using its speed to run away). If you are the defender, that means you can wait until combat automatically ends after 50 turns without ever having to engage in combat. Not a noble tactic, to be sure, but it can save marginally protected cities from being taken over or destroyed. Note, however, that computer opponents will stomp on your city squares to destroy buildings and citizens if they cannot attack you. So, be aware that waiting out the end of combat with a flying unit may result in considerable damage to your town.

Flight also lets your units attack flying opponents. This eliminates the one-sidedness of, for example, being attacked by great drakes, whose fiery breath only works when it initiates an attack. If you can

initiate an attack against them instead, you can bypass some of the additional damage caused by such first strike attacks (see Chapter 20).

Finally, having many flying units allows you to attack, with full stacks, nodes and Towers of Wizardry situated on islands. However, maintaining a flying corps of nine units raises the mana upkeep total to a rather high figure.

Invisibility

Invisibility confers phenomenal benefits to a unit. Invisible units cannot be targeted at range, by either weapons or spells. Invisibility also causes units attacking you to suffer a -1 penalty To Hit. The possibilities from combining this enchantment with missile units, magicians, or priests are virtually limitless, especially when you are going up against enemy missile units (like sprites).

The big downside to the wonders of Invisibility is that it costs a fortune to maintain. Even casting it in battle is expensive. Still, if you are in a battle and fighting with *only* invisible units, your opponents will not even *advance* on your troops—which could be very advantageous, indeed.

Flight *Summary Information*

Spell Rarity	Research Point Cost	Combat Casting Cost	Overland Casting Cost	Upkeep Cost Per Turn	Notes
Uncommon	560	25	125	3	None

Invisibility *Summary Information*

Spell Rarity	Research Point Cost	Combat Casting Cost	Overland Casting Cost	Upkeep Cost Per Turn	Notes
Rare	960	35	175	10	None

Wind Walking *Summary Information*

Spell Rarity	Research Point Cost	Combat Casting Cost	Overland Casting Cost	Upkeep Cost Per Turn	Notes
Rare	1,040	N/A	250	10	None

Note: Units that have immunity to illusions or that are enchanted by the Life spell, True Sight, are immune to Invisibility's effects.

Wind Walking

Wind Walking gives the enchanted unit the ability to fly and move three squares per turn. In addition, all units stacked with the enchanted unit can travel with it, and at the same speed. Thus, a speedy Wind Walking hero, for example, can allow you to move full stacks of units anywhere fairly quickly.

Unfortunately, units stacked with the Wind Walking unit cannot fly (although they *can* fight over the ocean) in battle. Note that Wind Walking is a good way to transport whole stacks of units to nodes and Towers of Wizardry sitting on tiny islands where you can't stack up armies before attacking.

The thing to remember about Wind Walking is its upkeep cost relative to casting Flight spells on individual units (at three mana per turn each). While it's always great to have a flying corps of troops, use Wind Walking to move units efficiently in large numbers and individual Flight spells for smaller stacks or units that need to have the advantage of flight in combat. Remember, though, that if your Wind Walking unit has its enchantment dispelled during combat over water, your stack will not be able to move again, until one of its units has Wind Walking cast on it or until the immobilized units have been enchanted with Water Walking.

Banish

Banish is, in essence, the attempt to kill each individual figure in an enemy fantastic unit. Each figure gets a chance to resist; each figure that fails disappears.

For each additional five mana spent in casting Banish, the defending figures' resistance decreases by one. This is a good spell when you have an inadequate army fighting against strong fantastic units (particularly at blue nodes, where this spell won't fizzle). Don't be too cheap with additional mana after you make that 20 mana down payment, either; spend enough to do the job right!

Stasis

Have you ever wished you had more time to gather an army to defend your city against an approaching stack of enemy units? Stasis is the solution to that problem (assuming you can cast it in time).

Banish *Summary Information*

Spell Rarity	Research Point Cost	Combat Casting Cost	Overland Casting Cost	Upkeep Cost Per Turn	Notes
Rare	1,120	20 to 100	N/A	N/A	targets resist at -3 plus -1 resistance per +5 mana

Stasis paralyzes an enemy stack of units for at least one turn. Thereafter, each paralyzed unit tries to free itself (at a penalty of -5 to its resistance) every turn. This should, hopefully, give you the time you need to muster an effective defense or counterattack. Note that computer players will automatically disband units that are immobilized by Stasis if they have a resistance lower than 7.

Stasis Summary Information

Spell Rarity	Research Point Cost	Combat Casting Cost	Overland Casting Cost	Upkeep Cost Per Turn	Notes
Rare	1,500	N/A	250	None	targets resist at -5

Magic Immunity

Magic Immunity is the king of creature enchantments. This spell protects the target unit from almost all spells and magic ranged attacks. It also protects the unit from most gaze, touch, and breath attacks (see Chapter 20). The only spells against which Magic Immunity has no effect are Nature's Cracks Call and Web.

Units enchanted with this spell are only susceptible to standard missile and melee attacks, giving them considerable advantages in most combat situations. All this for five mana per turn, too. This is the spell to cast on units before fighting critical battles against opponent wizards who have well-stocked mana reserves. At the very least, this spell is worth casting on the units in your best stack (the group that does most of your conquering, node collecting, etc.).

Note that units with magic immunity cannot be animated by an enemy casting the Death spell Animate Dead.

Haste

Haste is a creature enchantment that can only be cast during combat. It is extremely expensive, but its effects are phenomenal. This spell lets the enchanted unit move, attack, and counterattack twice as many times as normal!

This is clearly a spell to cast if you are wandering around, or defending, with a limited number of superb units. If your idea of a fine army is one or two outstanding heroes, or a few sky drakes or great wyrms, then Haste is the spell for you.

Magic Immunity Summary Information

Spell Rarity	Research Point Cost	Combat Casting Cost	Overland Casting Cost	Upkeep Cost Per Turn	Notes
Rare	1,600	50	250	5	None

Haste Summary Information

Spell Rarity	Research Point Cost	Combat Casting Cost	Overland Casting Cost	Upkeep Cost Per Turn	Notes
Rare	1,700	50	N/A	N/A	None

Creature Binding *Summary Information*

Spell Rarity	Research Point Cost	Combat Casting Cost	Overland Casting Cost	Upkeep Cost Per Turn	Notes
Very Rare	2,250	70	N/A	N/A	targets resist at -2

Haste is especially helpful when cast on units with first strike attacks, such as elven lords. This spell is also helpful when you know that you can kill a deadly opponent if you only had *one more* chance to fire missiles or initiate an attack before the opponent reached and attacked your troops. Casting this spell on a critical unit under such circumstances may be the push you need to assure victory in a close fight.

Creature Binding

Creature Binding is the ultimate way to use an opponent's summoned creatures against him or her. By casting this expensive spell, you attempt to steal an opponent's fantastic creature and make it fight on your side during combat! (Too bad, you don't get to keep it afterward; the bound creature disappears when combat ends.)

Naturally, the creatures worth stealing are the heavy hitters —behemoths, great wyrms, colossuses, great drakes, etc.—and these guys usually have a high resistance. Bear in mind that the target must resist the spell at a penalty of -2 to its resistance, but, even so, Crea-

ture Binding will not always work, and it will never work on creatures with magic immunity (such as sky drakes).

It is best to cast this spell with a hero who has spell save modifiers (see Chapter 18) or after you have cast a combat enchantment that lowers your opponents' resistances. (We're assuming that you wouldn't be casting Creature Binding if you didn't have a high spell-casting skill.) Then cast Creature Binding on the fantastic creature of your choice. The only creatures you can't get (at least not without further decreasing their resistance) are arch angels, colossuses, demon lords, great drakes, great wyrms, and sky drakes. Everything else, though, is up for grabs, and there are plenty of good creatures left that you can, shall we say, adopt?

Cautionary note: Fantastic creatures defending nodes have +2 modifiers to all of their statistics, including resistance. This makes a few more units inaccessible to Creature Binding unless you have cast a preliminary spell that lowers enemy units' resistances.

Combat Spells

Sorcery magic offers some of the most interesting combat spells in *Master of Magic*. Few of the blue combat spells are truly destructive in nature. Instead, they generally interfere with your opponents' abilities to fight.

Dispel Magic True

Sorcery magic has several extra-potent dispel spells, and this is one of them. Basically, when you are casting a dispel, you

Dispel Magic True *Summary Information*

Spell Rarity	Research Point Cost	Combat Casting Cost	Overland Casting Cost	Upkeep Cost Per Turn	Notes
Common	40	10 to 50	N/A	N/A	None

mean it. You really want to get rid of whatever enchantment you are targeting. Dispel Magic True offers *triple the effectiveness* over the standard Arcane spell Dispel Magic, *for the same mana cost* (see page 107 in the manual for how dispels work). Cast this spell when you are trying to remove negative enchantments from your units or positive enchantments from enemy units.

Interestingly, both this spell and Dispel Magic can be cast on a Magic Vortex (Chaos spell) to remove it from the battlefield.

Counter Magic

Counter Magic is best used against another wizard's (as opposed to neutral) armies since they usually have the most magic power backing them up in a fight. Enemy spells must overcome a dispel equivalent to the strength of the Counter Magic spell if they are to succeed—otherwise, they fizzle. Every time the Counter Magic barrier is tested against an opponent's spell, however, it is weakened a bit.

If you pay attention to your opponents' mana reserves before initiating combat, you will know whether they even have enough mana to cast spells. If they don't, unless they have spell-casting units or heroes in their armies, there is no reason to waste your mana on this spell.

Counter Magic Summary Information

Spell Rarity	Research Point Cost	Combat Casting Cost	Overland Casting Cost	Upkeep Cost Per Turn	Notes
Common	190	10 to 50	N/A	N/A	None

Counter Magic is especially advantageous in two circumstances. First, at a stage in the game where you are relatively weak and have few good combat spells, Counter Magic will at least make it difficult for your opponent to zap you with his; it evens the playing field a bit.

Second, later in the game, when your opponents have acquired devastating combat enchantments (like Wrack or Flame Strike), casting Counter Magic first will give you a chance to abort their spell-casting efforts before they can do serious damage to your armies (particularly when you are defending and, therefore, get the first opportunity to cast spells). Further, their casting attempts may very well exhaust the limit of their spell-casting skill, leaving the opposing player unable to cast any more spells.

Psionic Blast

Psionic Blast targets an opposing unit with an illusionary attack (ignoring their defenses) of strength five, plus one per every additional two mana spent on the spell. Unless the target unit has immunity to illusions, this attack can deal a fair amount of damage, depending on how much mana is spent casting the spell. Note that creatures immune to illusions include all Black Channeled creatures, all summoned creatures of

Psionic Blast Summary Information

Spell Rarity	Research Point Cost	Combat Casting Cost	Overland Casting Cost	Upkeep Cost Per Turn	Notes
Common	250	10 to 50	N/A	N/A	None

Blur *Summary Information*

Spell Rarity	Research Point Cost	Combat Casting Cost	Overland Casting Cost	Upkeep Cost Per Turn	Notes
Uncommon	300	25	N/A	N/A	None

Vertigo *Summary Information*

Spell Rarity	Research Point Cost	Combat Casting Cost	Overland Casting Cost	Upkeep Cost Per Turn	Notes
Uncommon	400	25	N/A	N/A	no resistance modifiers

Death, angels, arch angels, and sky drakes.

The amount of damage done by a Psionic Blast is enough to destroy some of the weaker normal units. However, spells like this are best for casting a killing blow on a particularly dangerous unit (such as an enemy-ranged-attack or spell-casting unit) before it can do further damage to your army. Of course, the relative threat of an enemy unit is an important consideration here. In evenly matched battles, this spell may be just the thing to give your army the edge it needs to press forward or hold off an enemy's advance and win the battle.

Mind Storm *Summary Information*

Spell Rarity	Research Point Cost	Combat Casting Cost	Overland Casting Cost	Upkeep Cost Per Turn	Notes
Rare	1,400	35	N/A	N/A	no resistance possible

Blur

Blur replaces Guises from pre-1.2 versions of *Master of Magic*. While in effect, this battlefield enchantment has a 10 percent chance of negating every hit against all of the caster's units (excluding those with immunity to illusions). The attempt to negate these hits occurs *before* units attempt to stop them with their shields (see Chapter 20). The net result is, the bigger the battle, the better the value of this combat insurance policy.

Vertigo

Vertigo reduces the target unit's ability To Hit and shields (by -2 and -1, respectively). Considering that this spell costs 25 mana to cast, that's only a modest gain. However, when fighting an army with only one really threatening unit, casting Vertigo on it is a good plan.

Vertigo also has devastating effects on missile units. This is because they already have a distance-dependent loss in accuracy (i.e., a negative To Hit modifier that increases with the range to their target). Reducing a missile unit's To Hit modifier still further with Vertigo can make it almost worthless.

Mind Storm

Mind Storm is the ultimate way to disarm a creature. This spell reduces by five each of a target creature's attacks, defense, and resistance. Better still, this spell cannot be resisted! That means that almost all units

Mass Invisibility *Summary Information*

Spell Rarity	Research Point Cost	Combat Casting Cost	Overland Casting Cost	Upkeep Cost Per Turn	Notes
Very Rare	2,500	80	N/A	N/A	None

are susceptible to Mind Storm; the only units that are not are those with immunity to illusions (see Chapter 20).

Mind Storm is moderately expensive, considering that it only affects one unit. However, there are many battles in which there is only one significantly dangerous foe in the army you are fighting. If that unit is too difficult for your army to kill, or if you aren't sure, Mind Storm will significantly improve your odds against it.

Note that the spell does not just decrease the attacks of the target monster. It also decreases its resistance to further spells during that battle. Thus, it can serve as the "one" punch of a one-two magical attack combination.

Mass Invisibility

Once you discover Mass Invisibility, you will find it hard to go back to any other spell or magic color. At a steep casting cost, this spell instantly makes all of your troops invisible, shielding all of them from ranged attacks and from spells that require targeting a unit.

Think of it...your missile and magician armies will suddenly be nigh unstoppable.

Your other armies will be able to deliver the full force of their blows before being picked off by enemy ranged units. Enemy spell casters will be foiled in their attempts to cast negative enchantments or destructive spells on your units. Enemy units that cannot see you will not bother advancing on your troops, leaving them wide open to your selective attacks. Finally, anyone who does manage to attack or counterattack you will suffer a -1 penalty To Hit!

What more can you ask? Mass Invisibility is expensive, but worth every mana point.

City Enchantments

Sorcery magic only offers two city enchantments, both of which are protective in function.

Spell Ward

This is a nifty city enchantment that provides the target city with complete immunity from any magic type you choose. That means that the city is protected from all global, city, and combat spells of that magic type. Also, all creatures of that magic type *may not enter* the city!

This is an especially good spell to cast on your Enchanted Fortress and border cities when you are at war with another wizard (particularly one skilled in destructive red and

Spell Ward *Summary Information*

Spell Rarity	Research Point Cost	Combat Casting Cost	Overland Casting Cost	Upkeep Cost Per Turn	Notes
Very Rare	2,000	N/A	350	5	None

Flying Fortress *Summary Information*

Spell Rarity	Research Point Cost	Combat Casting Cost	Overland Casting Cost	Upkeep Cost Per Turn	Notes
Very Rare	4,000	N/A	500	25	None

Wind Mastery *Summary Information*

Spell Rarity	Research Point Cost	Combat Casting Cost	Overland Casting Cost	Upkeep Cost Per Turn	Notes
Uncommon	620	N/A	400	5	None

black magic). By protecting your cities from a warring wizard's primary spell color, you can save yourself a lot of grief. Just be sure not to choose one of *your* primary magic realms for the Spell Ward because *you* will be barred from using that magic type in that city as well!

Flying Fortress

No, this spell does not summon a B-25 Flying Fortress bomber from World War II. Instead,

Figure 12-2. *Wind Mastery*

it makes your Enchanted Fortress much more difficult to attack. By lifting the Enchanted Fortress' city into the air, only flying units may enter it during combat. Non-flying units in the city may leave it to fight other units outside the city's perimeter, but they may not re-enter the city for the remainder of combat.

This spell is a good way to protect your Enchanted Fortress from the bulk of most computer opponent armies, albeit at a steep cost. Note that this spell will not protect your city or its occupants from dangerous combat spells or enchantments (such as Flame Strike or Wrack). The effectiveness of this tactic ultimately depends on which wizard you are fending off. Flying Fortress is best cast as a last-minute delaying tactic, while you work on better preparing yourself to meet your enemies.

Global Enchantments

Sorcery magic has the most annoying global spells. In fact, it is in this arena that blue magic really comes into its own. Just remember, though, casting spells that hurt other players can have long-term diplomatic repercussions (see Chapter 25).

Wind Mastery

Wind Mastery causes all of your ships, including Floating Islands, to travel at twice their normal speed, while your opponents' ships all move at half their normal speed. This spell is the perfect complement for an avidly expansionistic wizard because getting to new lands first is half the battle. Wind Mastery also lets you get to and conquer neutral cities, nodes, lairs, etc., faster than your opponents can.

In addition, this spell gives you the initiative during wars, allowing you to easily transport your troops to your enemies' shores long before their troops can get to yours. Unless you are traveling only with flying or water walking units, or unless you are having trouble with mana, there is no good reason not to cast this spell when you can.

Note that when two or more wizards cast this spell, their vessels each gain a 50 percent increase in speed, while all others' ships move at half speed.

Aura of Majesty

Aura of Majesty provides a fairly cheap way to maintain positive relations with other wizards. Each turn that this spell is in effect, relations between the casting wizard and computer opponents (this won't fool the human player, after all) will improve slightly (see Chapter 25 for all of the technical details). Over time, this can make some considerable difference on the diplomatic front.

Since blue is a slowly developing magic type, Aura of Majesty provides a good way for your wizard to keep out of trouble until he or she is ready for it; cast it as soon as you are able. If you are playing with both Sorcery and Death magic, this spell is particularly valuable because it can help counteract some of black magic's negative diplomatic side effects.

Aura of Majesty Summary Information

Spell Rarity	Research Point Cost	Combat Casting Cost	Overland Casting Cost	Upkeep Cost Per Turn	Notes
Uncommon	740	N/A	400	5	None

Great Unsummoning Summary Information

Spell Rarity	Research Point Cost	Combat Casting Cost	Overland Casting Cost	Upkeep Cost Per Turn	Notes
Very Rare	3,000	N/A	1000	5	targets resist at -3

Great Unsummoning

Before casting this spell, make sure you don't have any fantastic creatures you can't afford to lose. This spell tries to unsummon *all fantastic creatures* from both Arcanus and Myrror when cast. Each unit gets one chance to prevent this from happening (with a penalty of -3 to their resistance). Note that this does *not* affect the creatures in lairs or nodes!

Great Unsummoning is a good spell to cast late in the game if you find yourself up against one or more opponents who have had the time or mana to gather larger armies of fantastic creatures than you have had. Or, you might cast it if you have very strong normal units and you are planning to invade a wizard's cities in which large quantities of fantastic creatures are garrisoned. It's also handy if you're a Conjurer and can replace your lost critters more quickly than the other wizards can. Know, however, that this spell won't affect the strongest fantastic creatures, those with high innate resistances. You'll just be able to get rid of the less powerful ones with this spell.

Suppress Magic *Summary Information*

Spell Rarity	Research Point Cost	Combat Casting Cost	Overland Casting Cost	Upkeep Cost Per Turn	Notes
Very Rare	5,000	N/A	1250	40	500 dispel vs. all magic

Suppress Magic

Suppress Magic can really annoy people. It is a continuous dispel with a strength of 500 (see manual, page 107 for dispel equation) that attempts to stop all enemy overland (i.e., non-combat) spells and enchantments from being cast. This is one good way to keep your opponents from gaining the upper hand through global or city enchantments. It is especially useful when fighting wizards with heavy doses of Chaos or Death magic, since both of these have dangerous global and city spells.

While this spell is immensely pleasing if you have cast it, Suppress Magic is wildly irritating if someone else has. Get rid of this spell as fast as you can if it's not yours. Undercut the caster's mana sources, invade their cities, focus on building up your armies with normal units. Cast Disjunction or Disjunction True if you have it (at maximum strength, since this spell is tough to dislodge). Try to incite other wizards to attack the one who cast this spell. Until this spell is gone, your magic capabilities are too limited to discuss seriously—so do something about it.

Time Stop

Time Stop, the ultimate Sorcery spell, is wonderful if you have cast it and awful if you haven't. It stops all enemy actions, upkeep, income, and movement during the time in which it is active. In fact, the only thing that can go on, if you are the one who cast this spell, is that your troops can move and you must pay the 200 mana per game turn upkeep cost.

Time Stop is great to cast when you wish to march a lot of armies on your enemies' cities. You have to amass the armies *before* you cast the spell, however, since it stops production of troops and buildings as well as everything else. Casting this spell lets you focus your attacks concurrently on many or all of an opponent's cities, without them being able to re-garrison or prepare. It also gives you a good shot to succeed with a preemptive surprise attack. Finally, if another wizard starts casting Spell of Mastery before you can, Time Stop gives you a chance to strike at his or her Enchanted Fortress while keeping the wizard's spell-casting efforts on hold.

Special Spells

Blue magic offers a number of special spells. Many of these are aimed at destroying enemy enchantments or spell casting efforts.

Word of Recall

Word of Recall lets you instantly transport a friendly unit to your Summoning

Time Stop *Summary Information*

Spell Rarity	Research Point Cost	Combat Casting Cost	Overland Casting Cost	Upkeep Cost Per Turn	Notes
Very Rare	6,000	N/A	1500	200	None

Circle. This spell has a number of uses. First, if one of your cities is being approached by a dangerous-looking army, cast Summoning Circle on that city, then start casting Words of Recall on available units to quickly garrison that city. Second, you can cast Word of Recall on units to allow them to pass between planes, if you have cities on each plane, without having to go through Towers of Wizardry or other portals. This spell will even let you cross between planes through a Planar Seal.

Of course, at 20 mana a pop, casting Word of Recall merely to transport units for the heck of it is not really worthwhile, especially if you can easily construct fairly strong units in your cities. But there are times when it is necessary to amass an army quickly in a particular location. At such times, Word of Recall is a good spell for the task.

Disenchant True

Disenchant True is identical to the Arcane spell Disenchant Area, except that its effects are three times as powerful for the same price. Clearly, if you are trying to remove a city en-chantment or other localized enchantment, given a choice, you should always use Disenchant True.

Remember, the more mana you pump into these dispel spells, the greater your chance of success. But, for the same amount of mana you can cast the spell multiple times, which, statistically, will give you an even higher chance of success.

Enchant Road

Enchant Road converts all roads in a five by five square area into enchanted roads that cost no movement points to use (i.e., like the roads built on Myrror). This spell requires no upkeep and is fairly inexpensive to cast, too.

Enchant Road is great to cast on cities that form the nexus points of your road networks. In fact, it is good to cast this spell over most of your Arcanian roads, as enchanted roads allow such quickness of movement that defending your cities becomes a much

Word of Recall Summary Information

Spell Rarity	Research Point Cost	Combat Casting Cost	Overland Casting Cost	Upkeep Cost Per Turn	Notes
Common	160	20	20	N/A	None

Disenchant True Summary Information

Spell Rarity	Research Point Cost	Combat Casting Cost	Overland Casting Cost	Upkeep Cost Per Turn	Notes
Uncommon	350	N/A	50 to 250	N/A	None

Enchant Road Summary Information

Spell Rarity	Research Point Cost	Combat Casting Cost	Overland Casting Cost	Upkeep Cost Per Turn	Notes
Uncommon	500	N/A	100	None	None

Spell Blast *Summary Information*

Spell Rarity	Research Point Cost	Combat Casting Cost	Overland Casting Cost	Upkeep Cost Per Turn	Notes
Uncommon	680	N/A	50+	N/A	None

Disjunction True *Summary Information*

Spell Rarity	Research Point Cost	Combat Casting Cost	Overland Casting Cost	Upkeep Cost Per Turn	Notes
Rare	880	N/A	200 to 1,000	N/A	None

simpler and more inexpensive task. A few good units can defend many cities if they can get from one to the next in a single turn.

Spell Blast

If you have cast the Arcane spell Detect Magic, then you always know what your enemies are casting. If one of your enemies starts casting something noxious, you can cast Spell Blast to stop it. However, there is a string attached.

After casting Spell Blast, you must *also pay*, immediately, from your mana reserves, an amount equal to the mana the other wizard has invested thus far into casting his or her spell! If you don't have enough mana, your Spell Blast will fizzle. So, on a cautionary note, make sure you have plenty of mana before you start.

Note that it is always easier to stop a spell as it is being cast than it is to dispel it afterwards. Keep Detect Magic on if you have Spell Blast capability, and make sure you moni-

tor what the other wizards are doing. There's nothing like messing up an opponent's creature summoning or global enchantment before it gets off the ground.

Disjunction True

Disjunction True can be used to dispel global enchantments. Its strength is three times that of the Arcane spell, Disjunction, for the same amount of mana. Since most global enchantments are unpleasant (if you haven't cast them, that is), there is no reason to stint on the mana you spend when you cast Disjunction True (unless you are having trouble with your mana income). One of the luxuries of playing with a lot of blue magic is that your dispels are three times as strong as everyone else's—so make the most of it.

Spell Binding

The old saying goes, "Anything worth having is worth stealing." If you don't like another player's global enchantment, don't bother dispelling it, cast Spell Binding and simply steal it!

The spell costs 1,000 mana to cast; the upkeep you pay is the usual amount for the

Spell Binding *Summary Information*

Spell Rarity	Research Point Cost	Combat Casting Cost	Overland Casting Cost	Upkeep Cost Per Turn	Notes
Very Rare	3,500	N/A	1,000	Varies	None

global enchantment you steal. There is absolutely no reason not to cast this spell, if you can. All situations are right for it. We believe that Spell Binding is the best reason to specialize in Sorcery magic.

The Rainbow Connection

Now that we've sung the blues, it is time to consider the proposition that a wizard need not live by a single color of magic alone. In fact, combinations of colors often make for interesting game play in *Master of Magic*. Our next chapter premiers the latest in mix-and-match colors for the style-conscious wizard.

13

Seeing Rainbows

After the hard labor spent on each separate color of magic, we're now making a prism break. For fans of peppermint stripes, Neapolitan ice cream, and Aquafresh™ toothpaste, we have some cunning plans for showing your stripes by combining various colors of magic.

Although we've discussed the merits of trading off single color depth over rainbow breadth (see Chapter 6), let us consider now how particular colors complement one another. Afterward, we'll consider the order in which to research new spells and the factors that influence which spells to trade away when dealing with enemies.

Mix 'N' Match

First, we shall pair each color together and consider that combination's worth. Where appropriate, we've added our favorite cross-color spell combinations.

White and Black

Ha! You can't do this. (Ted Turner has already been here.)

White and Red

Life magic is the most protective, monster-poor magic form, while Chaos offers many fantastic units and many destructive spells. These two colors complement each other's deficiencies beautifully.

Some fun spell combinations include:

🐌 Endurance on the slow-moving chaos spawns and hydras

🐌 Chaos Surge and Doom Mastery mixed with Charm of Life for really deadly, long-lived units

White and Green

This combination (without other colors) is very defense-oriented, although green does bring some combat spells and fantastic units

to the party. If you want to play a long game, play this color combination and adopt a siege mentality. Otherwise, spice things up with a little Chaos magic.

Some super New York Jets green-and-white defense combos:

🐌 Lion Heart and Iron Skin for extra tough units

🐌 Endurance and Water Walking when your settlers are in a hurry to build an outpost on another continent

🐌 Invulnerability or Lion Heart on sprites for magic-ranged-attackers-from-hell

White and Blue

Although both Life and Sorcery magic are slow in development, they can really enhance one another's effects. Sorcery offers just enough fantastic units to supplement white magic's deficiencies in this area. In addition, blue's Aura of Majesty is the perfect crown to white's innately positive diplomatic effects.

Some Life and Sorcery spell combinations:

🐌 Mind Storm and Holy Word for massive destruction of fantastic foes

🐌 Holy Armor and Resist Magic for a budget-protective combination

Black and Red

This is the deadly duo. Both colors are strong in destructive spells and creature summoning. Combining them, however, is a like building a bigger nuclear bomb. (Who cares how many times you can blow up the world?) Nonetheless, the maniacal sadist inside you will have a jolly evil time with this black widow combination.

Some super-damaging spell combinations:

☙ Black Prayer with Disintegrate or other Chaos combat spells for quickly killing an obnoxious enemy unit

☙ Berserk on killer Chaos units with lots of hit points (like great drakes and hydras)

Black and Green

Now *this* is a balanced pair of colors. Between the positive, growth-enhancing spells that Nature offers, and the evil, nasty Death spells, there aren't many things that this greenback color combo can't do.

Rewarding combinations:

☙ Dark Rituals with Gaia's Blessing for tons of magic without the rebels and loss in population growth rate

☙ Regeneration and Black Channels (or any Death creature) to keep the non-healing Death units around longer

☙ Giant Strength or Stone Skin on weasly little skeletons and ghouls (these multi-figure groups benefit a lot from spells like this)

Black and Blue

While Sorcery is ordinarily a defensive color, it can greatly enhance the misery that Death magic causes others. While your black magic is out there doing heinous things to your enemies, blue magic can keep them from having any fun at all through its Spell Blast, Counter Magic, Dispel True, Suppress Magic, etc., spells. Also, Sorcery's Aura of Majesty can help compensate for the negative diplomatic effects caused by owning black spell books.

Black and blue bruisers:

☙ Mind Storm and Word of Death for decisive destruction of an enemy unit

☙ Invisibility on shadow demons to compensate for one of the few weaknesses this unit has

Red and Green

This pair of colors balances nicely. Between red's crushingly offensive spells, and green's positive urban and terrain magic, you will be prepared for almost anything. Both of these colors feature a multitude of fantastic units; with both Chaos and Nature magic units at your disposal, you can conjure up brutal fantastic armies. Finally, green's defensive unit enchantments complement red's offensive ones beautifully.

Red and green pairings that are like a stake of holly through the heart include:

☙ Regeneration on great drakes for an invincible death machine (of course Regeneration works well on anything)

☙ Stone or Iron Skin on hydras or chaos spawns will make them virtually impossible to kill

☙ With Raise Volcano and Change Terrain you can turn any city into a virtual paradise; Raise Volcano works on those otherwise nonproductive tundra squares, and Change Terrain can then convert those volcanoes into hills — and from there into other terrain types

Red and Blue

Since Sorcery magic goes well with anything, naturally, it goes well with Chaos magic. Chaos magic makes up for Sorcery's lack of non-combat unit summoning, and Sorcery gives Chaos a bit of defensive oomph. Blue magic clears the playing field in combat (Counter Magic, Dispel Magic True) and overland (Disjunction True, Suppress Magic, etc.), while your red magic spells devastate your opponents, making a nice one-two punch.

Blue and red spell combinations to consider:

- Blur, Invisibility, Flight, or Mass Invisibility combine with any destructive Chaos combat spells (Fireball, Warp Lightning, etc.) to keep your side protected while you magically damage enemies on the battlefield

- Flight on hydras will make them faster and more mobile in combat

- Mind Storm with Disintegration is a super *two strikes, you're out* combination, taking down some of the toughest units in the game

Green and Blue

A combination of Nature and Sorcery magic offers interesting possibilities. Together, they provide a wide range of effective combat spells. Nature magic's many fantastic units and positive enchantments are complemented by Sorcery's Spell Lock to nail them into place. Blue has some perfect complementary unit enchantments for green (Flight and Invisibility) that can make the land-bound Nature units nearly invincible.

Some possibilities for blue and green include:

- Stone Skin on phantom warriors will greatly help their shieldless condition, giving these illusionary attackers some staying power

- Flight on great wyrms (or basilisks, behemoths, colossuses, etc.) will cure the one problem these creatures have: they can't initiate attacks on flying units

- Enchant Road and Change Terrain for award-winning urban development

Two-Color Conclusions

While spreading yourself out over two colors of magic decreases the number of ultra-powerful spells you get, it opens up a range of casting and trading possibilities. With a broad array of basic spells from which to choose,

combining magic realms is less limiting than it is liberating.

A Broader Spectrum

So, what of choosing three or four colors instead of just two? We won't go into every possible combination, but you can use the preceding information to get an idea of what choosing even more magic colors can do for you. Selecting many colors has some specific advantages (and disadvantages) for your game:

- Node Mastery can only be chosen if you have at least one book each in red, green, and blue magic. This skill is useful because it lets you double the mana drawn from all your nodes and allows you to cast any spell at any node. For a high mana game (with considerable casting and research possibilities), choose at least one Chaos, Nature, and Sorcery spell book and Node Mastery.

- Trading options increase drastically with three or four magic colors, allowing you to trade with most other wizards in the game. Trading will increase your casting options, and each additional spell you acquire will add half its research value to the 60,000 research points required to learn Spell of Mastery.

Beware, though; your trading options in a magic realm will be limited to common and uncommon spells unless you choose at least *two* books of that color. Similarly, you will not be able to acquire very rare spells without at least *three* books in that color.

- Finding spells as treasure is subject to the same benefits and limits as trading spells; you'll find a more diverse array of spells, but they will be limited in rarity depending on the number of spell books you have in each color.

While diversity is good, spreading your spell picks over several magic colors limits spell quality. For example, you'll probably never get more than a few rare, and even fewer very rare, spells in a magic realm for which you only have two or three spell books. If you want to wield a color's powerful magic (and let's face it, some of those very rare spells are awesome), pick at least four or five spell books in that realm. You will still enjoy the benefits of many spell colors if you concentrate in one color while diversifying with one or two spell books in a few other colors.

For instance, say you like rare and very rare Chaos spells, but you want trading options or you want to be sure you don't accidentally find a black spell book as a treasure (for diplomatic reasons). Consider taking six spell picks in Chaos, one each in Sorcery, Nature, and Life magic and use your remaining two spell picks to get Chaos Mastery and Node Mastery. Now you can trade with almost everyone; your Life book prevents you from obtaining a Death magic book from some lair; and your mana production from nodes will be fantastically high.

These caveats aside, there are many great common and uncommon spells in every magic realm. There is nothing wrong with choosing a few spell books in even four colors, as long as you're aware of the limitations for doing so.

Spell Research Strategy

After diligently picking your spell books, the next question is, how do you choose what to research next? We have some theories about this....

First, know that the spells on your research list are arranged from the cheapest to most expensive, in terms of their base research value. You will always see the number of turns it will take, given your current researching level, to learn each spell.

Consider the following things when choosing your next spell to research:

🐌 Cheaper spells will make it into your spell book more quickly, which makes them available for casting and trading sooner. They also keep your options open for quickly making your next spell researching decision.

Note that in a particular magic realm, spells of greater rarity only become available once you have learned or are able to learn spells that are more common. For example, if there is some special very rare Sorcery spell you want, make a point of learning the more common spells, or else the spell you *want* may a take a long time getting into your research book.

🐌 If any of your opponents share spell book colors with you, consider researching spells you can trade with them. This, in turn, allows you to acquire more spells *from them.*

🐌 If there is a particular spell that you want or need, regardless of how long it takes to research, prioritize it. Examples: you may want to pick up Disjunction early, especially if your opponents specialize in magic colors with nasty global spells (black, red, or blue). If you are fighting the mistress of Life magic, Ariel, and you are playing a prince of evil, research your Darkness spell or similar spells earlier.

Experience will show you that a particular combat spell (like Flame Strike) or enchantment (such as Flight) is too good to pass up. Quickly research such spells. As a final example, if Tauron, the master of Chaos, erupts at you, raising volcanoes and corrupting lands, you'll find it helpful to research Gaia's Blessing as fast as you can.

That is pretty much it. Use common sense and keep an eye on your trading and casting possibilities.

Trading Spells

There you are, face-to-face with a wizard you must eliminate later in the game. You want his spells, but you don't want to give him any advantages over you. What do you trade for, and what do you trade away?

First, bear in mind that if you trade away expensive spells for cheaper ones (in terms of research point costs) you'll get a positive diplomatic boost (Chapter 25). This means that you should make trades like this when you are trying to avert wars and when you want to improve your relations with another wizard so that you can form wizard pacts or alliances. While such trading is helpful for your enemies, you can minimize the benefits they receive if you trade the right sorts of spells (i.e., spells that they can probably research anyway).

Spells to trade away:

 Every wizard knows all of the Arcane magic spells. Trade these freely because you're not giving them anything they can't already use against you. Since many have high research costs, they'll also net you some positive diplomacy points.

 In particular, go crazy trading away global Arcane spells like Awareness and the two summoning spells (Summon Hero and Summon Champion). When computer players have these spells, they cast them as soon and as often as they can. This keeps their casting efforts preoccupied with innocuous spells (after all, you're much better at putting your heroes to productive use than they are), rather than more dangerous ones.

 Go ahead and trade away less useful unit enchantments and summoning spells. The computer players love summoning (they'll do it anyway, so as long as you're not trading them a Hydra or Sky Drake spell, it won't make that much difference) and enchantments. The idea here is to get great spells from other wizards, while giving them spells they don't use nearly as effectively as you.

Never trade away:

 Destructive combat spells (even the cheesy ones)! There's no reason to arm your enemies so effectively.

 Destructive global or city enchantments: Computer players love to cast nasty global and city enchantments if they have them. Even when they *like* you, they won't hesitate to cast Armageddon if they have it. Regardless of your situation, you can do yourself great mischief by trading these spells to others.

Trade for:

 Spells that you're fairly sure won't be in your spell book (see Appendix D for decoding the runes) and that you can use. Always consider your *need* for a spell when weighing the value of what you must trade away for it.

 Any spells that you may have but that you need *now*. For example, say you want a Transmute spell, but it will take you 30 turns to learn it. Well, if it offers itself up for trade, you might want to grab it now. It's worth the same research point value toward casting the Spell of Mastery regardless of how you acquire it.

The only reason for not taking such a spell is if you shortchanged yourself on spell ranks when you chose your spell picks at the beginning of the game, in the hopes that you would acquire lots of spell books as treasure. In such a case, you may want to delay the inevitable researching of the Spell of Mastery (which will lock up your research efforts for hundreds of game turns), in the hopes that you acquire a few more spell books and, thereby, more spells to learn and cast.

Spells that you don't care about, but that you know you can trade to a different wizard for spells you want. For example, if you can acquire a Holy Armor spell from Ariel and trade it to Sss'ra for a Doom Bolt... why not?

Don't bother trading for:

Spells for which you see no good purpose, unless you are trying to boost your diplomatic status with a wizard or unless you plan to trade the spell away to another wizard for a better spell. Not all spells are equally useful, and without a greater goal, trading for ineffective spells is folly. For example, if you can already summon wraiths and shadow demons, you don't have many good reasons to trade for a Ghouls spell (unless you want an extra point when your score gets calculated at the end of the game; see Chapter 3).

Spells that you're only a few turns away from learning anyway. Again, the exception is if you are trying to make friends with a computer player.

When trading spells, just as when you are determining the next spell to research, let common sense be your guide.

I Put a Spell on You

At this point, you know enough to create an effective wizard and pick the right race. We've examined pre-game decisions and the spells of the six magic realms, and so, we close these spell books to open the maps. From here, we begin a new section that will help you commute and prosper in the worlds of Arcanus and Myrror, starting with the creation of the worlds and the best ways to discover them.

Section 4

Whipping Things Into Shape

14

Genesis, Master of Magic Style

As each game of *Master of Magic* begins, two worlds are generated: the lower, common world of Arcanus and the higher, special world of Myrror. This chapter is your key to these planes.

We will be the compass guiding you through the various features of both Arcanus and Myrror. We will explain the genesis of the worlds as they are created and help you to explore them. We will also make our legend of the terrain features and how best to navigate the worlds of *Master of Magic*.

Don't Fence Me In

The maps to both Arcanus and Myrror are 60 squares wide by 40 squares high, for a total of 2400 squares per world. Of this, each world should be covered with from 70 percent to 85 percent ocean squares. (See the Genesis section toward the end of this chapter for details on world creation.) Along the top and bottom (which can also be thought of as the north and south) edges are wastelands of tundra, denoting the polar caps. The maps have no east or west edges; units can go completely around the world in these directions. Ergo, the worlds of *Master of Magic* are cylindrical.

Putting the Cartographer Before the Host: Tips for More Effective Map Discovery

Except for the neighborhood around your starting city, the maps of both planes (Arcanus and Myrror) are covered in blackness. As units move around the board, squares near them are revealed. Basically, there are three ways to explore these maps: the hard way, the less hard way, and the easy way.

The Hard Way Made Easier: Square-by-Square Exploration

The hard way to explore the map is to take units with normal, one-square scouting

ranges, and maneuver them around, pushing back the blackness square-by-square.

One way to make this arduous method a bit more bearable is to move units diagonally, in a zigzag pattern (i.e., first up-and-to-the-left, than up-and-to-the-right). This will cut a wider swath of revealed squares in a unit's wake, as shown in Figure 14-1.

Another effective tool for exploring maps in this manner is to build units that can peruse the oceans. Ships, in particular, are good for this because they are cheap and move two to four squares per turn, depending on the ship type. *Be sure to explore the coastlines of newly discovered land masses thoroughly when using ships to probe the darkness. You never know what you'll find there.* Flying, water walking, and non-corporeal units are also good for trans-oceanic exploration but can be slower or more costly than ships. Besides, ships can always come back and pick up troops to take to interesting new continents you discover.

Hint: Use magic spirits for early exploration. They're cheap, they move two squares per turn (even across water) because they are non-corporeal, and they can peek into lairs quickly in hopes of finding the empty ones before the other players do.

Figure 14-1. *Revealing terrain is more effective when done in a zigzag pattern.*

Table 14.1 *City Scouting Ranges*

Scouting Range	Building or Spell
2	Unenhanced city
3	City walls (whether built or cast by a Wall of Stone spell*)
4	Oracle building
5	Nature's Eye spell**

*Wall of Stone is a common Nature city enchantment costing 50 mana to cast. The maintenance cost is the same as a normal stone wall, two gold per turn (see Chapter 11).

**Nature's Eye is an uncommon Nature city enchantment costing 75 mana to cast and one mana per turn to maintain (see Chapter 11).

The Less Hard Way: Scouting With The Best

Some units have longer scouting ranges than others. Normally, land and ship unit types have a scouting range of one square, while flying units have a range of two squares. During the early, exploratory stages of a game, you should exploit the higher scouting range of flying units.

Some of the heroes that often come by early in the game have special scouting abilities. These include Rakir and Greyfairer, both of whom have a scouting range of three, and Marcus, whose scouting range is two. Tossing either a Flight or Water Walking spell on these guys will make them very versatile scouts, indeed. See Chapter 18 for all the details on heroes.

The Easy Way to Discover The World: Magic

There are also magic spells that help you place features on the map. The best among them is Earth Lore. This common green spell reveals a whole screen's worth of terrain for a cost of 30 mana. If you've got this, be sure to use it, especially to track down where other player's units are coming from when you first encounter them. It is also great for rapidly discovering partially explored continents.

The rare Arcane spell of Awareness reveals all cities on both planes, including the squares directly adjacent to them. Awareness costs 500 mana, +3 per turn to maintain. Note that many cities revealed by this spell will appear within areas of unexplored blackness. While Awareness is maintained, any new cities that are built will also appear.

The ultimate version of Awareness is Nature's Awareness, a very rare Nature spell that reveals everything that isn't invisible. The cost is steep at 800 mana, +7 mana per turn to maintain, but only invisible units are hidden from you. All terrain, cities, and non-invisible creatures remain revealed for this spell's duration, including non-invisible city garrisons.

City Scouting Ranges

Every city and outpost has a scouting range, whether garrisoned or not. All cities have a base scouting range of two squares. Certain features and spells will enhance the scouting range of a given city. They are shown in Table 14.1.

A city's scouting range is its early warning detection system. It helps you spot troops in the neighborhood that may be preparing to attack your city. The farther out you spot approaching enemy units, the more time you

Table 14.2 *Standard Terrain Types*

Terrain	Food	Gold*	Production Bonus	Movement Point Cost	Required to Build
Chaos Node			5%	3	
Corruption**	0	0	0	***	
Desert	0	0	3%	1	
Forest	1/2	0	3%	2	Sawmill, Forester's Guild
Grasslands	1 1/2	0	0	1	Stable
Hills	1/2	0	3%	2	
Mountain	0	0	5%	3	
Nature Node	2	0	3%	3	
Ocean	0	0	0	1****	
River	2	20%	0	2	
River mouth	2	30%	0	2	
Shore	1/2	10%	0	1****	Ship Wright's Guild*****
Sorcery Node	2	0	0	3	
Swamp	1/2	0	0	2	
Tundra	0	0	0	2	
Volcano******	0	0	0	3	

*Gold refers to gold bonuses through trade

**Corruption supersedes all standard terrain types and special resources in that square

***The movement point cost to enter a corrupted square is the same as for the other terrain in that square

****Only ships and units with swimming or flying ability may enter this terrain.

*****Ship Wright's Guilds can be built on cities adjacent to *any* shore, including lakes!

******There should be a 2 percent chance each turn that a volcano will go dormant and turn into a mountain. Note, the contributions of nodes to food and production are not included in the information conveyed by the Surveyor button.

have to reinforce your threatened cities and prepare a proper defense.

For this reason, *always* considering enhancing the scouting ranges of your cities nearest to other players. Cities located near a Tower of Wizardry, along a well-traveled strait, or at a vital isthmus connecting two large land masses should also be provided with enhanced scouting ranges. Remember, *the early word gets a turn*. (I.e., with the early warning provided by enhanced city scouting abilities you may have an extra turn or two to prepare to counter an enemy's incursion.)

City Garrisons

Although cities remain on your map once revealed, their garrisons do not. Unless you currently have a city within the scouting range of one of your units (or have cast Nature's Awareness), you won't have any information available about its garrison. You will never see invisible units (such as the Dark Elf night stalkers) in any case.

Table 14.3 *Special Resources*

Resource	Gold	Mana	Unit Cost Reduction*	Weapon and Armor Bonus**	Food	Movement	City Protection with Dispel
Gems	5	0	0	0	0	0	-
Gold	3	0	0	0	0	0	-
Silver	2	0	0	0	0	0	-
Roads	bonus***	0	0	0	0	****	-
Crysx Crystals	0	5	0	0	0	0	-
Quork Crystals	0	3	0	0	0	0	-
Adamantium	0	2	0	+2	0	0	-
Mithril	0	1	0	+1	0	0	-
Coal	0	0	10%	0	0	0	-
Iron	0	0	5%	0	0	0	-
Wild Game	0	0	0	0	2	0	-
Nightshade	0	0	0	0	0	0	yes*****

*Applies only to normal units other than ships of any type, magicians, priests, shamans, and warlocks. Maximum cost reduction allowed is always 50 percent.

**These are bonuses in the melee attack strength and defense of units. Bonuses will only apply once the city has an alchemist's guild.

***Roads only provide gold bonuses through trade with adjoining towns.

****Arcanian roads allow travel at half a movement point per square entered. On Myrror, roads cost no movement points to travel on. Note: Units that fly *do* enjoy this road movement bonus; non-corporeal units do not. Units with the pathfinding skill treat every non-enchanted road land square as a normal road square for movement purposes *for their entire stack*.

*****Each nightshade plant casts its own 100 strength *dispel* on every negative city enchantment once per game turn.

Don't Forget Your Cartographer!

Master of Magic has many cool features, but one of the least appreciated is the maps provided by your cartographer. Pressing the Info button on the Main Movement screen shows the cartographer listed second (its hot key is F2). The overview maps they present of both Arcanus and Myrror are great for viewing *the big picture*. The cartographer provides a clear, geographic Polaroid of the locations of all known friendly and enemy units and cities. They are shown in relation to each other and to the position of the world's oceans and land masses. For those planning for a military campaign, unfurling these maps is a wise first step.

Adamantium: Is That Named After a Singer?

Now let's take a look around the map and see

the forests from the Nature nodes. First, a brief inspection of the various standard terrain types, including corruption and volcanoes, is in order. Table 14.2 sums this information up nicely.

In addition to its standard terrain type, a square may have a special feature. How those special features got there will be discussed later in this chapter. For now, lets consider what each one does. Table 14.3 lays this groundwork.

Moving Krakatowa East of Java: Working the Landscape

Four spells, two green and two red, alter the map's terrain or special features. In truth, these spells are a lot of fun to play with. Specifically, they are:

🐌 Change Terrain: This is the perfectionist's green spell for urban optimization. Although this won't change tundra, the Raise Volcano spell will. Playing a red-green color combination, therefore, can create plush cities for you in polar regions if you're willing to commit the time and mana to make them.

🐌 Transmute: This green spell interconverts gems and coal, iron and gold, plus silver and mithril. Thus, you can create cities that produce military units at a discount by switching their gem and gold production over to iron and coal. Note that altering silver into mithril is almost always worthwhile.

🐌 Raise Volcano: If you want to ruin a neighbor's day in a small way, this red spell can do it, particularly when cast on a special terrain square. Note that raising a volcano is a necessary first step for using the Change Terrain spell to convert tundra squares.

🐌 Armageddon: This massive volcano raiser will soon make everyone your enemy, so cast it at a point when you don't care. All the world, save the squares near your cities, will eventually be converted to volcanoes.

Special Sites

Special sites, generically known as *lairs*, include ancient temples, ancient ruins, fallen temples, mysterious caves, dungeons, abandoned keeps, and monster lairs. They serve two functions. First, they provide an opportunity for players to acquire treasure. Of course, such treasures are usually guarded (see Appendix C). Second, these guarded lairs can produce the occasional rampaging monster to terrorize the neighboring lands.

Once a lair's treasure has been removed, that lair disappears. The only new lairs created during the game are ruins left in the wake of rampaging monsters after they have completely destroyed a city.

Corruption

While a square is corrupted, all of the income it generates (food, gold, and mana) is lost. Corrupted nightshade no longer casts its autodispel, but corrupted node squares still have their full auras. Corruption does not alter the movement effects of the terrain in that square in any way.

Node Auras

Node auras, while not visible on the map until after a node has been conquered and melded, exist even when invisible. These squares do not affect movement in any way but do enhance the fighting ability of creatures from their same magic realm. See Chapter 20 for the details of node auras in combat.

You Can't Get There From Here, You Have to Start Somewhere Else

Moving units around in *Master of Magic* isn't so tough. The two main challenges are getting units across oceans and planes. Let's examine all forms of transportation and get things moving, shall we?

Walking

Units that walk by normal movement are predominant in the game. They cannot move on shore or ocean squares without transport. Furthermore, they must pay the movement point costs for entering land squares, as shown in Table 14.2. It is primarily for these units' benefit that you should build roads between strategic locations (such as cities, nodes, and Towers of Wizardry).

Floating

Units that move along the ocean's surface include ships, non-corporeal units, Lizardmen, Nagas, and units enchanted by the green spell, Water Walking. Short of flying, walking over the water is the surest way to cross the oceans whenever a unit needs to. However, embarking them on ships that move 3 or 4 squares per turn is often much faster.

Flying

The best way to travel is to fly (ask the Draconians; they all fly). Not only does every non-road land square cost just one movement point to enter, but oceans are easily crossed as well. Flying also provides a distinct advantage in combat (see Chapter 20).

Cargo Carrying

When it comes to ferrying landlubbers across the ocean blue, ships (and, in particular, galleys) are the ticket. Their large carrying capacities, fast movement rates, durability in combat, and reasonable maintenance costs make them ideal for hauling cargo across the

seas. Don't waste your money enchanting any (save, possibly, your best) troops with Water Walking or Flight just to get them across a body of water. Be practical and use ships instead.

In lieu of ships, the Sorcery spell Floating Island summons a unit that can carry eight others over the seas. It even allows them to fight an ocean battle as if they were on land! Because of a floating island's high upkeep cost, however, ships are usually more practical in the long run.

Note that the hero Jaer has a skill called wind walking. It allows him to fly and carry his entire stack through the air with him. If you can, hold onto this hero at all costs. He and other units that you've enchanted with the Sorcery spell, Wind Walking, are the ultimate transports in *Master of Magic*.

Similarly, heroes with the pathfinding skill can move their stacks over non-road land squares at the normal road movement rate of half a movement point per square. Pathfinders won't get their stacks across the water, but they sure can get them across undeveloped continents in a hurry!

Traveling by Plane

A pivotal point in every game of *Master of Magic* is reached when you can move units between the planes of Myrror and Arcanus. All units can do this via conquered Towers of Wizardry. Casting the Life spell Plane Shift will zap an entire stack to the other plane (provided that stack could move into the corresponding square on the other plane). Some units may also have the planar travel ability (shadow demons), allowing them to freely shift between planes by themselves.

Note that the Life spell Planar Seal prohibits all normal forms of trans-planar movement while it is in effect. At that point, the only way to get units through the Planar Seal is to cast Recall Hero or Word of Recall when

Table 14.4 What Special Terrain Feature Appears?

Terrain Type/ Specials	World/Percent Chance	
	Arcanus	Myrror
Desert		
Gems	66.7	20
Quark	33.3	60
Crysx	0	20
Hills		
Iron	33.3	10
Coal	16.7	10
Silver	22.2	10
Gold	22.2	40
Mithril	5.6	20
Adamantium	0	10
Mountains		
Iron	22.2	10
Coal	27.7	10
Silver	16.7	10
Gold	16.7	20
Mithril	16.7	30
Adamantium	0	20
Forests		
Wild Game	100	100
Swamp		
Nightshade	100	100

The number is the percent chance of that particular special appearing when its parent terrain square receives a special terrain feature.

your Summoning Circle is on the opposite plane as the unit recalled.

Stacking

Up to nine units can be stacked together in a single square. For efficient movement, however, try to form stacks with similar movement limitations. For example, adding one normal walking unit to a stack of eight Draconians means that stack isn't flying anywhere—the most restricted unit in the stack determines the entire stack's movement limitations.

Therefore, try to add units with forest and mountain walk (or, better still, pathfinding) to normal walking stacks. These will greatly ease their stack's way through difficult terrain.

Be careful when a stack reaches the end of a long move. Often, some units have used all of their movement points while other, faster units, still have a some remaining. If you continue that stack's move that turn, the slower units will automatically be left behind.

The Genesis of Worlds in Master of Magic

Before the game begins, one of three land mass sizes is selected for the continents of both Arcanus and Myrror: small, medium, and large. Small land masses cover approximately 360 of the 2,400 squares (15 percent) of each map with land. Medium land masses will take up approximately 480 squares (20 percent) on each world, while large land masses will spread out over 720 squares (i.e., 30 percent) of each world's area.

Large Terrain Groupings

There is a limit of 10 rivers, 8 major desert regions, and 8 major swamp regions on each plane (but no limit on large forests or mountain ranges). Tundra can only appear within seven squares of a top or bottom map edge.

Special Terrain Feature Placement

After the basic land squares are created, they are individually examined on both worlds to see if a special terrain feature is added. Each desert, hill, mountain, forest, and swamp square on Arcanus has a 1 in 17 chance of receiving a special terrain feature. These same squares on Myrror have a 1 in 10 chance of bearing goodies. The chance of a particular type of special terrain feature appearing on that square is shown in Table 14.4.

Tower of Wizardry Placement

There are always six Towers of Wizardry on each world placed in corresponding squares. That is, a Tower of Wizardry found on the 10th row up from the bottom and 20 squares over from some vertical reference point on Arcanus, will be placed on the identical square on Myrror. This is why, often, Towers of Wizardry are found on their own one- or two-square islands. Usually their corresponding location on the other plane is on a larger land mass.

The computer tries to place Towers of Wizardry at least ten squares apart from each other (but doesn't always succeed). They are *always* at least four squares from the nearest node, however. Note that Towers of Wizardry are always located on grassland squares (which can be important if you build a city near them). This is because the computer automatically changes the terrain in the square they're placed on to grassland.

Node Placement

There are always 16 nodes on Arcanus and 14 on Myrror. The neighboring terrain often determines the color of the node being placed. Because of the predominance of water on both worlds, there tend to be more blue nodes than either green or red ones. Therefore, the maximum number of blue nodes generated is limited to nine on Arcanus and four on Myrror.

Note that node power (i.e., the number of squares covered by its aura and the per-turn mana income it generates) on Arcanus ranges from a random 5 to 10 at the normal setting. On Myrror, node auras are a random 10 to 20 at the normal setting. The per-turn mana income they generate is halved when playing with weak nodes and increased by 50 percent when playing with powerful ones.

Lair Placement

When the worlds are created, 25 *normal* lairs (e.g., ancient temples, ancient ruins, fallen temples, mysterious caves, dungeons, abandoned keeps, and monster lairs) and 32 *weak* lairs are randomly distributed between the two planes. For all the poop on lairs' garrisons and treasures, see Appendix C.

Wizard's Starting City Locations

Each wizard's Enchanted Fortress (i.e., starting) city has to be at least two squares away from the top and bottom map edges. The computer tries to start players at least 16 squares apart but will settle for as few as 10 squares apart if the geography simply won't work out. The computer prefers to start Enchanted Fortress cities at least eight squares from a node, but will settle for as little as one, if it has to. It also tries to place each player's starting city at least four squares from a tower or lair, but this could also be as low as one, if necessary.

Neutral City Placement

There are 15 (total, for both planes) random neutral cities placed each game. Every contiguous land mass has a *continental race* selected for it. Each city on that land mass has a 75 percent chance of being inhabited by that continental race. Thus, continents tend to have homogenous races upon them. Usually, neutral cities within 10 squares of each other will be connected by roads. See Appendix E for more details on neutral cities.

The Differences Between Arcanus and Myrror

Reflecting on Myrror, we see that it is distinct from Arcanus in several ways. Besides the differences in color of the land and seas, other important differences are:

- Five special races (Dark Elves, Beastmen, Draconians, Dwarves, and Trolls) populate Myrror.

- The nodes and lairs are tougher on Myrror (and the treasures are better).

- The nodes on Myrror have larger auras.

- There are better minerals on Myrror, in particular crysx and adamantium.

- Myrran roads are all enchanted, costing units no movement points to use them.

Remember to stake a claim on the rich world of Myrror. Whether you opt to spend three picks to start as a Myrran or rush to conquer a Tower of Wizardry, the best cities you can found and conquer are almost always located on Myrran real estate. Get thee to it.

From Here to Maternity

With that, we fold up the maps of Arcanus and Myrror and zoom in on the city displays. In the next chapter, we will examine the assets available to you, from population to spell research, and how to maximize them. We will show you that you don't have to be a great accountant to make a good account of yourself in *Master of Magic*. However, knowing what cooks the books is often a savory secret of success at the end of a hard won game.

15

The Ledger Domain

ntil the leaf is adopted as legal tender, money won't grow on trees. For that matter, neither will resources, spell research, mana, or any other measure of power in *Master of Magic*. In order to optimize your resource gathering, we present this chapter. Here, we'll cook the books and *account* for your prosperity. Through careful, managed growth and development of those economic engines known as cities, as well as of other sources, you will never need to rely on your Grand Vizier, and you will have your economy humming like a tuning fork by the time you finish this chapter.

Warning: This chapter should not be read; it should be referenced. The contents are about as digestible as a stale fruitcake on New Year's Day. This the kind of stuff that only an economist could love and is included in this book for completeness' sake *as a reference*, not a pleasant read. The most efficient way to use this chapter, therefore, is to scan the formulas, lists, and tables right now. The formulas list the factors (buildings, terrain, etc.) that affect gold, mana, production, etc. in a city. You don't need to understand or analyze the formulas to use the information they contain; just look for the things that you can use easily, for instance, the buildings and minerals that increase your gold supply, if gold is your biggest concern. Table 15.11, at the end of this chapter, summarizes all of the spells, events, and building effects that impact the economic state of your city, so be sure to take a long gander at that when you skim through this chapter for the first time.

Master of Economics

Building your empire through expansion and conquest of cities is a fundamental part of *Master of Magic*. Cities provide most of the means and resources you draw upon to build fighting forces and cast spells. Understanding the game's basic economic facets is essential to make the best use of your resources.

And when you're playing at the higher difficulty levels where computer players get tons of extra resources (see Chapter 28), you'll have to make every point really count!

The City Limits

Each city draws on 21 nearby land squares for food, minerals, and production bonuses. These squares are shown in the City screen as illustrated in Figure 15-1 and are known throughout this book as its *city limits*. While some squares (tundra and oceans) produce nothing, most provide food, production, or some combination of both. The individual terrain types are discussed, where appropriate, in the following sections. A complete terrain analysis is provided in Chapter 14.

The Division of Labor

As you know, the people in your towns are responsible for producing everything: gold, food, production points (PPs), mana, and spell research—all of which are necessary for building your empire. Not every population point (e.g., 1,000 residents) is employed equally: some are farmers, some are workers, while others are useless rebels.

Figure 15-1. *A city draws on the resources provided within its city limits. These are the unshaded land squares on the upper right corner of the City screen.*

Those Who Must Farm

In *Master of Magic*, the minimum number of farmers required to support a town's people is clustered on the left side of the Population row in the City screen. The farmers cannot be changed into workers. How to calculate the minimum number of farmers necessary to feed the town is described in the formula box on this page.

The number of farmers required to support the local populace can be determined from three factors: city population, the amount of food produced by both buildings and wild game, and how much food each farmer can harvest. Because each citizen eats one food per turn, an amount of food at least equal to the city's population *must* be produced, or starvation ensues.

Farmers Versus Workers

Beyond the required number of farmers, all non-rebels can either be workers or farmers. Workers generate production points (PPs) which are necessary for building city structures and units. Workers also increase the yield when cities produce trade goods or housing. Farmers do contribute slightly to the production points of a city but are primarily used to make the extra food required to support troops.

Global Food Concerns (That Won't End World Hunger)

The proportion of farmers and workers should be viewed in two ways: on a per city basis and on a global basis. The global concern is the total number of farmers you need to maintain a positive net food production (as shown on the right side of the Main Movement screen). You must have enough food to support your troops *plus* a buffer in case one of your cities is conquered by an enemy that turn. Lack of a buffer could mean that you'll lose troops! (You won't get an opportunity to disband troops or readjust your food supply when your food supply drops drastically from the loss of a city; instead, the game automatically disbands your most recently acquired troops first.)

Formula for Minimum Farmers Required to Feed a City

Minimum Farmers = (City Population - Free Food) / Farming Rate

City Population = Number of population points in that city.

Free Food = +2 if the city has a granary; +2 if it has a forester's guild; and +3 if it has a farmer's market. These are cumulative (so the maximum would be seven if a city had all three of these buildings). More free food will be added if the city has wild game resources, at a rate of +2 for each unshared wild game and +1 for each wild game resource that is being shared with another city.

Farming Rate = Three for a Halfling city; three if the city has an animist's guild; or two in all other cases.

For example, say you have a completely built up city of 20,000 Orcs (i.e., 20 population point's worth). A total of 20 food units are required to support them. Subtract 7 food from this amount for the city's granary, forester's guild, and farmer's market, leaving 13 food that must be produced by local farmers. Each Orc farmer can, in this case, harvest 3 food (because the city also has an animist's guild). Dividing 13 by 3 gives 4.33. Rounding this number up gives the minimum number of farmers needed to support the local populace, which is 5.

Local Food Concerns

On a per city basis, the number of farmers and workers should be adjusted so that, *after* considering the global situation, you can optimize the rate at which buildings, troops, housing, or trade goods are produced. For example, you may want to accelerate production of a particular building or unit at a city. Converting as many of your people there into workers as possible will ensure the speediest production (short of buying it).

Such adjustments might require you to convert extra workers in other cities into farmers to maintain a positive net food supply. Similarly, making the most of trade goods and housing settings at a city requires maximizing the number of workers there.

Optimizing Needed Food and Resource Production

You do not necessarily need to convert *all* of your extra citizens to workers to produce a building or unit as quickly as possible. Here, you should experiment a little. You may find that having one or two fewer workers lets you produce the desired item *in the same amount of time*. Thus, you waste fewer resources from *overspending* to build that item. (It's not like those overspent resources are converted to gold or applied to your next construction project; they're simply lost.)

Economizing with your workers in this way can give a city extra farmers who are not needed as workers to produce the item being built there. This will decrease the need to readjust the farmer/worker ratios in other cities. It will also provide extra food, which gets converted into gold income (see later section).

With Production (and Humor), Timing Is Everything

On occasion, you may even *want* to slow down production of units or buildings! For example, you may have a city that is devoted to producing Dark Elf nightmare units. Each night-mare produced is expensive to maintain. Therefore, you may want to moderate the rate at which you make these units so that your overall economic situation can grow to meet the gold and food demands of your expanding army.

Let Them Eat Gold

There may also be times (when money is tight) that you wish to produce a slight excess of food. This is because surplus food gets converted to gold. For every two food produced in your global surplus, one gold is added to that turn's income. This surplus may mean the difference between running at a deficit and not.

At the end of a game turn, the ability to adjust the number of farmers and workers in different cities is a powerful tool. Certainly it is one of the best for fine tuning the economic well-being of your empire.

Rebels

Rebels are the non-productive members of society. Living well on State welfare, they consume food like other population points do, yet they produce neither gold nor production points in return. Rebels are generated primarily by two things: taxes and resentment between races.

Rebels and Taxation

The tax rate, which is set at one gold per person at the beginning of each game, makes one out of every five population points a rebel. Higher tax rates result in more rebels, while lower rates decrease their numbers. Table 15.1 shows how, as a city increases in population, new rebels will be created based on the prevailing tax rate. (The no gold per person rate is excluded from this table since it is impractical to produce no gold.)

Table 15.1 *Number of Rebels Caused by Taxation*

Population	0.5 Gold 10% Unrest	1.0 Gold 20% Unrest	1.5 Gold 30% Unrest	2.0 Gold 45% Unrest	2.5 Gold 60% Unrest	3.0 Gold 75% Unrest
1	0	0	0	0	0	0
2	0	0	0	0	1	1
3	0	0	0	1	1	2
4	0	0	1	1	2	3
5	0	1	1	2	3	3
6	0	1	1	2	3	4
7	0	1	2	3	4	5
8	0	1	2	3	4	6
9	0	1	2	4	5	6
10	1	2	3	4	6	7
11	1	2	3	4	6	8
12	1	2	3	5	7	9
13	1	2	3	5	7	9
14	1	2	4	6	8	10
15	1	3	4	6	9	11
16	1	3	4	7	9	12
17	1	3	5	7	10	12
18	1	3	5	8	10	13
19	1	3	5	8	11	14
20	2	4	6	9	12	15
21	2	4	6	9	12	15
22	2	4	6	9	13	16
23	2	4	6	10	13	17
24	2	4	7	10	14	18
25	2	5	7	11	15	18

Rebels and Conquest

The other primary rebel rouser is a city's racial tension. The race of the city where your Enchanted Fortress resides is viewed as your primary race. Any city you conquer that is inhabited by a different race may experience racial unrest due to the races' innate mistrust or hatred of each other.

Basically, conquering another city generates an *automatic percentage of rebels* ranging from 0 to 40 percent. (These rebels are added to any generated through taxation.) This number is always zero if the inhabiting race is the same as the conquering race.

The exact amount of unrest created by conquering a different race's city depends on both your primary race and the conquered race. Table 15.2 shows the automatic percentage of rebels created under each possible condition.

Rebels Added Through Malevolent Means

Besides taxation and racial tension, a number of spells and random events can directly generate extra rebels (these are listed in Table 15.11 at the end of the chapter).

To compound matters, many spells and events can *indirectly* increase the number of rebels in a city. This occurs when such spells destroy garrisoned troops and religious build-

Table 15.2 *Automatic Unrest Levels From Interracial Tension*

Interracial rebel increase = value (below) x 10% of the city's population.

Conquering Race	Half	Nomad	HiMen	Gnoll	Barb	Orcs	Lizard	Beast	Drac	Troll	H-Elf	Dwarf	Klack	Dk-Elf	Total
Half	0	0	0	0	1	0	0	1	1	0	0	0	2	2	7
Nomad	0	0	0	1	0	0	1	1	1	1	0	0	2	2	9
HiMen	0	0	0	1	1	0	1	1	1	1	0	0	2	2	10
Gnoll	0	1	1	0	1	0	1	0	1	0	1	1	2	2	11
Barb	1	0	1	1	0	0	1	1	1	1	1	1	2	1	12
Orcs	0	0	0	0	0	0	1	1	1	0	3	3	2	2	13
Lizard	0	1	1	1	1	1	0	1	1	1	1	1	2	2	14
Beast	1	1	1	0	1	1	1	0	2	2	2	2	2	2	18
Drac	1	1	1	1	1	1	1	2	0	2	1	2	2	2	18
Troll	0	1	1	0	1	0	1	2	2	0	3	4	2	3	20
H-Elf	0	0	0	1	1	3	1	2	1	3	0	3	2	4	21
Dwarf	0	0	0	1	1	3	1	2	2	4	3	0	2	3	22
Klack	2	2	2	2	2	2	2	2	2	2	2	2	0	2	26
Dk Elf	2	2	2	2	1	2	2	2	2	3	4	3	2	0	29
Total	7	9	10	11	12	13	14	18	18	20	21	22	26	29	

This table lists the races from the best loved (the Halflings) to the most despised (the Dark Elves). This was based on the total number of rebels they generate when conquering or being conquered by all other races. Notice that, except for Klackons and High Elves, all of the unfriendliest races are Myrran (something to consider when choosing your starting race).

Racial tension is a constant between two races. Regardless of which is the conquering race, the two races will always generate the same absolute unrest level. Remember, the numbers shown are multiplied by 10 percent to determine the added percentage of rebels in conquered cities. So a tension level of four will cause an additional 40 percent of a city's population to rebel.

ings, thus eliminating their calming effects on a city (see Table 15.11).

Calm Down, You Wascally Webels!

The actual unrest level in a city depends not only on the factors that increase the number of rebels, but also on the factors that *decrease* them. Some buildings exert pacifying effects on the local population. Religious institutions—shrines, temples, parthenons, and cathedrals—all decrease the unrest level by one rebel, as do animist's guilds. The presence of an oracle in the city will decrease its unrest level by two rebels.

Soldiers, too, will keep the disgruntled populace quiet. Non-fantastic (i.e., non-summoned) units in a city will decrease the number of rebels by one per two units. Because a city's garrison may hold up to nine units, a maximum of four rebels can be calmed by a full garrison of eight or nine normal units. (Note, fantastic units won't calm the populace, as their presence is unsettling and cowing in equal parts.)

The wizard skills Infernal Power and Divine Power increase the effectiveness of all *religious buildings*, raising the number of rebels they calm by 50 percent. (i.e., the existence of both a shrine and temple in a city will calm three rebels instead of two, while all religious buildings will calm six rebels instead of four). See Chapter 4 for tips on selecting these wizard skills.

There are also spells that decrease the number of rebels in cities. They are summarized in Table 15.11 at the end of the chapter.

Finally, the green city enchantment Move Fortress deserves some attention. By using it to move your Enchanted Fortress to a new city with a different race, you can alter the unrest levels in many or all of your cities! Table 15.2 shows what races will produce less rebellion in your empire if your Enchanted Fortress is placed in one of their cities. For example, you almost always want to move your Enchanted Fortress from a Dark Elf or Klackon city to one occupied by Halflings or Nomads, just to ease racial tensions.

Netting a Few Rebels

Use the following formula to determine the number of rebels in any city. Spell effects are not included in this equation.

Formula For Number of Rebels in a Given City

Taxation (see Table 15.1)

+ Racial Unrest (see Table 15.2)

-1 for each religious institution (shrine, temple, parthenon, and cathedral)

-1 for an animist's guild

-2 for an oracle

-1 for every two non-fantastic units in that city

= Total number of rebels in city*

*Excluding the effects of any wizard skills or city enchantments

Racial Limitations on Rebel Suppression

It is important to note that some structures cannot be built by certain races. For example, the Klackons cannot build temples and, thus, cannot build parthenons, cathedrals, animist's guilds, or oracles either, as they are all linked! Therefore, the Klackons can only build shrines or normal unit garrisons to help them limit their urban unrest levels. Fortunately for the Klackons, they have a *hive mentality*. When Klackons inhabit a player's Enchanted Fortress city, all Klackon cities owned by that wizard have their unrest level reduced by 2.

Basically, then, each race has its own limited ability to deal with rebels. This ability is the fixed number of rebels that can be quelled via garrisons (up to four) and the inherent building limitations of that race. Table 15.3 summarizes this information, showing how many rebels each race can pacify through building and garrison construction.

Table 15.3 clearly illustrates that some races are intrinsically better able to handle rebels than others. This table is based on each race's ability to reduce unrest with a full city garrison, having erected all unrest-quelling buildings they can.

Taxing Rebels' Racial Variables

Table 15.4, below, combines the information in Table 15.3 with the different races' abilities to handle unrest levels at the two most common taxation levels. The information it presents is based upon a fully built-up city, having a population of 25, with a column for two different tax rates: one gold per person and one and one-half gold per person.

The potential unrest level in a race's city depends on whether it is the primary race for its owner or a conquered race. The range of potential unrest for a given race is indicated at both tax rates and is determined by the extent to which that particular race gets along with other races.

Table 15.3 *Racial Rebel Suppression Maximums*

Race	Unrest Reduced by Buildings	Total Unrest Reduced with a Full Garrison Included*
Beastmen	7	11
Draconians	7	11
High Men	7	11
Nomads	7	11
Orcs	7	11
Dark Elves	6	10
Trolls	5	9
Halflings	4	8
Barbarian	3	7
High Elves	3	7
Dwarves	2	6
Gnolls	2	6
Lizardmen	2	6
Klackons	1 (3**)	5 (7**)

*The maximum amount of unrest, in terms of number of rebels, that can be decreased using all available city buildings and a garrison size of eight or nine normal units (including heroes).

**If a player's Enchanted Fortress city is occupied by Klackons, the number of rebels in each of that player's Klackon cities is reduced by two.

For example, Dark Elves automatically generate a 40 percent level of rebellion if they have conquered or been conquered by High Elves. So, at a tax rate of one gold per person, a 25-person city of Dark Elves will minimally generate five rebels (due to the 20 percent rebel production at this tax rate; see Table 15.1). If this Dark Elf city has been conquered by High Elves, that number is increased by 40 percent of the total population due to interracial tensions (see Table 15.2); so, there would be 15 rebels in this city (ouch!).

In addition to providing the range of potential unrest for each race's cities, Table 15.4 shows how many rebels per city can be pacified by that race (assuming all buildings have been constructed and the city's garrison is full, as shown in Table 15.3). Taking the difference between the potential number of rebels in the city and the number that can be pacified, the net expected unrest levels in fully built cities for each race are shown.

The lesson demonstrated in Table 15.4 is that some races are ill-equipped to deal with high rates of internal rebellion. Dwarves, Dark Elves, Klackons, High Elves, Lizardmen, Trolls, and Gnolls are particularly poor at handling excessive unrest. Barbarians, Halflings, and Orcs may find their abilities to deal with unrest strained at higher tax rates.

Table 15.4 *Race-Dependent Rebels Produced at Different Tax Rates*

Note: City size = 25 population (the maximum)

Race	The 20% (1 gold/person) Tax Rate Rebel Range*	Less the Maximum # of Rebels Calmed (Table 15.3)	Equals the Net Unrest Level in Rebels**	The 30% (1.5 gold/person) Tax Rate Rebel Range*	Less the Maximum # of Rebels Calmed (Table 15.3)	Equals the Net Unrest Level in Rebels**
Barbarians	5-10	7	0-3	7-12	7	0-5
Beastmen	5-10	11	0	7-12	11	0-1
Dark Elves	5-15	10	0-5	7-17	10	0-7
Draconians	5-10	11	0	7-12	11	0-1
Dwarves	5-15	6	0-9	7-17	6	1-11
Gnolls	5-10	6	0-4	7-12	6	1-6
Halflings	5-10	8	0-2	7-12	8	0-4
High Elves	5-15	7	0-8	7-17	7	0-10
High Men	5-10	11	0	7-12	11	0-1
Klackons	5-10	5	0-5	7-12	5	2-7
Lizardmen	5-10	6	0-4	7-12	6	1-6
Nomads	5-10	11	0	7-12	11	0-1
Orcs	5-12	11	0-1	7-15	11	0-4
Trolls	5-15	9	0-6	7-17	9	0-8

*Based on a city population of 25 (the maximum city size). The minimum number of rebels produced is five at a 20 percent tax rate or seven at a 30 percent tax rate. The higher number indicates the potential range based on interracial tensions when this race is conquered by others (see Table 15.2).

**The net unrest level is a range of numbers based on racial tensions. Remember, for Klackon cities, if that player's primary race is Klackon, there is an automatic reduction of two rebels.

The rest of the races, either through the ability to construct most of the rebellion-suppressing buildings or because of their peaceful natures, will generally be able to handle most of the rebels their cities can produce.

Rebel Reality

The important thing to note in this section is that a race's *ultimate* ability to squelch unrest has little to do with practical game play. Seldom is a city's economy fully optimized. Instead, cities are more often found in various stages of development. It is how you deal with rebels during a city's development that really matters.

Consider that many of the buildings that suppress rebels either are end-stage structures (requiring many prerequisite buildings) or are time-consuming to build themselves. They are usually expensive (both to build and maintain) and, sometimes, they exert few benefits beyond rebel pacification.

Also consider that supporting a normal unit garrison of eight or nine units in a city is impractical. Unrest levels, particularly in conquered cities, may be high for long periods of time until that city can build the shrines, temples, or other buildings it needs (or until your economy can support the more rapid construction of buildings and garrisons necessary to decrease their rebel population).

Finally, no matter what the rebel population *should be*, a city always maintains the minimum number of farmers required to support its people (unless there's a famine, of course). These subsistence farmers will *never* rebel. This also means that a city can have a *rebel debt*.

For example, your tax rate is set to 30 percent and your Enchanted Fortress is in a Troll city. You then conquer a Dwarven town. Thus, you generate 40 percent more rebels (in addition to the 30 percent from taxes) among the Dwarves (see Table 15.2). Because it's a hamlet with only three Dwarven population points, two of them automatically produce food to provide subsistence level food for the city. Therefore, only one rebel will appear when you conquer this berg, instead of the two rebels you should get from 70 percent of the three population points rebelling. When the population grows to four population points, a second rebel will be born because the city still only needs two farmers to make the four required food units (and that city is still "owed" a rebel). Every time a new Dwarf comes into being in that town, it will be turned into a subsistence farmer if more food is necessary to keep the citizens alive or it will be turned into a rebel until its rebel debt from taxation and interracial unrest is paid in full (through additional rebels or their suppression). Depending on the tax rate, there may be many more rebels to create before a new Dwarf will appear as a worker.

Note: If a city is garrisoned with at least two normal units, the *first* rebel it produces *will* be pacified and turned into a worker. It will *not* be turned into a rebel even if more are "owed."

Population Growth

The key economic factor in *Master of Magic* is the population size of cities. The more people you have, the more units you can support and the more valuable items you can produce. The maximum population of a city at a given site depends on the quantity of food the surrounding lands can produce and the race building a city. The Surveyor (F1 key) states how many people the land around that site can support (rounding one-half food up to the next highest whole population point). Certain buildings, namely the granary and farmer's market are accessible to almost all races and will increase the maximum number of people that can live in a city.

Determining a City's Maximum Size

Regardless of the surrounding terrain, the maximum population limit for a city is 25

Formula for City Maximum Size

   2.0 times the number of wild game specials

+ 2.0 times the number of river squares

+ 2.0 times the number of Sorcery nodes

+ 2.0 times the number of Nature nodes

+ 1.5 times the number of grassland squares

+ 0.5 times the number of hill squares

+ 0.5 times the number of swamp squares

+ 0.5 times the number of shore squares

+ 0.5 times the number of forest squares (even ones with wild game)

+ 2.0 if the city has a granary

+ 3.0 if the city has a farmer's market

= City Maximum Size (rounding up)*

*Actual population of a city, however, cannot exceed 25.

Note that the food contributions from nodes are incorrectly shown by the Surveyor button.

population points (i.e., 25,000 citizens). The following equation (in formula box) for the maximum population for a particular city at any given time is based on the squares within its *city limits* and any supporting buildings it has:

The Surveyor's information is always current when you query it about a site. For an undeveloped site, its calculations will not include any potential buildings. In addition, the Surveyor assumes the worst case for wild game squares that are two spaces away from the potential city site (therefore, it calculates their food value as one instead of two, as if those squares will be shared with another city).

Squares shared with another city only contribute half of their resources to each. Once built at a city, modifications to its maximum size for having a granary and farmer's market become included in the Surveyor's calculations. Note that oceans, mountains, Chaos nodes, tundra, volcanoes, deserts, and corrupted lands produce no food. They contribute nothing to a city's maximum size.

Magic Effects on a City's Maximum Size

The maximum size of a city, then, is dictated by the amount of food that can be produced in it and on the lands surrounding it. The only other things that can influence a city's maximum size are spells or events that either change the total food production of the available lands or alter the land itself. These are all listed in Table 15.11 at the end of the chapter. In all cases, a city's population, regardless of terrain, buildings, or spells, can never exceed 25 population points.

The Population Growth Rate

The rate at which a city grows is based upon its maximum city size, as previously explained, and is increased by the presence of a granary and farmer's market. Not all races grow at the

Table 15.5 *Racial Growth Rate Modifiers*

Race	Growth Rate Modifier
Barbarians	+20
Lizardmen	+10
Beastmen	none
Halflings	none
High Men	none
Orcs	none
Draconians	-10
Gnolls	-10
Klackons	-10
Nomads	-10
Dark Elves	-20
Dwarves	-20
High Elves	-20
Trolls	-20

The number is that race's inherent increase (or decrease) in population growth per city per turn

same speed. Table 15.5 shows how the races differ in their rate of population growth.

Besides depending on its maximum potential size, a city's growth rate also depends on whether its citizens are producing housing. The following equation summarizes the factors relevant for determining the population growth rate of a city:

As a consequence of the above formula, the population growth rate will be some multiple of 10 (with every 10 points equivalent to one percent of a citizen, such as a worker or farmer population point). This is the number of people (and we use the term loosely) that the city grows by every turn. Each citizen in a city's Population row (i.e., population point) represents 1,000 such people.

In effect, a growth rate of 100 means that in 10 turns, the city size will increase by one citizen (100 people x 10 = 1,000 people = 1

Formula for City Growth Rate

Base Growth Rate = (City Maximum Size - Current Size + 1) / 2 (rounding up)*

(Base Growth Rate x 10)
+ 20 if granary
+ 30 if farmer's market
+ Racial Growth Modifier (see Table 15.5)
+ Housing Bonus (see below)

= **Population Growth** (in numbers of citizens, rounded down to the nearest multiplier of 10)

*You can also think of this variable as that city's *room for growth*. For example, a city with a maximum size of 22 (based on surrounding terrain and buildings) that already has 12 population points would have a Base Growth Rate of: (22 - 12 +1) / 2 = 4.5, rounded up to 5.

Note, the Death spell Dark Rituals reduces a city's final population growth by 25 percent.

Formula for Housing Bonus

Workers / Population
+ .10 if sawmill
+ .15 if builder's hall

Total of above factors x **Population Growth Rate** = **Housing Bonus**

Workers = the total number of population points in that city that are workers
Population = the total number of population points in that city (including workers, farmers, and rebels)
Population Growth Rate = as determined in the preceding formula
Housing Bonus = the number added to the Population Growth Rate, rounded down to the nearest 10.

Note that the Housing Bonus is *always* 50 percent for a city with only one population point.

For example, a city with 13 population points has 8 workers and is currently growing at a rate of 40 people per turn. When its production is set to housing, in addition to those 40 people per turn for its Population Growth Rate, a housing bonus of +20 would be added. The math works out like this: (8 / 13) x 40, or 24.6, rounded down to the nearest 10, which makes the result 20.

population point). If the growth rate is 200, it takes five turns to gain another population point, etc. Every time another 1,000 people have been added to the city, another character (farmer, worker, or rebel) appears in the Population row of the City screen.

Making More Babies

Beyond the aforementioned construction of a granary, or farmer's market, there are ways by which a city's population growth rate may be increased. Specifically, they are:

☙ Cast the Nature spell Change Terrain, so that the squares around a city are converted to more fertile types of land. This will increase both the city maximum size and the population growth rate of the city.

☙ Stream of Life is a white spell that doubles the target city's population growth rate. Note that the Population Boom event does the same thing.

🕯 If you set your city's production to *housing*, additional tens of people will be added to the city's population growth rate according to the following formula box on page 196.

The Population Death Rate

When a city can't feed all of its population points (sudden land corruption, the Death spell Famine, or if the ending of a Gaia's Blessing spell has left more people in that city than its food production can support), instead of a growth rate it has a *death rate*. For every unit of food the city is short of producing, the death rate rises by -50 people per turn. (Negative food is shown on the City screen as black bread.) As the population drops to below whole 1,000s, another population point disappears.

When a city is under the effects of a Pestilence spell, a full population point might die every turn if the city's present population is *greater than* the result of a d10 (see Chapter 9).

Feeding the Masses

Speaking of food, know that it has three important uses:

1. Supporting a city's population points.
2. Supporting your empire's normal units.
3. Earning extra gold from the sale of surplus food (players gain one gold for every two surplus food produced that turn).

The computer always sets aside the minimum number of farmers required to feed a particular city. They are automatically separated from the rest of its population as indicated by their placement to the left of a break in the city's Population row. You, however, are responsible for ensuring that there are enough

Table 15.6 *Food Harvesting by Races*

No Animist's Guilds Always 2 Food/Farmer	Animist's Guilds *Eventually Harvest* 3 Food/Farmer	No Animist's Guilds *But Innate* 3 Food/Farmer
Barbarians	Beastmen	Halflings
Dwarves	Dark Elves	
Gnolls	Draconians	
Klackons	High Elves	
Lizardmen	High Men	
	Nomads	
	Orcs	
	Trolls	

farmers to produce the additional food necessary to feed your troops.

Food comes from the lands surrounding a city and from special structures built at that city, specifically: a granary, farmer's market, and forester's guild. The total food that can be produced on the basis of a city's lands and buildings directly determines the maximum population that the city can hold (see the City Maximum Size equation in earlier section).

By Bread Alone: The Food Harvesting Rate

While the amount of food that a city site can produce to support its citizens may be constant, the rate at which the food can be harvested will vary based on the city's race and development. Most ordinary farmers can only harvest two food each per game turn. Only Halflings can harvest more. Each Halfling farmer harvests three food per game turn.

Several races can eventually increase the efficiency of their farmers by building animist's guilds. These allow the city's farmers to harvest three food each per turn. Table 15.6 summarizes which races can build animist's guilds and harvest at the rate of three food per farmer per turn.

The rate at which a city's farmers harvest food can affect the city's production rate. The fewer the citizens that have to be devoted to farming, the more that are left to serve as workers and increase the city's production point output. The capability to free farmers for other forms of productive labor is part of what makes building a granary, farmer's market, and forester's guild so valuable. These buildings not only increase the city's maximum size by allowing it to support more people, they also produce food for free (i.e., without requiring any farmers).

The Failure of Agribusiness: Diminishing Harvest Returns

Once a city is producing an amount of food equal to that required to support its maximum population (whether it has grown to its maximum population level or not), any surplus farming in that city yields only *half* the food that it ordinarily would (rounding down any odd unit of food). At this point, according to designer Steve Barcia, "the land is being *overworked* and the farmers [at that city] have reached a point of diminishing returns."

For example, a city can support only 10 Halflings. (Hey, it was built on a crummy site.) If five of the Halflings are farmers, with each producing three food, the city does *not* produce 15 food. Instead, it produces only 12 because the five surplus food production beyond that needed to feed the city' maximum population of 10 gets halved and rounded down.

Production Points (PPs)

The worker and, to a lesser degree, farmer population points generate the production points (symbolized by pick and shovel icons and abbreviated here as "PPs") necessary to construct buildings, troops, trade goods, and housing at a city. The total production points of a city is modified by the city's buildings and surrounding terrain.

The base production generated by a city depends on its division of labor. Rebels, of course, produce nothing. All farmers generate half a production point per turn. Except

---

Formula for The Production Point

Base Production Points (BP) =
(Number of Workers x 2*) + (Number of Farmers / 2, rounded up)

*Three for Klackons and Dwarves

---

for Dwarves and Klackons, the workers from all races generate two production points per turn; Dwarven and Klackon workers contribute three. See formula box above for the equation summarizing the contributions to base production.

Raising Your PP (Enhancing Production Point Output)

Sawmills, forester's guilds, miner's guilds, and mechanician's guilds increase a city's PPs. Various terrain types do so, as well. All of these PP modifiers are added together before their cumulative effects are applied on the Base Production Points, described in the preceding formula. This means that the modifiers *don't* multiply each other like compound interest, but, in a sense, multiply themselves independently by the Base Production (BP) a city generates (which is true for most of the income enhancement equations in *Master of Magic*, by the way).

The equation on page 199 describes how the total production for a city is calculated.

Klackons, Dig: An Analysis of Productivity by Race

To sum up, the PPs a city generates depend upon the number of workers (and, to a lesser extent, farmers) in it, types of buildings supporting increased production, and that city's race. It is important to consider that some races must devote a greater proportion of their citizens to farming than others because they

Formula for Total Production Points Generated in a City

Base Production (BP), as explained in the previous formula
+ BP x the sum of the following:

	.25 if the city has a sawmill
+	.25 if the city has a forester's guild
+	.5 if the city has a miner's guild
+	.5 if the city has a mechanician's guild
+	the sum of all the city's terrain production bonuses*
=	Total PPs generated in that city

*Terrain Production Bonus:

	.03 x the number of hill squares within the *city limits***
+	.03 x the number of forest squares within the city limits
+	.03 x the number of desert squares within the city limits
+	.03 x the number of Nature nodes within the city limits
+	.05 x the number of mountain squares within the city limits
+	.05 x the number of Chaos nodes within the city limits
=	Total Terrain Production Bonus

***City limits** are those surrounding squares that a city uses to support its local economy (see Figure 15-1).

Note that after the Total Production Points are calculated, the final value is truncated (i.e., any fraction is dropped, so the value is rounded down to the nearest whole number).

For example, a city with a Base Production of seven only has a sawmill contributing to its productivity. That sawmill will only add one PP to the total! This is because 25 percent of 7 is 1.75 which, when truncated, is rounded all the way down to one.

cannot build animist's guilds to increase their food harvesting rates.

Other races cannot construct one or more of the building types that provide production bonuses. Since both the harvesting rate and the production bonuses generated from buildings have a significant impact on the productivity of different races, we have analyzed them here. Table 15.7 provides our view of the relative productivity of *Master of Magic*'s different races.

Magic Effects on Production Points

A city's production level can be affected directly or indirectly by spells and random events. Indirect effects on productivity are exerted by:

- Spells that lower or increase the population size of a city.
- Spells that can destroy the buildings that increase city productivity.
- Spells that can destroy troops in city garrisons can increase the rebel population, decreasing production levels.
- Spells that change the number of rebels can increase or decrease the number of workers in a city.
- Spells that alter terrain can increase or decrease the productivity bonuses from the lands surrounding the city.

Table 15.11 at the end of the chapter lists all the spells and random events that can directly or indirectly alter productivity in a city.

Throwing Money at the Problem: Using Gold to Supplement Production

Productivity levels alone do not determine how quickly a city can build something. *Master of Magic*'s "Golden Rule" is: If you have the gold, you can always opt to speed up your produc-

Table 15.7 *Relative Productivity of Each Race*

Excellent	Good	Passable	Poor	Embarrassing
Beastmen	Dwarves	Barbarians	Trolls	Lizardmen
Dark Elves	Draconians	Gnolls		
High Elves	Halflings			
High Men				
Klackons				
Nomads				
Orcs				

(column header: **Relative Productivity Level***)

*The relative productivity is based on all races having cities:

1. of equal size;

2. with the minimum number of farmers required to feed that city (and, hence, the maximum number of workers available);

3. that have built all the relevant production enhancing buildings available to that race (i.e., sawmill, forester's guild, miner's guild, mechanician's guild, and animist's guild).

Note that the least productive race is the Lizardmen. They can't build sawmills, forester's guilds, miner's guilds, mechanician's guilds, or animist's guilds. Ack!

tion by simply buying the building or unit you want.

The cost of buying something instead of building it depends on how many production points have already gone into making a given building or unit. If you try to buy something from scratch, it costs considerably more gold per unspent PP for that item than if you had already accumulated PPs for its purchase. Specifically, buying something from scratch (with no PPs currently invested in its purchase), costs four gold times that item's PP cost. A unit that would normally cost 60 PPs would cost you 240 gold if you ordered it now for delivery next turn.

This premium on the gold required to complete an item drops the closer the item gets to completion via normal production means (i.e., as PPs are invested in its purchase over time). Specifically, if more than none and less than half of the item's PP cost is already invested in its purchase, it will cost three gold per re-

maining PP to buy the item. If half or more of the item's PP cost is already invested, the premium on gold is only two per PP cost remaining for that item. The moral? It's cheaper not to rush things; even investing one turn's worth of production before purchasing an item can save you a fortune in gold.

For example, the same 60 PP item that, bought from scratch, would cost you 240 gold, would be much cheaper if you waited even *one* turn before purchasing it. Let's say the city only generated a *single* PP toward its purchase. The price in gold for its purchase drops from 240 to 177 (59 is the amount of PPs required to complete the item, times three, the gold premium multiplier when the item is more than none and less than half paid off by PPs). A considerable saving of gold for a single turn's wait!

Discount Purchases from Minerals

Some cities can produce troops (*not* buildings!) at a discount because of their proximity to coal and iron deposits. These mines decrease the production costs of most normal units by five percent and 10 percent, respectively, increasing the rate at which units can be built. Miner's guilds increase bonuses from these deposits by 50 percent, and Dwarves get double the production bonuses from all special deposits, including coal and iron. Better still, these deposits can exert cumulative effects, allowing a maximum discount of 50 percent for the building of new units.

Hint: Build cities near multiple coal and iron deposits whenever possible and make them your *soldier factories*. When they have enough heavy metal playing in their background, these cities can crank out new units like they're going out of style.

Mana

Magic power, or *mana*, is your wizard's life blood and puts the "Magic" in *Master of Magic*. Used to cast spells that summon powerful creatures, enhance your troops and cities, or harm your enemies, mana is an indispensable tool for winning this game. Mana alone can even win the game through casting the Spell of Mastery (although you will still need some troops to defend your empire throughout play).

The Game Set-Up "Magic" Button

Whenever you start a game, you can define its *magic setting*. This magic setting governs the strength of magic nodes (i.e., the amount of mana they produce). Stronger nodes (at the powerful setting) are occupied by more dangerous creatures, but yield 50 percent more mana. At the weak setting, magic nodes will be occupied by relatively easier monsters and will yield 50 percent less mana to a control-

ling wizard. The magic setting, then, determines the premium placed on occupying magic nodes for that particular game. The relative importance of city sources of mana (buildings, certain race's population points, and mineral deposits) will change in opposition to the strength of that game's magic nodes.

Mana is not only used to cast spells; it also contributes to the speed at which the wizard's spell-casting skill improves, determines how quickly a wizard's researching efforts progress, and can be converted into gold through alchemy.

Mana From Heaven: Income Sources

Mana comes from urban sources, including the population points of magical races and a city's special mineral deposits and religious buildings, in addition to magic nodes. There is almost nothing that affects all sources of mana, save for a devastating event called Mana Short (see Chapter 26).

Urban Sources of Mana

Your urban mana production is going to depend on some of the earliest decisions you make in the game: the skills your wizard picks and the race you choose to lead. Afterward, your ongoing urban development scheme and choices for new city sites will profoundly influence your urban mana production. The formula for total mana production from a city is shown on page 202.

If you choose Myrran as a wizard skill at the beginning of the game, your initial city (and Enchanted Fortress, therefore) will be situated on Myrror. Note the additional five mana production in the formula for an Enchanted Fortress located on Myrror.

A Myrran may also select from among *all* the player races to start the game, including many special races that are of a magical nature. These races, as listed in the formula box below, contribute a set amount of magic per

Formula for City Mana Production

+ 1 per spell rank chosen at the beginning of the game for your Enchanted Fortress
+ 5 if your Enchanted Fortress is on Myrror
+ 1 per Dark Elf population point
+ 1/2 per Beastman, Draconian, or High Elf population point (rounded down, per city)
+ 1 per shrine*
+ 2 per temple*
+ 3 per parthenon*
+ 4 per cathedral*
+ 3 per alchemist's guild
- 3 per wizard's guild**
+ 5 per crysx crystal deposit
+ 3 per quork deposit
+ 2 per adamantium deposit***
+ 1 per mithril deposit***
= City Mana Production

*To build up to a cathedral, a city must have built a shrine, temple, and parthenon first. Between all of these four *religious institutions*, therefore, a city would receive +10 mana per turn (roughly the average strength of a node).

**Although a wizard's guild costs three mana and five gold to maintain, it gives eight research points and is, therefore, worth building in most cases.

***Dwarves get double the mana from adamantium, mithril, crysx, and quork deposits.

Note that the presence of a miner's guild will increase the mana production from special deposits by 50 percent.

population point every game turn. The only Arcanian race with this magical property is the High Elves.

They Think They're Magic: A Comparison of Urban Mana Production by Race

Besides inherent magic production, you will have noticed that races also differ in their abilities to build the institutions that provide mana. Based on the mana-generating buildings available to each race, as well as their inherent mana production capabilities, Table 15.8 ranks all races in terms their ability to generate urban mana in support of a wizard's cause.

Mo' Mana, Please: Urban Mana Production Enhancements

A city's race also has an indirect effect on mana production in that some races can build miner's guilds. These provide a 50 percent bonus on any special mineral deposits, including those producing magic power. The only races that cannot take advantage of this are the Lizardmen and Trolls.

The amount of a city's mana production is also affected by whether your wizard has Divine Power or Infernal Power as a skill. These skills increase the *total* mana production from religious institutions (i.e., shrines, temples, parthenons, and cathedrals) in a wizard's cities by 50 percent. Note that the Death spell Dark Rituals doubles the mana production from these buildings. A combination of Dark Rituals and Infernal Power will *triple* the mana production from a city's religious buildings.

Magic and Urban Mana Production

Many spells and random events can directly or indirectly affect the amount of mana produced by your cities. Indirect changes in mana production occur when terrain squares with mineral deposits are altered; when buildings that generate mana are destroyed; and when magic-producing denizens of a city are killed.

Table 15.8 *Relative City Mana Production of Each Race*

Relative City Mana Productivity Level*			
Excellent	**Good**	**Not So Good**	**Execrable**
(19 to 22 mana/turn)	*(9 to 13 mana/turn)*	*(exactly 6 mana/turn)*	*(1 to 3 mana/turn)*
Beastmen	Barbarians	Dwarves	Gnolls
Dark Elves	Halflings	Klackons	
Draconians	High Elves	Lizardmen	
	High Men		
	Nomads		
	Orcs		
	Trolls		

*Mana production levels are based on:

1. a city of population 20;

2. that has no special mineral deposits;

3. with all of its building types that directly increase or decrease city mana production considered built.

Spells and events that alter urban mana production are listed in Table 15.11 at the end of the chapter.

Nodes

Magic nodes that have been captured and melded with a magic or guardian spirit are excellent sources of mana, especially when their pre-game setting is at normal or powerful. The game's magic setting determines the amount of mana generated by all nodes.

At the normal setting, nodes on Arcanus produce from 5 to 10 mana per turn, and those on Myrror produce from 10 to 20 mana per game turn. At the weak magic setting, all nodes produce half as much mana, while at the powerful setting they produce 50 percent more mana (with that node's total rounded down, in both cases). This won't affect the actual number of squares covered by a node's affected area or *aura* (as shown by the twinkling lights in that node's controlling player's color). Instead, each such square only produces 1/2, 1, or 1 1/2 mana on the weak, normal, and powerful levels, respectively.

1 Node Dat! (Node Wizard Skills)

Other pre-game choices determine how much actual mana you can draw from nodes. Chaos Mastery, Nature Mastery, and Sorcery Mastery allow you to draw *double* the mana from captured nodes of the corresponding magic type. Node Mastery lets you make exceptional use of *all* nodes, allowing you to draw *double* the mana from each. If you have both Node Mastery and one of either Chaos, Nature, or Sorcery Mastery and capture a node of the corresponding color, its mana income to you is *quadrupled*.

Because nodes are a constant, valuable source of mana, make it a high priority to capture a few nodes during the early stages of a game. Captured nodes should be quickly melded to magic spirits or, for added safety, guardian spirits. In addition, you should garrison them with a patrolled unit or two. Computer players value nodes very highly, and they will *always* try to steal the nodes from you if they are not garrisoned.

Magic and Nodes

There are a few spells and events that can affect nodes:

Warp Node is a Death magic spell that perverts a node so that it draws five mana per turn *out* of the controlling wizard's mana reserve, rather than adding any mana to it.

Conjunctions are celestial events that influence the amount of mana produced by nodes. Conjunctions always double the amount of mana produced by nodes of corresponding type, while halving the mana produced by nodes of each different type.

Node-able Notes

Because nodes can be acquired by any player and require no special racial abilities to access, they are extremely useful sources of mana, especially for races that cannot generate large quantities of mana on their own (i.e., Dwarves, Gnolls, Klackons, and Lizardmen). When playing as one of these races, be sure to place node acquisition high on your strategy list!

Minding Your Manas: Other Sources of Mana Production

There are a few other means to accumulate mana: through alchemy, by the destruction of magic artifacts, and by finding mana as treasure. The problem with these mana sources is that they are not steady, per turn sources of *mana income*. As such, mana from these sources cannot be allocated toward researching spells or improving your spell-casting skill. These supplemental mana sources only contribute to your mana *reserve*, allowing you to cast more costly spells and to maintain many or more expensive enchantments for longer periods of time.

Money Is Magic: Mana Production and Alchemy

Alchemy is the process by which gold is converted into reserve mana and vice versa. Unless you have the Alchemy skill, this conversion will always be inefficient, resulting in a loss of 50 percent of the starting material. With the Alchemy skill, gold and mana are transmuted on a straight, one-for-one basis.

Unless your whole game strategy hinges on using alchemy to convert gold to mana (or mana to gold), only employ the alchemy process under desperate circumstances. Such desperate times would include when you stand to lose critical enchantments, units, buildings, or even cities through inadequate mana or gold maintenance. When your gold supply is insufficient to maintain your units and buildings, extra units will be disbanded by the computer, starting with the latest units you acquired (i.e., the last in is the first out). Also, when your mana reserves are tapped out, you risk defeat in battle by being unable to project magic there, so it is always good to have some defensive combat mana in your mana reserve.

The Anvil Chorus: Mana From Broken Artifacts

Magic artifacts can be broken on the anvil in the Items screen. Breaking items is a fast way to boost your mana reserves by denuding your heroes. This action is best left as a mechanism to get rid of items that you no longer have room to store, and even then it is better to break the cheap stuff first and try to hold on to your more powerful magic items so your heroes can use them as best they're able.

Crystal Light: Mana Crystals as Treasure

Especially at the beginning of the game (and during Mana Shorts), finding mana crystals (i.e., reserve mana points lying around loose) by exploring and conquering lairs is a worthwhile task. Being able to maintain a few fantastic creatures early in a game (even when running a per turn mana deficit, you can still maintain creatures for a time if you have sufficient reserves), can really get the ball rolling for some important early conquests.

Being able to cast a few additional Earth Lore spells, for example, or summoning a floating island for a few turns so that you can move to another continent, having additional mana to help you capture a neutral city, etc., are all productive uses for these boosts from early mana finds. Don't neglect this important source of mana. It may make all the difference at the most important stage of the game—the beginning.

Molding Mana: My Three Wands

The mana you earn each game turn gets distributed among three areas as determined by your wand settings on the Magic Summary screen. The wand marked "Mana" shows the amount added to your reserves—the mana upon which you draw when you cast spells and pay for upkeep on enchantments and summoned creatures. The middle "Research" wand's mana gets converted into spell research points—representing your ongoing effort to learn new spells. Finally, the "Skill" wand's mana contributes to your wizard's efforts to improve his or her spell-casting skill—determining the rate at which you can contribute mana to spell *casting* and how much potential mana you, personally, can expend during a battle.

You can readjust how much of your mana income gets allotted towards each of these categories by readjusting the level of liquid in each of the three wands. Note that adding or reducing the mana going to one wand automatically readjusts the amount in the other two. If you want to shift your mana ratio between two of the three wands, click on the gemstone at the top of the wand whose mana

income ratio you want keep fixed. How and why you should adjust these ratios are discussed in the following sections.

More Power! Your Mana Reserve and How to Increase It

Your mana reserve is your mana checking and savings account rolled into one. Here is where part of your mana income should go every turn. Here is where the mana you find in lairs, release from artifacts, and convert from gold gets deposited. Your mana reserve is *from* where the mana comes for all your spells: your overland spells, combat spells, summonings, creation of artifacts, and maintenance of enchantments and fantastic creatures. It is all that you have in the world during a Mana Short to pay for everything from your ongoing spells to future combat. In short, your mana reserve is your mana bank.

The object is always to have enough mana in reserve to pay for what you want to cast, when you need to cast it. Therefore, you want to generate a net positive mana income (meaning the sum of the mana required for upkeep on fantastic creatures and enchantments is less than the mana you are earning from all your per turn sources: nodes, buildings, people, and terrain).

Anything, therefore, that increases your net mana income: Node Mastery, Chaos Mastery, Nature Mastery, Sorcery Mastery, and various spells (such as Dark Rituals), will improve the condition of your reserves. Keeping mana upkeep costs down, within reason, is also important, but you do not want to be hampered in your objectives. Clearly, you should remove enchantments that are no longer helpful (remove a Water Walking spell from your settlers after they encounter dry land again, for instance). However, it is always better to increase your income rather than decrease your spell casting (hmm... sounds like a politician's view the federal budget).

Skills, Spells, and Your Mana Reserve

Aside from paying attention to the obvious question of income and costs, there are a number of wizard skills that can keep your mana reserves healthier. Channeler, Artificer, Conjurer, Mana Focusing, the Mastery skills (Chaos, Nature, and Sorcery), and Runemaster skills save you mana when you cast some or all spells. One of the more useful of these, for this purpose, is Mana Focusing. It effectively gives you a 20 percent discount on all spells (i.e., for every 80 mana placed into your mana reserves, 100 mana are deposited there for future spell casting and maintenance, see Chapter 4). Channeler is also extremely useful in that it not only eliminates combat casting cost modifiers, but also halves all spells' maintenance costs! In addition, acquiring eight or more spell ranks in a particular magic type will give you discounts ranging from 10 percent to 40 percent, depending on how many spell ranks you have, in the casting costs of spells of that type.

There is one more wizard skill that can sometimes improve your mana reserves. Charismatic allows a wizard to purchase magic artifacts presented by merchants for a 50 percent discount. Charismatic wizards get the same amount of mana for breaking artifacts as other wizards do (i.e., they get half the gold value of the item back in mana), even though they only paid half the gold value of the item in purchasing it. Therefore, such purchased artifacts, if broken, will yield double the mana, relative to the cost of the item, for Charismatic wizards than for others (i.e., they get back, in mana, the full amount of gold they paid for the item).

Of course, the size of your mana reserve can be viewed as a relative measurement. As long as your reserve is bigger than your opponents', you're in pretty good shape. To address any imbalance in your relative mana reserves, use a spell called Drain Power. This Death spell (for those envious wizards amongst you) drains 10 to 200 mana from one opponent's mana reserve. That should help keep the balance tipped in your favor....

Your Skill Level: The Great Limiting Factor

Your own spell-casting skill level is an important consideration. It determines the total amount of mana your wizard can cast during any combat (not including the distance modifier penalty assessed for casting spells in combats far from your Enchanted Fortress). It also determines how much mana you can funnel into an overland spell during each game turn. Basically, your skill level is your personal speed limit on how powerful a spell caster you can be.

No Practice Necessary: Improving Your Skill Level

Your spell-casting skill improves as you divert mana income into this skill according the formula below.

Therefore, the more mana you earn per turn, and the more allocated to improving your skill level, the faster your wizard's spell-casting skill will increase. In addition to the things that increase your mana income, there are other ways to improve your spell casting skill:

Skill Level Improvement Formula

Amount of mana investment required to raise a wizard's skill level by 1 = (2 x Present Skill Level)

For example, you have a skill level of 12. Investing twice your present level of 12, which is 24, mana in improving your skill will raise it to level 13. Mana invested beyond the exact amount required to reach a new skill level is applied toward the next level.

The wizard skill Archmage improves your ability to increase your spell casting skill by 50 percent (for every two mana applied to your spell skill per turn, three mana points worth show up beneath your Skill wand and are applied to improving your spell skill). An Archmage also starts with a +10 bonus to his spell skill.

You start with two spell-skill per book, so pick more spell books at the beginning of the game.

Heroes with spell-casting skill can artificially increase the spell-casting skill of your wizard. When such heroes are stationed at your Enchanted Fortress, half of their spell-casting skill contributes to that of your wizard for purposes of casting overland spells (not for casting magic in combat!). The maximum contribution from such heroes is equal to your current spell-casting skill. If, for example, you have a hero with a spell skill of 23 at your Enchanted Fortress, you will be able to funnel an additional 11 mana per turn into casting overland spells.

The Death magic spell, Cruel Unminding, will improve a wizard's spell-casting skill relative to that of his opponents. This spell permanently destroys 10 percent of the total mana that the target wizard has invested into improving his spell skill, decreasing it commensurately.

Research: Looking It Up

All spells cost a certain number of *research points* before they are moved from your research list to your spell book and, therefore, become available for casting. Three things go into paying the required research points when learning a new spell: spell research that is earned from special buildings such as libraries, mana income that is diverted into research efforts, and any discounts a wizard receives for researching some or all spells.

Formula for City Research Point Production

+2 per library
+3 per sage's guild
+5 per university
+8 per wizard's guild
= City Research Point Production

Scrolls & Books: Research Points

The only direct source of research points that is not subject to drying up during a Mana Short are those that come from buildings. A city's contribution to research points can be calculated by the formula above.

Need That Spell Fast! Investing Mana in Spell Research

In addition to research points contributed by libraries and other institutions of learning, mana may also be allotted to spell research. One mana point becomes one research point, as the middle of your three mana allocation wands on your Magic Summary screen shows. Anything, then, that affects your mana income, either positively or negatively, will exert its proportional effect on the speed by which you can research new spells from funneling your mana income into spell research.

Not all races can build all the institutes of higher learning. Each city belonging to Barbarians, Dwarves, Gnolls, Halflings, Klackons, Lizardmen, and Trolls can, ultimately, produce no more than five research points per turn. Note that these same races also tend to be the poorest mana producers. When playing them, spend more time conquering nodes for mana production and focus more of your mana on research. Also, you had best pick skills that enhance the availability of mana or that lower your research costs.

Study Shortcuts:
Spell Research Bonuses

In addition to the direct contributions of both spell-research points and mana income allotted to spell research, your skills and spell ranks will further determine whether you receive any discounts on spell research costs.

🐸 Conjurer gives a 25 percent discount on research of summoning spells.

🐸 Chaos, Nature and Sorcery Mastery provide a discount of 15 percent on the researching of new spells of the corresponding magic realm.

🐸 Runemaster gives a discount of 25 percent on learning Arcane magic spells.

🐸 Sage Master allows you to research all new spells at 25 percent less than the usual cost.

🐸 Eight or more spell ranks in a particular magic realm entitles your wizard to a 10 to 40 percent discount, depending on the number of spell ranks, in researching new spells from that magic realm.

As you can see, the choices you make when constructing your own wizard have important effects on the speed with which you learn new spells.

One final, but important, contribution to the rate at which you learn new spells concerns heroes with the Sage ability. The value of your heroes' Sage ability ratings translates directly to that amount of per turn spell research.

Slowing Down Research

There are times, however, when you may wish to spend less of your mana on researching new spells; i.e., if you spent most of your spell picks at the beginning of the game on wizard skills rather than on spell books. In such a case, you may wish to reduce the proportion of mana income going to spell research, giving you time to find extra spell books (and new spells) in nodes and lairs before your research-ing efforts are occupied with learning the Spell of Mastery.

Also, diverting mana income from research to your spell skill and mana reserves, once you have acquired a steady research point income from universities or other buildings, will greatly speed the rate at which you accumulate greater casting power, while giving you the mana in reserves to support your casting efforts.

E=MC²: Researching the
Spell of Mastery

Learning new spells quickly is fairly important. The reason to do so is twofold. First, the faster you can learn spells, the faster you will know and be able to cast them, both during and outside of combat.

Second, the game winning Spell of Mastery has an immense research cost of 60,000 research points. All of the spells you have learned or acquired have half of their research point values (ignoring any discounts that you may have received) summed before you start learning the Spell of Mastery. This sum is mercifully subtracted from the number of research points required to learn the Spell of Mastery. You are, then, only required to spend the remaining research points to learn this spell. Note that wizards with eleven spell books in one color get an additional 3,000 points deducted from the researching cost of this spell. After you have learned the Spell of Mastery, you can start casting it at any time as your bid to win the game.

Gold: Carat & Schtick

The most versatile of *Master of Magic*'s commodities discussed in this chapter is certainly gold. This element can be converted into mana through alchemy, and can boost production through the purchase of buildings and troops. Gold lets you hire mercenaries and heroes, buy exotic artifacts from wandering merchants, bribe your opponents, and maintain your normal units. While gold is not all that glitters in this game, it's second to none.

The Taxman Cometh: Getting Your Hands Into Other's Pockets

The amount of gold income your wizard collects depends primarily on your tax rate, set through your Tax Collector. Various terrain features enhance the amount of gold a city earns, as do special financial institutions and the production of trade goods. The base gold income of a city is a crucial accounting concept in *Master of Magic* and is determined according to the formula below.

Dwarves are the only race to receive double their base gold income. On the basis of the formula below, clearly anything that increases the number of citizens under your jurisdiction will almost certainly increase your income, as will anything that decreases the number of rebels.

More Than Greed: Enhancing Gold Income

The *total* gold income that a town will generate at a given tax rate and number of citizens depends on whether the town has a marketplace, bank, and merchant's guild or not. Income will also depend on sea trade, by being adjacent to shores, and trade over land, via roads. In the absence of a city's devoting its production efforts to making trade goods, its income in gold can be described by the formula below.

Ships Laden with Gold: Trade by Sea

Note that the bonuses for sea trade will vary. The trade bonus is initially set at zero; it rises to 10 percent if the town is located on a shore (even a lake shore—the test is whether that city can build a ship wright's guild; if so, that city is on a shore). The trade bonus increases to 20 percent if the city is built on a river square. Note that building a city on a river mouth (the end of a river located on a shore

---

Formula for Base Gold Income for a City

Tax Rate x Number of non-rebels in that city
+5 gold per gem deposit*
+3 gold per gold mine*
+2 gold per silver mine*
= **Base Gold Income**

*Note that when a city produces a miner's guild, any gold bonuses from gold, silver, and gem deposits will increase by 50 percent (of their total, rounded down). On a comparative basis, the only races that can't build miner's guilds and, therefore, will not be able to enjoy the full benefits of such deposits, are the Lizardmen and Trolls.

Formula for Total Gold Income for a City

Base Gold Income (BGI), as explained in the previous formula
+   (BGI x .5) per marketplace
+   (BGI x .5) per bank
+   (BGI x 1) per merchant's guild
+   (BGI x .1) for shore (trade) bonus*
+   (BGI x .2) for river (trade) bonus**
+   road (trade) bonus (see below)*
= **Total City Gold Income**

*A town's total trade bonus, from both land and sea trade, is limited to three percent times the number of its citizens.

**A city must be built *on* a river square to get this trade bonus.

square) provides *both* of these bonuses, for a combined 30 percent.

Caravans of Coinage: Trade by Land

The shore and river bonuses represent the contribution of sea trade to your city's income. When your city is *directly* connected to others by roads, the bonus from all trade increases. So, roads provide an additional factor to the above equation. Each other city connected by a road to the city concerned contributes to that city's income by one percent per person in the adjoining cities. Note that the maximum contribution from all forms of trade (i.e., the sum of the road, shore, and river bonuses) is three percent per person in the city concerned.

The trade bonus from roads depends on the race in the cities to which the city receiving the bonus is connected (actually, *all* cities interconnected by roads receive this bonus, but we're focusing on a single one of your cities for the purposes of explaining how this all works). If the other city's race is the same as your city's, then the trade bonus is halved, i.e., it is half a percent, not one percent. Only

trade between different races generates the full bonus of one percent per person.

Go GATT Some More: Maximum Gold from Trade

No matter how many cities you are connected to by roads or what bonus you receive from sea trade, the absolute maximum combined trade bonus that a city can ever collect is limited to three percent per person in that city. The maximum contribution to a city's gold income from trade, therefore, is described by the formula below.

Merchants from Afar: Nomads and Trade

Nomads are a trading race. In addition to their trade by water and road, Nomads get an automatic 50 percent added to their trade bonus. Note that this Nomad trade bonus is subject to the same limitation in the maximum gold allowed from trade as are all the other races.

This means that Nomads can always receive their maximum trade bonuses in cities while they are developing, whereas other races will have a tough time building up to a city's

---

Bonus From Trade Ceiling Example

For example, your city is at its maximum of 20 people. As it sits on a shore, your sea trade bonus is 10 percent. Since it is also connected by a road to another city with 12 people, the following equation describes how much of a gold bonus your city can receive from trade:

    .01 x 12 people in adjoining town,
       which is .12
 +   .10 for shore bonus
 = . 22 x **Base Gold Income**
 =   a Bonus From Trade of 22 percent of that
       city's BGI

Formula for Maximum Gold Received from Trade Bonus at a City

(.3 x Number of people in that city) x **Base Gold Income**
= Maximum Gold Bonus that city can receive from trade

Continuing the above example, then, in which there are 20 people in your city, the maximum gold the city can receive from the combined effects of trade (roads, shore, river) is 60 percent of the city's base gold income.

trade bonus maximum. Other races are usually only able to generate their city's maximum trade bonuses after carefully situating their cities in favorable locations and building roads.

For example, what can you expect if you have a Nomad city located on a river mouth but unconnected by roads to any other city? Let's say your Nomad city has eight population points. In this case, the current maximum trade bonus for this city is three percent per person, or 24 percent of the base gold income. The river mouth, alone, provides a 30 percent trade bonus. Therefore, the Nomad's special trade bonus will not have any impact on the city's gold production until that 30 percent river mouth bonus has been exceeded (i.e., until after the town's population exceeds 10 Nomads).

Let's take another look at this city 15 persons later. With 23 people in it, its maximum trade bonus rises to 69 percent (3 percent times 23). The Nomad city is still generating its maximum trade bonus, though, because the river's 30 percent trade bonus is combined with the Nomads' natural 50 percent trade bonus, for a combined maximum trade bonus of 80 percent. Heck, it would take 27 population points in that city before its maximum trade bonus was exceeded! (And a city's normal maximum size is only 25 population points—making Nomads excellent traders, indeed!)

Trade Goods: The Ultimate Export Item

The final city-based gold income producer is trade goods. The trade good setting in a city's production choices will convert a city's production points into gold at a rate of two to one.

Magic Effects on Gold Income

The total gold income from a city can be altered directly or indirectly by spells and random events. Indirect effects include spells or events that:

- alter production, which can change a city's gold income from trade goods.
- destroy or corrupt terrain, which can destroy or, temporarily, prevent the use of mineral deposits, such as gold, silver, and gems.
- destroy buildings, which can eliminate the buildings that increase gold income.
- change population size, which will affect gold income by altering the number of taxable and productive individuals.
- affect the number of rebels in a city, which can change the number of productive (non-rebel), taxable citizens.
- destroy troops in city garrisons, which can temporarily increase the non-taxable, non-productive rebel population.

Spells and events that affect a city's bottom line are listed in Table 15.11 at the end of this chapter.

Gold: Expenses and The Bottom Line

The total gold that a wizard brings in per turn depends on influences other than city-based gold income and expenses. All non-fantastic units, except for *noble* heroes (see Chapter 18), require an upkeep cost in gold and bread. A wizard's gross upkeep in gold is the sum of the upkeep for all that player's city structures and units. In addition, any surplus food produced during a game turn that is not required to feed troops is converted into extra gold at a ratio of two food to one gold.

Trade Goods: Production Points to Gold Conversion Formula

Total City Production / 2 (rounded down) = Trade Goods Gold Income Bonus

---

Besides an income in gold (dependent largely on taxes, trade, and maintenance costs), a wizard's gold reserves may increase through finding treasure in monster lairs, receiving a generous donation (an event, see Chapter 26), or capturing cities. Reserve gold may be used to purchase artifacts, heroes, and mercenaries as opportunities present themselves (see Chapter 4) or to purchase buildings and normal units as the need arises.

Gold may be plundered when cities fall or lost from the Piracy event. Finally, gold may be obtained in a pinch from mana reserves through the use of alchemy, an action that costs two mana per one gold gained unless your wizard has the Alchemy skill (in which case mana is transmuted to gold on a straight one-for-one basis).

Ethnic Values: Analyzing Aggregate Resource Income by Race

One of the simplest ways to get a clear picture of the relative strengths of each race in *Master of Magic* is to examine what each race is capable of producing *in toto*. The races' ability to produce each of the key economic ingredients, gold, mana, production points, and research points, is important in assessing their relative strengths and weaknesses.

Not all races produce equivalent amounts of gold. These differences are due either to their inability to build financial institutions that are more advanced than marketplaces, or due to other inherent racial characteristics.

It is difficult to analyze the relative abilities of the races in producing gold. There are several reasons for this. First, an analysis of gold production should include a study of necessary maintenance costs. Because different races can develop their cities to widely varying extents, these differences must be reflected in upkeep costs and net income. Second, races differ in their net productivity, which will influence the income they can generate by making trade goods. Third, an analysis should consider whether to base a comparison on cities while they are producing trade goods or not.

All Things Being Equal

The following tables compare the races in terms of relative economic strength. Here, we've examined a city's net earnings in gold, production, research, and mana, and varied its output strictly by race. For comparative purposes, each race is assumed to have a standardized city with a maximum population of 20, completely filled with citizens. All calculations are based on the supposition that the city is fully built (all possible structures have been created) and that its base trade bonus from roads and coastal locations is 30 percent (about half what the population could use, as explained above).

Further, it is assumed that the local terrain supports the production of all other building types (stables, sawmills, forester's guilds). No production, gold, or mana bonuses are given for special terrain effects. (Such features vary significantly between cities and, therefore, have no basis in a cross-comparison.)

Each city is assumed to have a minimal garrison of two native swordsmen units, costing an additional two food and two gold per game turn for upkeep and to pacify one rebel. The number of farmers and workers used for comparison assumes that the town is producing the food required to feed only itself and its garrison. In applicable cases, rebels that cannot be pacified by the existing buildings and garrisons are assumed to be in a state of rebellion. Consequently, they are not contributing to either gold or other production.

Note that, in Table 15.9, it is assumed that the local taxation level is at one gold per population, producing a base 20 percent rebel population. Table 15.10 uses a 1 1/2 gold per population taxation level, producing a base 30 percent rebel population. We thought a look

at both average taxation rates would make
an interesting comparison in itself.

Table 15.9 *City Economics at a One Gold per Person Tax Rate*

Race	Farmers	Gold + Trade	Base Prod	Total Prod	Mana	Net Unrest	Research Points	Upkeep	Net Gold	Net Gold With Trade Goods
Barbarians	9	30 + 6	27	54	9	0	5	-48	-12	+15
Beastmen	6	40 + 6	31	77	20	-4	18	-75	-29	+9
Dark Elves	6	60 + 6	31	77	22	-3	18	-84	-18	+20
Draconians	6	60 + 6	31	62	19	-4	18	-76	-10	+21
Dwarves	9	57 + 11	35	70	6	+1	5	-37	+31	+66
Gnolls	9	28 + 5	25	50	3	+1	2	-32	+1	+26
Halflings	6	30 + 6	31	62	13	-1	5	-40	-4	+27
High Elves	6	60 + 6	31	77	12	0	18	-77	-11	+27
High Men	6	60 + 6	31	77	10	-4	18	-86	-20	+18
Klackons	9	30 + 6	38	76	1	0	2	-32	+4	+42
Lizardmen	10	28 + 5	23	23	3	+1	2	-22	+12	+23
Nomads	6	60 + 12	31	77	13	-4	10	-83	-11	+27
Orcs	6	60 + 6	31	77	10	-4	18	-92	-26	+12
Trolls	6	30 + 6	31	46	10	-2	2	-43	-7	+16

Farmers means the minimum number of farmers necessary to support the population of 20 with the garrison of two normal units.

Gold + Trade refers to the gold income of the city from taxation and buildings, plus the contribution from a 30 percent trade bonus. Note that the Nomads are getting a full trade bonus of 60 percent because of their inherent high trade bonus.

Base Prod is the total Base Production output of farmers and workers.

Total Prod refers to the production level after including building contributions.

Mana shows the net mana production in the city from its people and buildings.

Net Unrest is the number of rebels in that city. A negative value here simply means that many more rebels can be pacified in the city under the prevailing conditions.

Research Points means the number of research points produced.

Upkeep refers to the maintenance cost in gold of the buildings and garrison.

Net Gold is the difference between the total gold income and upkeep.

Net Gold with Trade Goods shows the difference between the total gold income and upkeep if that city's production is changed to trade goods.

Table 15.10 *City Economics at a 1 1/2 Gold per Person Tax Rate*

Race	Farmers	Gold + Trade	Base Prod	Total Prod	Net Mana	Unrest	Research Points	Upkeep	Net Gold	Net Gold with Trade Goods
Barbarians	9	40 + 8	23	46	9	+2	5	-48	0	+23
Beastmen	6	60 + 9	31	77	20	-2	18	-75	-6	+32
Dark Elves	6	90 + 9	31	77	22	-1	18	-84	+15	+53
Draconians	6	90+ 9	31	62	19	-2	18	-76	+23	+54
Dwarves	9	76 + 15	29	58	6	+3	5	-37	+54	+83
Gnolls	9	37 + 7	21	42	3	+3	2	-32	+12	+33
Halflings	6	42 + 8	29	58	13	+1	5	-40	+10	+39
High Elves	6	81 + 8	27	67	12	+2	18	-77	+12	+45
High Men	6	90 + 9	31	77	10	-2	18	-86	+13	+51
Klackons	9	40 + 8	32	64	1	+2	2	-32	+16	+48
Lizardmen	10	37 + 7	19	19	3	+3	2	-22	+22	+31
Nomads	6	90 + 18	31	77	13	-2	10	-83	+25	+63
Orcs	6	90 + 9	31	77	10	-2	18	-92	+7	+45
Trolls	6	45 + 9	31	45	10	0	2	-43	+11	+33

Farmers means the minimum number of farmers necessary to support the population of 20 and the two unit garrison.

Gold + Trade refers to the gold income of the city from taxation and buildings, plus the contribution from a 30 percent trade bonus. Note that the Nomads are getting a full trade bonus of 60 percent because of their inherent high trade bonus.

Base Prod is the total Base Production output of farmers and workers.

Total Prod refers to the production level after including building contributions.

Mana shows the net mana production in the city from its people and buildings.

Net Unrest is the number of rebels in that city. A negative value here simply means that many more rebels can be pacified in the city under the prevailing conditions.

Research Points means the number of research points produced.

Upkeep refers to the maintenance cost in gold of the buildings and garrison.

Net Gold is the difference between the total gold income and upkeep.

Net Gold with Trade Goods shows the difference between the total gold income and upkeep if the city's production is changed to trade goods.

Table 15.11 *Things That Alter City Mana, Gold, Food, and Rebels*

Factors	Rebels Inc	Rebels Dec	Food* Inc	Food* Dec	Production Inc	Production Dec	Mana Income Inc	Mana Income Dec	Research Inc	Research Dec	Gold Income Inc	Gold Income Dec	Notes**
Chaos Spells													
Armageddon	2			○		○	●	○				○	global enchantment: raises volcanoes (which provide mana to caster)
Call the Void	○			○		○		○		○		○	city spell: destroys units and buildings; causes corruption
Chaos Rift	○			○		○		○		○		○	city enchantment: destroys units and buildings
Corruption				○		○		○				○	targets map square
Fire Storm	○					○						○	targets map square: can destroy units
Great Wasting	1			○		○		○				○	global enchantment: causes corruption
Meteor Storms	○			○		○		○		○		○	global enchantment: destroys buildings
Raise Volcano	○			○		○	●	○		○		○	targets map square; destroys buildings and land; volcanoes provide mana to caster
Death Spells													
Black Wind	○					○						○	targets map square: can destroy units
Death Wish	○					○						○	global spell: destroys units
Cursed Lands	1				-50%							○	city enchantment
Dark Rituals	1					○	0-10					○	city enchantments: decreases population growth rate by 25%; double mana from religious buildings
Evil Presence	0-4					○		0-10				○	city enchantment: negates calming effects and mana production of all religious buildings
Famine	+25%			-50%		○		△				○	city enchantment
Pestilence	2					○		△				○	city enchantment: can kill up to 1 citizen per turn

Table 15.11 Cont. *Things That Alter City Mana, Gold, Food, and Rebels*

Factors	Rebels Inc	Rebels Dec	Food* Inc	Food* Dec	Production Inc	Production Dec	Mana Income Inc	Mana Income Dec	Research Inc	Research Dec	Gold Income Inc	Gold Income Dec	Notes**
Life Spells													
Inspirations					+100%						○		city enchantment: increase in production = to that from 2 miner's guilds
Just Cause		1			○						○		global enchantment: increases fame
Prosperity											+100%		city enchantment: acts like a merchant's guild
Stream of Life		all			○			△			○		city enchantment: eliminates all unrest in target; doubles population growth rate
Nature Spells													
Change Terrain			△	△	△	△							targets map square: changing terrain alters food and production from land
Earthquake	○			○				○	○			○	city spell: destroys buildings and units
Gaia's Blessing		2	+50%		●			△			○		city enchantment: production bonus = doubled production from forests and Nature nodes
Ice Storm	○					○						○	targets map square: can destroy units
Move Fortress	△	△											city spell: changing primary race can alter unrest levels
Nature's Wrath	○			○		○		○		○		○	global enchantment: destroys buildings and units
Transmute							△	△			△	△	can change minerals
Sorcery Spells													
none													

Table 15.11 Cont. *Things That Alter City Mana, Gold, Food, and Rebels*

Factors	Rebels Inc	Rebels Dec	Food* Inc	Food* Dec	Production Inc	Production Dec	Mana Income Inc	Mana Income Dec	Research Inc	Research Dec	Gold Income Inc	Gold Income Dec	Notes**
Events*													
Population Boom													doubles population growth rate
Bad Moon							▲	▲					increases mana from religious buildings by 50% if you have Death books; decreases this by 50% if you have Life books
Depletion								△				○	
Donation											●		
Good Moon							▲	▲					opposite of Bad Moon
New Minerals							△				△		
Piracy												●	
Plague	2							△				○	
Earthquake	○			○				○		○		○	just like the spell
Great Meteor	○			○		○		○		○		○	just like Call the Void
Buildings													
Alchemist's Guild							3						
Animist's Guild		1	●										increases harvesting to 3 food per farmer
Bank											+50%		
Cathedral		1					4						
Farmer's Market			+3										
Forester's Guild			●		+25%								2 food units are harvested for free
Granary			+2										
Housing													increases population growth
Library									2				
Marketplace											+50%		
Mechanician's G.					+50%								
Merchant's Guild											+100%		
Miner's Guild					+50%		△						
Oracle		2											
Parthenon		1					3						
Sage's Guild									3				
Sawmill					+25%								increases population growth for a city making housing
Shrine		1					1						
Temple		1					2						
Trade Goods												●	+1 gold per 2 production points
University									5				
Wizard's Guild							3	8					

217

Table 15.11 Cont. *Things That Alter City Mana, Gold, Food, and Rebels*

This table lists the spells, events, and buildings that can affect your cities' economic status. Effects are shown under Inc or Dec columns of the economic factor they affect, depending on whether they increase production of that factor or decrease it.

Key:

● = This spell, event, or building directly affects this attribute.

○ = This spell, event, or building *indirectly* affects this attribute.

▲ = This spell, event, or building may directly affect this attribute.

△ = This spell, event, or building may *indirectly* affect this attribute.

Indirect effects are due to:

* loss of buildings (for example, the loss of a shrine will increase rebels and decrease mana production in a city)

* destruction or alteration of land or resources eliminates their food, production bonuses or other contributions to a city

* destruction of troops garrisoning a city affects number of rebels and alters the city's productivity and income from taxes

* changes in rebel population (affecting production, gold, etc.)

* changes in city size (for example, deaths in a city populated by a mana-producing race will decrease mana production)

* changes in production can alter gold earned from trade goods

Note that temporary as well as permanent effects are included in this table. For example: Corruption can be cleaned, volcanoes changed into hills, buildings rebuilt, people regrown, and garrisons replenished.

*Increases in food production will increase the maximum size of a city and the city's population growth rate if the city has not already reached maximum size. Note that Famine and Gaia's Blessing affect the food production by farmers in the city; they do not alter the food produced by buildings or wild game.

**This column describes effects of spells and events that help explain some of the other column entries. Note that when this column says "can destroy units," it means that a city's garrison can be injured or destroyed.

***See Chapter 26 for more information on random events.

Summary of Spells, Events, and Buildings Affecting City Economics

We have summarized the myriad of effects that the enormous array of spells and random events in *Master of Magic* have on the economic status of cities in Table 15.11. Virtually all the events, spells, and buildings that can impact on most of the things discussed in this chapter (rebels, food production, mana, gold, production points, random events) have been included in this reference table.

Give My Regards to Broadway

That, good wizard, is the ledger domain of world domination. For those of us without the skill of Spreadsheet Mastery, this analysis of production and spending in *Master of Magic* should prove useful to you. In particular, the racial comparisons can go a long way toward helping you pick certain supporting spell colors and wizard skills. Goodness knows you deserve a medal (and a drink) if you've read this dry chapter on economics from beginning to end.

Next, we're going to play the *Master of Magic* equivalent of *SimCity*. Urban planning is the cornerstone of a smoothly running economic engine. Without a sound economy to subsidize your ambitions, how can you ever expect to be the Master of Magic? Let's take it one city at a time and see what blueprints we can find.

16 Urban Planning

While *Master of Magic* is no *SimCity*, urban planning is still a vital concern. Cities are the economic and military engines that drive the game, and we must pay special attention to their growth and development. So, from outpost to capital, we present you with our guide to urban development and resource management from the ground up.

Born in a Log Cabin: Outpost Growth

New cities are founded by converting a settler to an outpost. *Where* to found a new city will be discussed shortly. First, we will show you what makes an outpost grow into a full-fledged, newborn city (called a hamlet).

The growth rate of an outpost depends primarily on lands within its city limits and the race establishing the outpost. An outpost begins with three-tenths of a person (represented by the three houses filled in on the row of 10, as shown in Figure 16-1, and representative of 300 inhabitants). Every game turn, there is a chance that the outpost might grow by one- to three-tenths of a population point (i.e., 100 to 300 people) or shrink by one- to two-tenths of a population point. Table 16.1 shows how this is determined.

In addition to the a chance to grow every turn, outposts also have a chance to *decrease* in size. This is why, occasionally, outposts die before ever growing into hamlets. The chance of this occurring is explained in Table 16.2, below.

Degrees of Outpost Growth and Shrinkage

The exact amount by which an outpost grows or decreases in size every turn depends on several die rolls. First, a d100 is rolled against the outpost's chance to grow, as per Table 16.1. If it succeeds, the outpost will grow one- to three-tenths of a population point, as determined by a d3.

After growth is checked and added, shrinkage is determined in the same manner. A d100 is rolled against the outpost's chance to shrink. If it does, the outpost will shrink by one- to two-tenths of a population point, as determined by a d2. Note that outposts *can* grow *and* shrink in the same turn and, if they do and their die rolls are identical, there will be no net change in the outpost's current size.

Outpost Growth Analysis

In summary, remember that your outposts are most likely to flourish in the same places you would choose to build new cities: sites that have high population maximums and are rich in valuable minerals (see Chapter 15). Later in the game, if you have access to the Nature magic spell of Gaia's Blessing or the white magic spell, Stream of Life, you can improve your outposts' (and cities') growth rates. Conversely, if you know some darker spells such as Chaos Rift and Evil Presence, you can cast these on your enemies' outposts (and cities) to decrease their growth rates.

Setting Your Sites

Before pulling a Plymouth Rock and founding a new city, you should always take the

Figure 16-1. *An outpost is born with three-tenths of a population point (i.e., 300 people)*

Table 16.1 *Base Outpost Positive Growth Rates by Race*

Race	Base Outpost Growth Rate
Barbarians	15%
Halflings	15%
High Men	10%
Lizardmen	10%
Nomads	10%
Orcs	10%
Dwarves	7%
Beastmen	5%
Draconians	5%
Gnolls	5%
High Elves	5%
Klackons	5%
Trolls	3%
Dark Elves	2%

Base Positive Growth Rate Modifiers:*

+1% per point of the Maximum City Size**

+5% per Iron deposit

+5% per Silver deposit

+10% per Coal deposit

+10% per Gems deposit

+10% per Gold deposit

+10% per Mithril deposit

+10% per Adamantium deposit

+10% per Quork deposit

+10% per Crysx deposit

+10% while enchanted by Stream of Life spell

+20% while enchanted by Gaia's Blessing spell

*Mineral deposits must be within the *city limits*, meaning those squares on or within two squares of the city site, excluding the four squares that are diagonally two squares away from the city site (see Figure 15-1).
**The maximum city size refers to the maximum population of a city built at the outpost site, under the present circumstances (i.e., not including the building of a granary or farmer's market). This number is shown when you use the Surveyor at the outpost site.

For example, the High Men (10 percent) plant an outpost on a site that could support a city maximum size of 13 (+13 percent). Within the city limits are two gold deposits (at +10 percent each) and an iron deposit (+5 percent). This would give that outpost a total Base Positive Growth Rate of 48 percent. Not bad!

Table 16.2 *Base Outpost Negative Growth Rates*

Base Outpost Negative Growth Rate = 5%

Base Negative Growth Rate Modifiers:*
+5% while enchanted by an Evil Presence spell
+10% while enchanted by a Pestilence spell
+10% while enchanted by a Famine spell
+10% while enchanted by a Chaos Rift spell

For example, let's look at an ordinary outpost, with its base 5 percent chance of shrinking in size every turn. If an enemy wizard cast a Famine spell (+10 percent) on that outpost, it would have a 15 percent chance of decreasing in size every turn.

telescope out and survey the area. After all, some places are better to found your cities on than others. Choosing a location for a new city requires that you consider many factors. For example:

☙ Always use the Surveyor to assess the maximum city sizes, production bonuses, etc. allowed at different sites before making a decision.

☙ If you have already expanded to some extent, you will want to decide with which race (your starting race or some conquered one) you wish to build an outpost.

☙ Consider the advantages of various minerals and other special terrain features.

☙ Placement along a coast may be a priority so that you can build ships to explore farther, launch attack forces, or build merchant's guilds.

☙ Consider potential trade benefits (i.e., what cities can you connect to your new city via roads).

☙ Military considerations, such as a location's proximity to Towers of Wizardry, nodes, or other important squares may also play a part in the choices you make.

As an experienced player, you know that every game features its own unique challenges. Some combinations of race and circumstance place you in a position where finding enough gold or enough mana, supporting troops with food, etc. are particular problems. They call new city building units "settlers" for a good reason. Founding outposts that meet your special needs is a good way to "settle" these problems before they become unmanageable.

Surveying Terrain

One of the most useful features in *Master of Magic* is the F1 key (the Surveyor button). It assesses the exact value of all potential sites in terms of a city's maximum population and its nearby terrain-based gold and resource bonuses. (It leaves you to determine a site's other relative advantages, however.) Note that your surveyor *does not* factor in nearby terrain that you have yet to discover! To insure the complete accuracy of a surveyor's report, therefore, make sure that all the squares within the city limit radius of the one examined have been revealed.

This surveyor function also allows you to examine already established cities. Be aware that the current surveyor information *includes* any increases in production, gold, and maximum city size that occur as roads and new

Figure 16-2. *The Surveyor's important information is imparted from the Status window on the right.*

structures for that city are built. Finally, the surveyor also indicates the special advantages of most terrain features.

The big question when surveying potential new city sites is, "Should I choose the site that gives me more people, more production, or maybe even more gold?" Usually, it's better to pursue larger city sizes than higher production or gold bonuses. There are many reasons for this, but two are particularly important.

First, a larger potential city means that your new city, and outpost, will grow at a more rapid rate. The growth rate of a city depends on the difference in the number of its current inhabitants and its maximum population size. A faster growing city will more quickly be able to produce necessary resources, such as gold, mana, research points, and units.

Second, a larger population also has positive rippling economic effects (as well as the ability to give you a lot of points, should you win the game—see Chapter 3). Specifically:

🐍 Gold income depends on taxation which, in turn, depends on the number of people to tax in your cities.

🐍 A city's maximum trade bonuses (see Chapter 15) from roads and rivers or shorelines also depend on how many people there are in a city.

🐍 Gold received from trade goods depends on production that, in turn, depends on how many workers there are.

🐍 Production bonuses (provided by mountains, deserts, hills, and forests) only apply to the productivity of individual workers. Still, the more workers, the better.

It is true that, all other things being equal, smaller cities may produce as much as, or more than, larger cities if they are built on sites that feature large terrain-based production bonuses. When making your new city site decisions, bear in mind our golden rule of thumb: Each additional person can contribute an amount of income roughly equal to a 10-15 percent production bonus. This should help you decide what to do between two similar sites where one offers a larger potential population.

Of course, there are also straight, site-dependent gold bonuses from shores and rivers to consider. They are similar to trade and road bonuses (see Chapter 15) and, as such, the limits of their benefits are defined by the city's population size. In any event, sites near rivers and shores tend to be reasonably fertile, as well.

Note that building a city next to a coastal square can be crucial for two reasons. First, it allows that city to produce ships. Second, the most economically useful institution, the merchant's guild, is only allowed with improved ship building.

Special Placement of New Cities: A Look At Terrain Features

Choosing a site for a new city is more complicated, however, than merely trying to go for the largest population or the greatest producer

Table 16.3 Boosting Gold Production in Cities

Building Type Progression:

Mine Type	Base Value	Market place	Bank	Merchant's Guild	Miner's Guild*
Silver	2	3	4	6	n
Gold	3	4	6	9	n
Gems	5	7	10	15	n
Silver	3	4	6	9	y
Gold	4	6	8	12	y
Gems	7	10	14	21	y

* The presence of a miner's guild will increase the base gold you earn from silver, gold, and gem deposits by 50 percent. The increase in gold from marketplaces, banks, and merchant's guilds depends on the base gold value. The first set of numbers is for the gold you would get if the city had no miner's guild; the second set shows how much gold you would get from these mines if you built a miner's guild in the city.

that you can find. Granted, if your primary concern is achieving economic growth, then finding the closest city sites with the largest maximum size is the route to take. In general, this is the best policy.

However, there are times you may wish to consider other things, such as producing food or mana , building large quantities of troops, situating yourself favorably for your military operations, etc. Depending on your needs, you may find it expedient to sacrifice some potential population size or production potential so that your city will include a mine, quork crystals, or nightshade (etc.).

The resources with the greatest, most enduring effects are coal, iron, adamantium, mithril, and nightshade. The rest: quork and crysx crystals, gems, gold, silver, and wild game, provide quick boosts to mana, gold, or food, but exert fewer long-lasting effects. This is because once you have developed several cities and alternate sources of mana and gold, such deposits become relatively less important. Let's examine the effects of these deposits and measure how relatively important they are.

Before going on, though, remember, as you choose city sites, that some races cannot take full advantage of special minerals! Lizardmen and Trolls, for example, cannot build miner's guilds. Consequently, they will never reap the full benefit of mines and crystals.

Gold, Gold, and More Gold!

Gems, gold, and silver mines boost your gold production. Table 16.3 shows the greatest boost you can get from including these mines within a city's territory. Gold mines, of course, provide 50 percent more gold than silver mines, and gems provide the equivalent of the sum of one gold and one silver mine. Remember, too, that many races cannot even build banks or merchant's guilds! The only races that can take full advantage of these mines by erecting all of these building types are Dark Elves, High Elves, High Men, Nomads, and Orcs. Note that Dwarves receive double the gold value from these mines.

Food: I'm Game if You Are

Wild game provides a straight bonus of two food per turn, freeing up one farmer in your city forever, or providing food for two normal units. This has two significant effects. First, wild game can free up your first citizen to work instead of farm, giving a strong boost to the production of new city structures. Second, wild game will increase the maximum population, and thereby the growth rate, of your new city.

Crystal Eyes

Quork and crysx crystals look extremely attractive when you are examining sites for new cities. Bear in mind, though, that like gold and silver, they provide minor, permanent boosts in that city's per turn mana income. Quork crystals provide three mana per turn, crysx five. A miner's guild in a city will increase the mana production from these deposits by 50 percent. If you can build a miner's guild, these crystals will yield four and seven mana per turn, respectively (half their value again, rounded down). As for other mineral deposits, Dwarves also get double the value (mana) from crysx and quork crystals.

While, at the beginning of the game, additional mana from crystals such as these can exert significant effects on your spell-related skills (research rate, spell skill development, and storage of magic power), later in the game, their effects are far less significant.

The Frugal Army

Coal and iron mines are quite useful in your cities. They reduce the cost of constructing troops and exert additive effects when multiple mines adorn a city, up to a total reduction in building costs of 50 percent! The time and gold you save in building troops in such locations may save your bacon many times over. These mines, like all special mineral deposits, also increase in effectiveness if you can build a miner's guild in the city.

The Magic in Your Weapon

Adamantium and mithril mines are a godsend for troops in *Master of Magic*. These mines not only provide additional mana for your wizard, they also, once an alchemist's guild has been built in the city, permanently improve the weapons, attack strength, and defense of all units produced by that city. Since the effects of adamantium and mithril are not only impressive but ongoing, we feel these mines are the best resource in the game.

Building cities that include adamantium and mithril mines is worth significant sacrifices in maximum population size of the city when selecting a new city site. These mines result in stronger troops that can help your cause many times over. The only races that cannot make use of the weapon-enhancing effects of adamantium and mithril, because they cannot construct alchemist's guilds, are Gnolls, Klackons, Lizardmen, and Trolls. When playing those races, consider the wizard skill of Alchemy instead (see Chapter 4). Note that Dwarves receive double the mana from adamantium and mithril mines (but not double the attack and defense bonuses).

Dispelling The Mysteries of Nightshade

Nightshade grows in swamps and, every turn, provides a city with a permanent chance to dispel all negative city and global enchantments directed at or affecting that city. Each nightshade plant effectively casts a Disenchant spell (of strength 100; see page 107 of the game manual) during every turn. Because these little plants do their job unceasingly throughout the game (and for free!), they are well worth the trouble of finding and incorporating into new cities. The only requirement for making use of nightshade is that a city have a shrine or other religious building. All races can build one or more of these structures, so the benefits of nightshade are available to all.

Table 16.4 *Special Terrain Features Ranking*

Authors' Summary of Terrain Specials to Include in New Cities

	Special Terrain Feature	Bonus Effect Description
Most Useful ↑	Adamantium	+2 mana, +2 attack strength, +2 defense
	Coal	10% unit discount
	Mithril	+1 mana, +1 attack strength, +1 defense
	Iron	5% unit discount
	Nightshade	standing Disenchant spell
	Crysx	+5 mana
	Quork	+3 mana
	Gems	+5 gold
	Wild Game	+2 food
	Gold	+3 gold
Least Useful ↓	Silver	+2 gold

Summing Up Special Terrain Features

To recap, then, Table 16.4 ranks the various special terrain features from, in our opinion, best to worst.

Other Considerations When Choosing City Sites

Besides maximizing city population and incorporating valuable resources into your city limits, other factors may influence your decision about where to plant a new outpost. In particular, you may wish to locate your new city near special places. Accessibility to other cities may be important for building roads and generating trade, for example. Nearness to other cities may also be important for more easily building well-balanced armies! For example, you may wish to construct a force of Lizardmen javelineers, Dark Elf warlocks, and Klackon stag beetles. Positioning cities with these three races near each other will facilitate your construction of specially designed "killer armies."

Coasting Home

You may also wish to build new cities on coastal sites so they can build ships to transport settlers and troops to other places. This is especially important at the beginning of the game for everyone except Lizardmen and Draconians. Early on, your wizard may not know how or be able to afford to cast Water Walking, Wind Walking, or Flight spells. However, having cities on coastal sites is also important at later stages of the game, since transporting troops with galleys or warships is much faster, and less wasteful of mana, than enchanting all your troops with Water Walking or Flight. Of course, building cities on coasts allows them to take advantage of trade bonuses and, if the founding race is able, to build merchant's guilds that double the revenue collected from taxes and gold-producing mines.

Suburban Nodes

Another consideration is to build your cities next to nodes whose color magic is the same as a type your wizard knows. There are two reasons for building cities adjacent to nodes. One is practical; if you can capture a node next to your city, you can keep an eye on it with ease. Enemies frequently try to "stake out" nodes, so it is a good policy to garrison them. Magic nodes that you have captured that are next to one of your cities do not need to be protected this way, since you can quickly mobilize the city's units to defend the node from would-be intruders.

The other reason for building a city next to a node and, in particular, a node that matches the magic type in which your wizard is proficient, is that nodes have auras. The node's aura contributes to the combat ability, including attack strengths, defense, and resistance (see Chapter 20), of fantastic units that come from the same magic realm as the node's magic type! For example, if your wizard knows a lot of Chaos magic, Chaos creatures (such as fire elementals and hell hounds) summoned or created by your wizard, fighting within squares protected by the node's aura, will fight better than they would elsewhere. This makes your cities easier to protect. One word of caution: If you decided that it is best to garrison nodes with fantastic units from corresponding magic realms, be careful. One Great Unsummoning spell can suddenly leave a good portion of your nodes unprotected.

Towering Shadows

Another consideration is an outpost's position relative to a Tower of Wizardry. Since these towers provide the only normal means for movement between Arcanus and Myrror, accessibility to them is quite important for expansion and exploration, as well as for monitoring the activities of your enemies. It is a good strategy to build a city next to each such tower you control so that you can quash enemy units attempting to use them.

Playing Spoil Sports

Your idea of a useless city site may not be shared by your opponents. You may wish to build cities at poor locations merely to prevent another wizard from establishing a city there, especially if the potential city site is too close to one of your cities. You don't want to get too chummy with your neighbors, after all.

Choosing a Race

Once you have chosen the ideal site for your new city, you may have the luxury of deciding which race to settle there. Your choice may be as simple as determining which of your growing cities can afford to peel off a settler and get it to your chosen site as fast as possible. In the above discussion, it was noted when certain races cannot make full use of terrain specials. Table 16.5 recaps the different races and what they can or cannot build when considering what terrain is within their city limits.

One of the most important things to consider when choosing a city's founding race is balance. Once you have conquered your first few races, you can develop a grand design for your armies and cities. How do you want to structure your expansion efforts so that you produce a reasonable amount of all the important resources and develop the strongest armies possible? The conclusions you draw will depend on the races at your disposal which will, in turn, depend largely on chance and on the initiative you take in conquering nearby neutral or enemy cities. You may even take such thoughts into consideration when you prioritize which cities to conquer first; the earlier a start you have with a particular race, the further it can go towards helping you win the game!

The Power of Magic

Some spells modify a city's resource income. In particular, Nature and Life magic spells are the most powerful for improving a city's lot. Here, we must refer you back to Chapter 8 to refresh your memory on the spells Inspiration and Prosperity and to Chapter 11 to reexamine the spells Change Terrain, Transmute, and Gaia's Blessing. Even without all this hocus pocus, however, carefully planning where to build your cities will go a long way toward making your game play more successful.

Pumping Cities Up

Whenever you establish an outpost that grows into a hamlet, capture a reluctant and underdeveloped city, or even start a new game of *Master of Magic*, you need to think about how to build up your new city. Even as your cities finish developing the most basic structures, you will need to devote some thought toward what you should build next. At times, your most pressing needs—for gold, mana, food, research points, troops, or specific units—will govern your choices. Often, though, the answer of what to produce next at a given city is not so obvious.

Starting from Scratch

City development is an important part of *Master of Magic*. While you can use the toggle and allow your Grand Vizier to manage your cities for you, don't. *Real* wizards do it themselves.

Before a city can start contributing significantly, it must develop a rudimentary population base and a few basic buildings. Early in the game and in most cities' lives, certain things will cause other, temporary priorities to weave their way through your standard construction agenda. You may need garrisons, exploration teams, settlers. Depending on your city's race, its unrest level (especially for conquered races), your resource requirements, the local situation (are you constantly being swarmed by raiders or rampaging monsters?), and your own priorities, you will often have to disrupt your normal construction plans to produce buildings or units that meet more pressing needs.

There are several stages in building a new city. First, you have to found a wee outpost and wait for it to grow into a hamlet. Once an outpost is founded (and well guarded, of course, with at least two units), you may be in a lucky position to hasten its growth by casting either Gaia's Blessing or Stream of Life on it (see Table 16.1).

Next, that hamlet usually needs to grow in population a bit (unless there is wild game in your city limits) before buildings or other structures can be built in a reasonable number of game turns. (Unless you're so rich that you can dump a ton of gold into a city to build it up at warp speed, let it produce housing early on.) Setting the city's production to housing will increase the city's growth rate by 50 percent if there is one person in the city and by a percentage equal to the ratio of workers to total population in the city when the population is two or more (see Chapter 15).

Third, once the hamlet has reached between two and four population points (two is adequate if there is plenty of food in your city; four is better if you are using a slow-growing race), you should start building *the basics*. The consensus among the authors of this book is that establishing the most rapid growth rate possible, as early as possible, is the best route to take. This means producing a builder's hall, granary, smithy, marketplace, and farmer's market as quickly as you can. This approach also provides you with the monetary benefits of the marketplace as rapidly as possible. Note that shrines, barracks, and ship wright's guilds are also important early buildings and may take precedence, depending on your situation, over the other buildings mentioned here.

Military needs may interrupt this construction agenda. A city might need an extra spearmen to defend itself or an extra unit to explore with as quickly as possible. Early jumps in exploration will not only reveal

Table 16.5 *Racial Limitations on Taking Full Advantage of a City*

No Limits: Can exploit every possible terrain feature

Dark Elves
High Elves
High Men
Orcs

No Banks and/or Merchant's Guilds: Destined to earn less potential gold

Barbarians
Beastmen
Dwarves
Gnolls
Halflings
Klackons
Lizardmen
Trolls

No Shipyards and/or Maritime Guilds: Give less consideration to coasts

Beastmen
Dwarves
Klackons
Lizardmen
Nomads
Trolls

No Need for Plains: Because they can't build stables/fantastic stables

Dwarves
Halflings

No Use for Forests: Because they can't build sawmills/forester's guilds

Lizardmen

No Alchemist's Guilds: So take skill of Alchemy for magical weapons

Gnolls
Klackons
Lizardmen
Trolls

No Miner's Guilds: So consider another race to fully exploit minerals

Lizardmen
Trolls

fertile areas for new settlers but occasionally will provide you with rewards from investigating empty lairs and ruins. You may even luck into finding a neutral or enemy city so early in its development that you can either destroy it, if it is an outpost, or capture it. An early capture of a neutral city can provide a tremendous boost to your early game economics and development options!

While maximizing growth rate early in the life of a city is one approach to preparing cities for future development, another approach is to boost production a little first by constructing a sawmill. However, as it turns out, there is not much time saved by this approach. Getting a rapid production rate going too soon may actually cause more trouble than it's worth by allowing you to construct expensive buildings before you can adequately support their upkeep.

If your mana or research needs are not being met, it is wise to build a shrine early on. Finally, if you do not have enough room to expand, build a ship wright's guild early so that your development is not critically slowed by a lack of access to suitable city sites.

After the Basics

Finally, after you have developed the city to where it has all of these essential buildings, the city moves into a long period of continued growth we call the final development stage. Here, you must decide whether you want to build the city up all the way or whether you want to specialize the city; for example, if you only need it to make a particular kind of unit, don't construct any buildings superfluous to that need. Below are discussed some of the kinds of approaches you may wish to take, or to balance, in achieving your goals.

Resource Considerations

The need for increasing your gold, mana, and food income and spell research must be met from both urban development and the con-

quest of nodes, lairs, and other cities. There are several lines of development that can be pursued.

The Military Economy

Whether of desire or necessity, one approach to urban development is to focus heavily on military needs and, in particular, the construction of new units. Rapid development of barracks, fighter's guilds, stables, etc. that bolster the military become a priority.

In addition, sources of food and gold must be developed so that you can maintain your new armies. Army maintenance necessitates the rapid development of financial institutions, forester's guilds, animist's guilds (to improve farming efficiency), and perhaps even buildings that increase productivity (for earning more gold from trade goods, eventually).

New units can fortify existing garrisons, protect outposts, conquer other cities, and capture nodes and lairs. This approach is fairly sound for both expanding your empire and acquiring the necessary magic power, through capturing nodes, to fuel your spell research. Your fame will also increase quickly (see Chapter 4) with this approach, furthering your development of effective armies through the intelligent distribution of new mercenaries and heroes.

Of course, a military agenda must be balanced with some careful urban development so that your empire is not overburdened financially or though lack of adequate food supplies. Additionally, aggressive development of fighter's guilds and war colleges (which produce regular and veteran status units) in a few cities is a necessary ploy to further your army's capabilities.

Throwing the Book at 'Em

The opposite of the strong military approach is to prioritize protecting your frontiers, develop internally as rapidly as possible (concentrate on conquering nearby nodes and lairs), and concentrate on spell research. This approach is best implemented if you start with a race that produces large quantities of magic power and that is capable of building the institutes of higher learning (i.e., the Beastmen, Draconians, Dark Elves, or High Elves). Other races, however, can use this economic strategy to good effect, especially when it is complemented by some militaristic and expansionist policies. One advantage to this peaceful approach is that you will automatically be focusing on the sorts of buildings that decrease civil unrest, so that the thrust of your efforts will not be diverted toward soothing rebellious citizens.

Picks & Shovels

Instead of lunging for troops or research points, you may look toward delaying that development for a while and focus your efforts on improving a city's production rate. Building sawmills, forester's guilds, miner's guilds, and mechanician's guilds as early as possible is one way to place your cities into a position where they can later produce units and buildings with considerable speed. This enhances your flexibility for later stages of the game, forming a platform upon which to build other agendas: militaristic, spell-research-oriented, and expansionist.

Note, if you are going for increased productivity, the best order (based on building cost and benefits provided) is to build a sawmill, a miner's guild, a forester's guild, and finally a mechanician's guild. Consider building a mechanician's guild before building other expensive end-stage structures, such as cathedrals, wizard's guilds, and war colleges. The production bonus you get from building a mechanician's guild first will significantly reduce the time it takes you to build these expensive structures.

Colonizing

Peaceful expansion is a good way to develop your wizard's power. While this may initially be a slow way to develop, it will cause a dramatic and steady increase in your capabilities as the game progresses and make you far fewer enemies during the early stages of the game when you are particularly weak. Aggressively building settler units with small, two-unit garrisons and deploying them to establish outposts is a (literally) constructive approach, particularly for both the slow-growing (Dark Elf, High Elf, Troll, and Dwarf) and fast-growing (Barbarian) races.

Colonize or Conquer?

Expansion through outpost building has the advantage over the largely military form of expansion through conquest because your empire will remain largely homogenous, decreasing unrest problems. In addition, your cities will eventually reach the point where they can form massive armies with ease. Military forms of expansion discourage outposts, since a higher premium is placed on military units. This delays the starting race's expansion, even to the point where such expansion loses its meaning. Military expansion makes later outpost expansion more difficult and less profitable. In fact, later expansion through settlers will not exert significant effects on the course of events.

Early military expansion, however, encourages racial heterogeneity, allowing you to select among the capabilities of many races for powerful armies and making use of all races' positive attributes. If a sufficient number of neutral or enemy cities can be conquered, military expansion can give you a vast array of unit types, with their inherent, racial differences in physical abilities, buildings, etc., to call upon, which can quickly and greatly increase your power.

The Balanced Approach

Finally, of course, there is the balanced approach. Balancing the military, peaceful expansion, industry, and the development of spell research and spell skill is, at least to some extent, an integral part of developing a powerful wizard and empire. Balancing all of these goals, as a basic approach, can often be a difficult but worthwhile approach. Flexibility, however, remains important at all times to meet the ever-changing demands and events in *Master of Magic*.

General Methods of City Development

While you must focus your efforts in many different areas to fully succeed in *Master of Magic*, there are a number of possibilities that relate to how you develop your cities.

Buy Cheap

Cities can be developed slowly, using the *peeling an onion* approach. You can build the cheapest buildings first and, slowly but surely, work your cities up from the ground. This approach is a good way to establish a balanced effort. By not concentrating too heavily on any area, your cities will provide you with a steady, balanced increase in the resources you need to increase your power. On the other hand, developing high-powered armed forces will take much longer when using this approach.

Go Specialized

Another approach, used by most computer players, is perhaps the most economical: specialize each city for a specific purpose. For example, make one city a producer of Lizardmen javelineers, another city the producer of dragon turtles, etc. To minimize costs, only build the structures necessary to create these units, to quell civil disobedience, to protect your city, and to pay for what you build. This method sacrifices flexibility for efficiency, but it is a viable approach as long as the specialized areas are not so far apart as to cause

long lapses of time gathering armies for specific purposes. One potential weakness is that it is easy to under develop the structures that speed your spell research efforts.

Resource Orientation

You may, instead, choose to devote your efforts almost exclusively on a particular resource-oriented approach. You may build mostly religious and educational institutions in your cities to maximize the production of spell research points and magic power, focusing your efforts on expansion only when needed to acquire or build more cities to further this agenda.

You may opt to focus entirely on the military and conquest, erecting city structures that allow you to build troops and to support them (with gold and food). Within this approach, you may either specialize or allow for unit-building flexibility. The only problem with heavily slanting your priorities is the potential to neglect the other areas needed to develop your wizard's power to its fullest.

Bow to the Strategic Plan

Finally, you may prefer to emphasize development in one area before expanding your urban centers. For example, you could focus largely on the military at early stages of the game, later developing the spell research and mana producing capabilities of your cities. Conversely, you could focus first on getting your spell research well under way and then later form powerful armies, aided by the spells you have learned, to expand and to conquer your neighbors.

Whichever route you choose, being flexible to circumstances, while maintaining a general sense of purpose and scheme for reaching your goals, is your best ally as you battle your way to becoming the Master of Magic.

A Few Comments on Imperialism

One of the fastest and best ways to develop your empire early in the game is to conquer neutral and, if they are relatively weak, enemy cities. The benefits you gain from such actions are many. Conquering other cities is a way for you to capitalize on the investment that others before you have made. Neutral and enemy cities are already partially, if inadequately, developed. They already have a large enough population base, generally, that you can start building units or useful structures immediately. Conquering fairly large cities will net you fame points which, in turn, will save you money on maintaining your troops and will encourage better mercenaries and heroes to approach your wizard.

Besides the benefits gleaned from not having to painstakingly build cities from scratch, conquering other cities gives you more choices by giving access to more races' abilities and troop types. Some races are inherently stronger than others, while some races specialize in vital magic power production. Other races, the Draconians and Lizardmen, have great exploration value. Some races grow quickly; others have superb specialized units. Having several races and troop types while you are expanding your empire both militarily and through settlers, will give you more flexibility.

Finally, by conquering neutral and enemy cities, you will eliminate threats to the stability of your existing cities. Not having to worry about raiders and enemies who encroach too often on your territory is a very positive aspect of devoting some of your efforts on conquest.

There are two real drawbacks to unbridled conquest. The first is that not all races get along equally well. There is generally some unrest in conquered cities when the city's race is different from the race in your wizard's Enchanted Fortress city. While often the level of unrest is low enough that it causes little concern, there are other times when it can slow production in conquered cities to a halt.

High levels of natural enmity between races can cost you a lot. Large numbers of units are needed to garrison such cities; either do that or plan on spending lots of production or money erecting religious institutions. Of course, the level of unrest only worsens if your tax rates are high, which might be the case if you have large numbers of units or specialized buildings to maintain. This can be a real downward spiral that you must be aware of to avoid.

The second drawback to military expansion is diplomatic. If you take other wizards' cities, it is a *casus belli* (a case for war) and you will automatically be at war with them. If you banish another wizard by taking his or her Enchanted Fortress, all remaining wizards eye you with additional disfavor. Finally, if you expand too rapidly, your neighbors will get envious and, eventually, seek ways to even the score.

City Spells

There are a number of spells that permanently or temporarily affect cities in *Master of Magic*. Some of the spells merely make a change, such as Summoning Circle, an Arcane spell that moves your Summoning Circle to a new city. Some spells clearly exert positive effects for the casting wizard, while others are quite destructive. Table 16.6 provides a thumbnail synopsis of the different city spells in this game. Also included are spells that can directly affect cities, even though they are not cast directly upon them.

With this spell information summary in hand, you can decide which types of magic will best suit you, in terms of building or busting cities. Since cities are the engines that drive the game, knowing how they are tuned or tortured by spells is vital to your game.

Table 16.6 *Spells and Cities: A Complete Reference*

Spell	Nature	Effect Description	Nature of Effect
Altar of Battle	Life	All units created by city are Elite to start	Positive
Gaia's Blessing	Nature	Increases food by 50%; Improves terrain; Eliminates corruption	Positive
Stream of Life	Life	Increases growth rate, healing, and eliminates unrest	Positive
Dark Rituals	Death	Generates extra mana at cost of growth and added unrest	Increase Mana
Inspirations	Life	Increases base production by 100%	Increase Production
Prosperity	Life	Increases gold from taxes by 100%	Increase Gold
Cloud of Shadow	Death	Increases death creatures' / decreases life creatures' combat	Protective
Consecration	Life	Protects from Chaos and Death magic; dispels enchantments	Protective
Flying Fortress	Sorcery	Fortress can only be attacked by flying creatures	Protective
Heavenly Light	Life	Increases Life creatures' / decreases Death creatures' combat	Protective
Nature's Eye	Nature	Scouting range of city increases to 5 squares	Protective
Spell Ward	Sorcery	Protects from all spells and creatures of chosen magic type	Protective
Wall of Darkness	Death	Protects garrison from ranged attacks	Protective
Wall of Fire	Chaos	Units crossing wall suffer from fire attack	Protective
Wall of Stone	Nature	Creates a stone wall	Protective
Astral Gate	Life	Creates a portal to other plane	Redecorating
Change Terrain	Nature	Alters the terrain in target map square	Redecorating
Earth Gate	Nature	Creates a means to teleport between cities	Redecorating
Enchant Road	Sorcery	Enchants all roads in 5X5 area	Redecorating
Move Fortress	Nature	Moves Enchanted Fortress to new city	Redecorating
Summoning Circle	Arcane	Moves Summoning Circle to a new city	Redecorating
Transmute	Nature	Changes mineral types in existing mineral deposit	Redecorating
Armageddon	Chaos	Raises volcanoes everywhere (see Raise Volcano)	Positive/Negative
Eternal Night	Death	Casts global Cloud of Shadow	Positive/Negative
Raise Volcano	Chaos	Raises volcano on target square, destroying production; Gives casting wizard one mana/turn	Positive/Negative
Black Wind	Death	Rains disease on all figures in target square or city	Destructive

Table 16.6 cont. *Spells and Cities: A Complete Reference*

Spell	Nature	Effect Description	Nature of Effect
Call the Void	Chaos	Can devastate a city's buildings, citizens, and garrison	Destructive
Chaos Rift	Chaos	Subjects city and garrisons to lightning attacks every turn	Destructive
Corruption	Chaos	Eliminates food and mineral production from target	Destructive
Cursed Lands	Death	Increases unrest by 1 and decreases production by 50%	Destructive
Earthquake	Nature	Can destroy buildings and garrison	Destructive
Evil Presence	Death	Increases unrest and causes loss of city's mana production	Destructive
Famine	Death	Halves food production by city's farmers; increases unrest	Destructive
Fire Storm	Chaos	Rains fire attack on all units in target square or city	Destructive
Great Wasting	Chaos	Causes corruption everywhere	Destructive
Ice Storm	Nature	Rains ice attack on all figures in target square or city	Destructive
Meteor Storms	Chaos	Chance of destroying any building in any city every turn	Destructive
Nature's Wrath	Nature	Causes earthquakes for casters of Death and Chaos magic	Destructive
Pestilence	Death	Causes death and increases unrest by 2	Destructive

Positive effects give the caster some specific benefit, such as increased mana or fewer rebels. Spells that positively affect specific economic variables or that protect a city from specific types of units or magic are indicated as such.

Spells that alter a city's structures, terrain, or terrain features are listed as "redecorating" spells.

Positive/Negative are as follows:
Armageddon and Raise Volcano are positive in that they result in a stream of mana income (1 mana per volcano per game turn) to the caster. They are clearly negative because they destroy lands and resources used by others. Eternal Night is both Positive and Negative because creatures of Death benefit from this spell, while creatures of Life are hindered by it and because it exerts its effects in all areas of Myrror and Arcanus.

Destructive effects cause damage to the target city's buildings, population, and/or units or foment rebellion and misery.

Forward, March!

Okay, put away those spreadsheets and roll up the ledgers. You've earned your diploma in *Master of Magic* economics.

Now we will take you from mild-mannered accountant to warlord deluxe. The next chapter begins our comprehensive analysis of military matters, beginning with what goes into a unit. Inspection will begin as soon as you turn the page.

Section 5

Who Goes There?

17

Vast, Unending Armies

An enormous number of different unit types appear *in Master of Magic*, with different abilities, strengths, and weaknesses. Making sense of your options when forming armies and garrisons requires an understanding of how to capitalize on the unique properties offered by the different unit types in *Master of Magic*. Unit properties are also an important concern when choosing your first city's race at the beginning of the game.

How to Read a Combat Unit

All units, from the lowliest spearman to the fearsome sky drake, share basic attributes: attack strengths, defensive abilities, resistances, etc. These attributes are shown on their unit displays and are broken down in the following way:

🐌 The number of figures in a unit is indicated on the unit's display. Each unit has one to nine figures. The statistics on the rest of the unit display are *for each figure* in the unit. That's a vital concept, so grasp it firmly as you read further.

🐌 Movement type and speed are indicated at the top of the unit display. See Table C in the game manual for information on the different modes of movement in *Master of Magic*. The number of movement points that the unit has per game and battle turn is indicated by the number of movement icons (boots, wings, waves, etc.). For example, a unit with three boots has three movement points of normal, overland movement to spend per game and battle turn.

🐌 Melee Attack Strength is shown as a series of swords on the unit display (and we use the terms "Melee Attack Strength" and "swords" interchangeably). Each sword represents one potential *hit* against an enemy unit when engaging in hand-to-hand combat. Note that *each figure* in the unit has the indicated at-

tack strength, so the potential damage that the whole unit can deal out is equal to the number of swords on the unit's statistics multiplied by the number of figures remaining in the unit. Chapter 20 has a full explanation of damage and defense in combat.

🐌 Ranged Attack Strength is shown in two ways. First there is an attack type: bows and rocks indicate different normal missile attacks and fireballs indicate magic ranged attacks. Magic ranged attacks only differ significantly from normal missiles in that they are not subject to decreases in accuracy over long distances. They are also subject to certain immunities (discussed in Chapter 20). The strength of a figure's ranged attack is shown by the number of bows, fireballs, etc.

🐌 Defense is shown as shields and indicates the number of chances each figure in the unit has to defend itself against incoming melees or ranged attacks. It is also the number of chances that unit has to defend against damage from certain destructive magic spells (see Chapter 21).

🐌 Resistance is shown by crosses and indicates the chance that the unit (or figure, when applicable) has to defend itself against spells and certain special attack types, such as gaze attacks (see Chapter 20).

🐌 Hits or hit points are shown as hearts on the unit display. This is the number of damage points each figure in the unit can take before dying. Hearts darken as a figure takes damage.

Whenever units get special bonuses to their basic statistics, such as attack bonuses from enchantments or artifacts, these are visible on the unit display as golden swords, shields, etc. Note that things are not always what they seem to be. Certain enchantments or abilities only apply under specific circumstances and their attribute bonuses are, in this case, not shown on the unit display. For example, the +10 shields and +10 crosses given by the spell Elemental Armor only apply when the enchanted unit is defending against a Chaos or Nature spell or certain ranged attacks. The enchantment's bonuses, therefore, are not shown on the unit's display.

Experience From Experience

All normal units also have an experience level. Recruits start out at zero experience. Tables H and K in the game manual indicate the statistical bonuses given to normal units and heroes as they gain experience levels. Our thoughts on the importance of experience levels follow. (Note that the unit lists are not exhaustive; primarily generic combat units are listed.)

🐸 Simply going from recruit to regular will *double* the melee attack strengths of bowmen and spearmen.

🐸 Many elite normal units (bowmen, magicians, priests, shamans, spearmen, swordsmen, etc.) are more than twice as difficult to kill as recruits. This is because each figure in the unit gets an extra heart (doubling the unit's hit points) and an extra shield when it reaches elite status.

🐸 If you are a Warlord or have cast the Life magic spell Crusade, the ultra-elite experience level increases units' ability To Hit by one and doubles (or more) the defenses of many basic unit types (e.g., bowmen, cavalry, catapults, spearmen, swordsmen, and triremes).

🐸 Accuracy, the ability *To Hit* another unit during melee or missile fire, starts to improve at the elite experience level, which is the highest level most units will ever reach. Accuracy is important for all units, but especially for missile units, such as bowmen, because the accuracy of these weapons decreases with distance (the farther away the target, the lower its To Hit chance).

🐸 Experienced units are significantly better than their green counterparts and don't cost any more to maintain! So, when you've got a unit up to a high level, think twice before throwing it away on hopeless engagements.

🐸 Every experience level gives a normal unit a 10 percent increase (additive) in its ability to resist spells and special attacks (such as life-stealing or poison). In other words, an additional cross. That means that at the elite experience level, a unit has a 30 percent greater chance of resisting dangerous spells than when it started as a recruit.

🐸 The ultimate point is this: the weaker the unit, the more it gains, proportionally, from increases in experience levels. The only exceptions are the heroes because their gains, per experience level, are dramatic, and because they can gain so many levels.

Specific Experiences

So what can unit experience *really* do? How does it work in combination with special bonuses? Let's take a look at a few specific examples:

🐸 Orc spearmen are about as basic and lowly a unit type as can be found in *Master of Magic*. Their units are comprised of eight spearmen, each with a melee attack of one strength, a defense of two shields, one heart each, and a 40 percent chance of resisting any spell (i.e., four crosses). From this raw recruit stage, their attacks double when they hit the next experience level and increase to three times their initial value when Orc spearmen become elite. Their defenses also double by the time they are elite, as do their hit points.

Looking at this in the most simplistic way, at the elite level, these units are three times stronger and four times harder to kill. At the elite level, they also gain a +1 To Hit, making their inherent accuracy jump from 30 percent to 40 percent. Finally, their ability to resist spells increases by 10 percent per level, giving them a base resistance of 70 percent by the time they are elite.

Of course the gains are even more impressive if the units can get to higher experience levels; i.e., if you are a Warlord, if you've cast Crusade, or if you are sitting on top of a mithril or adamantium mine. The significance of these statistics in combat is discussed in detail in Chapter 20.

🐸 Halfling slingers are the end-stage, power Halfling unit. When slingers first come off the assembly line, it is a little difficult to appreciate their finer qualities. Recruit slinger units have eight figures each with a two-strength missile attack, two shields, eight crosses, and one heart. (We're neglecting slinger melee attacks, since this is not their forte.)

Let's take these units straight to the elite level. When elite, slingers have a four-strength missile attack (that's eight guys with four attacks each) with a 50 percent chance To Hit. The extra 10 percent chance To Hit comes from the fact that all Halfling units are lucky, giving them an extra 10 percent modifier for almost everything they do. This extra To Hit chance is especially important here because slingers are missile units; their accuracy depreciates over distance. So, the higher their base accuracy, the better they'll hit under any circumstance. Furthermore, elite slingers have double the shields, double hit points, and a resistance of 11.

So far, they don't look too bad. Let's combine their advantages with an alchemist's guild and an adamantium mine (we may as well go all the way with these guys). We suddenly get another +1 To Hit from the guild, giving the slingers an accuracy of 60 percent. On top of that, the adamantium bonus gives the slinger units two extra attacks, so at the elite level, the slingers will have eight attacks of strength six each. Finally, they'll be even harder to kill because the adamantium bonus gives units an extra two shields. Their final stats will be a total attack strength of 48 (with a deadly 60 percent accuracy), six shields and two hearts per figure, and a resistance of 11. Not bad considering their humble origins as recruits!

🐸 Our last example will be Dwarven hammerhands. These units are brutally strong, even when they're newborn. Hammerhands have six figures, each with a strength eight melee attack, three shields, four hearts, and a resistance of nine. Dragging them up to an elite level will gain them a strength 10 attack (with a 40 percent To Hit chance), five shields, five hit points, and a resistance of 12. Add adamantium and an alchemist's guild, and you'll have a melee attack of 12 (that's a net attack strength of 72 hits) with a 50 percent To Hit chance, and seven shields per figure in the hammerhand unit. That gives fully developed hammerhands more attacks, net shields, and hearts than a great drake! None of this means that a single hammerhand unit can kill a great drake. A great drake's fiery breath attack can wipe out a lot of figures before the hammerhand unit can strike back. And, as a unit loses figures during combat, it loses a lot of strength (see Chapter 20). However, a *team* of developed hammerhands *can* kill great drakes.

At the end of the day, be aware that experienced units significantly outclass recruits. This makes some of the expensive buildings, like the war college, important to have in your main production cities. While adamantium and mithril bonuses are discussed further in this chapter, remember that their bonuses to attack and defense strengths, especially for races that can build alchemist's guilds (i.e., all races but Gnolls, Klackons, Lizardmen, and Trolls) are enormous, especially for multi-figure units.

Normal Unit Types

Aside from basic attributes, many units have inherent special abilities (also indicated on their displays). Some of the more important special abilities present in basic unit types are as follows:

 Healing and purification of corrupted land can be performed by priest and shaman units. Some races, Dwarves, Gnolls, High Elves, and Klackons, cannot build these units and suffer a significant disability when playing against wizards with Chaos magic (due to red magic's Corruption and Great Wasting spells).

 Strong magic ranged attacks and destructive combat spells are basic abilities of magician and warlock units. These units are powerful, especially at advanced experience levels, and are particularly useful in garrisons. Offensively, these units are at risk because the defending side always gets to move first in combat and usually prioritizes weak units with a ranged attack. Defensively, magicians and warlocks can use their full destructive power before an attacker's first battle turn.

 Wall-crushing abilities can break down city walls and are inherent in engineer and catapult units. By destroying sections of city walls, garrisoned units in the squares with broken walls are accessible to accurate missile fire and melee attacks. If missile units form the bulk of your city-conquering force, catapult units, with their long ranged attacks, are the perfect complementary unit.

 First-strike weapons and rapid movement are part of basic cavalry units. These units can rush up to enemies and get in the first wallop before being hit or counterattacked. Their speed makes them particularly useful for quickly taking out enemy missile units. Their first-strike capability may also enable them to take less damage when they attack enemy units (Chapter 20 elaborates on the first-strike concept).

 Large shields possessed by swordsmen units provide added protection against enemy missile fire and can aid in defending cities against enemy bowmen, especially when you haven't built any city walls yet.

 Negate first strike is the one special ability of all halberdier (and pikeman) units. Halberdiers are the most powerful standard unit available to most races. These units have added strength because of their ability to prevent enemy units (like paladins, elven lords, griffins, and death knights) from damaging them before they get a chance to counterattack. Being able to return blows is at least important as being able to take them, and halberdiers excel at both.

As you glance over the offerings of standard unit types, you can see that balancing armies for specific purposes (e.g., taking a host of cavalry and swordsmen to conquer towns with bowmen-stocked garrisons) or to provide for almost all contingencies with a smattering of many different unit types is an important facet of this game. When constructing armies, you should be aware of the particular skills and limitations of each unit type available, especially early in the game when your options are limited to essentially weak, basic unit types.

Special Unit Types That Are Race-Specific

Besides the standard unit types (spearmen, bowmen, priests, swordsmen, etc.) that are available to many or all of the races, there are also units specific to each race. The race-specific units have their own special abilities and properties. What follows is a discussion of one or more units specific to each race (not all unit types are discussed):

🐸 Berserkers are the tough, powerful unit of Barbarians. Aside from their strong fighting ability, they have a two-strength thrown attack that lets them target flying units, something most ground troops cannot do. Thrown attacks are also first strike attacks and so can be used to get in a swing before opponents can counterattack. As end-line units go for the different races, berserkers might not seem too impressive. However, at elite levels and en masse, they can form a powerful backbone to most all-purpose armies or garrisons.

🐸 Minotaurs are the units of choice when you're playing with the Beastmen. These are strong, hardy units with an inherent +2 bonus To Hit. This gives even minotaur recruits a 50 percent chance of landing every blow. Imagine their possibilities when built near an adamantium mine! Elite minotaurs built in adamantium-rich cities can even be used to tackle the most ferocious units in the game: drakes (especially if you can web those drakes first) and great wyrms.

🐸 Nightmares are the flying, killer units of Dark Elves. (Note that Dark Elves also have the powerful, Doom Bolt-wielding warlocks.) Nightmares are fast, flying units with strong melee attacks, many hit points (10 each to start) and a magic ranged attack. Their flying and ranged attacks make them great units for invading and conquering neutral or poorly garrisoned cities. Their speed also helps when confronting other dangerous flying units.

The warlocks' uses are more obvious. With their strong magic ranged attacks and their Doom Bolts, flocks of warlocks can take down a lot of units before they're stopped, especially

in situations where they are not fighting other ranged units.

🐸 Air ships are the most powerful Draconian units. Although all Draconians can fly, most of their units are disappointingly fragile, especially for a Myrran race. The air ships compensate a good deal for this, however. Capable of powerful, wall-crushing rock attacks, air ships are also extremely fast, with four movement points per turn. A couple of ships can seriously dent or kill many units and, because they fly, they are hard to take down.

Flying units, in general, are excellent for another reason: their inaccessibility to many other units' melee attacks allows you take flyers into situations where you can dominate a battlefield just by casting deadly spells. One flying unit, in conjunction with all-purpose killers like the Death spell Wrack or Chaos' Flame Strike, works well as a city conquering strategy. Alternately, casting summoning spells to do your flyer's fighting for you is another viable battlefield technique.

🐸 Hammerhands are the all-powerful Dwarven units. At their peak (even without any special bonuses from mithril or adamantium), these little guys can pack a net punch of 60 swords when they attack or counterattack, placing them on par with the toughest units in the game. When they're enhanced with special spells or magic weapons, hammerhands in large groups are almost unbeatable.

Dwarves can also produce golems. These strong units are immune to Death magic and poison and wield a powerful 12-strength melee attack. In addition, their high resistance to spells (15 crosses), and sturdy nature, make these units very hard to kill.

Dwarves have another particularly useful unit, the steam cannon. Steam cannons are remarkably sturdy ranged attack units that are resistant to spells and relatively inexpensive (at least for Dwarves). Steam cannons are also the *only* Dwarven ranged attack unit and nicely balance an all-Dwarven army.

🐾 Wolf riders are the power unit of Gnolls. Their greatest asset is their speed. At three movement points per turn, there isn't much they can't run down, or outrun, on the battlefield. If you don't have flying units, fast units are the next best thing. Speed lets you escape bigger, badder ground units (outrunning them until combat ends) and lets you get to the enemy's rearguard missile units quickly, before they can decimate your ranks.

🐾 Slingers are *the* Halfling units. Before you get these guys, Halfling units aren't worth a whole lot, although their luck gets these weaklings through a lot. Once you have slingers, though, you can meet most challenges. Wait for the slingers to gain experience before you use them, and only build them near mithril or adamantium mines, if you can (otherwise you're shortchanging their potential).

It's worth waiting until you have a solid army of top-of-the-line slinger units. Because of their inherent accuracy, they can take down the toughest units in the game and laugh about it afterward. A host of experienced slingers can pull down a couple drakes, demon lords, or great wyrms without a problem. If you can make them fly, through Sorcery's Flight or the Chaos Channel spell, or enchant them in other useful ways, small sets of slingers can take over towns and nodes very efficiently.

🐾 Longbowmen are a superb, early unit available to High Elves. Longbowmen are like super bowmen; they have long-range attacks and so they never suffer a penalty greater than -1 to their ability To Hit their targets. On top of this, they get a +1 bonus To Hit and have stronger missile attacks than regular bowmen units. Longbowmen can take you far into a game with High Elves, which is good because

this race grows slowly and it takes some time to get to its end-line units.

Those end-line High Elf units, though, are powerful and worth the wait. Elven lords have armor-piercing (halves shields), first strike attacks with an inherent +2 To Hit. That gives them a base accuracy of 50 percent, before they gain any experience at all. Their attacks are completed before defending units can counterattack, and they effectively get twice as many hits because of the armor-piercing nature of their attacks. Elven lords are so strong that there really isn't any special need to give hints on using them well. Just let them get in the first attack, if they can.

🐾 Paladins are the final High Men units. Forget everything else; once paladins are out there, your worries are over. These units are capable of conquering virtually everything except, perhaps, nodes infested by multitudes of drakes or great wyrms. They have immunity to magic, so they can't be taken down by spells or magic ranged attacks. Their attacks are armor-piercing and first strike, just like the elven lords discussed above. On top of that, they have a holy bonus that raises all friendly units' stats at the battle by one. Packs of paladins, thus, are deadly. When enchanted by spells (Eldritch Weapon, Lion Heart, Flight), little can stop them.

🐾 Stag beetles are the big Klackon units. These are solid, strong units. They have a fairly strong fiery breath attack and so can be used to attack flying units. Their greatest asset is that they can be built early in the game, if you've started with Klackons, often before other wizards are building their powerful units. This can give you an early initiative in conquering neutral cities. Consider building on large land masses if you are starting with this race, so that you can really avail yourself of this unit's strength.

🐢 Dragon turtles are the Lizardmen's equivalent to the Klackon's stag beetle. They are virtually identical except for one essential and important difference: dragon turtles swim (so you don't need big land masses). Build these units early and send them everywhere. Combining them with the Lizardmen's crack missile unit, javelineers, will give you the physical strength to take many neutral cities and to successfully explore lairs early in the game.

🦅 Griffins are the end-stage Nomad unit. These flying creatures have first strike, armor-piercing attacks. While flight is an inherent advantage, particularly if your spell-casting abilities give you powerful means to destroy enemy units, the attack capability of griffins is also useful. Because they fly, griffins can frequently choose what and when to attack; this lets them use their first strike ability to its utmost. Use griffins to selectively eliminate physically weak units with dangerous attacks first. However, griffins are only moderately sturdy, so don't use them as the backbone of a killer army unless you have no viable alternatives.

🐉 Wyvern riders are the Orcs' one big contribution to originality in *Master of Magic*. Their greatest assets are that they are fast flying units, at three movement points per turn, and that they have a strength six poison attack on top of their normal melee attack. These units are fast enough to escape most enemies, and their flying ability generally lets them choose their targets. Wyvern riders are strong enough to include in an army as a solid basic unit. Make the most of their flying ability though; that's where their greatest strength lies.

🧌 War trolls are the killer units from hell; like most Troll units, they keep coming and coming and coming. As they are strong and regenerating, not much can stop these units.

Their regeneration ability, in combination with their relative speed (two movement points per turn), lets them do *attack dancing* when they want. That is, they get to close in to melee, but when they're dangerously injured they can use their speed to run away on the combat field until they've regenerated enough hit points to close in and start swinging again. War trolls are awesome units that can hold their own against almost anything.

As you can tell from the notes above, there is a lot of variety in the types of units you may have available when you play *Master of Magic*. When you know a unit's strengths and weaknesses, you have all the tools you need to determine how it can be used in forming solid armies or special attack squads.

Comparison of Armies by Race

One of the most basic questions in *Master of Magic* is which races form better armies than others. The following tables are designed to give you a feel for which races are better militarily than others. Table 17.1 shows how the statistics of standard unit types differ among the various races.

Fantastic Units

The fantastic units differ from normal units in that they are summoned, rely on mana for upkeep, and don't gain experience levels. Each of the fantastic units is discussed in the appropriate spell chapter (see Chapters 7 through 12); all of their special attacks and defenses are discussed in Chapter 20. Here, we will discuss some key fantastic unit types and their special abilities. This will give you a feel for the sorts of options you have when you create armies with them. Note that *only common and uncommon units are discussed here*, since these are accessible when you choose even one spell book of a particular magic color. Look under the appropriate spell

Table 17.1 *Comparison of Standard Unit Statistics by Race*

Race	Attacks (Swords)	To Hit	Defense (Shields)	To Defend	Resistance (Crosses)	Hit Points (Hearts)	Notes
Barbarians					+1		some have thrown attacks
Beastmen	+1				+1	+1	
Dark Elves					+3		ranged magic attacks
Draconians			+1		+2		fiery breath and flying
Dwarves					+4	+2	
Gnolls	+2						
Halflings	-1	+1		+1	+2		+ To Hit/ Defend from luck
High Elves		+1			+2		
High Men							
Klackons			+2*		+1		
Lizardmen			+1			+1	swim
Nomads							
Orcs							
Trolls	+2				+3	+3	regenerate; 4 figures/ unit

This table lists the statistical differences for standard unit types (spearmen, swordsmen, bowmen, triremes, cavalry, halberdiers, etc.) among the different races where it varies from the standard for that unit type. For example, most spearmen units have one hit point per figure. Every race's spearman units will have this value unless a different number is indicated in the Hit Points column. Lizardman spearmen each have an additional hit point, or a total of two hit points, per figure.

Note that the default ability To Hit is three (or 30 percent chance to land a blow). The default ability To Defend is also three (or 30 percent). Each +1 in these areas and in resistance indicates a +10 percent in this ability.

*The Klackon defense bonus does not apply to its engineer unit type.

chapter for information on rare and very rare fantastic creatures.

🐍 Chimeras, cockatrices, gargoyles, and doom bats are all flying units with solid attacks and defenses. The added attacks enjoyed by most of these units (stoning touch, fiery breath, immolation) make nice additions to their already stout ratings. These units can be used to form a *flying corps* and, in combination with spell casting in combat, can de-

feat many mid-strength armies, garrisons, and lairs.

🐍 Fire elementals, phantom warriors, and phantom beasts can be summoned during combat for increased attack capabilities or diversionary maneuvers (drawing attacks away from more valuable units). The illusionary (armor-ignoring) attacks of phantom warriors and beasts are particularly welcome in pruning hit points off of enemy units. Their attacks are particularly effective against multi-figure units because the resulting loss of figures in such units makes their subsequent attacks against your troops less fearsome.

🐌 Hell hounds, war bears, nagas, magic spirits, guardian spirits, and skeletons are generally nothing to write home about. They are the cheap, stable units from each magic realm. As such, they are essentially magical grunts, primarily useful in fleshing out your armies at the earliest stages in the game. Since their upkeep costs are in mana, these units are particularly welcome when your gold and food supplies are limited.

Other than these benefits, the best things that can be said about these units types are 1) guardian and magic spirits are good for exploration because they move fairly quickly and can travel over every terrain type; 2) nagas swim, albeit slowly, and can explore and conquer weak lairs and ruins on other continents; 3) hell hounds have fiery breath that can attack flyers and toast weak units; 4) war bears are actually pretty strong and more than a match for many spearmen and other weak units; 5) a skeleton's biggest asset is its immunity to missiles and its extra cheap casting and upkeep cost, making large armies of these undead units very affordable.

🐌 Ghouls are minor units with one big plus: they can create undead units out of enemies they kill. Use ghoul armies when marching on weakly garrisoned towns, but never attack with a full stack of nine units, or enemy units can't be raised to flesh out your ranks. New undead units can be used right away to garrison the newly conquered town when your ghouls move on.

🐌 Sprites are defense kings. Bursting with little magic ranged attacks, these flying units are the perfect pre-shaman and pre-priest units to supplement a garrison. They're dynamite when garrisoning a Nature node, in

particular, because of bonuses they receive there (see Chapter 20). Furthermore, armies of sprites are great for conquering neutral cities early in the game (except for cities garrisoned with Dark Elves or other ranged attack units).

🐌 Giant spiders are almost always useful. Their Web spell can be cast anywhere (nodes don't dispel their webbing ability) and can ground drakes and other fearsome flying critters. Take a few with you whenever you can.

🐌 Shadow demons are like super sprites. They have eight brutal magic ranged attacks and they regenerate! Better still, they are noncorporeal (so they can't be webbed) and they fly. This allows them to bob out of range of most other units and complete their deadly ranged attacks before stooping to melee combat.

🐌 Unicorns are sturdy, mid-strength units whose chief asset is that they can teleport. This lets them pounce upon your enemy's rearguard ranged attack units on your first battle turn. Furthermore, as long as they aren't up against any remaining ranged units, they can outrun

Figure 17-1. *Small armies of sprites can be effective for conquering neutral cities.*

anyone on the battlefield (which makes them very useful as a garrison unit since they can easily wait out an enemy's 50 battle turns).

Most fantastic units aren't necessarily any better than the units you can build in your cities. What they provide are options: different forms of upkeep and different abilities to supplement your armies.

One final special unit type deserves a brief mention here: undead units. Undead units include all creatures summoned or permanently altered by black magic (werewolves, zombies, ghouls, black channeled units, animated units, etc.) Their defining characteristic is that they do not heal. The only way their hit points can be restored is if the units have the regeneration ability or life-stealing attacks (see Chapter 20). The best thing about undead units is that they are completely immune to all Death magic spells.

Some Enchanted Units

In *Master of Magic*, you have to work with what you've got. If your potential army units are pretty poor in nature, you still have options: you can always enchant them. Even the weakest units can become incredibly powerful if the right spells are cast on them. Table 17.2 lists the ways different enchantments affect unit statistics.

Table 17.2 lists both positive and negative enchantments. The most important thing to remember when casting spells designed to alter unit attributes is that the greatest effects will occur when you cast these spells on units *with multiple figures*. This is because effects are *always* on a per figure basis, not a per unit basis.

For example, adding two attacks to a stone giant simply adds two swords, total. But if you add two attacks to a halberdier unit, which has six figures, you add a total of 12 swords to that unit. Casting enchantments on multi-

figure units is the *key* to deciding when and where to cast unit enchantments.

Even when you don't have the option of choosing multi-figure over single-figure units, enchantments are worth casting whenever you wish to improve your battle odds. They can turn even the meekest units into killers. In fact, some enchantments (Lion Heart and Invulnerability) are so good that they're worth casting on almost any unit. These spells turn the most fragile units, like magicians, into Schwarzeneggeresque killer commandos.

No matter what your starting material is, you will generally have spells or other ways to mold it into something tremendous. When it comes to building effective units, it's not what you're dealt, but what you make of it when the chips are down.

From Here to Heroics

Now you have a microscope's eye view of a unit in *Master of Magic*. The comparisons of various unit types and their statistics, as modified by experience, race, and enchantments, are pivotal concepts for forming victorious armies. However, those who lead these armies in the field, your heroes, are the most important units of all. For them, we have dedicated the next chapter.

Table 17.2 *Bonuses to Unit Attributes and Abilities*

Spell, Mineral, Skill, Other	Unit	Melee To Hit	Melee	Thrown	Breath	Magic Ranged	Bows and Slings	Rocks	Ranged To Hit	Shields	To Defend	Hits	Resist	Comments
Chaos Unit Spells														
Chaos Channels	norm				2					+3				flying; only one effect
Eldritch Weapon	norm		All*	All			All				Opp-1			
Flame Blade	norm		+2*	+2			+2							
Immolation														+4 fiery touch
Shatter	norm		1	1	1	1	1	1						
Warp Creature			halve							halve			0	only one effect
Warp Wood	norm						All							lose missile ammo
Chaos Combat, City, or Global Enchantment														
Chaos Surge	Chaos		+2	+2	+2	+2	+2	+2		+2			+2	
Doom Mastery	norm													see Chaos Channels
Metal Fires	norm		+1*	+1			+1							
Warp Reality	non-Ch	-2							-2					
Death Unit Spells														
Berserk			double							0				
Black Channels	norm		+2	+1	+1	+1	+1	+1		+1		+1	+1	
Black Sleep														automatic damage
Cloak of Fear														decrease enemy attacks
Lycanthropy	norm													werewolf
Weakness			-2	-2			-2							
Wraithform														non-corporeal; weapon immunity
Death Combat, City, or Global Enchantments														
Black Prayer			-1	-1	-1	-1	-1	-1		-1			-2	
Cloud of Shadow														see Darkness
Darkness	Death		+1	+1	+1	+1	+1	+1		+1			+1	
	Life		-1	-1	-1	-1	-1	-1		-1			-1	
Eternal Night														see Darkness
Mana Leak														-1 magic ranged ammo or -5 mana per turn

Table 17.2 Cont. *Bonuses to Unit Attributes and Abilities*

Spell, Mineral, Skill, Other	Unit	Melee To Hit	Melee	Thrown	Breath	Magic Ranged	Bows and Slings	Rocks	Ranged To Hit	Shields	To Defend	Hits	Resist	Comments
Life Unit Spells														
Bless			B&R		All	B&R				+3			+3	vs. B&R spells
Endurance														+1 speed
Heroism	norm													elite level
Holy Armor	norm									+2				
Holy Weapon	norm	+1	*	All			All	All	+1					
Invulnerability														weapon immunity first 2 hits do no damage
Lion Heart			+3	+3			+3	+3				+3	+3	
Righteousness					All	B&R				(50)			+30	vs. B&R spells
True Sight														illusion immunity
Life Combat, City, or Global Enchantments														
Altar of Battle														elite level
Charm of Life												+25%		
Crusade	norm													+1 level
Heavenly Light														see True Light
High Prayer		+1	+2						+1	+2	+1		+3	Opp -1 To Hit
Holy Arms	norm	+1	All*	All			All	All	+1					
Prayer		+1							+1		+1		+1	Opp -1 To Hit
True Light	Life		+1	+1	+1	+1	+1	+1	+1				+1	
	Death		-1	-1	-1	-1	-1	-1	-1				-1	
Nature Unit Spells														
Elemental Armor					All	G&R				+10			+10	vs. G&R spells
Giant Strength			+1	+1										
Iron Skin										+5				
Regeneration														+1 heart per turn in combat
Resist Elements					All	G&R				+3			+3	vs. G&R spells
Stone Skin										+1				
Water Walking														+ swimming
Web														lose flying; temp paralysis
Nature Combat, City, or Global Enchantments														
Earth to Mud														lose moves
Entangle														-1 speed

Table 17.2 Cont. *Bonuses to Unit Attributes and Abilities*

				←	Ranged	Attacks		→						
Spell, Mineral, Skill, Other	Unit	Melee To Hit	Melee	Thrown	Breath	Magic Ranged	Bows and Slings	Rocks	Ranged To Hit	Shields	To Defend	Hits	Resist	Comments
Sorcery Unit Spells														
Flight														+ flying
Guardian Wind							All			(50)				missile immunity
Haste														double number of attacks and counter-attacks
Invisibility		Opp-1												no targeting at a distance
Magic Immunity					All	All				(50)			+30	immunity to most spells, touch and gaze attacks
Mind Storm			-5	-5	-5	-5	-5	-5	-5				-5	
Resist Magic													+5	
Vertigo		-2							-2	-1				
Wind Walking														+ flying and moving stack with wind walker
Sorcery Combat, City, or Global Enchantments														
Blur														negates 10% of all hits
Mass Invisibility		Opp-1												Invisibility
Wind Mastery														double ship speed; halve enemy ships'
Alchemist's Guild and Resources														
Alchemist's Guild	norm	+1	*	All			All	All	+1					
Mithril	norm	+1	+1*	+1			+1	+1	+1	+1				
Adamantium	norm	+1	+2*	+2			+2	+2	+1	+2				
Wizard Skills														
Alchemy Skill	norm	+1	*	All			All	All	+1					
Warlord Skill	norm													+1 level
Effects of Structures on Combat Statistics														
City Walls										+3				**
City Walls-broken										+1				**
Node Aura	Same		+2	+2	+2	+2	+2	+2		+2			+2	

Table 17.2 Cont. *Bonuses to Unit Attributes and Abilities*

Spell, Mineral, Skill, Other	Unit	Melee To Hit	Melee	Thrown	Breath	Magic Ranged	Bows and Slings	Rocks	Ranged To Hit	Shields	To Defend	Hits	Resist	Comments
Unit Skills														
Armor-Piercing	Opp								halved					
Charmed													+30	Heroes only
Large Shield				All	All	All	All	All	+2					
Lucky		+1							+1		+1		+1	Opp -1 To Hit
Magic Immunity					All	All			(50)				+30	
Missile Immunity				All			All		(50)					
Weapon Immunity			All						(10)					only if foe not using magic weapon
Unit Skills that affect all friendly units on the battlefield														
Holy Bonus			+1 +2						+1 +2				+1 +2	modifiers depend on Holy Bonus
Leadership	norm		+1 +2 +3 +4	+1 +1 +2	+1 +1 +2		+1 +1 +2	+1 +1 +2						bonus level depends on hero level
Prayer Master													+max	***
Resistance to All													+max	***

Column headings:
Unit: indicates the unit types that can be affected by the spell or skill.
Melee or Ranged *To Hit*: is the accuracy of the unit's melee or ranged attacks.
All listed attack types: indicate the strengths of those attacks; for example a +2 under melee means that the unit's melee attack strength is increased by two swords. A number without a plus or minus means that the spell results in the exact value shown. For example, Shatter reduces the attack strength from all attacks to one.
Shields: is the unit's defense.
To Defend: is the inherent ability of each shield to defend against a hit.
Hits: refers to hit points or hearts.
Resist: is the unit's resistance or crosses.
Comments: lists other effects that should be noted.

Clarification of how the values in this table affect a unit's combat performance is in Chapter 20.

Abbreviations:
All: The effects shown in the other columns apply to all attacks of this type. For example, Magic Immunity provides 50 shields against all magic ranged and breath attacks.
B&R: The numerical effects shown in the other columns only affect black (Death) and red (Chaos) spells or attacks of this type. Note: B&R melee attacks are those made by Death or Chaos units.
Chaos: Affects Chaos creatures only, including Chaos Channeled units.
Death: Affects Death creatures only, including Black Channeled and Animated units and those that have risen from the dead.
G&R: The numerical effects shown in the other columns only affect green (Nature) and red (Chaos) spells or attacks of this type.
Life: Affects Life creatures only.
non-Ch: Affects all units except for Chaos creatures.

Table 17.2 Cont. *Bonuses to Unit Attributes and Abilities*

norm: Affects normal units only. Summoned, Chaos Channeled, Black Channeled, and undead units are *not* normal.

Opp: Armor-piercing halves enemy units' shields in *melee combat.*

Opp-1: The indicated effect (-1) applies only to enemy units engaged in combat with the enchanted unit. Note that the Opp-1 To Hit modifiers for High Prayer, Prayer, and Lucky (like Invisibility) only affect enemy units' abilities To Hit during *melee combat.*

Same: Indicated bonuses only apply to creatures from the same magic realm as the node.

vs. 'X' spells: This spell causes the enchanted unit to have the indicated defense and/or resistance bonuses when it defends against spells of 'X' type.

(): Indicates that this value cannot be modified by spells or by armor-piercing attacks.

*This spell or influence changes the character of the unit's attack from non-magic to magic. Remember that magic attacks are just like regular attacks. The only difference is that magic weapon attacks can inflict damage on creatures with weapon immunity (see Chapter 20).

**All units within city walls, whether friend or foe, gain these benefits.

***Prayer Master and Resistance to All are basically the same skill; on the battlefield, the unit with the highest value for these skills applies the appropriate bonus to all other friendly units' resistances.

Note, mithril and adamantium only exert their effects once an alchemist's guild has been built in the city producing the unit.

Also, armor-piercing, Charm of Life, Warp Creature, and Berserk exert their effects on unit statistics *after all other* modifiers (such as unit or global enchantments) have exerted their effects.

Heroes

Of all the units in *Master of Magic*, he—roes have the greatest unrealized po—tential when you first acquire them. Through experience and by equipping pow-erful artifacts (Chapter 19), your heroes can become your greatest assets. Like Napoleon with his Marshals, you must learn to make the best use of your subordinate's abilities.

The Heroes

Each wizard in *Master of Magic* begins the game with an identical pool of 35 heroes. That means that "Brax the Berserker" is available to every wizard; he may not always be called Brax, but all of your opponents can have their *own* Berserker who is identical to Brax. The same is true for all the other heroes. In fact, you can get a fair idea of which heroes you're up against when you look at your enemies' armies, because the heroes all have unique classes. For example, if you see that your en-emy has a "Druid," that means he or she has some version of Greyfairer the Druid (see Table 18.1).

Some of the starting heroes may not be available in a game since they require a wiz-ard have certain spell books (Death or Life) before they will join that wizard. Table 18.1 lists all of the heroes in *Master of Magic*. This table includes the fame level your wizard must achieve before heroes will offer their services, the heroes' hiring and upkeep costs, and the special skills they *always* come with. Most heroes vary slightly between games because they have a certain number of randomly de-termined "picks" or skills when they appear. This will be discussed more in a later section of this chapter.

Explaining the Hero List

Table 18.1 shows the starting statistics for all the heroes in *Master of Magic*. These are the minimal starting values for these heroes. The actual values may be higher if a hero starts with additional random hero skills. These ran-dom hero skills are indicated in the *Rndm* col-umn. For example, some heroes will get one Fighter pick in addition to the skills shown here. Depending on the skills that hero already has, he may then get Might, Constitution, Agility, Blade Master, Luck, Charmed, etc.; or, if he already has one of those skills, he may get its *super* version. Table 18.2 lists the different Fighter, Mage, and Any random hero picks.

In addition to showing the starting at-tributes for all heroes, each hero has a second set of numbers listed below his base statistics. This second set is the minimum value for the hero's attributes once he reaches *demi-god* status. Again, the hero's actual statistics will depend on the additional skills he has (and the artifacts he is carrying). However, know-ing a hero's potential demi-god stats can give you a good idea of that hero's growth potential.

Fame shows the minimum fame required before the indicated hero will step forward and offer his services. Note that Summon Hero and Summon Champion can be used to acquire heroes with higher fame requirements than that possessed by the casting wizard.

Atk is the melee attack strength of the hero, and the hero's accuracy is indicated in the To Hit column. A To Hit of 3 represents a 30 percent chance of hitting the target for each attack the hero makes.

Rng is the ranged attack strength of the hero (breath and thrown attacks are considered ranged attacks because they allow units to attack flyers).

Type refers to the kind of ranged attack the hero has. Arrows, breath, thrown, and magic-ranged attacks are indicated. In addi-tion, the color (green, red, or blue) of any magic ranged attacks are included. Note that different enchantments (Righteousness, Resist Elements, Elemental Armor, and Bless) con-fer protection against specific colors of magic attacks. For example, Elemental Armor pro-

Table 18.1 *List of Heroes*

Hero Name	Fame	Class	Atk	To Hit	Rng	Type	Def	Res	Hits	Hire	Maint	Rndm	Skills	Hero Skills	Spells
Brax	0	Berserker	5	3	-	-	4	10	10	100	2	None	Mountain Walk	Constitution	-
(demi-god)			13	6	-	-	8	18	27						
Gunthar	0	Barbarian	13	3	3	Thrown	4	6	9	100	2	None	-	Might	-
(demi-god)			22	6	11		8	14	17						
Zaldron	0	Sage	1	3	6	Blue Magic	3	6	5	100	2	None	-	Sage, Spell Caster 7	Counter Magic, Dispel Magic, True
(demi-god)			9	6	14		7	14	13					Spell Caster 67	
B'Shan	0	Dervish	4	3	4	Arrow	4	6	7	100	-	None	-	Noble	-
(demi-god)			12	6	12		8	14	15						
Rakir	0	Beastmaster	5	3	-	-	5	6	6	100	2	None	Forest Walk, Scouting 3	Spell Caster 5	Resist Elements
(demi-god)			13	6	-	-	9	14	14					Spell Caster 45	
Valana	0	Bard	4	3	-	-	4	7	8	100	2	None	-	Leadership, Spell Caster 5	Confusion, Vertigo
(demi-god)			12	6	-	-	8	15	16					Spell Caster 45	
Bahgtru	0	Orc Warrior	6	3	3	Thrown	5	6	5	100	2	1 Ftr	Mountain Walk	-	-
(demi-god)			14	6	11		9	14	13						
Serena	0	Gypsy Healer	3	3	6	Green Magic	3	7	7	100	2	1 Mage	Natural Healer	Spell Caster 7	Healing
(demi-god)			11	6	14		7	15	15					Spell Caster 67	
Shuri	0	Huntress	5	3	4	Arrow	3	6	7	100	2	1 Ftr	Forest Walk, Mountain Walk, Pathfinding	Blade Master	-
(demi-god)			13	10	12	-	7	14	15						

Table 18.1 Cont. *List of Heroes*

Hero Name	Fame	Class	Atk	To Hit	Rng	Type	Def	Res	Hits	Hire	Maint	Rndm	Skills	Hero Skills	Spells
Theria	0	Thief	5	3	-	-	5	6	37	100	2	None	-	Agile / Charmed	-
(demi-god)			13	6	-	-	18	14	45						
Greyfairer	5	Druid	1	3	8	Green Magic	5	6	5	150	3	None	Scouting 3 / Purification	Spell Caster 7	Ice Bolt / Petrify / Web
(demi-god)			9	6	16		9	14	13					Spell Caster 67	
Taki	5	War Monk	6	3	-	-	5	6	6	150	3	1 Ftr	-	Super Agile	-
(demi-god)			14	6	-		22	14	14						
Reywind	5	Warrior Mage	4	3	4	Red Magic	4	6	7	150	3	1 Any	-	Spell Caster 5	Flame Blade / Shatter / Eldritch Weapon
(demi-god)			12	6	12		8	14	15					Spell Caster 45	
Malleus	5	Magician	1	3	8	Red Magic	5	10	5	150	3	1 Mage	Missile Imm	Arcane Power / Spell Caster 10	Fire Bolt / Fireball / Flame Strike / Fire Elemental
(demi-god)			9	6	25		9	14	13					Spell Caster 90	
Tumu	5	Assassin	3	3	0	None	5	6	6	150	3	1 Ftr	-	Blade Master	-
(demi-god)			11	10	-		9	18	14						
Jaer	10	Wind Mage	1	3	6	Green Magic	5	6	5	200	4	1 Mage	Wind Walking / Missile Imm	Spell Caster 7	Word of Recall / Guardian Wind
(demi-god)			9	6	14		9	14	13					Spell Caster 67	
Marcus	10	Ranger	6	3	5	Arrow	5	6	8	200	4	None	Mountain Walk / Forest Walk / Scouting 2	Might / Spell Caster 5	Resist Elements / Stone Skin
(demi-god)			23	6	13		9	14	16					Spell Caster 45	

Table 18.1 Cont. *List of Heroes*

Hero Name	Fame	Class	Atk	To Hit	Rng	Type	Def	Res	Hits	Hire	Maint	Rndm	Skills	Hero Skills	Spells
Fang	10	Draconian	7	3	5	Breath	5	6	8	200	4	2 Ftr	Flying	Might	-
(demi-god)			24	6	13	-	9	14	16						
Morgana	10	Witch	1	3	8	Red Magic	5	36	5	200	4	2 Mage Missile Imm		Charmed Spell Caster 10	Darkness Possession Black Prayer Mana Leak
(demi-god)			9	6	16	-	9	44	13					Spell Caster 90	
Aureus	10	Golden One	6	3	6	Red Magic	6	6	6	200	4	2 Any	-	Spell Caster 5	-
(demi-god)			14	6	14	-	10	14	14					Spell Caster 45	
Shin Bo	20	Ninja	6	3	0	None	5	6	7	300	6	2 Ftr	Invisible	Blade Master	-
(demi-god)			14	10	-	-	9	14	15						
Spyder	20	Rogue	7	3	0	None	5	6	8	300	6	1 Ftr	-	Leadership Super Legendary	
(demi-god)			15	6	-	-	9	14	16						
Shalla	20	Amazon	7	3	4	Thrown	4	36	8	300	6	1 Ftr	-	Charmed Might Blade Master	
(demi-god)			24	10	12	-	8	44	16						
Yramrag	20	Warlock	1	3	8	Red Magic	5	10	5	300	6	1 Mage Missile Imm		Spell Caster 15	Lightning Bolt Doom Bolt Warp Lightning
(demi-god)			9	6	16	-	9	18	13					Spell Caster 135	
Mystic X	20	Unknown	5	3	5	Red Magic	4	10	8	300	6	5 Any	-	Spell Caster 5	-
(demi-god)			13	6	13	-	8	18	16					Spell Caster 45	

Table 18.1 Cont. *List of Heroes*

Hero Name	Fame	Class	Atk	To Hit	Rng	Type	Def	Res	Hits	Hire	Maint	Rndm	Skills	Hero Skills	Spells
Aerie	40	Illusionist	1	3	5	Blue Magic	4	6	5	500	10	2 Mage	Illusionary Attacks, Missile Imm	Spell Caster 10	Psionic Blast, Vertigo, Mind Storm
(demi-god)			9	6	13	-	8	14	13					Spell Caster 90	
Death-stryke	40	Swordsman	6	3	0	None	5	6	10	500	10	1 Ftr	-	Constitution, Arms Master, Leadership, Legendary, Might	-
(demi-god)			23	6	-	-	9	14	27						
Elana	40*	Priestess	2	3	8	Green Magic	5	14	5	500	-	None	Natural Healer, Purification	Charmed, Arcane Power, Spell Caster 12, Noble, Super Prayer Master	Dispel Evil, Healing, Prayer, Holy Word
(demi-god)			10	6	25	-	9	36	13					Spell Caster 112	
Roland	40*	Paladin	9	3	0	None	5	6	8	500	10	1 Ftr	First Strike, Armor-Piercing, Natural Healer, Magic Immunity	Super Might, Prayer Master, Legendary	-
(demi-god)			30	6	-	-	9	14	16						
Mortu	40**	Black Knight	9	3	0	None	5	6	10	500	10	1 Ftr	First Strike, Armor-Piercing, Magic Immunity	Legendary, Might, Blade Master, Constitution	-
(demi-god)			26	10	-	-	9	14	27						
Alorra	40	Elven Archer	5	3	8	Arrow	6	6	6	500	10	3 Any	Forest Walk, Mountain Walk, Pathfinding	Blade Master	-
(demi-god)			13	10	16	-	10	14	14						

Table 18.1 Cont. *List of Heroes*

Hero Name	Fame	Class	Atk	To Hit	Rng	Type	Def	Res	Hits	Hire	Maint	Rndm	Skills	Hero Skills	Spells
Sir Harold	40	Knight	8	3	0	None	5	6	9	500	-	1 Ftr	First Strike, Armor-Piercing	Constitution, Super Leadership, Super Legendary, Noble	-
(demi-god)			16	6	-	-	9	14	26						
Ravashack	40**	Necromancer	1	3	7	Red, Magic	5	6	5	500	10	2 Mage	Life-stealing Attacks, Missile Imm	Arcane Power, Spell Caster 12	Weakness, Black Sleep, Animate Dead, Wrack
(demi-god)			9	6	24	-	9	14	13					Spell Caster 112	
Warrax	40	Chaos Warrior	8	3	8	Red, Magic	5	9	8	500	10	3 Any	Armor-Piercing Attacks	Constitution, Spell Caster 10, Arcane Power	-
(demi-god)			16	6	25	-	9	14	25					Spell Caster 90	
Torin True Light	***	The Chosen	12	3	0	None	8	17	12	***	12 mana	2 Any	Missile Imm	Magic Immunity, Constitution, Super Leadership, Prayer Master, Spell Caster 15	Super Might, Healing, Holy Armor, Lion Heart
(demi-god)			33	6	-	-	12	20	29					Spell Caster 135	

*You must have Life spell books to get this hero.

**You must have Death spell books to get this hero.

***Torin is summoned by the Life magic spell, Incarnation.

tects against green and red magic ranged attacks (see Chapter 20).

Def, Res, and *Hits* refer to the shields, crosses, and hearts that hero has.

Hire and *Maint* are the hiring and upkeep costs of the hero.

Rndm indicates the number and type (*Ftr,* for Fighter; *Mage* or *Any*) of additional skills the hero gets.

Using the Hero List

All of the heroes in Table 18.1 are in your starting pool unless you lack necessary spell books. If you have no Life spell books, you cannot acquire Torin the Chosen, Elana the Priestess, or Roland the Paladin; similarly you cannot get Mortu the Black Knight or Ravashack the Necromancer if you have no Death books. Heroes return to this pool of accessible heroes if you decide to dismiss them. If the heroes die, they can be brought back through the Life spell Resurrection.

Heroes that manage to return after their dismissal do so at one experience level higher (but at a maximum level of Commander) than they were when dismissed. Resurrected or resummoned heroes return at the same experience they were when they left. If you win a battle in which a hero dies, you obtain all of the fallen hero's artifacts, unless the hero dies from Banish, Cracks Call, Disintegrate, Dispel Evil, Holy Word, Word of Death, Petrify, stoning gaze, or stoning touch.

Random Hero Picks

All heroes have their standard features (as shown in Table 18.1), and many have random features. The stable features include many of the starting attributes, such as attack strength, type of ranged attack, To Hit, etc. Stable features may also include certain skills. For example, the gypsy healer has an inherent ability to cast spells, including the Life spell Healing. In addition to their stable features, many heroes vary each game by nature of their randomly chosen special abilities. Table 18.2 shows the special abilities that can be randomly assigned for the *Fighter, Mage,* and *Any* picks given to heroes.

The random hero picks can greatly enhance a hero's abilities. Carefully observe every new hero's *skills*. Their skills are the basis upon which you should judge whether to hire that hero. The question to always ask each prospective new hero is: are you bringing skills I can use to the party? It's okay to be picky and turn away heroes whose skills you can't use in the near future.

For example, Valana the Bard is not a strong hero. However, her natural leadership ability makes her useful early in the game. Having her travel with your armies of swordsmen, bowmen, or other early game units, will improve the combat skills of these normal units and greatly improve their chances of winning battles.

Super Skills

Because of these random skill picks for heroes, luck might find them picking the same particular skill twice (if they are allowed more than one pick or if they already have that skill as one of their standard features). A skill that has been thus picked twice becomes a *super* version of that skill. Super versions give a 50 percent greater benefit than that skill's normal version.

For example, let's say that we have a hero who has no natural special abilities but who does have two random Fighter picks. If he chooses might two times, that hero will arrive at your door with one skill: super might. Instead of gaining one extra point to melee attack strength with every level, that hero will gain one and one-half extra points instead.

In a second example, if a hero naturally has arcane power and is allowed one random Mage pick, that hero may pick arcane power. In this case, the hero will start with super arcane power and nothing else.

Table 18.2 *Random Hero Picks*

Available Picks	Brief Description	Fighter Picks	Mage Picks	Any Picks
Agility	improves hero's defense	yes		yes
Arcane Power	improves hero's ranged magic attacks		yes	yes
Arms Master	gives experience points every turn to units stacked with hero	yes		yes
Blade Master	improves hero's To Hit	yes		yes
Charmed	hero gets +30 to resistance	yes	yes	yes
Constitution	improves hero's hit points	yes		yes
Leadership	improves all normal, friendly unit's combat statistics	yes		yes
Legendary	improves wizard's fame	yes		yes
Luck	gives hero +1 To Hit, To Defend and resistance	yes	yes	yes
Might	improves hero's melee attack strength	yes		yes
Noble	hero has no upkeep cost and wizard gets 10 gold per turn	yes	yes	yes
Prayer Master	gives resistance bonus to all friendly units in combat		yes	yes
Sage	gives wizard extra spell research points		yes	yes
Spell Caster*	increases hero's spell skill		yes	yes

*A Spell Caster skill improves the hero's base spell skill value by two and one-half, rounded down (see Table 18.3). This base value is multiplied as the hero gains levels. The hero's spell skill determines how many spells he can cast in combat and, if he also has arcane power, how many magic ranged attacks he can launch (each magic ranged attack costs three spell skill points).

Note that a hero can get several of his Mage or Any picks in the Spell Caster skill. For each such randomly assigned pick, the hero's base spell skill will improve by two and one-half.

Heroes may not get a Spell Caster or Arcane pick if they do not already possess these skills (see Table 18.1).

Heroes with spell-casting skill that are at your Enchanted Fortress contribute half their Spell Caster skill to *your* spell casting skill when you are casting spells outside of combat. For example, a hero with a spell skill of 30, when in your fortress city, will allow you to funnel an extra 15 mana per game turn into any non-combat spells you are casting (provided, of course, you have the mana available).

Certain hero skills cannot be picked twice: noble, charmed, and luck. Once these have been picked they are no longer available for that hero's random skill picks. Also, all skills, except for spell caster, may not be picked three times; if the hero has a super version of a skill, that skill will not be included in his remaining random picks.

Table 18.3 lists the contributions each hero skill makes per experience level, depending on whether or not the hero has a normal or super version of the skill. As you can see from Table 18.3, hero skills can exert tremendous effects, especially as heroes gain experience levels. Before your heroes can gain levels, however, you first have to actually acquire them.

Hero Acquisition

There are three ways to get new heroes. They may come to you looking for work; you may free them from lairs; or you may summon them by casting Summon Hero, Summon Champion, or Incarnation (see Chapters 7 and 8). In fact, Torin the Chosen can *only* show up if you summon him specifically by casting the Life spell, Incarnation.

Regardless of how you obtain heroes, you may never collect more than six. Once you have six heroes, no more can appear, by any means, until one or more of your current heroes is dismissed or dies.

Knock, Knock

Heroes are particular about the wizards they serve. Most heroes will only work for wizards with enough fame to attract them (see Table 18.1). By casting Summon Hero or Summon Champion, you can acquire heroes even if you don't have enough fame to normally get their attention.

The chance that a hero offers his services to you on any given game turn depends on several things (the exact formula is in Chapter 4):

🐢 The higher your fame, the more likely it is that a hero stops by.

🐢 If you are Famous, your chances of getting a new hero are higher than if you do not have this skill.

🐢 The more heroes you already have, the less the chance of a new one knocking at your door.

🐢 If you had a chance to get a new hero on a particular game turn, but if you did not have the money to hire him, that hero doesn't even bother to knock. Worse, you're not even notified that you were passed over due to your poor financial state.

If you don't have the fame or money to attract heroes, never fear; you can find them in the more fashionable dungeons or summon them with spells.

Brax Unchained!

Every lair you conquer (with the exception of Towers of Wizardry) has a base chance of 6.7 percent of having a hero imprisoned there that you can free (see Appendix C for more details on finding treasures and heroes). Of course, if you already have six heroes or a full stack of nine units, you won't find any as prisoners. However, exploring lairs remains a sound way for you to add heroes to your ranks.

These shackled heroes are the same ones you can acquire by casting Summon Hero (i.e., the first 25 heroes on the list in Table 18.1). Heroes already in your employ or resting in peace cannot, obviously, turn up as prisoners. Note that prisoners are undiscriminating and couldn't care less about your fame; and you do not need to pay the grateful escapee's normal hiring cost.

Summons To Appear

When your fame is low, your luck rotten, and you face empty hero slots, serve a summons to appear. Spells that can summon heroes are:

🐢 The Arcane spell, Summon Hero, will summon one of the first 25 heroes listed in Table 18.1.

🐢 The Arcane spell, Summon Champion, will summon any one of the last 10 heroes listed in Table 18.1, except for Torin the Chosen or heroes that you cannot have because you lack the necessary type of spell books.

🐢 The Life spell Incarnation summons Torin the Chosen, the most powerful hero in *Master of Magic*.

No heroes will respond to your summoning spells if you already have six heroes. Except for Torin the Chosen, heroes you've buried cannot be summoned. Dead heroes are gone forever unless you cast the Life spell Resurrection.

Table 18.3 *Effects of Hero Skills by Experience Level*

Hero Skill	Affected Ability	Bonus to Attribute by Level								
		Hero	Myr	Capt	Comm	Champ	Lord	Grand	Super	Demi
Agility	defense (shields)	+1	+2	+3	+4	+5	+6	+7	+8	+9
Super Agility		+1	+3	+4	+6	+7	+9	+10	+12	+13
Arcane Power	ranged magic attack strength	+1	+2	+3	+4	+5	+6	+7	+8	+9
Super Arcane Power		+1	+3	+4	+6	+7	+9	+10	+12	+13
Arms Master	experience pts per turn*	+2	+4	+6	+8	+10	+12	+14	+16	+18
Super Arms Master		+3	+6	+9	+12	+15	+18	+21	+24	+27
Blade Master	To Hit (accuracy)	0	+1	+1	+2	+2	+3	+3	+4	+4
Super BladeMaster		0	+1	+2	+3	+3	+4	+5	+6	+6
Charmed	never fail resistance rolls	-	-	-	-	-	-	-	-	-
Constitution	hit points (hearts)	+1	+2	+3	+4	+5	+6	+7	+8	+9
Super Constitution		+1	+3	+4	+6	+7	+9	+10	+12	+13
Leadership	improved friendly combat**	0	0	1	1	1	2	2	2	3
Super Leadership		0	1	1	2	2	3	3	4	4
Legendary	wizard's fame	+3	+6	+9	+12	+15	+18	+21	+24	+27
Super Legendary		+4	+9	+13	+18	+22	+27	+31	+36	+40
Luck	improve To Hit, To Defend and resistance by 1	-	-	-	-	-	-	-	-	-
Might	melee attack strength (swords)	+1	+2	+3	+4	+5	+6	+7	+8	+9
Super Might		+1	+3	+4	+6	+7	+9	+10	+12	+13
Noble	no upkeep, +10 gold	-	-	-	-	-	-	-	-	-
Prayer Master	friendly resistance***	+1	+2	+3	+4	+5	+6	+7	+8	+9
Super Prayer Master		+1	+3	+4	+6	+7	+9	+10	+12	+13
Sage	wizard's spell research	+3	+6	+9	+12	+15	+18	+21	+24	+27
Super Sage		+4	+9	+13	+18	+22	+27	+31	+36	+40
Spell Caster x****	hero's spell skill	x	2x	3x	4x	5x	6x	7x	8x	9x

The column headings for hero experience levels are abbreviations for Myrmidon, Captain, Commander, Champion, Lord, Grand Lord, Super Hero, and Demi-God, respectively. The abbreviations, *atk* and *pts*, refer to "attack" and "points," respectively.

*Arms Master gives all normal units stacked with the hero the indicated number of experience points per game turn, regardless of what the stack of units is doing.

**The Leadership skill comes in four levels. This skill increases the swords of all friendly normal unit's figures stacked with the hero by an amount equal to the Leadership level of the hero. In addition, all other attack strengths, except for magic ranged attacks, are also increased by an amount equal to half the Leadership level of the hero. For example, a hero with Leadership level three gives +3 swords to every figure in all normal units fighting on his or her side. However, those units' thrown, breath, and missile attacks only improve by +1 (half of three is one and one-half, and the value gets rounded down).

***All friendly units gain the indicated amount of resistance during combat. Since Prayer Master and the non-hero skill, Resistance to All, are equivalent, only the highest bonus from all the friendly units' Prayer Master or Resistance to All skills applies. For example, if there are two heroes with Prayer Master on the battlefield, one with a bonus of +9, to other with a bonus of +6, all friendly units gain nine crosses (the higher value).

Table 18.3 Cont. *Effects of Hero Skills by Experience Level*

****Spell Caster is a skill that can have several different base values, indicated here by an "x," ranging from 5 to 20. As the hero gains experience levels, every additional level increases the hero's spell skill by +x per level (rounded down). So, at the third experience level, a hero will have three times his starting value in spell skill, as indicated on the table by "3x."

Heroes can start at different levels of the Spell Caster ability. These levels, and the number of spell points they give the hero per his experience level, are shown below:

Spell Caster Ability	Spell Points per Experience Level (x)
1	5
2	7.5
3	10
4	12.5
5	15
6	17.5
7	20

Losing Heroes

Heroes can be lost in two ways. You may dismiss heroes you no longer want, which frees up space for new and, hopefully, better heroes. Or, heroes may die in battle.

If you win a battle in which heroes die, you will be able to retrieve any items they were carrying, unless the heroes died from being unsummoned, banished, disintegrated, stoned, or killed by Cracks Call. If you lose heroes in such a battle, however, you also lose half a fame point per level of the heroes slain.

For example, if you lose a hero who is at the Myrmidon level (the second level), you will lose one fame point. If a Demi-God hero dies in a battle in which you were defeated, you will lose four fame points! All in all, it is better to dismiss weaker heroes that no longer serve a useful purpose than to risk their lives (and your fame) in battle.

Making The Most Of Your Heroes

Whenever you get a new hero, there are three things you should do. First, examine the hero's abilities and statistics. For this, you may find Table 18.1 convenient. In addition to a hero's initial stats, it also lists their minimum demi-god level statistics. Always consider hero's skills and *potential* when deciding whether you wish that hero to join you.

Second, if the hero is offering his or her services (i.e., the hero isn't appearing because of summoning), take a quick peek at your financial situation and the hero's hiring and upkeep costs. You may decide to forgo the offer until your finances are in a better state.

Third, determine how that hero can most help your cause. Heroes can basically be categorized into three, often overlapping groups: heroes that increase your skills and options, heroes that help other units in their stacks, and heroes that are useful in combat in their own right. The following sections assess the value of the different hero skills and how these skills dictate the best ways to use your heroes.

Wizard Aides

Some heroes have skills that specifically benefit you, the wizard:

Noble heroes are helpful because they give you an extra 10 gold per game turn. While they are often vital at the beginning of a game, you eventually will want heroes that provide some bang for their bucks. After your financial situation stabilizes, re-examine the heroes you hired for their nobility and decide whether their blue blood is still worth keeping.

Sage heroes are also useful at the beginning of the game (when it seems that researching every new spell takes an eternity). These heroes can make a great relative contribution to your spell researching abilities over time. Eventually, though, you will develop other sources of spell research points. At this point, consider giving your sages the brush.

🐸 Legendary heroes bring you fame. If you look at Table 18.3, you will see that their increases to your fame can be significant (up to 40 for a demi-god hero with super legendary abilities). Fame not only discounts how much gold per turn you pay in upkeep costs for your armies, it also influences the quality and frequency of the artifacts, heroes, and mercenaries that come your way. Legendary heroes are always worth keeping, even if they offer few additional benefits. (See Chapter 4 for more details on the value of increased fame.)

🐸 Spell casters are the most powerful and useful heroes in *Master of Magic*. When left in your Enchanted Fortress, they contribute half their spell skill to yours when you cast spells outside of combat. Thus, when casting summoning spells or overland enchantments, these heroes can considerably decrease the time each spell takes.

In addition, spell-casting heroes can cast spells when present at a battle without drawing on your mana reserves. They can spend up to their own spell skill level in mana at every battle they fight. Especially at later experience levels, when spell casters can have spell skills of over 100, but also earlier, these heroes are formidable units to have on your side.

Many of the spell casters also come with their own spells that they can cast in battle (in addition to any combat spells that *you* know). These extra spells can round out your combat options in several ways. First, they may know spells from a realm in which your wizard has no spell books. That means they

can cast spells at nodes where your spells would ordinarily fizzle.

Second, some of their spells are extremely useful or expensive to cast. As examples, Malleus knows Flame Strike; Morgana knows Black Prayer; and Serena knows Healing. No spells cast by heroes are subject to distance modifiers in casting cost (see Chapter 21), and if a hero is equipped with items that reduce an enemy's resistance (spell saves), such spells are much more likely to exert their effects than if *you* had cast them.

Finally, many spell-casting heroes can equip artifacts you have made (wands and staffs) that contain spell charges. They can cast spells from these artifacts at no mana cost! (More details on artifacts can be found in Chapter 19.)

Heroes with spell casting ability can, then, be used to good effect both by having them garrison your Enchanted Fortress and by sending them out with your armies to conquer lairs, nodes, and cities.

🐸 Some heroes (Rakir the Beastmaster, Greyfairer the Druid, and Marcus the Ranger) have an innate scouting ability. While this skill isn't limited to heroes, a hero that scouts can be useful, especially early in the game. Aside from casting Flight or Water Walking on them, send these heroes out on ships to rapidly explore neighboring continents.

Stacks

Some heroes have skills that enhance the units they are stacked with. If you have several heroes of this type, it is best to spread them out over several armies so that their benefits can be conferred to as many of your units as possible.

🐸 Arms master gives all units stacked with the hero added experience points every game turn. Since normal units profit a great deal from higher experience levels (Chapter 17), stacking them with an arms master is a useful way to raise their statistics in the shortest possible time. Consider using the arms master heroes to ferry stacks of new units from production centers to battle sites; perhaps they will have improved a level or two by the time they arrive there. Note, other new heroes that you summon or hire can also benefit from being stacked with arms masters until their experience levels are higher.

Clearly, later in the game, when you've built war colleges or fighter's guilds in your major production cities, arms master heroes will be less useful. Depending on the experience levels at which your new troops emerge, you should take stock of these heroes for other ways in which they can be useful to you.

☙ Heroes with leadership are extremely valuable if the bulk of your armies is comprised of normal units. Leadership increases the melee, thrown, breath, and missile attack strengths of all friendly, normal units stacked with the hero. These increases are especially significant for weak and medium-strength units (i.e., swordsmen and halberdiers). The added melee attack strengths can be as high as four swords, if the hero has super leadership skills. Since these bonuses are on a per figure basis, multi-figure units stacked with leadership-wielding heroes can become immensely powerful. Always keep heroes with the leadership ability and form stacks of normal units around them for combat.

☙ Prayer master gives all units stacked with that hero a bonus in resistance to spells, gaze, and touch attacks. This bonus can be as high as 13 crosses, making your armies completely resistant to almost all spells that can be resisted (see Chapter 21). Most such spells are Death magic spells, although several Life and Sorcery combat spells must also be resisted. Therefore, a hero with the prayer master skill is helpful for your armies when campaigning

against wizards that specialize in Death, Life, or Sorcery magic. In other cases, this skill is less useful.

☙ Some heroes are natural healers and, while this is not a hero skill as such, it is fairly useful. Natural healers accelerate the rate at which their stacks heal, thus keeping armies in peak condition as they travel between battles. This isn't a skill that you have to go out of your way to keep or acquire, but is nice when you have it. Unless you feel a natural healer hero is too inferior to keep for other reasons, you may as well hang on to him or her.

☙ Jaer is the only wind walking hero, but he is *extremely* useful for that reason alone. Stacked with other units, he can rush them overseas and over all kinds of terrain quickly. Since mobility is essential to victory in *Master of Magic* (getting your armies where you want them can often take a long time), hold on to Jaer at all costs.

The Fighting Hero

Many heroes were born for battle. They should fight, especially after you beef them up with a few artifacts or enchantments. Aside from the aforementioned advantage of the spell casting skills, the following skills are useful to your combat heroes:

☙ Heroes with strong fighter skills, such as agility, might, constitution, and blade master, especially their super versions, can eventually become formidable players on the battlefield. Some heroes can even achieve melee attacks or defenses stronger than a great drake's! However, when devoid of artifacts, other special abilities, and enchantments, you must carefully look after these fighter heroes in battle. Give them time to raise their experience levels before sending them off on suicide charges.

The ability to pick off targets at range should never be underestimated. Heroes with missile weapons are beneficial to your main army, especially if they can move quickly. Although these missile heroes can't do much at low experience levels, with the proper items and training they will be able to kill mid-strength units with a single shot.

Rejoice if you have a missile-equipped hero that is also a blade master (thus boosting its To Hit rating). With a high enough accuracy, these twanger heroes might never miss.

Arcane power increases the strength of a hero's magic ranged attacks. As you've probably observed, magic ranged attacks are deadly, even at fairly low attack strengths. With arcane power, many heroes acquire magic ranged attacks stronger than 20 per attack. Considering that it only costs these heroes three mana (of their spell skill) to throw a magic ranged attack, these heroes can launch upwards of 20 such attacks per combat at high experience levels!

A hero with both arcane power and blade master is a force indeed. Between the fact that magic ranged attacks suffer no distance penalty (see Chapter 20) and the added accuracy from blade master, a hero can wreak considerable havoc on foes. Note, only Aureus, Mystic X, and Warrax can ever be blessed with this skill combination; but be on the lookout for it!

Equip arcane-powered heroes with items that increase their movement and defenses, so that they can stay out of harms way while taking out enemy units. Arcane power is an A+ skill, valuable for any hero leading armies into battle.

Lucky and charmed are the two least valuable hero skills. Charmed is moderately helpful because a hero with this skill is automatically resistant to all spells that must be resisted and to all gaze and touch attacks (except Immolation, see Chapter 20). This will make a hero stand up fairly well under certain dangerous combat conditions.

Luck is of more dubious merit. This skill gives the hero a +1 To Hit, To Defend, and +1 cross. These are such relatively small increases compared to other random hero picks that getting luck (instead of another random hero pick) may be deemed unlucky.

The greatest advantage conferred from luck is the +1 To Defend, making shields more effective at stopping incoming attacks (see Chapter 20). This gain is far from insignificant, but there are more valuable skills a hero can have. In any event, if there are two skills *not* to favor when reviewing a hero, they are lucky and charmed.

A few heroes, Torin, Mortu, and Roland, come with magic immunity. This is not a hero skill, but it is tremendously useful. Such heroes are immune to most spells and to all magic ranged, breath, and most gaze attacks. Since so much damage to units is the result of these very things, a hero with magic immunity is almost indestructible on the battlefield (particularly if you give him or her artifacts with high defense modifiers). Glom on to every such hero that crosses your path!

First strike and armor-piercing attacks are inherent skills of some of the most awesome fighter heroes (Roland, Mortu, and Sir Harold). The ability to do damage before taking any upon attacking and, simultaneously, halving opponents' defenses are a potent combination on the battlefield. These heroes were born to lead your fighting forces; use them that way.

There are three odds-and-ends type skills, each possessed by one of the heroes: invisible (Shin Bo), flying (Fang), and life-stealing attacks (Ravashack). Each of these skills is useful in combat situations for slightly different reasons. Their merits are discussed fully in Chapter 20.

Adding Beef To Your Hero

Heroes can become powerful through experience, but there are many ways to make them even better. Like other units, heroes can be enchanted to the point of virtual indestructibility. Go ahead and zap your favorite fighting heroes with powerful enchantments. Your goal is to keep them alive in battles so that, over time, they'll attain high experience levels. See Chapter 17 for a complete list of unit enchantments.

Some of our favorite hero enchantments include Regeneration (Nature), Invulnerability (Life), and Magic Immunity (Sorcery), but almost all positive enchantments are useful. Enchantments like Wind Walking and Flight (both Sorcery spells) and Water Walking (Nature) will make your heroes more mobile and useful in combat. Invisibility (Sorcery) will make your spell-casting, ranged attacking, and fighter heroes virtually impossible to target by enemy ranged attacks and spells, allowing them to cast their spells, launch attacks, or sneak up on opponents undisturbed.

Aside from enchantments, the big advantage heroes have over all other unit types is

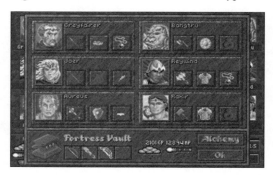

Figure 18-1. *A full roster of heroes equipped with artifacts.*

that they can wield artifacts (see Chapter 19). Even the cheapest items can significantly improve a hero's abilities. Artifacts can alter a hero's movement speed or type (flying, water walking, pathfinding), giving the hero more options for overland travel and during combat. They can also increase hero attributes, such as attacks, To Hits, defenses, and resistances.

For spell-casting heroes, artifacts can be an incredible boon. If the artifacts have *spell saves*, all spells (except for combat enchantments, like Wrack) that hero casts in battle will be harder for enemy units to resist. In addition, by charging a spell caster's artifacts with spells (i.e., Doom Bolt, Cracks Call, various enchantments, etc.), such heroes can cast these spells in combat without drawing on their mana reserves. Combinations of spell saves and spell charges in artifacts can be particularly deadly.

Remember that a judicious distribution of found artifacts and the considered creation of specific new ones is the best way to improve your heroes. Even inferior heroes can become extremely valuable when well outfitted. (See Tables L and M in the game manual for a list of ways items can enchanted, and Chapter 19 for more information on this subject.)

The Baton of Passing

Thus we have discussed the bread, meat, and cheese of heroes. Lettuce say, if you can cut the mustard with them, your heroes will stuff your enemies and force them to ketchup with you. So when it appears you're in a pickle and your chips are about to be barbecued, add a good hero and you should be able to beer the worst of it. Our next chapter covers other items on the menu that you can add, à la carte, to heroes. For some spice, turn the page.

19

Magic Items

hile half the value of heroes is innately due to their abilities and experience levels, the other half is something over which you have more control. Each hero can carry three items. These items can enhance the hero's attributes, enchant that hero with a special ability, or, for heroes that can wield a staff or wand, offer them spells to throw in battle at no mana cost. A good hero is one thing; a well-equipped hero, however, can be a juggernaut.

Lost and Found

Items come to you for parceling out to your heroes in a variety of ways. Occasionally, a merchant will come by, inspect your treasury, and see if you can afford his wares (see Chapter 4, Table 4.6). You might luck into an item as part of the loot received from a horde of treasure (see Appendix D, Table D.3). Alternately, with the spells Enchant Item and Create Artifact (see Chapter 6), you can cast your own custom items—something that we'll discuss later in this chapter.

Items are destroyed in a couple of ways. First, if the hero who wields an item dies horribly (specifically, through disintegration, banishment, petrification, stoning, or Cracks Call), the item is lost along with the hero. Heroes who die normally during a battle yield their items to the winning side after the battle.

Alternatively, you can break items by selecting them and clicking over the anvil on the Items Screen. This act gives you half their value back in mana (added to your mana reserve).

What to Look for in a Magic Item

What you're trying to achieve with magic items is *optimization* of your heroes. In other words, matching the right item to the right hero. For instance, Brax, the stout fighter, will have no use for a wand with +10 spell skill

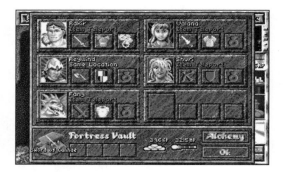

Figure 19-1. *Items can be broken for half their mana by clicking them over the anvil in the lower-left corner of the Items Screen.*

and -2 resistance. Conversely, a +3 To Hit bow won't do Zaldron the sage any good.

The first step in optimizing your heroes through magic items is to determine what you expect each hero to do for you, particularly on the battlefield. Heroes that must slug it out in melee should have items that raise those stats or enchant those abilities. Heroes lobbing off magic should seek items that add spell-casting skills, and then consider what sort of magic they'll use on the battlefield. Combat mages who like direct, ranged magic attacks should look for items that increase their Attack and To Hit ratings. Those who cast negative spells on enemy units should seek items that lower the enemy's resistance.

The goal in examining each hero is that you'll know, specifically, what you want that hero to do in a combat situation. Your goal then becomes finding (or, better still, creating) items tailored to optimize that hero's task in battle. *You must stay focused on this concept to use items effectively.*

Item Creation and Philosophy

As previously mentioned, items can be created though the Arcane spells Enchant Item and Create Artifact. (Tables L and M in the game manual list the enchantments that you can place in different artifacts.) While found items and those brought to you by merchants come as is, these spells allow you to custom tailor items to meet a specific hero's exact needs.

Creating custom items costs time and mana (like any other spell). Because the value of an item (and, hence, the time and expense involved in creating it) is player-defined (the more cool things that item does, the more expensive it will be and the longer it will take to cast), greed is a serious problem. Many players try to conjure items with the highest modifiers and best spells packed into them, only to find that they bankrupt their mana reserves in no time, leaving them magically destitute for many turns to come.

Don't fall into this trap. Items you create need never be the best you can possibly conjure. Instead, always create items that fit within your budget. Know before you design an item how much mana you have in reserve, what your per turn mana income is, and what your spell-casting skill is. Between these three factors, determine what you can afford before you commit yourself to the creation of an

important magic item. *Never* overreach your ability to afford a new item!

Although we discuss the philosophy of creating items in the sections that follow, we decided to leave many exact combinations a mystery. Armed with the knowledge found throughout this book, you can easily solve the puzzles of superior item creation for all occasions without our giving everything away. We thought we'd leave you at least *one* (relatively minor, but intricate) realm to explore in *Master of Magic.*

Naked Heroes

Strive to pack your heroes with at least one, or better two, items. New heroes arrive devoid of these stat boosters, and the newer the hero is, the more a hero needs them (usually, just to survive).

Therefore, we believe in the value of creating a few relatively cheap items that concentrate on improving a hero's defense. Naturally, selecting armor- or shield-type items is the best way to go because of their inherent defensive benefits (see the Effects column of Table L in the game manual). Even when better items come along to replace them, keep a cheesy defensive item or two in your vault for the next new hero who joins your cause. You'll be glad you did.

How Enchanting

Table M at the back of the game manual lists all of the enchantments that an item can possess. These enchantments bestow their abilities upon the hero who wields them, often as if that hero were enchanted by the spell of the same name. Slipping these enchantments into items and awarding them to heroes has some distinct advantages:

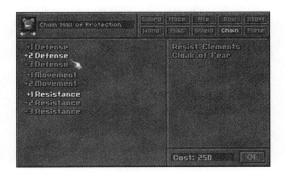

Figure 19-2. *Even cheesy defensive items can be crucial to the longevity of new heroes.*

 You don't have to pay to cast that enchantment on the item-wielding hero.

Table 19.1 *What Heroes Can Tote*

Item List	Hero Titles
Bow, Shield and Ring	Dervish, Huntress, Ranger, Elven Archer
Sword or Staff, Shield and Ring	Warrior Mage, Unknown, Chaos Warrior
Staff, Ring and Ring	Sage, Druid, Magician, Wind Mage, Witch, Warlock, Illusionist, Priestess, and Necromancer
Sword, Shield and Ring	All others

Item Slot	What Items Can Go In It
Bow	bow, ax, mace, or sword
Ring	only miscellaneous (orb, helm, gauntlet, ring, amulet, etc.)
Shield	chain mail, plate mail, or shield
Staff	staff or wand
Sword	ax, mace, or sword

🐸 Better still, you don't have to pay to maintain that enchantment every turn.

🐸 Item enchantments can't be dispelled.

Note that some of these enchantments, as you have probably learned the hard way, are mighty expensive to throw in combat. Boosting your hero's abilities permanently with an enchanted artifact can be a much more practical way to go.

Packing Punch in Wands and Staffs

When you have a hero who can wield a wand or staff (See Table 19.1), you should create something special for him. In particular, it is wise to create items that can cast expensive or all-purpose area enchantment spells. Think of all the mana you will save in battle (affording the hero more spell-casting options in combat) if the staff your hero wields has Doom Bolts, Lion Heart, Invulnerability, etc. ready to cast for free in every battle!

Web spells, Confusion, Blur, Prayer, Darkness, Entangle, and other useful area effect spells also make good choices to pump into wands and staffs. Even combat summoning spells are useful if, like the battlefield area enchantments, you plan on using them as your standard battle tactics.

An important key, though, is to provide your spell-casting hero with items that reduce the enemy's resistance. This resistance lowering effect is called "spell saves" and is associated with a negative number. Each negative point lowers by one the number of crosses the enemy has available to resist that hero's spells (see Chapter 20 for how crosses and resistance work). *Lowering enemy resistance to your spells is crucial.*

Note, spell saves do not alter enemy units' resistances to combat enchantments (such as the Wrack); they only come into play for spells that target individual units.

The final consideration comes back to that old bugaboo, affordability. Items with good spells and multiple charges (i.e., the ability to throw them for free that many times per battle) can cost a small fortune in mana to create. Again, watch yourself! Don't get caught up committing more mana to making an item than you have or can quickly replace. Deficit spending, as it were, when casting spells (like when you're creating an expensive item) can be ruinous.

With An Eye On Accuracy

As a rule, improving a hero's ability *To Hit* an opponent in combat is more important than getting a boost in attack strength. So, when enchanting new artifacts, consider placing some To Hit modifiers in the item, especially for your missile-bearing heroes, instead of adding attack strength.

Potpourri

While most artifacts only affect attacks for which they are specifically designed (i.e., a bow's attack strength and To Hit modifiers only affect the hero's ranged attacks; a stoning attack on a wand will only affect a hero's magic ranged attacks, etc.), miscellaneous items affect *all* of the hero's attacks! For example, placing a +2 To Hit in a miscellaneous item will improve the accuracy of all of the hero's attacks.

The upshot is that, although it costs more, you should consider placing some of the critical enchantments into miscellaneous items rather than into defensive items or weapons.

Hack and Slash 101

In this chapter we have provided some thoughts and philosophies for creating and wielding magic items. The hero/magic item relationship is an important one, not to be underplayed. Remember that effective spell combinations (see Chapter 13) are every bit as applicable to magic items. Just watch your spending when creating your own items!

The next chapter is the biggest in this book. With sword drawn and shield in hand, we are about to enter the fray of combat. Don your armor before turning the page. You'll need it.

Section 6

Magic & Might

20

Normal Combat: A Drop of Blood, A Load of Dead and Thou

Ah, the clash of swords, the whooshing of arrows, the growling of monsters; this is the stuff of *normal* combat in *Master of Magic*. This chapter covers all non-spell casting aspects of conducting your own battles, which is certainly one of the most fascinating elements of this game.

Weigh To Go

First, before any battle, you should assess the situation (see Figure 20-1). Are your forces sufficient to win, will it be close, or are you outclassed? To answer these questions, take stock of the relative strengths of your enemies and your own troops. (The information in Appendix F may help you do this.)

After you have assessed the risks, it's decision time. First, do you flee? If you opt to fight, will you let the auto combat AI routines fight for you or will you command the battle yourself? We recommend that you only use auto combat to handle battles that you can easily win. You should take personal command if the battle will be close or if you are using a battle to chip away tough units garrisoning a node or city. Note that whittling down units at well-defended sites might cost you a few

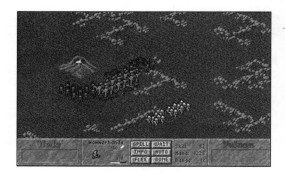

Figure 20-1. *Assessing your battle odds: Walking into this node with three hammerhands was probably not a good idea.*

stacks of units, but it is a viable way to capture a difficult objective.

Saving Lives

The surest way to master combat in *Master of Magic* is to practice. Fortunately, the game provides a great tool that allows you to enter battles you initiate with no risk. It's called saving the game. Do so before you move your stack and engage any enemy that you aren't sure you can beat. If things don't go well, simply reload that saved game after the battle, and you'll be no worse (and perhaps wiser) for your efforts. Failure to save the game before every important battle could be hazardous to your army's health.

Fleeing

If your army is hopelessly outclassed, or if you suddenly discover that you took your newest or favorite hero into a battle against 20 sprites, fleeing becomes an attractive option. Unfortunately, if you initiated this battle, you can only flee after your opponents have had their turns. When a side flees, each of its non-hero units has a 50 percent chance of dying and each hero has a 25 percent chance (on Intro and Easy levels, fleeing won't kill heroes). The enemy suffers naught and you avoid losing heroes in combat, which can cost you fame (see Chapter 4). In addition, you will lose their magic items, which become prizes for the other player, if your heroes die as you flee from a battle against another wizard's forces.

Fleeing is always a last resort. It is best considered when you know you will lose the battle without inflicting a worthwhile number of losses on your enemy. It is also worth considering if you do not want to lose a particular unit or hero and don't have the spell or mana necessary to recall it from the battlefield. (And why are you wandering around with a unit that you are unwilling to lose, anyway?). You can certainly entertain the notion of seeing a battle to its bloody finish if you have the Life magic spell Resurrection. This spell will let you reclaim any of your fallen heroes (but not their artifacts).

Still, fleeing is synonymous with disaster, and preventing disasters from affecting your position in the game is the reason you should save before every major battle. If it's time to flee, then it's probably time to reload your last saved game.

Auto Combat

When it looks like you'll romp in battle, or if you're feeling lazy, select auto combat and have the computer fight your battle while you watch and enjoy the spectacle. Note that the artificial intelligence routines in *Master of Magic* won't approach combat in the same way that you should. When it is a particular unit's turn to move and fight, the auto combat routine tries to assess where that unit can inflict the most damage. It looks for units that it can take out with one or two attacks and uses this information to weigh its options. This is why you will see computer opponents going after your bowmen, wizards, and priests—the units that have the fewest hearts and shields.

Mark Your Targets

You, however, should fight differently. Go after the most dangerous units first, assuming you have a reasonable chance to kill them. For example, you will last longer by removing that pesky sky drake before focusing on its supporting hordes of phantom warriors, so guide your actions accordingly. Auto combat, however, will do a great job trying to eliminate the phantom warriors on your behalf while the sky drake kills your units one by one. *That* is the fundamental difference between fighting with auto combat and using

your time, patience, and good sense to fight your own battles.

Auto Magic

The computer will not touch your mana reserves during auto combat, but it does use the spell-casting abilities of heroes. Unfortunately, the AI tends to expend the mana of spell-casting heroes on spells (that may or may not be useful) rather than having them lob off their effective magic ranged attacks.

The computer rarely picks the spells you would in battle. However, you *can* pick up interesting ideas from watching the computer's techniques in auto combat. You may quickly get a feel for how well different spells work, particularly spells that didn't seem so interesting to you when you first considered them.

Life is Cheap in Auto Combat

Auto combat does not consider unit survival. Do not expect the computer to rotate your units to and from engagements so that more of them survive. The computer does not worry about preserving the army as a whole entity in which each unit has a purpose beyond the current battle. Engineers, heroes, priests, etc. can all be seen rushing blindly into the fray only to meet their demise.

The AI does not fall back with fragile units engaged in melee combat, even when more suitable units are right there to do that kind of fighting. In the later versions of *Master of Magic*, the computer *does* wait to charge units into melee combat until its ranged attackers have done their bit. Often, you, too, should wait before closing in for melee combat, in order to give your archers and magic users time to do their damage first. Unlike you, the AI never protects fragile units by physically moving bodies (i.e., stronger units) between them and enemies. Finally, the computer will never order your forces to flee, period.

The upshot is, use auto combat when you have nothing to lose or when you know you should easily win the battle. As with all things, when you really care about what happens, you'll get the best results if you do it yourself. For that, we have the whole rest of this chapter.

Leading Your Battles

Unless you have only killer armies, you will want to control your units during part or all of your battles. Sometimes, making the opening moves for your troops on the battlefield is all you need to do before switching to auto combat. This will allow you to reign in your melee units so they don't charge prematurely and/or to cast just the *right* combat spells before turning the battle over to the AI.

While there are several things to consider when conducting a battle, they all boil down to one principle: use your forces efficiently. That is, don't waste 'em: neither through losses inflicted by your foes nor by letting them languish idle on the battlefield.

Pre-Battle Questions

Approaching a battle requires use of your Organatron Infinite Megahertz computer (i.e., your brain). You must analyze both sides' troop dispositions, determine a battle plan, and estimate your chances of winning. Specifically, what kinds of missile weapons are there? Who can use magic, and how much, to influence the battle (the subject of the next chapter)? Are any creatures particularly helped by of city enchantments or a nodal aura? Are certain creatures or units immune to particular forms of magic or weapons? Which are the most dangerous pre-melee enemy units (usually the ones with a strong ranged attack) and which are the most vicious enemies once they are closing for melee combat? Who has what flying creatures and how will that influence the battle?

What about the battlefield? At what speed can both side's forces move? Can you slow enemy troops with Web or Earth to Mud? Will roads or rough terrain affect movement during battle? Can you crush the walls surrounding a city you're attacking?

The Board

The battlefield is set up as a grid. Moving into each square of the grid takes one movement point unless you are traveling along a road, in which case it takes half a movement point, or unless you are entering rough terrain, which requires two movement points to enter (or one if that is all the unit has). As long as you have any movement points left, you can enter any type of terrain. If, however, you have more than the number of movement points required to enter a square, you will use up the full complement of movement points when you enter that square.

Flying creatures do not gain any movement benefits or penalties from terrain, unless they were webbed earlier in combat. Non-corporeal units pay one movement point per square and can walk through walls. Pathfinding and wind walking have no movement effect on the battlefield.

Sequencing Unit Movement and Combat

An awareness of the effect on movement of various terrain types can be important during difficult battles. If you enter a square and have any movement points left (even one-half) you can still attack! The order in which units move and fire is also vital. Softening up a target with a missile attack before risking your own forces in melee is an appropriate tactic. However, if you shoot a missile, you use up all your movement points. Therefore, if you move that missile unit first, assuming it has any movement points left after moving, it can *also shoot on the same turn.* Casting a spell (for heroes, magicians, priests, shamans, and warlocks) works similarly: All that unit's movement points are used up when they cast

Table 20.1 *Combat Statistics for Attacking in Normal Melee*

Total Attack Strength ("Swings") = Number of Figures x Number of Swords

The Total Attack Strength is the maximum damage, in hit points, that an attacking unit can do in one round of melee combat. This is also the number of "swings" that unit makes in a melee round. Thus, each sword represents a separate "swing," and each swing can do one hit point of damage.

Chance of a Hit = 30 percent + (10 percent x sum of all To Hit modifiers)

Each swing has a chance of landing a blow and becoming a hit point of damage inflicted upon the enemy unit. This base chance of success can be modified by unit enchantments, artifacts, special weapons produced by alchemist's guilds, special abilities, etc.

Average Number of Hits Landed = Total Attack Strength x Chance of a Hit

For example, a full strength unit of Gargoyles has four figures. Each figure has four swords with a +1 To Hit. So, the total attack strength for this unit is 4 figures x 4 swords, or 16 swords total. The chance of a hit is 30 percent + (10% x +1), or 40 percent. Finally, the average number of hits landed by a full strength gargoyle unit would be 40 percent of 16, or 6.4 hits.

spells. Therefore, move these units first if you want to move and cast in the same battle turn.

The difference between attacking and defending is also important. If you are fighting *against* units with first strike capabilities, you want to wait patiently for them to exhaust their movement points getting adjacent to your troops. That way, you have a chance to attack them on your turn when their first strike weapons won't have any effect, rather than allowing them to hit you first, when their first strike weapons *will* have an effect. The opposite holds true when you command units with first strike capability; aim your movement so that you can get in the first attack. First strike weapons and the advantages of attacking over defending are discussed later in this chapter.

The Nitty Gritty of Combat

Many unit statistics influence combat results (see Chapter 17). The question is, what is really happening when you hear the clash of swords, the twang of a bow, and the grunts of

pain? Combat takes many forms and, for each type of combat, different statistics and calculations come into play. In this section, we will describe what happens under most (i.e., "normal") combat situations. Although magic in combat is discussed in its own right (see Chapter 21), spells that alter unit statistics and, hence, their combat skills are mentioned where appropriate.

Basic Melee Combat: Up Close and Personal!

Now let's take a look at what really happens when two units come sword-to-sword. When two units engage in melee combat, both get to swing their swords, spears, halberds, etc., simultaneously. They also get to duck behind their shields at the same time. Allow us to present an examination of how damage is determined between two units engaged in melee combat:

Both units engaged in melee combat swing at each other and duck the other unit's attack

Table 20.2 *Modifying Melee Attacks*

Altering Attack Strength and To Hit Abilities Through Increasing Experience:

Arms Master, a hero skill

Warlord, a wizard skill

Altar of Battle, a Life spell

Crusade, a Life spell

Heroism, a Life spell

Changing Attack Strength:

Hero Skills: Leadership and Might

Unit Skills: Holy Bonus (Paladins, Angels, Arch Angels)

Alchemist's Guild: If city is on an adamantium (+2) or mithril (+1) deposit

Chaos Spells: Chaos Surge (+2), Flame Blade (+2), Metal Fires (+1), Shatter (1*), Warp Creature (half strength)

Death Spells: Berserk (doubles strength), Black Channels (+2), Black Prayer (-1), Cloud of Shadow (***),
   Darkness (***), Eternal Night (***), Weakness (-2)

Life Spells: Heavenly Light (***), High Prayer (+2), Lion Heart (+3), True Light (***)

Nature Spells: Giant Strength (+1)

Sorcery Spells: Mind Storm (-5)

Changing To Hit Abilities:

Hero Skills: Blade Master

Unit Skills: Bonus to Hit (varies), Invisibility (-1****; Nightblades, Air Elementals, Night Stalkers),
   Luck (+1; Halflings)

Rarity of Fantastic Units: common and uncommon units (+1); rare units (+2); most very rare units (+3)

Wizard Skills: Alchemy (+1)

Alchemist's Guild: (+1)

Chaos Spells: Warp Reality (-2)

Life Spells: High Prayer (+1), Holy Arms (+1), Holy Weapon (+1), Prayer (+1)

Sorcery Spells: Invisibility (-1****), Mass Invisibility (-1****), Vertigo (-2)

*If successful, Shatter causes the target's weapons to break, giving them an attack strength of one.

**Effect may not occur all the time.

***These effects vary from +1 to -1 depending on whether units are creatures of Life, Death, or neither.

****These spells decrease the To Hit ability of enemy units in direct melee combat with the enchanted unit.
Note that in addition to increasing the target units' abilities To Hit, High Prayer, Prayer, and Luck are like
Invisibility in that they also decrease enemy units' To Hit abilities by one.

Note, artifacts can raise these attributes as well.

   Also, the Sorcery spell Haste doubles the number of melee attacks and counterattacks a unit makes per
melee round.

Table 20.3 *Dodging Blows*

Total Defense = Number of Figures x Number of Shields

Each shield can stop one hit that the attacker has landed (see Table 20.1) on the defending unit. Each shield has a certain chance To Defend, or to negate, a successful hit:

Chance To Defend = 30% + (10% x sum of all To Defend modifiers)

The average number of hits that a full strength unit can stop through its shields alone is:

Average Number of Hits Blocked = Total Defense x Chance To Defend

simultaneously. This is because the defending unit simultaneously *counterattacks* the attacking unit. Consequently, damage and defense calculations are made for both units before the results are applied to either.

Taking Damage (Ouch!)
The way in which damage is meted out is discussed below. As a reminder, when swords, shields, hearts, bows, crosses, etc. are mentioned, they refer to the icons on the Unit Statistics Display. They, therefore, refer to *per figure* statistics.

Table 20.1 describes the essential statistics for determining the melee attack capabilities of a unit.

From Table 20.1, you can see that the amount of potential damage a unit can do depends on three things, all of which can be altered: attack strength in swords, the chance To Hit, and the number of figures in the unit. The number of figures in a unit can be modified in the obvious ways (i.e., death or healing, regeneration, raising from the dead, etc.).

The attack strength and To Hit abilities of units can also be modified. These modifications are listed in Table 20.2.

Changes in a unit's "To Hit" ability exert profound effects on combat. For example, a combat enchantment that modifies all friendly units' To Hit ability by +1, such as Prayer or High Prayer, will result in all your normal units landing up to 33 percent more hits than they otherwise would.

Similarly, changing the attack strength of units will alter the average number of hits they can land on their enemies. Units with many figures will gain relatively more from an increase in attack strength per figure than units with only one or two figures.

Blocking Damage (Saved!)
Of course, any change in a unit's attack-related attributes will exert relatively greater consequences on units with a higher innate combat survivability. After all, improving a unit that won't be around the battlefield for long is a waste.

After a unit has landed a certain number of hits on its target, but before damage is calculated, the target unit has a chance to defend itself from these hits. Table 20.3 describes how this occurs.

Unfortunately, unless a unit is comprised of a single figure, the *first figure* in the unit bears the entire brunt of an attack. Once its shields have done their job (checking to see if they successfully repel any hits), all non-blocked hits are subtracted from the figure's hit points (shown as blackened hearts on the unit's statistics). Hits exceeding that figure's remaining hearts are then applied to the next

Table 20.4 *Per Figure Defense in Melee Combat*

Each figure in a unit can absorb a certain number of hits from a single attack before dying:

Average Hits Blocked = Number of Shields x Chance To Defend + Number of Hearts

For example, war bears come in pairs, with each bear having three shields and eight hearts. The average number of hits that the first bear can block before taking damage is equal to its defense of three shields multiplied by the chance for each shield to block a hit, in this case 30 percent. So the average bear will block an average 0.9 hits with its shields before the damage directed at it will start taking hit points away. Given that the bear has 8 total hit points, this means that the first war bear will die after an average of 8.9 successful hits from a single attack have been directed at its unit.

If the first bear does not die from the first attack, on the following attack, its full three shields will get another chance to block their 0.9 hits before the bear starts taking damage again. Therefore, the more shields each figure in a unit has, the more damage it can block before it starts losing hit points from each attack. The longer a figure lasts, the longer it can exact damage from units it is fighting.

---

figure in the unit, which gets to roll for all of its shields, etc.

The final important consideration in determining the outcome of a melee encounter is the total number of hit points of a unit. Here is the formula:

Total Hit Points = Number of Figures x Number of Hearts per Figure

Perhaps a more useful way to assess the survivability of a unit is to look at the total blocking potential of the individual figures in it. Table 20.4 shows this information.

Both the defense and the hit points per figure in a unit are important parameters in assessing a unit's durability in combat. These values can be modified by a number of things, as described in Table 20.5.

Anything that increases the durability of a figure or unit in combat greatly enhances its utility. The longer a unit lasts, the longer it can deal damage, and the more likely it will survive to fight again. To this end, adding shields tends to be more advantageous than

adding an equivalent number of hit points (unless, of course, you already have a lot of shields but very few hearts per figure). Shields block hits and get a chance to do so *every time* the unit is attacked. Each heart can only absorb one hit, and then it is gone (at least for the remainder of that particular combat). Hearts can only return during combat if healing spells, including Raise Dead, are cast, or if the unit can regenerate.

In this section we discussed what occurs during normal melee combat, i.e., when two units are using normal weapons and have normal attributes and no additional special attack types. Now, not all melee combat follows the basic rules. However, most melee engagements build upon the combat routine outlined above, so make sure you have a good grip on this material before pressing on. From here, we will cover special attacks, magical weapons, and immunity to various attacks, all of which affect what actually happens when swords clash.

Table 20.5 *Changing Unit Defenses to Melee Attacks*

Changing Unit Defenses and Hit Points Through Increasing Experience:

Arms Master, a hero skill
Warlord, a wizard skill
Altar of Battle, a Life spell
Crusade, a Life spell
Heroism, a Life spell

Changing Unit Defenses*:

Hero Skills: Agility
Unit Skills: Holy Bonus (Paladins, Angels, Arch Angels)
Alchemist's Guild: If the city is on an adamantium (+2) or mithril (+1) deposit
City Walls: Intact (+3 to units inside city); Broken (+1 to units inside city)
Chaos Spells: Chaos Channels (+3**), Chaos Surge (+2), Warp Creature (half defense**)
Death Spells: Berserk (no defense), Black Channels (+1), Black Prayer (-1), Cloud of Shadow (***), Darkness (***),
    Eternal Night (***)
Life Spells: Bless (+3**), Heavenly Light (***), High Prayer (+2), Holy Armor (+2), True Light (***)
Nature Spells: Iron Skin (+5), Stone Skin (+1)
Sorcery Spells: Mind Storm (-5), Vertigo (-1)

Changing Unit Ability To Defend:

Unit Skills: Luck (+1; Halflings)
Chaos Spells: Eldritch Weapon (-1****)
Life Spells: High Prayer (+1), Prayer (+1)

Changing Unit Hit Points*:

Hero Skills: Constitution
Unit Skills: Regeneration***** (Trolls, Hydras, Shadow Demons, Werewolves)
Death Spells: Black Channels (+1)
Life Spells: Charm of Life (+25%, minimum +1), Lion Heart (+3)
Nature Spells: Regeneration (+1 hit point per unit, per turn*****)

Special Effects:

Invulnerability is a Life magic spell that not only provides weapon immunity but also prevents the first two hits that get past a figure's shields from causing damage.

*Special attacks that restore hit points or eliminate shields are not included here, as this table only examines normal melee combat. Similarly, healing spells of various types, except for the skill and enchantment of Regeneration, are not included in this discussion.
**This effect may not occur all the time. Bless only provides its defense bonus to attacks from Chaos and Death creatures.
***The actual effect on defense varies from -1 to +1 and depends on the nature of the unit and the spell.
****Decreases the effectiveness of the target unit's defenses against the enchanted unit's attacks.
*****Effectively gives unit an extra hit point per combat round.

Heroes' artifacts may also alter the parameters listed here.

The Sorcery spell Blur negates 10 percent of all hits landed by enemy units during combat before friendly units must start defending themselves from attacks.

Weapon Immunity and Magic Attacks

Weapon immunity is a unit skill that protects the unit from attacks by normal weapons by increasing its defense to such weapons to (not *by*, *to*) 10 shields. If a unit has 10 or more shields already, weapon immunity would be no help at all.

Only the creatures listed below have weapon immunity inherently. Be aware that fantastic creatures completely ignore this skill! So, your unit's weapon immunity is useless when you're facing summoned monsters, as in lairs, nodes, etc.

Units with Inherent Weapon Immunity:

Air Elemental
Death Knights
Demon
Demon Lord
Shadow Demons
Werewolves
Wraiths
Weapon immunity is granted by enchanting a unit with the Life spell Invulnerability or with the Death spell Wraithform.

Aside from overwhelming the defense of 10 shields granted by weapon immunity, the only way a normal unit can hit a unit with this skill during normal melee combat is with a magic weapon of some type (or a special attack, discussed in following sections). All normal units (from cities) have normal weapons, unless you see a sword icon on the unit. The sword icon indicates that the unit has magical weapons.

Magic weapons are, by definition, those capable of hitting units with weapon immunity. Units with weapon immunity defend against magic weapons as though they would against a normal melee attack. We have listed the items, outside of artifacts, that can make a unit's weapons capable of hitting those with weapon immunity:

"Magic" Weapons List:

The Wizard Skill Alchemy
Alchemist's Guilds
Chaos Spells: Eldritch Weapon,
    Flame Blade, Metal Fires
Life Spells: Holy Arms, Holy Weapon

Since most units are susceptible to normal melee attacks, you will generally not *need* magic melee weapons. However, both alchemist's guilds and enchantments that create magic weapons increase units' combat statistics and, for this reason, have considerable value in *all* melee combat situations.

Bypassing Defense: Illusionary and Armor-Piercing Attack

There are special attacks, illusionary and armor-piercing, that completely or partially bypass the target unit's defenses. Attacks of this type can be devastating to defending units, so an awareness of what types of units possess these abilities is crucial.

Illusionary Attacks and Immunity to Illusion

Illusionary attacks *ignore* a defending unit's shields unless the defender is immune to illusions. That's right, every hit (attack strength multiplied by the To Hit of the unit) by an illusionary unit lands!

In Table 20.6 you can see that very few monsters are capable of illusionary attacks, but that being immune to illusions confers many benefits beyond protection from such attacks. It is also useful to observe that sky drakes, the worst denizens of Sorcery nodes, are not affected by attacks from phantom beasts and phantom warriors. That's a pity since these are the only creatures that can be

Table 20.6 *Illusionary Attacks and Defense*

Illusionary Attacks	Immune to Illusion*
Phantom Beasts	Angels
Phantom Warriors	Arch Angels
Illusionist (hero)	Sky Drakes
	Skeletons
	Ghouls
	Night Stalker
	Werewolves
	Demons
	Wraiths
	Shadow Demons
	Death Knights
	Demon Lord
	Zombies
	Immunity to illusions is provided by the Life spell True Sight and the Death spell Black Channels*.

*Immunity to illusions allows units to see and target invisible units with ranged weapons and provides protection from the following spells: Blur, Confusion, Creature Binding, Invisibility, Mass Invisibility, Mind Storm, Psionic Blast, and Vertigo.

easily summoned when fighting at Sorcery nodes (unless, of course, you have Node Mastery, see Chapter 4).

Armor-Piercing Attacks

Armor-piercing attacks halve the number of shields, rounded down, accessible to a defending unit. There is no specific immunity to the armor-piercing nature of such attacks or counterattacks. However, units with magic immunity (paladins, sky drakes, and units enchanted by the Sorcery spell) are also immune to armor-piercing attacks. Note that lightning attacks are armor-piercing by nature.

Units with armor-piercing attacks:

Elven Lords
Griffins
Paladins
Pikemen
Death Knights
Storm Giants (both ranged and melee attacks)
Black Knight, Knight, Chaos Warrior (both ranged and melee attacks), and Paladin heroes

Other Special Melee Attacks and Resistance

A number of other special melee attacks are possible. Some units have poison, stoning, life-stealing, or other attacks that occur simultaneously with their ordinary melee attacks. The thing that all of these special melee attacks (except immolation) have in common is that *they must be resisted*, not defended. Therefore, the defending unit's shields are ignored and its crosses determine whether it success-

Table 20.7 *Resisting Special Attacks and Spells*

The chance that a unit or a figure, depending on the spell or attack, successfully resists the spell or attack depends on three things:

1. The unit's resistance (i.e., the number of crosses it has)
2. The sum of any acting Resistance Modifiers from unit skills, spells, or artifacts
3. Any modifier to the saving throw

The saving throw modifiers basically alter the number of crosses a unit or figure has to resist a spell or attack. If the spell or attack acts at a -2 save, for example, then the defender must resist it with two fewer crosses than it can normally use to resist spells and attacks.

Each cross the unit has is worth a 10 percent chance to resist a spell or attack. Thus, a unit with six crosses would have a base 60 percent chance when resisting. The total chance that a unit has to resist something is given by:

Chance to Resist = 10% x (Number of Crosses + Sum of Resistance Modifiers + Saving Throw Modifier)

fully defends against the attack or not. Table 20.7 describes how resistance to these attacks and spells is determined.

A unit's ability to resist spells and special attacks can be modified, just like any other attribute. Table 20.8 describes the things, aside from artifacts for heroes, that can modify unit resistances.

Be aware that a unit's resistance affects its ability to survive a variety of attacks, including many touch attacks, gaze attacks, and stoning. Resistance also determines a unit's ability to withstand many of the spells that may be directed against it (see Chapter 21).

Life-Stealing Attacks and Immunity to Death Magic

Life-stealing is a special attack made concurrently with (*and in addition to*) the unit's normal melee attack. A unit with a life-stealing attack (see Table 20.9) rolls a d10 for that attack. For each point that die roll is above the defender's resistance, the defender takes a hit and the attacking unit *gains* one heart!

For example, if a unit with a resistance of five is hit by a life-stealing attack, a d10 is rolled for the strength of that attack. Let's say that the result of this die roll is eight, then the unit will have three (8 minus 5) hearts stolen from it, while the attacker gains three.

In addition to this blood-sucking heart transplant (ouch!), if a unit's side loses the battle and the unit that died had more than half of its hit points stolen by life-stealing attacks, the unit rises from the dead and serves the winning side as an undead unit. (**Hint:** if you have an army of life-stealers, never go into battle with a full stack of nine units. Leave a hole or two that can be filled by resurrected enemy units after you win the battle.)

Avoid fighting life-stealers in melee combat at all costs! Take them down with spells or missile weapons, if you can.

Poison Attacks and Immunity
Poison attacks occur simultaneously and supplementally to normal melee attacks. Like

Table 20.8 *Changing Unit Resistances*

Through Increasing Experience:

Arms Master, a hero skill

Warlord, a wizard skill

Altar of Battle, a Life spell

Crusade, a Life spell

Heroism, a Life spell

Changing Resistance:

Hero Skills: Charmed (+30), Prayer Master

Unit Skills: Holy Bonus (varies; Paladins, Angels, Arch Angels), Luck (+1, Halflings), Magic Immunity (+30),
  Resistance to All (varies; Guardian Spirit, Unicorn)

Chaos Spells: Chaos Surge (+2), Warp Creature (0*)

Death Spells: Black Channels (+1), Black Prayer (-2), Cloud of Shadow (**), Darkness (**), Eternal Night (**)

Life Spells: Bless (+3***), Heavenly Light (**), High Prayer (+3), Lion Heart (+3), Prayer (+1), Righteousness
  (+30***) True Light (**)

Nature Spells: Elemental Armor (+10***), Resist Elements (+3***)

Sorcery Spells: Magic Immunity (+30), Mind Storm (-5), Resist Magic (+5)

*Effect only occurs some of the time.

**Effect ranges from -1 to +1, depending on whether a unit is made up of creatures of Life, Death, or neither.

***The enchantment is only effective against spells, magic ranged attacks, and special attacks that are 1) green
or red for Elemental Armor and Resist Elements, 2) red or black for Bless and Righteousness (see Table 20.22)

most touch attacks, however, poison attacks must be resisted, instead of defended against.

For the purposes of determining melee results when poison attacks are involved, be aware that the strength of such an attack determines the number of resistance rolls a unit must make. For each failed resistance roll, the unit will lose one hit point. So, the strength of the poison attack is the maximum amount of damage a defending unit can take, depending on how many failed resistance rolls it makes. Note that units with poison attack capabilities also use this attack type when they counterattack.

While resistance is involved in defending against poison attacks, some units are completely immune to such attacks. Table 20.10 lists all units capable of and immune to poison attacks.

Stoning Touch

Only cockatrices are capable of attacking with a stoning touch without the aid of an artifact. (Note, basilisks have a stoning *gaze*, discussed later.) The stoning touch, which also occurs during counterattacks, causes each figure in the target unit (per figure in the attacking unit) to resist at -3 or be stoned (killed outright) after the other parts of melee combat have been resolved.

A number of units are immune to stoning; all elementals are immune, as are gargoyles, stone giants, and the colossus. Units with magic immunity are also unaffected by this attack. A more complete discussion of stoning immunity can be found later in this chapter in the Stoning Gaze section.

Table 20.9 *Life-Stealing Attacks and Death Immunity*

Life-Stealers:
Death Knights (-4)
Demon Lords (-5) for both melee *and ranged* attacks
Wraiths (-3)
Necromancer (0; hero) for both melee *and ranged* attacks

The Death spell Life Drain directs a life-stealing attack at a target enemy unit. This spell can, therefore, also create undead units, when used either alone or in conjunction with other life-stealing attacks.

Note that all the life-stealing units are listed with a number following them. This number signifies the Saving Throw Modifier to the defending unit. For example, a unit defending itself against a life-stealing attack from death knights will resist with four fewer crosses than normal.

Ghoul attacks are not life-stealing attacks, but they can create undead units. When units on the losing side die in battle with more than half their hit points eliminated by ghoul attacks, the killed units rise from the dead.

Note, a combination of ghoul attacks and life-stealing attacks that take more than 50 percent of the hearts from a unit (on the losing side) that dies in battle will also result in the fallen unit rising from the dead.

All units that are immune to Death are immune to life-stealing attacks.

Immune to Death magic:
All Undead units (all of Death's fantastic creatures, Black Channeled,
Animated units, and those that have risen from the dead after being killed by life-stealing or ghoul attacks)
Golems
Floating Islands
Phantom Beasts and Warriors
All units with magic immunity (Paladins and Sky Drakes)

Units enchanted with the Life spell Righteousness or the Sorcery spell Magic Immunity are immune to life-stealing attacks. Units that have been enchanted by Bless get three added to their resistance when defending against such attacks.

Dispel Evil Through Touch

The ability to dispel evil through touch is the exclusive province, outside of artifacts conferring such an ability, of the angel (*not* arch angels). The only creatures susceptible to this attack are Chaos and Death creatures, including undeads.

Dispel evil operates during both attacks and counterattacks and is resolved simultaneously with normal melee combat. The touch attack operates under the same resistance penalties (-4 for Chaos creatures and Death creatures and -9 for undead units, i.e., those that have risen from the dead) as the spell of the same name. It also works in the same way as the spell in that each figure in the target unit (per figure in the attacking unit) must resist separately. Note, since angels are single-figure

Table 20.10 *Poison Attacks and Poison Immunity*

Units with Poison Attacks*	Immune to Poison**
Manticores (6)	Golems
Nightblades (1)	Air Elementals
Wyvern Riders (6)	Colossus
Chaos Spawn (4)	Earth Elementals
Ghouls (1)	Fire Elementals
Giant Spider (4)	Gargoyles
Great Wyrm (15)	Stone Giant
Nagas (4***)	Unicorns
	Phantom Warriors
	Phantom Beasts
	Floating Island
	Animate Dead Units
	Black Channel Units
	Death Knights
	Demons
	Demon Lords
	Ghouls
	Night Stalkers
	Shadow Demons
	Skeletons
	Werewolves
	Wraiths
	Zombies

*Number in parentheses is the strength of the poison attack.

**Note that all elementals and creatures of Death, except for undead units formed from life-stealing or ghoul attacks, are immune to poison attacks.

***Nagas' poison attack is a first strike attack that occurs and is resolved before other parts of melee combat.

units, they can only kill one figure in target units per melee round through their dispel evil touch. When a figure fails to resist dispel evil, it is banished. Units enchanted by the Sorcery spell Magic Immunity are unaffected by this attack.

Immolation or Fiery Touch

Similar to the poison attack, immolation occurs in addition to, but concurrently with, normal melee combat. Immolation is active in both attacks and counterattacks and has a strength of four (which is not that hot, since what little damage it does is blocked by the enemy unit's shields). Nevertheless the attack is equivalent to a Fireball spell and will hit

Table 20.11 *Magic Immunity*

Units with Magic Immunity:

Paladins

Sky Drakes

Black Knight, Paladin, and the Chosen heroes

The Sorcery spell Magic Immunity endows a unit with this ability.

Magic Immunity confers immunity to:

All breath attacks

All gaze attacks (except for Doom Gaze)

All other special attacks (life-stealing, stoning, armor-piercing, etc.) except for illusionary and poison attacks

Virtually all spells (except for Web and Cracks Call)

Magic Immunity also increases defense to 50 shields against all magic ranged attacks, except for illusionary ones

every figure in the target unit. Only the doom bat has an innate immolation attack, but the Chaos spell of the same name can endow any unit with this ability.

An immolation attack is defended, instead of resisted, but certain units are naturally immune to fire: the efreet, fire elemental, and fire giant. Creatures with magic immunity (paladins, sky drakes, or units enchanted with Magic Immunity) are also unaffected by immolation.

Before Melee Combat Begins: First Strike Attacks

Some kinds of melee attacks actually occur, and are resolved, *before* normal melee combat. These include breath attacks, gaze attacks, thrown attacks, and attacks by first strike weapons. Except for the gaze attacks, none of these attack types can be used by a defending unit (i.e., when a unit counterattacks during the opponent's battle turn).

Therefore, to get the benefit of these attacks, a unit has to do the attacking! Like comedy, the secret is timing. Plan your approach with these units so that if they are yours, they will get in the first attack or, if they are your opponent's, you get the first at-

tack on them. This is the key to these first-strike units!

Except for ordinary first strike weapons, all of these attack types can be used against flying creatures. This is important since, as discussed later in this chapter, ground troops cannot attack flying creatures under ordinary circumstances. If, however, your troops have breath, gaze, or thrown attacks, or if they wield missile weapons, they can directly attack flying units and force the flying units to engage in melee combat. The following sections describe each of these pre-melee attack types in detail.

Breath Attacks, Magic Immunity, and Fire Immunity

There are two types of breath attacks: fiery breath and lightning breath. Fiery breath is the more common since only sky drakes have the armor-piercing lightning breath attacks.

All breath attacks occur before normal melee combat begins and can only be used when the unit is actually attacking; i.e., a unit cannot use its breath when counterattacking. Breath attacks are defended against with normal defenses or shields. Units with large shields (i.e., swordsmen and minotaurs) get

Table 20.12 *Fiery breath, Immolation and Fire Immunity*

Fiery breath*	Immolation**	Immunity to Fire***
Draconians (1)****	Doom Bat	Efreet
Doom Drakes (6)		Fire Elemental
Dragon Turtles (5)		Fire Giant
Stag Beetles (5)		
Chimera (4)		
Great Drakes (30)		
Hell Hounds (3)		
Hydras (5)		
Draconian hero (4 to 13)		

*The strength of each fiery breath attack is indicated in parentheses after the unit.

**Immolation is a strength four fiery touch attack.

***Immunity to fire confers immunity to a number of spells and creatures in addition to immunity to fiery breath and immolation. These units are immune to the following spells Fireball, Fire Bolts, Fire Storm, Flame Blade, Flame Strike, Immolation, Metal Fires, and Meteor Storms.

****All Draconian units except for bowmen, shamans, and magicians have a strength one fiery breath attack per figure.

Note that units with magic immunity are not affected by breath attacks or immolation.

the benefit of an extra two shields when defending against breath attacks.

Units with magic immunity are completely immune to both types of breath attacks. See Table 20.11 for more information about magic immunity.

Fiery breath attacks occur before normal melee combat begins and can only be used when the unit is attacking. These breath attacks have a given strength which has the same To Hit ability as the unit's other attacks. Each fiery breath attack that lands can be blocked by the defender's shields, in the same way as during normal melee combat. The only difference is that the fiery breath attack is resolved before normal melee combat begins.

Units with immunity to fire cannot be affected by fiery breath attacks, nor can they be affected by the immolation attacks discussed earlier. Table 20.12 shows the units capable of fiery breath attacks and immolation and those units immune to fire.

There are a number of spells that affect breath attacks:

🔥 Black Channels (Death) increases a unit's breath attack strength by one.

🔥 Black Prayer (Death) decreases enemy units' breath attack strengths by one.

🔥 Bless (Life) increases a unit's defense to breath attacks by three.

🔥 Chaos Channels (Chaos) can permanently give units a fiery breath attack of strength two.

🔥 Chaos Surge (Chaos) increases all Chaos units' fiery breath attacks by two.

🔥 Cloud of Shadow, Darkness, Eternal Night, Heavenly Light, and True Light can increase or decrease units' breath attacks by one, depending on the spell and the nature of the unit.

🔥 Elemental Armor (Nature) increases a unit's defense to breath attacks by 10.

Table 20.13 *Thrown Attacks*

Units with Thrown Attacks:*
Barbarian Cavalry (1)
Barbarian Spearmen (1)
Barbarian Swordsmen (1)
Barbarian Berserkers (2)
Barbarian (3 to 11), Orc Warrior (3 to 11), and Amazon (4 to 12) heroes

*The strength of the thrown attack is in parentheses following the unit type. Note, the strength of hero thrown attacks does not include modifications from the hero skill might or from miscellaneous artifacts and axes.

Note that all spells and skills that affect melee attack strength and the unit's To Hit ability during a melee attack also affect thrown attacks (see Table 20.2). The only exceptions or variations are:
Unit Skills: Holy Bonus (no effect on thrown weapon strength), Leadership (offers half the bonus to thrown attacks as it does to melee attacks)
Chaos Spells: Warp Creature (decreasing a target's melee attacks has no effect on that unit's thrown attacks)
Death Spells: Berserk (has no effect on thrown weapon strength), Black Channels (increases thrown attack strength by one)
Life Spells: High Prayer (no effect on thrown weapon strength)
Artifacts: Axes and miscellaneous items with + attacks and + To Hits.

Magic Immunity (Sorcery) increases a unit's defense against breath attacks to 50 shields.

Mind Storm (Sorcery) decreases targets' breath attacks by five.

Righteousness (Life) gives 50 shields to units when they defend against breath attacks.

Resist Elements (Nature) increases a unit's defense to breath attacks by three.

Shatter (Chaos) will decrease a targeted unit's breath attack to one.

Although Immolation does not affect fiery breath attacks, it does give the target unit a strength four fiery touch attack.

Besides the spells listed above, normal units in the presence of a hero with Leadership ability get up to two strength added to their fiery breath attacks (see Chapter 17).

The only other type of breath attack is the lightning breath attack, which is only found among sky drakes. Their breath attack is strength 20 *and* is armor-piercing (halving

shields). Units best able to withstand these fierce attacks are those with magic immunity, such as paladins, other sky drakes, or units enchanted with either the Sorcery spell Magic Immunity or the Life spell Righteousness.

Unless your units are immune to breath attacks, they should always try to initiate attacks against units with fiery or lightning breath, since these attack types are not involved in counterattacks.

Thrown Attacks

Thrown attacks are conducted before normal melee combat and can only be used when a unit is initiating an attack. Units use their shields to protect themselves from thrown weapons. Units with large shields (i.e., minotaurs and swordsmen), get an added protection of +2 shields when defending against thrown attacks. Units with missile immunity (magicians, warlocks, skeletons, and demons) are immune to these attacks. Thrown attacks

Table 20.14 *First Strike Units and Negate First Strike Units*

First Strike	Negate First Strike
Cavalry	High Men Halberdiers
Colossus	Lizardmen Halberdiers
Death Knights	Nomad Halberdiers
Elven Lords	Troll Halberdiers
Griffins	Pikemen
Paladins	
War Mammoths	
Black Knight (hero)	
Knight (hero)	
Paladin (hero)	

Note that negate first strike does *only* that. It does not affect the timing of breath, gaze, or thrown attacks.

are resolved before normal melee combat begins. Note that ground units with thrown weapons can attack flying units.

Only Barbarians units and some heroes come with thrown weapons. These units are listed in Table 20.13 along with the skills and spells that can affect the strength and accuracy of thrown attacks.

Similar to those with breath attacks, units with thrown attacks should be moved so that they can initiate combat in order to take advantage of this capability. Remember to use these units when you're fighting flying creatures, since units with thrown attacks can initiate melee combat with them!

First Strike Weapons

Some units can use their swords first in melee combat. This first strike capability means that their attacks get resolved before the opponent's counterattack. Hence, the defending unit will suffer the damage from the first strike attack before its counterattack is even calculated. If you use first strike capabilities effectively, you can wipe out enemy units (or at least deplete their strength) before they have a chance to counterattack.

Note that the first strike capability simply means that a unit gets to hit before it gets hit back; it does not get extra attacks from this ability. Also, first strike attacks are defended against in the normal way. The only way that a unit's first strike ability will not exert its effects is if the enemy units have the ability to negate the first strike.

The ability to negate first strike changes the attacking unit's timing so that it makes normal, simultaneous melee attacks. This gives the defender a chance to counterattack at the strength at which it started the combat round (instead of the depleted strength it might otherwise have after suffering a first strike attack). Table 20.14 lists the units with first strike and negate first strike capability.

Note that some of the deadliest units: death knights, elven lords, and paladins, have this ability. If you have these units, make an effort to use their first strike abilities wisely. Remember that death knights also have a life-stealing attack that allows them to attack first *and* replenish their hit points while attacking, so charge into enemies freely with them.

Table 20.15 *Death and Doom Gazes*

Death Gaze:

Spells and skills that increase a unit's resistance will increase the chance of figures successfully withstanding this gaze. Figures failing their saving throws die before they can attack or counterattack.

Units with Death Gazes*:

Chaos Spawn (-4)

Night Stalker (-2)

*The Saving Throw Modifier is shown in parentheses following the unit. A value of -4 means that the defending figure's resistance is lowered by 4 crosses before it gets a chance to resist the gaze.

Doom Gaze:

Chaos Spawns are the only creatures with a doom gaze. This gaze has an attack strength of four and automatically does four damage to the opposing unit before melee combat begins. Note that at Chaos nodes (where all like-colored creatures get +2 to all of their attributes), the Chaos spawn's doom gaze will do six automatic damage to enemy units.

Note that Magic Immunity confers immunity to all gaze attacks except Doom Gaze.

In combination with their flying ability, which often allows them to pick and choose their opponents, death knights can be a tremendous asset to a wizard specializing in Death magic.

Gaze Attacks and Stoning Immunity

Gaze attacks come in three types: death gaze, doom gaze, and stoning gaze, and all are nasty. These attacks occur before melee combat and are *also* used in defense (when a unit counterattacks). Gaze attacks must be resisted, and their effects are resolved before melee combat is conducted.

Death and stoning gaze attacks affect all figures in the targeted unit, with each figure attempting to resist separately. Both the death gaze and the stoning gaze kill figures outright. The doom gaze offers no opportunity for resistance; it simply does its damage to the opposing unit before melee combat commences. Note that gaze attacks can be used by ground troops to attack flying units.

Magic immunity offers a unit the ability to escape the consequences of all gaze attacks except the doom gaze. Paladins and sky drakes innately have this skill; other units may only acquire it through the Sorcery spell of the same name. See Table 20.15 for summary information on death and doom gazes.

The stoning gaze attack works the same way as the death gaze. Targeted figures have an opportunity to resist *before* melee combat begins (thus, stoning *gaze* is resolved *before* melee combat; stoning *touch* is conducted *concurrently* with melee combat). Figures failing to resist get stoned the hard way (i.e., die). Some units are completely resistant to stoning. A summary of units and spells that try to kill by stoning, as well as those units immune to stoning is shown in Table 20.16.

Many of the units that are immune to stoning effects are those that can be summoned during combat, if you have the appropriate spells. This makes such summoning spells es-

Table 20.16 *Stoning and Immunity to Stoning*

Units with Stoning Attacks and Stoning Immunity:

Stoning Gaze*	Stoning Touch**	Stoning Immunity***
Basilisks (-1)	Cockatrices (-3)	Air Elementals
Chaos Spawn (-4)		Colossus
Gorgons (-2)		Earth Elementals
		Fire Elementals
		Floating Island
		Gargoyles
		Phantom Beasts
		Phantom Warriors
		Stone Giants

*Saving Throw Modifiers are shown in parentheses.

**Saving Throw Modifiers are shown in parentheses. Note that stoning touch occurs concurrently with normal melee combat and that artifacts are capable of conferring this ability to heroes (but only at a -1 Saving Throw Modifier).

***Stoning immunity also protects against the Nature spell Petrify.

A stoning touch enchantment (or any other touch enchantment, such as disintegrate or life-stealing) in an artifact will exert its effects with that item's normal attacks. For example, stoning touch in wands will travel and occur simultaneously with magic ranged attacks. Similarly, stoning touch in a sword will occur simultaneously with the hero's melee attack. If the hero's attack happens to be first strike, then the stoning touch attack will also occur as a first strike attack.

Note that magic immunity (in Paladins, Sky Drakes, or via the Sorcery spell) confers protection from stoning attacks.

pecially useful when combating units that can stone others.

Sequence of Melee Combat

All of the attacks we have discussed so far are, officially, part of melee combat. They only occur when one unit attacks another adjacent to it. The discussed attacks occur and are resolved in a certain sequence. In addition, some of these forms of combat can only be used when a unit is attacking. These facts are summarized in Table 20.17.

Units with breath, thrown, and first strike capabilities should always *attack* in a melee

situation—rather than wait to receive an enemy attack—so that they can exploit their special advantages. Conversely, it is always to your relative advantage to initiate attacks against enemies with these abilities to prevent their effective use of these abilities.

To Attack or Defend in Melee Combat?

The evidence overwhelmingly shows that it is always better to attack than defend, assuming that you wish two units to engage in melee combat. This is because the defending units do not enjoy the benefits of first strike, thrown

Table 20.17 *Timing of Melee Combat*

Phase 1: Breath*, Gaze (Attacker), Thrown Attacks*

These attacks are conducted and appropriately defended or resisted, simultaneously, before the next phase begins.

Phase 2: Gaze (Defender)

Defender's gaze attacks are conducted and resisted, before the next phase begins.

Phase 3: First Strike*

The attacker's first strike attack is conducted and defended. If defender has Cloak of Fear, the first strike unit must resist this before attacking.

Phase 4: Normal Melee Combat, Life-Stealing, Poison, Other Touch Attacks

The phase 4 attacks are conducted and appropriately defended or resisted simultaneously. If the defender has Cloak of Fear, the attacker must first resist it.

* = These attacks are not available to a defending unit. Only the attacking unit (i.e., the one spending movement points and initiating combat) may engage in these types of attacks.

---

attacks, or breath attacks; instead, they are subjected to such attacks by their enemies. Similarly, your units with these capabilities can only use them when they attack! In any case where unit capabilities differ in this area, if at all possible, be sure that your troops are the ones initiating the attacks.

Basic Ranged Combat: Missiles

Missiles can play a pivotal role in combat. Launching missile attacks on your enemies for several combat rounds before melee combat begins, as they slowly make their way toward your units, is one of simplest ways to minimize damage to your own forces and *tenderize* approaching enemy units.

Unfortunately, missiles of any type—bows, rocks, slings, javelins, or even magic missiles (discussed later)—can only be launched once per unit per battle turn. Missile units are usually among the most fragile units in an army; therefore they draw a lot of enemy fire.

Carefully consider where to use your bowmen, slingers, or other missile units. Only take

them where they can actually do some good. A lair full of sprites, for example, would not be the place to take your missile units unless they were well enchanted or quite experienced, i.e., having more defenses and hit points than new units. Otherwise, they'll die from withering enemy fire before they can be used to their full effect.

Missile attacks are similar to normal melee attacks in all ways but three:

🔹 Missiles are limited in quantity. Most troops cannot fire more than eight arrows or other missile ammunition per combat.

🔹 Missile units always fire their missiles, even when adjacent to units they could melee, as long as their ammunition holds out. You can't make them stop shooting arrows and pick up their swords. On the up side, when firing missiles, even from an adjacent square, missile units cannot be counterattacked.

🔹 Missile units suffer a distance penalty. The farther away the target, the greater the penalty to the missile unit's To Hit modifier (the

Table 20.18 *Damage from Normal Missile Attacks*

Total Attack Strength = Number of Figures x Number of Missiles

This number represents the maximum damage in hit points that an attacking missile unit can do in one round of combat, since the unit can only fire once. This number is equivalent to the total number of arrows fired at the target. Some arrows will miss, and some will hit. Of those that hit, some will be stopped by the target's shields. Each unstopped arrow causes one point of damage. The chance that a missile hits its target follows:

Chance of a Hit = 30% + (10% x sum of all To Hit modifiers, including Distance Modifier)

Distance Modifier = (Squares from Target/3, rounded down) x -1

After determining the probability of actually hitting the target, the average number of hits that a missile unit can land on its target unit can be determined by:

Average Number of Hits Landed = Total Attack Strength x Chance of a Hit

penalty is -1 To Hit for every three squares' distance).

Table 20.18 describes how damage from missile attacks is determined.

The damage calculation for missile attacks is the same for regular melee attacks with the addition of a Distance Modifier. Because of the dramatic distance penalty, though, spells or skills that alter the chance To Hit have especially significant effects for missile units.

A number of skills and spells can affect the strength and accuracy of missile units. Most spells or skills that affect attack strength and the ability To Hit exert the same effects on normal missile attacks. Besides modifications from artifact enchantments, there are a few spells and skills that are specifically applicable to missile attacks. These are described in Table 20.19.

Units defend themselves from missile attacks in the same way as they do from normal melee attacks. Units with a large shield ability (i.e., minotaurs and swordsmen), get an additional two shields whenever defending against missile attacks.

It is possible for units to be completely immune to most normal missile attacks, because of either an inherent resistance or a resistance through enchantments. Table 20.20 summarizes the things that affect a unit's ability to defend against missile attacks.

The Death spell Wall of Darkness protects garrisoned troops from ranged weapons. In fact, this spell confers complete protection from all ranged attacks on such troops. Only units with True Sight can fire missiles at units behind a Wall of Darkness.

When fighting with bowmen or other units with normal missiles, the most important thing to be aware of is distance limitations. (Although knowing not to shoot enthusiastically at skeletons and magicians is helpful, too.) Since your ammunition is usually limited, it may be advantageous to wait one combat round for the range to close up a bit before starting to fire your missiles. This is especially true if you have normal, possibly expendable, ground troops who can delay the approach of enemy units to your missile units, or if you can summon units, such as phantom warriors, to do this.

Table 20.19 *Modifying Missile Attacks*

Exclusively Affecting Missile Attacks:
Long Range is a unit skill that allows it to fire missiles with a maximum distance modifier of -1 To Hit (i.e., when firing at a range of three or more squares). Catapults, longbowmen, and warships have this skill.

Warp Wood is a Chaos spell that destroys all of the target unit's remaining ammunition for bows or slings (rocks are unaffected).

Other Skills and Spells that Affect Missile Attacks*:
Hero Skills: Blade Master (To Hit), Leadership (varies)
Unit Skills: Luck (+1 To Hit; Halflings)
Wizard Skills: Alchemy (+1 To Hit)
Alchemist's Guilds: (+1 To Hit), with Mithril (+1), with Adamantium (+2)
Chaos Spells: Chaos Surge (+2), Eldritch Weapon (-1** to target's ability To Defend), Flame Blade (+2**), Metal
     Fires (+1**), Shatter (1***), Warp Reality (-2 To Hit)
Death Spells: Black Channels (+1), Black Prayer (-1), Cloud of Shadow (****), Darkness (****),
     Eternal Night (****), Weakness (-2**)
Life Spells: Heavenly Light (****), High Prayer (+1 To Hit), Holy Arms (+1 To Hit), Holy Weapon (+1 To Hit), Lion
     Heart (+3), Prayer (+1 To Hit), True Light (****)
Sorcery Spells: Mind Storm (-5), Vertigo (-2 To Hit)

*Numbers in parentheses refer to changes in attack strength, unless otherwise indicated.
**Change affects only bow and sling attacks; does not affect rocks.
***Shatter reduces the target unit's missile weapon strength to one.
****These spells can add one, subtract one, or exert no effect on a unit's missile attack strengths, depending on the spell and the unit's color.

As always, being aware of what you're up against before you walk into a combat situation (right-click on cities and stacks before you step on them) is the best way to ensure that you will be prepared. If you are up against a lair full of night stalkers, don't walk in with an all-missile army. If you plan to invade a town full of bowmen, consider an army of missile-immune units. This rock-paper-scissors approach is simple, but it works.

Magic Ranged Attacks

Magic ranged attacks are similar to normal missile attacks, so we are discussing them here rather than in the next chapter (which covers the use of magic in combat). Units defend themselves from such attacks in the normal way, using shields. Targeted units may not counterattack, even if the attack is launched from an adjacent square. Note that units with large shields (minotaurs and swordsmen) still get their +2 shields against magic ranged attacks.

Magic ranged attacks are different from normal missile attacks, however, in other ways:

🦎 Magic ranged attacks do not lose accuracy over distance.
🦎 Magic ranged attacks are usually supplied with less ammunition than normal missile attacks. Most units (other than heroes) cannot

Table 20.20 *Protection from Normal Missile Attacks*

Increased Protection:
Large Shields (+2 to defense): Minotaurs and Swordsmen

Missile Immunity*:
Demons
Magicians
Skeletons
Warlocks
Magician, Wind Mage, Witch, Warlock, Illusionist (heroes)

Invisibility:**
Air Elementals
Nightblades
Night Stalker
Ninja (hero)

*Missile immunity confers complete protection (50 shields)to the unit from bow and sling attacks. Rock attacks can still hit targets with missile immunity. The Sorcery spell Guardian Wind enchants the target unit with this same ability.

**Invisible units are impossible to target with ranged weapons unless the targeting unit is immune to illusions or has been enchanted by True Sight. Units can be made invisible by casting the Sorcery spells Invisibility or Mass Invisibility.

launch more than four such attacks per combat.

In addition, different spells and abilities are used to protect units from missile and magic ranged attacks. Table 20.21 provides a synopsis of the specific skills and spells that affect magic ranged attacks, including units that are immune to these attacks.

All magic ranged, breath, and gaze attacks are colored. Certain spells protect units from specific colors of magic ranged attacks. These spells and the colors of various attacks are listed in Table 20.22.

Magic ranged attacks have some wonderful features. First, they are not subject to distance dependency and are equally accurate at all ranges. Second, the strengths of magic ranged attacks tend to be greater than normal missile attacks and, against susceptible creatures, the damage done to units tends to be higher. Third, fewer units are inherently immune to these attacks than those immune to normal missiles.

When building armies, include a few ranged attack units, unless your army is made up of only the toughest units. Ranged weapons, regardless of type, can whittle away the most formidable opponents before they can reach your units. Balancing your armies is the key (see Chapter 22). Remember, unless you have enchanted your missile and magic ranged units with lots of protective spells, they are very susceptible to being picked off by enemy units of the same type (don't forget about those sprites!).

Table 20.21 *Magic Ranged Attacks*

Spells and Skills Affecting Magic Ranged Attacks Through Increasing Experience:
Arms Master, a hero skill
Warlord, a wizard skill
Altar of Battle, a Life spell
Crusade, a Life spell
Heroism, a Life spell

Hero Skills:
Arcane Power (affects strength of attack)
Blade Master (affects accuracy of attack)
Spell-Casting Skill (affects number of attacks at three mana expended/attack)

Unit Skills:
Large Shield increases unit's defense to magic ranged attacks by two (Minotaurs and Swordsmen)
Magic Immunity gives a minimum defense of 50 versus non-illusionary magic ranged attacks (Paladins, Sky Drakes)
Invisibility prevents targeting that unit (Air Elementals, Nightblades, Night Stalkers)

Defense Spells:
Bless (Life, +3 defense to black and red magic ranged attacks)
Magic Immunity (Sorcery, same as skill)
Invisibility (Sorcery, same as skill)
Mass Invisibility (Sorcery, same as Invisibility)
Righteousness (Life, +50 defense to red and black magic ranged attacks)
Elemental Armor (Nature, +10 defense to green and red magic ranged attacks)
Resist Elements (Nature, +3 defense to green and red magic ranged attacks)

Spells Affecting Magic Ranged Attack Strength:
Chaos Surge (Chaos, +2 strength)
Shatter (Chaos, strength goes to one)
Black Channels (Death, +1 strength)
Black Prayer (Death, -1 strength)
Cloud of Shadow, Darkness and Eternal Night (Death, +1 strength for Death creatures and -1 for Life creatures)
Heavenly Light and True Light (Life, +1 strength for Life creatures and -1 for undeads)
Mind Storm (Sorcery, -5 strength)

The Death spell Mana Leak will remove one ammunition from all opponents' ranged magic attacks per combat turn.

Table 20.22 *Colors of Magic Ranged and Special Attacks*

Comparison	Colors of Attacks			
Color	Red Magic	Green Magic	Blue Magic	Black Magic
Units	Dark Elves Demon Lords Efreet Magicians Shadow Demons Storm Giants Warlocks	Djinn Priests Shamans Sprites		
Heroes	Draconian Golden One Magician Necromancer Unknown Warrior Mage Witch	Druid Healer Priestess Wind Mage	Sage Illusionist	
Attack Types	Doom Gaze Fire Breath Lightning Breath	Stoning Gaze Stoning Touch	Illusionary	Death Gaze Life-Stealing
Artifact Attacks*	Destruction			Cause Death**
Protective Spells	Resist Elements Elemental Armor Magic Immunity Bless Righteousness	Resist Elements Elemental Armor Magic Immunity	Magic Immunity	Magic Immunity Bless Righteousness

Note, all magic ranged, gaze, and breath attacks have a color attached to them. Certain spells can confer protection to specific attack colors. Units and heroes with colored magic ranged attacks, special colored attack types (poison attacks are considered colorless; and dispel evil, not listed above, is considered a white attack), and protective spells are listed in this table.

* Attacks only found in artifacts.
** Cause death is a special attack that occurs concurrently with an artifact's attacks and must be resisted at -3 by the target.

Combat Variations: Flying, Water, Walls, and More

Before you engage an enemy host, you should consider the impact of the basic combat types discussed above, as well as other things that can affect your battle. The following sections discuss some special factors—flying, teleporting, walls, ocean combat, node auras, etc.—that may influence your plans in a particular battle.

Moving Prospects

Units differ in their movement types and speed, which is an important consideration when you are trying to achieve offensive initiative (as discussed earlier in this chapter). The following sections examine the specific effects of special movement types in combat.

Flying

Many units in *Master of Magic* have the ability to fly. These units tend to have a great advantage during combat.

Flying units may only be attacked by other flying units or units with breath, gaze, thrown, missile, or magic ranged attacks. Because of these special requirements for attacking flying units, such units can often choose when and what they will attack during combat. This luxury of choice means that flying units pitted against ground troops can get in their first strike attacks during each melee round. It also makes it easier to rotate flying units in and out of melee combat to help spread out physical damage among all your units present at a battle. Under ordinary circumstances, you might have to run an injured unit around the battlefield merely to avoid its being attacked. Flying units, generally, don't have to do that.

Because flying units are indifferent to terrain (being able to fly over water, mountains, and grasslands with equal ease), they can fight in naval battles (see below). In addition, the flying units' indifference to terrain type means

they are unaffected by the Nature spell Earth to Mud.

Flying units have an additional feature: They do not have to attack, enter, or exit cities through breeches or openings in a city wall. They can move and attack over walls.

Below, we have listed spells that can affect a unit's flying ability.

Spells Affecting Flight:

The Nature spell Web can tie up the target in its sticky strands for a while. Better than this, though, is that once a flying unit has been webbed in combat, it can no longer fly for the remainder of the battle. Note, there are two non-corporeal flying units: shadow demons and wraiths. Neither of these can be webbed because of their non-corporeal nature.

The Sorcery spell Flight is a unit enchantment that can be cast during and outside of combat. You can cast this spell in a pinch, when you suddenly find that you have brought an all-ground army with no projectile weapons into combat against an army of flying units. This spell is also good for taking a ground unit out of harm's way when you are fighting a deadly battle against other ground troops. This spell can be particularly helpful when you've been invaded and your garrison is inadequate for the task of defending your city. Casting Flight on one of the defenders can prevent that unit from being attacked (assuming the invaders have no means to attack a flying unit). Then you can simply outlast the invasion by flying around until combat ends. Note, however, if you do this, enemy units deprived of a target will stomp on your city and try to destroy its buildings and people.

Table 20.23 *Non-corporeal Units*

Non-Corporeal Units:

Guardian Spirit

Magic Spirit

Phantom Beast

Phantom Warriors

Shadow Demons

Wraiths

Wraithform (a Death spell that makes a unit non-corporeal)

Non-corporeal units are immune to the Nature spell Web and the webbing skill of giant spiders. These units are also unaffected by the Nature spell Earth to Mud.

During combat, part of prioritizing your attacks or other options depends upon examining the capabilities of all the units on the field. Flying is an ability to pay close attention to. For example, your all-ground army without missile weapons cannot tackle an army of flying units, unless your army is stronger than your enemy's or you have the Web spell and enough mana and skill to cast it as required. To assess relative army strength in such a situation, you should consider first strike potential available to the flying units vs. any first strike potential you will lose because you cannot attack. A flying unit with first strike ability is much more dangerous to you if you have no flying units and no Web spell.

The discussions in this section suggest a few interesting options, depending on your wizard's magic types. For example, consider casting the Death spell Wraithform, which makes units non-corporeal, on flying units to prevent them from being webbed by enemies. Conversely, it isn't necessarily redundant to cast the Sorcery spell Flight on non-corporeal units. Or even, if you are a master of both blue and black magic, consider casting both of these spells on the same deadly units! Imagine a troop of flying, non-corporeal paladins or elven lords. Casting Invisibility on flying

units can make them even more dangerous because it removes them as targets for ranged attacks and spells. Consider casting flight on your missile units before entering great wyrm lairs (wyrms cannot attack fliers). Also, consider casting Earth to Mud *after* you have cast Web on a flying unit, because these units are otherwise not affected by Earth to Mud.

Non-Corporeal Units ("Wafting") and Webbing

The non-corporeal skill allows a unit to "waft" over *all* terrain types as if it were moving over normal roads. Therefore, units can travel over water without any difficulty. This skill also confers an immunity to the Nature spells, Web, Cracks Call, and Earth to Mud.

While some units are innately non-corporeal (see Table 20.23), this skill can be conferred onto other units either through special artifacts, for heroes, or by enchanting units with the Death magic spell Wraithform. Note that although Wraithform allows units to move over all terrain types, as if they were moving over roads, this speed benefit only affects overland travel; a non-corporeal unit's movement speed is not affected during combat.

Non-corporeal movement affects combat in two ways. First, non-corporeal units can attack and pass through city walls, which can

Table 20.24 *Teleporting Units*

Teleporting Units*:

Djinn (3, flying)

Great Wyrm (3)

Unicorns (2)

*Movement speed and type, if unusual, are indicated in parentheses after the unit name.

Note that no spell confers the ability to teleport and none removes it.

be useful on both attack and defense. Second, non-corporeal units cannot be webbed or hindered by an Earth to Mud spell. This means that they cannot be stopped or slowed by these Nature spells or by the webs cast by giant spiders. Since webbing has the greatest adverse effects on flying units, as it prevents them from flying for the remainder of combat, non-corporeal flying units, such as shadow demons and wraiths, can be valuable.

Teleporting

A few units, djinns, great wyrms, and unicorns, can teleport anywhere on the battlefield for the cost of one movement point (see Table 20.24). Teleporting units can get right next to their chosen targets and attack. When your army has stepped onto a map square inhabited by teleporting units, there is nothing you can do about it: those enemies will get in the first attack and they will attack whichever unit they prefer. So you should make an effort to prepare for such battles *before* you initiate combat.

Because teleporting units may go wherever they please on the battlefield, they can run around and avoid attacks against them from stronger units (assuming those units have no ranged weapons). This may be helpful in defending cities. Remember that the accuracy of non-magic ranged weapons has a distance dependence, except for the long ranged weapons of longbowmen, catapults, and warships.

This means that if you have a teleporting unit against a strong missile-based army, you can keep your teleporting units substantially away from harm by teleporting them to the farthest ends of the battlefield until the enemy's missiles are exhausted.

Each of the teleporting units is somewhat unique. Understanding their strengths and weaknesses will help you determine how and when to attack lairs, nodes, or cities populated by these creatures. It will also give you a feel for what you can do if you summon one of them.

Great wyrms and unicorns are incapable of attacking non-webbed flying units. But, the wyrms are exceedingly powerful in melee combat. One of the simplest ways to kill them (without using much magic) is to send in armies of flying missile units, such as slingers that have been enchanted by Flight. Flight will allow these units to attack without risking the great wyrm's deadly counterattack (unicorns are not nearly as tough to fight).

Djinns are flying teleporters. Consider casting the Nature spell Web on them before you do anything else. This will give you a chance to attack them in relative safety with flying missile units. In any event, Djinns are not usually too difficult to fight since they generally cast a spell, such as Phantom Warriors or Guardian Wind, before they start attacking your army. Also, they will use up their magic ranged attacks before teleporting and engag-

Table 20.25 *Unit Movement Speeds*

Unit Movement Speeds During Combat*:

Infinitely Fast**	5 Squares	4 Squares	3 Squares	2 Squares	1 Square
Djinn	Air Elemental	Air Ship	Angel	Basilisk	Berserkers
Great Wyrm		Arch Angel	Death Knights	Behemoth	Bowmen***
Unicorns		Doom Bat	Doom Drakes	Cavalry	Catapult
		Sky Drake	Efreet	Centaur	Chaos Spawn
		Warship	Galley	Chimera	Engineers
			Nightmares	Cockatrices	Fire Elemental
			Pegasi	Colossus	Ghouls
			Wolf Riders	Demons	Golem
			Wyvern Riders	Demon Lord	Guardian Spirit
				Dragon Turtle	Halberdiers***
				Elven Lords	Hammerhands
				Fire Giant	Hydra
				Floating Island	Longbowmen
				Gargoyles	Magicians***
				Giant Spider	Magic Spirit
				Gorgons	Minotaurs
				Great Drake	Nagas
				Griffins	Nightblades
				Hell Hounds	Phantom Warriors
				Horsebowmen	Pikemen
				Javelineers	Priests
				Manticores	Settlers
				Night Stalker	Shadow Demons
				Paladins	Shamans***
				Phantom Beast	Skeletons
				Rangers	Slingers
				Sprites	Spearmen***
				Stag Beetle	Steam Cannon
				Stone Giant	Swordsmen***
				Storm Giant	Warlocks
				Trireme	Zombies
				War Bears	
				War Mammoths	
				War Trolls	
				Werewolves	
				Wraiths	

*All movement speeds are indicated by the number of squares per combat turn the unit may move. Actual movement may depend on the terrain type and any enchantments affecting the unit's movement.
**These units are capable of teleporting and can, therefore, travel to any free square on the battlefield.
***Draconian units of this type have a movement speed of two.

Note that floating islands, although listed here, never physically take part in a battle; they merely provide a battle platform for the units they are carrying.

Heroes may carry artifacts that increase their movement speeds to extremely high levels. Since a hero's actual movement speed depends on his or her artifacts, heroes are not included in this table.

Table 20.26 *Breaking Down Walls*

Wall Crushers*:

Air Ships
Catapults
Colossus
Earth Elemental
Engineers
Fire Giant
Stone Giant
Storm Giant
War Mammoths

In addition to units that can destroy walls, the Chaos magic spell Disrupt and the Nature spell Cracks Call can be used to destroy a targeted wall section.

*Wall crushers have a 50 percent chance of destroying the wall section when attacking a unit on a square bordered by a wall. If they are melee attacking across the wall, their attack is only completed if the wall section is destroyed. Wall crushers attacking at range (such as catapults) only have a 25 percent chance of destroying a wall section. A ranged attack through the wall section can be defended with the wall defense bonus of +3 shields if the wall section does not break. If it breaks, the ranged attack is defended with +1 shield.

ing in hand-to-hand combat with enemy units. For all practical purposes, then, enemy Djinns rarely jump over and whack at your units until you've had plenty of time to do something about it.

Speed

The speed at which your units can move during combat sometimes means the difference between winning and losing. Units that move quickly can often avoid the negative effects of repeated missile attacks. They can avoid attacks from stronger opponents, and they have a great chance of setting things up to preserve the initiative value of attacking with available first strike weapons. Furthermore, some quickly moving missile units can out-run enemies while continuing to shoot at them until their ammunition is exhausted.

There are only three spells that will alter the movement speed of units on a battlefield:

- Endurance is a Life magic spell that increases a unit's movement speed by one. This spell cannot be cast during combat and, so, will only exert effects if you've done some thinking and casting before starting a fight.
- Entangle is a Nature spell that slows *all* enemy movement by one square per turn. Enemy units with only one movement point per turn may not move at all when you cast this spell, nor may they attack. Such units can counterattack, however. Note, one turn will go by after casting the spell before enemy movement is slowed.
- Flight is a Sorcery spell that, in addition to giving a unit the ability to fly, gives the unit a movement speed of three. Considering the fact that front lines in combat are exactly six spaces apart, this means that a unit enchanted with Flight can reach and attack opponents during the second round of combat. Flight can be cast during combat and can, therefore, be

pulled out of your spell book in an emergency situation.

Table 20.25 lists the units in *Master of Magic* in terms of their relative movement speeds, including teleporting units (that travel infinitely fast).

One other spell, Nature's Earth to Mud, affects movement in the sense that it affects movement points. A unit that enters a muddy square forfeits the remainder of its movement points for that combat turn. Only flying, teleporting, and non-corporeal units are unaffected by this. The Earth to Mud spell is a good way to slow opponents while you leisurely cast combat spells and fire missiles at them. In fact, this spell is so cheap to cast (15 mana per mud patch), that—since computer opponents prioritize leaving the mud patch over heading towards your units—you can cast several mud patches, keeping your opponents struggling for a long time while you finish them off at range.

City Factors

When you invade or defend a city, the presence or absence of city walls, including magic walls, can alter the course of combat. In addition, Sorcery magic has a spell, Flying Fortress, that can suspend a target city above the ground, which can exert a profound effect on combat. The following sections take a brief look at such structural factors and their impact on combat tactics.

Wall of Stone

You can build city walls either through the city Production screen or through the Nature spell Wall of Stone. These walls, whether built or cast, confer various levels of protection to your garrison.

City walls provide an additional three shields to all units within the city against all attacks; destroyed city walls only provide one shield. This makes city walls a prudent city accessory when invading troops stop by. While there is no necessity for permanent city walls (after all, they cost two gold per turn in upkeep), such permanent walls provide additional defense by increasing a city's sighting range to three map squares. This usually gives you an additional turn to prepare your city to meet enemy invasions.

City walls also provide a physical barrier to incoming troops in combat, forcing all normal units to attack or get through the wall's entrance, unless they have some means to avoid walls. Some units have an inherent ability to destroy walls (the wall crusher skill), and the Chaos magic spell Disrupt can be used for the same purpose. Table 20.26 summarizes information on destroying walls.

Note that non-corporeal units—guardian spirits, magic spirits, phantom beasts, phantom warriors, shadow demons, and wraiths—can attack and pass through walls. Similarly, flying units can attack and fly *over* walls. Both flying and non-corporeal units are useful, then, in attacking walled cities, since they can avoid the troops guarding the city's entrance.

When attacking a walled city, remember that your attacks will be far less effective than normal. Consider moving your missile units forward (after enemy missile fire is exhausted) so that their attacks are more accurate. Make liberal use of your ranged magic weapons, since their attacks don't get a distance penalty and, therefore, will have some chance of damaging the well-shielded units inside. In fact, you might go so far as to replace your regular missile units with magic ranged attackers, such as magicians and priests, before invading walled cities.

Many of the cities you attempt to conquer will have stone walls. If you happen to have wall crusher units in your army when making such an attempt, certainly use them, but it is perfectly simple to take cities without such units. So don't let an absence of wall crushers in your army stop your ruthless expansion efforts. Also, be aware that certain spells, like

Confusion and Magic Vortex, can wreak considerable havoc on enemies garrisoned behind city walls because of the tendency of enemy units to stay behind such walls.

When you are defending a city, think carefully before leaving the safety of your city's walls. If you are faced by a stack of enemy missile units, stay behind the wall until their ammunition is exhausted. The increased defense provided by the wall will keep your troops around a lot longer when you're subjected to missile fire. Otherwise, weigh your options carefully. If you have a solid front row and a set of missile units behind it, stay behind your wall until your ammunition is spent. Otherwise, think about leaving the city, because battles over city squares will damage your buildings and kill citizens. Leaving the city walls will give you more mobility and options in combat. This can also help you lure your attackers away from vulnerable city squares.

Wall of Darkness

The Death magic spell Wall of Darkness can be cast as a long-term city enchantment or during combat. This wall protects garrisoned troops from *all* enemy missile fire, except for fire from enemy units enchanted with the Life spell True Sight.

A Wall of Darkness spell can save you many times over. Enemy stacks are frequently full of shamans and bowmen, deadly to a garrison made largely of inexpensive spearmen or swordsmen. A Wall of Darkness, cast during combat or as a standing city enchantment, protects these troops and forces the enemy units to march towards your garrison, allowing you to kill them one at a time. Additionally, you will have a chance to cast spells, and your units can fire missiles or magic ranged attacks at the oncoming enemy hordes from a safe position until they finally close for melee combat.

Casting Wall of Darkness as a long term enchantment can generate considerable expense, however (each costs five mana per turn in upkeep). It may be more efficient to cast this enchantment only on cities bordering disputed territories. For other cities, casting it as needed in combat is probably sufficient.

Wall of Fire

Chaos magic offers the Wall of Fire, the only other type of magic wall besides Wall of Darkness. A Wall of Fire is a structure that damages units: either those entering the city across the wall or those outside of the city attacking across the wall. Such units suffer a strength five fire attack when they do so. This is not a strong attack and there are units—efreets, fire elementals, fire giants, and units with magic immunity—who are immune to this damage. Nevertheless, this fire attack can seriously damage weaker units.

The Wall of Fire is fairly inexpensive to maintain (two mana per turn), relatively expensive to cast in combat (30 mana), and doesn't do that much damage. Consequently, it is not worth fortifying cities with this wall as a matter of course. It may be worthwhile, however, since every little bit helps, to cast this wall on border cities when you are warring with other wizards. Casting during combat instead of as a city enchantment makes the most sense when enemy invasions appear sparsely scheduled. A Wall of Fire is of greatest use when you are defending a slightly weaker garrison from stronger units, particularly if the invading forces are not well equipped with missile or ranged weapons.

If you are planning to invade a city that is enveloped by a Wall of Fire, use an army that consists largely of missile or ranged attack units. Be careful, though, that you don't invade with only those unit types if the target

Table 20.27 Naval Combat and Ships

Carrying Unit	Carrying Capacity*	Speed**	Ranged Weapon Type (Strength)***	Cargo Combat?****
Air Ship	0	4	10 Rocks; 8	N/A
Floating Island	8	2	*****	yes
Galley	5	3	8 Bows; 3	no
Trireme	2	2	8 Bows; 2	no
Warship	3	4	Unlimited Rocks; 10 (long ranged)	no
Wind Walking Units	8	******	******	yes

*Carrying Capacity refers to the number of units that can be carried by the indicated unit. This number does not include heroes, flying units, water walking units, swimming units, or other transports, all of which may also be stacked with a full transport.

**Movement speed can be doubled for friendly ships and halved for enemy ships if the Sorcery spell Wind Mastery has been cast. Note that Wind Mastery will not affect the movement speed of stacks being carried by wind walking units.

***Ranged Weapons shows the number of attacks, type of attack, and attack strength. Thus, air ships have 10 rock attacks, each with an attack strength of eight.

****A "yes" in this column indicates that the units carried by the indicated unit will be able to engage in combat over water, even if they cannot normally do so! A "no" means that such units remain on the craft for the duration of combat. If a transport dies, so will its cargo.

*****Floating islands do not physically engage in combat and, so, have no weapons.

******Wind walking units are those that either have the wind walking skill naturally or have had the Sorcery enchantment Wind Walking cast on them. These units can travel over water and automatically carry their entire stack with them wherever they go. The speed of travel depends on the wind walking unit's speed (three or more), and the presence of ranged weapons depends on the wind walking unit type, as well.

Unit Types That Can Fight On Water:

Ships

Non-corporeal Units

Draconians, Flying units, and Units enchanted with Flight (Sorcery)

Lizardmen, Nagas, and Units enchanted with Water Walking (Nature)

Units enchanted with Wind Walking (Sorcery)

Units enchanted with Wraithform (Death)

city's garrison is similarly composed. You will want a couple of hardy units who can survive the flames and march into the city to finish off any remaining enemy units cowering therein.

Flying Fortress

The Sorcery spell Flying Fortress is a city enchantment that cannot be cast during combat; i.e., you have to plan ahead. This spell elevates the Enchanted Fortress city above the ground. The flying city can only be entered by flying units during combat. Even *your* non-flying units, once they leave the protective confines of the city perimeter, may not re-enter the city during combat unless you enchant them with Flight. This situation puts an interesting twist on combat, pitting flying units against flying units and heavily skewing combat to favor missile and magic ranged attack units (since they can launch their attacks at the city's garrison from afar).

If you are attacking a Flying Fortress, you clearly want to bring along units that fly and, preferably, ones with strong missile or magic ranged attacks. Casting Flight on your attacking missile units before invading may be helpful but is probably unnecessary, unless you are also planning to take them in for hand-to-hand combat with the garrison. Rather, you will want some strong flying units so that you can easily enter the city for this purpose after you have softened up the inhabitants with your ranged attack units.

If you are defending a Flying Fortress city, the same rules apply. Lots of strong missile and magic ranged units and a few really good flying units should be sufficient protection. This will provide a place for your melee units (the fliers) to retreat if they are too wounded to continue and if you just want to wait out the end of combat so that the invaders will be forced to retreat. Don't exit the city with ground troops unless 1) you view them as expendable—because you can't bring them back, 2) you know they are strong enough to defeat the enemy, or 3) you are desperate.

Other than slanting planned combats by forcing you and your opponents to alter the make-up and tactical combat of your armies slightly, the Flying Fortress basically only has a significant impact on combat involving unprepared armies. If you blunder into a Flying Fortress city with an army of cavalry units, well, you deserve what you get. If you take your time and prepare your army to meet this situation, you will have no more trouble capturing a Flying Fortress city than you would capturing a regular city.

Naval Warfare

There are several types of combat and transport ships *in Master of Magic*. These units and others can engage in combat over ocean or lake map squares. Table 20.27 summarizes ships and ship-like units in terms of some their relevant combat characteristics.

There are many facets to naval combat, but the most important thing to remember is that the units on board your ships cannot usually fight. Their lives are in the oars of their carriers. Warships are particularly useful carriers, although they can only hold three units at a time, because they have such strong, accurate, and unlimited fire power. Floating islands are the least combat-reliable, as they don't even appear during a battle. Only the units they are carrying can fight.

Take great care when you initiate an ocean battle. You don't want your floating island, carrying precious troops, to intercept a couple of enemy warships. The inexhaustible missile power of the warships, combined with their speed, could destroy your units far too quickly. On the other hand, running down enemy stacks with your warships may be a good way to take the wind out of your enemies' sails (hehehe).

For weaker ships, especially triremes whose essential function is to carry cargo and not to engage in combat, consider escorting them with strong flying units or other units that can travel over water. Such armies cannot generally be moved as a stack, but you can move the components so that they end up on the same map square at the end of the game turn. As a last comment on triremes, try to avoid getting these units into combat. They simply won't last.

Guarding your port cities by patrolling warships, or galleys if you have nothing else, outside may be a good defensive maneuver against transcontinental invasion forces. Finally, be aware that the computer AI is set up so that enemy ships will often flee if they are attacked by flying units. This is one way to keep them out of certain areas. It is also a way to wrack up fame points (if four or more units are lost during the fleeing) by attacking their navies with even the cheesiest single flying unit you have.

Node Effects

Outside of city enchantments and other magical influences on combat, the last really important factor in some battles is the aura of magic nodes. Magic nodes have a range of influence that you can see when a spirit is melded to the nodes, by the colored aura that appears. Important: This aura exerts an effect regardless of whether a spirit has melded to the node or not.

The effect of the nodal aura is to enhance, by +2, the combat statistics of units that come from the same magic realm as the node. That means shields, swords, bows, magic ranged attacks, other attacks, and resistance, all increase by two. For example, Sorcery creatures, such as phantom warriors and djinns, will enjoy these improved combat abilities when they are doing battle in an area under the influence of a Sorcery node. This improvement to combat abilities for creatures benefited by a nodal aura is so great, that it is a wonder how normal units ever succeed in conquering nodes.

If your wizard is specializing in Chaos, Nature, or Sorcery magic, you may want to consider node auras when you initiate combat. For example, if you are planning to invade a city that is built right next to a Nature node and you happen to be able to summon Nature creatures, such as basilisks or cockatrices, you may want to include a few such creatures in the invading army (unless you have significantly better normal or fantastic

units than those you can summon through that magic type).

Similarly, when you are building cities and forming garrisons, you may want to keep the same considerations in mind. Try to guard your nodes with their like-colored creatures (but be forewarned: an enemy casting Great Unsummoning can then strip your nodes' garrisons). Finally, if, for example, you are near an enemy stack with an army full of efreets or fire giants, you may want to wait to pounce on that stack until they are outside the aura of a nearby Chaos node. Circumstances will not always favor such offensive or defensive strategies, but be on the lookout for them so that you can take advantage of the opportunities that present themselves.

The magic dispelling properties of nodes are discussed in Chapter 21.

Specific Tips, Tactics, and Techniques for Normal Battles

Foremost, learn how to fight battles from your own experiences, rather than relying solely on *our* experience. By saving the game prior to every battle, no matter how hopeless your odds are before going in, you can always experiment and then reset the pieces afterward by reloading the saved game, losing but a moment of your time.

We have mentioned several specific combat tips in this chapter and the reasons for them. Here, we have summarized them and included a few new ones. Stick these in your battle plans and smote them.

🐌 When you have first strike, thrown, gaze, or breath attacks, always maneuver so that the first melee engagement will be conducted during *your* turn. These special advantages don't apply when counterattacking during the enemy's battle turn.

🐌 Don't let a wounded unit die. Instead, rotate it out of harm's way (if at all possible) and put a fresh unit between it and the enemy. Preserve your units. It is better to wait for them to heal than to have to acquire new ones from scratch.

🐸 Similarly, Trolls and other units that regenerate during a battle had better learn to jog. By running away on the battlefield for a few rounds they can regain considerable oomph (at the rate of one heart per turn). Remember that discretion is the better part of valor, and jog these guys around the battlefield a bit to build their strength before their next melee.

🐸 Computer players seldom sally from their cities to attack invading armies. Therefore, always close in with your normal missile units to reduce their range To Hit penalty before you commence firing with them.

🐸 Always strive to squeeze every missile shot you can from your ranged units before closing in for melee attacks. Do this when you have ranged weapon superiority in that battle.

🐸 Because computer players pick on weak units that they hope to kill in a single shot or swing, your second-line units (bowmen, magicians, and shamans) are its favorite targets. Therefore, you might want to beef them up defensively (either through magic or experience) before committing them to particularly nasty battles.

🐸 Again, because computer players target the weak, you can bait them with weakened units (or phantom warriors) to draw their attention away from other units. You can even lead them into traps where you withdraw behind some of your stronger units who can then whack at your weak unit's pursuers.

🐸 Try to bring enemy flyers down with a Web spell whenever possible. Flight is too great an advantage in combat when the enemy has it.

🐸 When you have ranged attack units with a movement allowance greater than one, use scoot 'n' shoot tactics. That is, move them half or less of their movement allowance (usually away from a closing enemy unit) and *then* fire with them! Firing first consumes their *entire*

movement allowance, thus making them unable to move in the same turn.

🐸 Remember, heroes' normal ranged magic attacks consume three mana each. If you want to know how many shots your spell casting heroes have, do the math.

🐸 Node what creatures to bring to an aura battle. That is, always have creatures of the same magic type as a node's aura in battle so that they'll enjoy that +2 bonus to each figure's ratings. Wow!

🐸 Whether attacking or defending, never flee if you can play for time. Each battle lasts 50 rounds. If you can survive through them all, the battle ends with the attacker retreating out of that square. However, that should be good enough for you if you're defending (particularly when defending a node or city). When you're attacking, it allows you to get your survivors out of a battle without them rolling to see if they die while fleeing. Patience—wait out those 50 battle rounds if you can't gain a decisive victory on the battlefield.

🐸 Here's a tip we call the corner confusion technique (see Figure 20.2). To help you waste

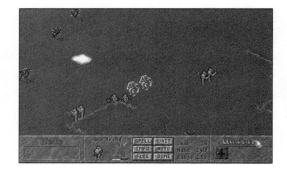

Figure 20-2. *The Corner Confusion Technique: The phantom beasts defending this node don't know which Troll unit to attack and are wasting their combat turns while the Trolls regenerate.*

those 50 battle rounds, send equally strong units to opposite corners of the battlefield. Each round, a computer player unit decides which enemy unit to pursue. Often, it will change its mind between turns. If your troops spread out far enough, the enemy units will go back and forth between your groups, wasting time and not landing any blows against you. This trick is especially useful when you have something nasty like Call Lightning or the Wrack chipping away at their poor, confused forces every round!

A Note About Strategic Combat

Strategic Combat, which is a toggle you can set, conducts your battles using the same calculations that computer players use when they fight each other. Units are assigned gross values and weighted by skills and spells. After a quick calculation that is far too complex to briefly explain here, the outcome is determined by one side being completely eliminated. The victorious side might have some units killed or damaged. Regardless of who wins a strategic combat battle, both wizards *automatically* spend their maximum mana in that battle (i.e., whatever their spell casting skill level is) if it is available.

You can use the Strategic Combat setting as a cheat. Because of the values the computer assigns to different units, sometimes a battle that would be hopeless if you used tactical combat is an easy win if you switch over to the Strategic Combat setting for that battle. Try not to get hooked on this, though. You can frequently pull out decisive victories using tactical combat under situations that would net you a loss using the Strategic Combat system.

Great Balls of Fire

The battle is not yet over. Although you are now armed with the knowledge for conducting normal combat, using magic in combat can prove decisive. Here, this tome switches from a military play book to a spell book. It's time to make a little magic and upset the odds in battle.

21

Magic in Combat

Think of this chapter as a *spelling* lesson (spell-ing, get it?). If *Master of Magic* were a wargame, we'd be discussing combat support elements, off-map artillery, and NBC (Nuclear, Biological, Chemical) warfare. Fortunately, because of the game's more fanciful and gentler subject, we're merely talking about hurling fireballs, calling up lightning storms, and finding other imaginative ways to help and hinder units on the battlefield. Shooting and swinging in combat is one thing. Backing your troops with the right selection of mana-made magic is another.

Here we examine spell casting in combat. We consider the costs in mana, battlefield troop summonings, area enchantments, unit enchantments, etc. that can alter the relative balance of forces in battle. When you consider what an army can do in battle, it is important to have a grasp on your combat casting possibilities.

Defining the Limits

Combat spells may be cast either by player wizards (like you) who control a side at the battle, or by heroes and special units (djinns, efreets, arch angels) who are on the scene and have spell-casting ability. In the former case, the amount of mana that can be spent casting combat spells is limited by either the player wizard's skill level or mana reserve (whichever is *less*). Premium charges are also deducted for player wizards who cast combat spells at a distance from their Enchanted Fortress.

Mana in Reserve

Before casting combat spells, you must have sufficient mana in your reserves. All spells have a base casting cost (see Chapters 7 through 12), but the amount of mana *actually spent* to cast a spell depends on four things:

🐍 Battle Location: When combat takes place within your Enchanted Fortress city, all your combat spells automatically cost 50 percent less than usual.

🐍 Distance from Enchanted Fortress: Spells cast in battles taking place far from your Enchanted Fortress can take up to three times more mana to cast than normal (see Table 21.1).

🐍 Wizard Skills: The Channeler ability allows all combat spells outside of your Enchanted Fortress to cost the normal amount. Chaos, Nature, and Sorcery Mastery give a 15 percent discount on casting spells of the same type. Conjurer gives a 25 percent discount on casting summoning spells, so combat summoning spells (fire, air, and earth elementals; phantom warriors and beasts) will also be cheaper to cast. Runemaster gives a 25 percent discount on casting all Arcane magic spells. See Chapter 4 for more details on wizard skills.

🐍 Number of Spell Ranks: If you have eight or more spell ranks in one magic realm, you will receive from 10 (for eight spell ranks) to 40 percent (for eleven spell ranks) of a discount on casting all spells of that type (see Table A in the game manual).

Spell-Casting Skill

In addition to having the mana necessary to cast combat spells, you must have enough spell-casting skill (see Chapter 15). The sum of all the base casting costs of the spells you cast during combat cannot exceed your spell-casting skill.

For example, if your only combat spell is the Life magic spell Healing, which has a base casting cost of 15 mana, and your spell skill is 25 mana, you can only cast this spell once during combat. The leftover 10 spell skill points (25 skill minus 15 mana casting cost) will remain unused. On the other hand, if you have 11 ranks in Life magic, you get a 40

Table 21.1 *Combat Casting Cost Distance Multiplier*

Squares From Enchanted Fortress	Multiplier
0	1/2
1 to 5	1
6 to 10	1 1/2
11 to 15	2
16 to 20	2 1/2
21+	3

Note, the multiplier for transplanar casting between Arcanus and Myrror is always three.

percent discount on casting Life spells. In this case, your casting cost for Healing would be nine mana. With a 25-mana spell skill, you could cast Healing twice during combat, leaving you with seven unused spell skill points.

All of the *discounts* from wizard skills, number of spell ranks, and battles within your Enchanted Fortress apply to the casting costs of spells before these costs are subtracted from your available spell-casting skill points. But, distance *penalties* for casting spells in battles far from your Enchanted Fortress only apply after you have removed the base casting cost of the spell from your remaining skill points. Hence, the distance penalties put an additional drain only on your mana reserves, not your combat spell abilities.

Continuing with the example above: Again, you have 11 Life spell ranks, 25 spell skill, and the one combat spell, Healing. Let's say you are engaged with an enemy at a distance so far from your Enchanted Fortress, that the full distance penalty (three times the spell's casting cost) applies. In this case, you could *still* cast Healing twice if you had enough mana in your reserves. Each Healing spell would still drain nine mana (its base casting cost with your discount for concentrating in Life magic) from your *spell skill*. Because of the distance penalty, however, each casting would drain three times that, or 27 mana, from your *mana reserves*.

Hero and Unit Casting

Many heroes and some creatures (djinns, efreets, and arch angels) can cast spells during combat. These units all have a specific spell-casting skill. For heroes, this skill level increases as they gain experience levels (see Chapter 18); it will also increase when you equip them with artifacts that provide spell-casting skill. For the other units, however, their maximum skill level never changes: 20 spell skill points for djinns and efreets and 40 for arch angels.

Units with spell-casting skill also automatically have enough mana to cast their own spells, so none of your mana is drained when they cast spells from their own "spell books" in combat. Each of these unit types is described here briefly:

🐌 Heroes can cast all of the spells you know as well as a few of their own (see Chapter 18 for specifics). They receive all of your casting cost discounts but suffer no distance penalties. Since they can cast any of the spells you know, they can save you significant quantities of mana if you use them to cast combat spells in your place.

🜨 Djinns have 20 spell points for casting Sorcery spells during combat. *All* blue combat spells costing 20 mana or less are available to them at the beginning of every battle. None of your casting discounts or penalties apply to djinns under your control.

🜨 Efreets have 20 spell points for casting Chaos spells during every combat. As for the djinns, your casting discounts and penalties do not apply.

🜨 Arch angels have 40 spell points for casting Life magic spells during every combat. This gives them access to virtually all white combat spells. Again, your casting penalties and discounts do not apply to these creatures.

Items

Magical artifacts occasionally contain embedded spells. You can also create your own artifacts, placing any of your favorite combat spells into custom wands and staffs. See Chapter 19 for a discussion of magical items.

Artifact spells can be cast for *free* during combat; they will drain no mana or spell-casting points from either you or your hero. Their cost is even listed at "Item" in the hero's combat spell book to symbolize that no mana is spent. For example, if you have created a magic wand that contains two Invulnerability spells, the hero who is equipped with this wand can cast Invulnerability twice during every combat for free.

Magical artifacts provide a powerful way to supplement your spell casting abilities in combat. They provide valuable alternatives to draining your mana reserves when fighting numerous battles far from home. The ability to wield such items, in fact, may be one of the best reasons to include mage-type heroes in all of your major armies.

Nodes

The various nodes in the Arcanian and Myrran landscapes provide a true challenge to most wizards. These nodes all have a standing, 50-strength "dispel spell" against any combat spells of a different magic type than the node. Attempting to cast spells at nodes can drain your spell skill (for that battle) and your mana reserves for nothing more than the pleasure of watching your spell fizzle.

Any spell to be cast successfully at a magic node must either be of the same magic type as the node (blue spells at Sorcery nodes, red spells at Chaos nodes, and green spells at Nature nodes) or be able to withstand the dispel. (See page 107 of the game manual for the dispel equation.) As a rule of thumb, spells costing 15 mana have about a 25 percent chance of success, and spells must have a base casting cost of 50 mana to have a 50 percent chance of not fizzling at a node. Thus, the greater the cost of the spell cast against a node's dispel, the better the chance it won't fizzle. Note that the wizard skill Node Mastery allows you to cast all your combat spells at nodes without any chance of fizzling.

Resisting Spells and Saving Throws

Many combat spells that debilitate, damage, or kill your enemies must first overcome the target's resistance or defense before exerting their effects. Spells that do physical damage, such as Fire Bolt, work in the same way that melee combat does (see Chapter 20); the damage is defended by the target's shields. For each damage point unsuccessfully defended, the target loses a hit point (heart).

Many other spells must be resisted, however. Their effects depend on the target *failing its saving throw*. Let's talk about that....

Every unit has an ability to resist spells. This resistance is represented by the number of crosses on their Unit Display window. Each cross is equal to a 10 percent chance to resist.

For example, if you have a unit with three crosses, this unit and the figures in it each have a 30 percent base chance of resisting spells. The computer program rolls a d10 to determine whether the spell will affect the unit (this is known as a *saving throw*). If the die roll is greater than the unit's resistance (greater than three in this case) the unit will be affected by the spell. If the die roll is three or less (in this case), the unit will escape the spell's harmful effects.

Many spells also have inherent resistance (i.e., saving throw) modifiers. These modify the number of crosses the target unit uses to defend against the spell's effects. For example, the Death spell Weakness has a saving throw modifier of -2. So a target unit with a base resistance of three, will only get three minus two, or one, cross with which to defend itself from Weakness. That means it only has a 10 percent chance of escaping the effects of this spell. Some spells, such as the Death spell Wrack, have positive resistance modifiers that increase the target unit's ability to resist the spell (but woe to those who fail!).

Heroes can equip items that have "spell saves" (see Chapter 19). These spell saves lower the resistance of units that the hero targets with his spells. Note that spell saves exert no effects on enemy units' resistances to combat enchantments.

Finally, some spells simply cannot be resisted or defended unless target units are specifically immune to their effects. Such spells include Cracks Call, Web, and Mind Storm. Units with immunity to illusions cannot be targeted by Mind Storm. Non-corporeal units cannot be webbed, and only non-flying, corporeal units are affected by Cracks Call.

Chapter 20 gives a formula for determining a unit's (or figure's) resistance to spells or to special attacks, like poison attacks, that must resisted. In the following sections, descriptions of all combat spells that target enemy units will also indicate whether shields (defense) or crosses (resistance) are used to protect the target from the spell's effects.

Kinds of Spells to Cast in Combat

Combat spells fall into several categories. Some spells summon creatures to fight for your side during the battle. Other spells are enchantments that continuously affect combat. In addition, there are spells that enhance the abilities of individual friendly units, while others damage, debilitate, or directly destroy enemies.

Summoning Spells

The ability to summon units during combat is a powerful tool. Summoned creatures can dramatically alter the odds of winning a battle. Table 21.2 lists the summoning spells that can be cast during combat.

Summoned creatures provide a number of benefits:

🐚 They allow you to undergarrison your cities (and nodes of the same color as the creatures you can summon) and to attack with fewer units than you might otherwise. This

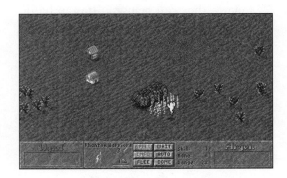

Figure 21-1. *Summoning units like phantom warriors during combat can help you ward off disaster.*

Table 21.2 *Combat Summoning Spells*

Summoned Units	Magic Realm	Rarity	Casting Cost	Special*
Air Elemental	Sorcery	Rare	50 mana	fast/flying/invisible
Earth Elemental	Nature	Rare	60 mana	25 melee attack
Fire Elemental	Chaos	Common	20 mana	fire immunity
Phantom Beasts	Sorcery	Uncommon	35 mana	illusionary attack
Phantom Warriors	Sorcery	Common	10 mana	illusionary attack

*Not all special abilities are necessarily mentioned in this column; only the more useful skills are included.

can save you time forming and using armies effectively.

🐸 They can provide extra attack strengths to beat down enemy troops. Several of these units—air elementals, earth elementals, and phantom beasts—are particularly useful for this purpose. For example, a phantom beast can wipe up several units of skeletons, zombies, etc. before dying.

🐸 They provide alternative targets for enemy missile and melee attacks and can, therefore, draw fire away from some of your special units, such as magicians, bowmen, and heroes.

🐸 They can act as physical barriers to keep rushing enemies from your fragile units.

🐸 Finally, they can help you stay in battle long enough so that your more devastating combat enchantments can finish off your enemies.

All in all, being able to cast these spells is akin to pulling a rabbit (a big one, with teeth) out of your wizard's cap. Once you start using these spells, you will find a myriad of circumstances where they prove beneficial.

Battlefield Enchantments

All of the colored magic realms have combat enchantments. These spells can be cast during battle and exert effects that last for the duration of combat. In addition, they are like global enchantments in that their effects cover

all relevant targets. Table 21.3 lists these spells as well as briefly describing their effects.

Combat enchantments should be cast for any of several reasons:

🐸 Cast spells that lower enemy resistances and defenses before casting offensive combat spells. This will give your subsequent spells a better chance of success. For example, cast Black Prayer before Wrack, if you can, particularly because the Wrack gives defending units a resistance bonus to protect themselves from its effects. The opposite order works well for this example too, however; Wrack is a combat enchantment, so it will stick around for the remainder of the battle. Getting a Wrack started before casting Black Prayer works as well as the other way around.

🐸 Cast spells defensively when appropriate. For example, when confronting an enemy army of missile units, you can cast Wall of Darkness, if they've invaded your city, or Mass Invisibility. When confronted by masses of magic ranged attack units (sprites, magicians, shamans), cast Mana Leak or Mass Invisibility.

🐸 Combine slowing spells, like Earth to Mud or Entangle with offensive punch, like Wrack or Call Lightning. This gives the offensive spells more time to wreak destruction on your enemies.

🐸 Improve your own troops whenever possible, especially if they are composed largely of multi-figure units. These types of units

Table 21.3 Combat Enchantments

Enchantment	Magic Realm	Some Important Effects	Defend	Resist (*)
Magic Vortex	Chaos	Mini tornado sweeps battlefield, damaging units, buildings	Yes**	-
Metal Fires	Chaos	All friendly normal units get magic, increased attacks	-	-
Wall of Fire***	Chaos	Encircles city in protective, damaging wall of flames	-	-
Warp Reality	Chaos	All non-Chaos units suffer -2 To Hit	-	-
Black Prayer	Death	Curses all enemy units, lowering their stats	-	-
Darkness	Death	Improves Death units' stats; decreases white units' stats	-	-
Mana Leak	Death	Leaks 5 mana from reserves of enemy spell casters every turn; Also causes enemy magic ranged units to lose 1 ammo per turn	-	-
Terror	Death	Enemies must try to overcome fear to attack every turn	-	Yes (+1)
Wall of Darkness***	Death	Encases city in black cloud, preventing incoming missile fire	-	-
Wrack	Death	Tries to take 1 heart from every enemy figure every turn	-	Yes (+1)
High Prayer	Life	Blesses friendly units with superb increases in stats	-	-
Prayer	Life	Blesses friendly units with increases in stats	-	-
True Light	Life	Improves Life unit's stats; decreases black unit's stats	-	-
Call Lightning	Nature	Lightning strikes enemy units 3 to 5 times per turn	Yes	-
Earth to Mud***	Nature	Throws a 5x5 mud patch on the battlefield, slowing movement	-	-
Entangle	Nature	Slows enemy moves by 1; can eliminate the ability to attack	-	-
Blur	Sorcery	10% of all hits by your enemy miss automatically	-	-
Counter Magic	Sorcery	Attempts to "fizzle" all enemy spells	-	-
Mass Invisibility	Sorcery	Friendly units cannot be targeted by ranged attacks	-	-

This table indicates when spell effects are resisted (crosses) or defended (shields).

*The number in parentheses is the modifier to the target unit's or figure's resistance. After being modified, the target unit's resistance is used to determine whether the given spell exerts its effects on that unit.

**Magic Vortices do automatic damage (five hits) to units that occupy any square it crosses, unless those units have magic immunity. However, a vortex also emits lightning attacks at units in neighboring squares. These lightning attacks are defended using the units' shields.

***These spells are more like "area" effects. They won't necessarily affect all relevant units, but only those units attempting to act across them (in the cases of walls) or crossing them (Wall of Fire and Earth to Mud).

benefit the most from the statistical increases provided by combat enchantments like Metal Fires and Prayer because they're received on a *per figure* basis.

 When in doubt, Counter Magic is always useful to cast against enemy wizards. Cast it first and at as high a level as you can afford,

taking into account anything else you may wish to cast later.

Note that several city and global enchantments that cannot be cast *during* combat can also influence the course of combat under spe-

Table 21.4 *Non-Combat Enchantments Affecting Battles*

Enchantment	Magic Realm	Type	Important Effects
Chaos Surge	Chaos	Global	Increases all Chaos units' attacks/defenses
Doom Mastery	Chaos	Global	New friendly units are "Chaos Channeled"
Cloud of Shadow	Death	City	Same as Darkness spell
Eternal Night	Death	Global	Same as Darkness spell
Charm of Life	Life	Global	Increases all friendly units' hit points
Crusade	Life	Global	Friendly units get 1 extra experience level
Heavenly Light	Life	City	Same as True Light spell
Holy Arms	Life	Global	Friendly units get Holy Weapon (+1 To Hit)
Flying Fortress	Sorcery	City	Only flyers can enter Enchanted Fortress
Spell Ward	Sorcery	City	All units and spells of specific type are prohibited in target city
Wind Mastery	Sorcery	Global	Friendly ships move faster; enemies' slower

cific circumstances. These enchantments are described briefly in Table 21.4.

Most of the city and global enchantments in Table 21.4 that influence combat do so primarily by altering unit attributes. For the most part, unless you're suffering from a mana shortage, there's no reason not to cast these spells. Some, of course, are only useful under specific circumstances. For example, you would probably only want to cast Chaos Surge if most of your armies were comprised of Chaos units and if none of your enemies specialized in Chaos magic. All of these spells are described in the appropriate chapters and are listed here for convenience.

Targeting Enemy Units

Half the fun of casting combat spells is doing damage to enemy units. *Master of Magic* provides a multitude of ways to hurt the bad guys. Table 21.5 lists these, as well as the ways target units attempt to defend themselves (shields or crosses) from specific spells.

Destructive combat spells that must be defended using shields instead of resistance are treated similarly to normal melee or ranged attacks. Each of the damage points that a destructive combat spell can theoretically incur has an intrinsic ability To Hit of 30 percent. So if an attack can do 10 damage to a target, each damage point has only a 30 percent chance of getting through. Each damage point that makes it is then defended, as normal, by the target's shields. Note that the "To Hit" abilities of destructive spells are not modified by anything that alters To Hits. Chapter 20 has a complete discussion of attack types and defenses.

Before casting destructive combat spells, be sure to cast any appropriate combat enchantments that lower the resistances or defenses of enemy units. This should provide the final push required to get the maximum destructive effect you are seeking.

Don't neglect the part that heroes have to play in all of this. Heroes with spell saves in their items are tremendously effective when their spells require target units to resist the spell's effects! Note, the spell saves do not

Table 21.5 Destructive Combat Spells

Spell	Magic Realm	Effects	Defend	Resist (*)
Disenchant Area	Arcane	Tries to remove all enemy enchantments from battlefield	-	-
Dispel Magic	Arcane	Tries to remove enchantments from target unit	-	-
Call Chaos	Chaos	Random effects on *all* enemy units, most are negative	**	**
Disintegrate	Chaos	Obliteration of target unit	-	Yes***
Doom Bolt	Chaos	Automatically causes 10 points of damage to target unit	****	****
Fireball	Chaos	5 to 25 strength fire attack on all figures in target unit	Yes	-
Fire Bolt	Chaos	5 to 25 strength fire attack on target unit	Yes	-
Flame Strike	Chaos	15 strength fire attack on *all* enemy figures	Yes	-
Lightning Bolt	Chaos	5 to 45 strength armor-piercing attack on target unit	Yes	-
Shatter	Chaos	Attempt to reduce to strength 1 all of target normal unit's weapons	-	Yes (none)
Warp Creature	Chaos	Tries to destroy target's resistance or halve its attack or defense	-	Yes (-1)
Warp Lightning	Chaos	Series of diminishing strength armor-piercing attacks on target unit	Yes	-
Warp Wood	Chaos	Automatically destroy all of target normal unit's missile ammunition	****	****
Animate Dead	Death	Raise a unit from the dead to fight and remain with your army	-	-
Black Sleep	Death	Knock out target unit for rest of combat	-	Yes (-2)
Death Spell	Death	Tries to kill *all* enemy units	-	Yes (-2)
Life Drain	Death	Life-stealing attack on target unit	-	Yes*****
Possession	Death	Changes allegiance of target unit for duration of combat	-	Yes (-1)
Weakness	Death	Reduce target's attack strength by 2	-	Yes (-2)
Word of Death	Death	Tries to kill target enemy figures	-	Yes (-5)
Dispel Evil	Life	Tries to kill all figures in target Chaos or Death unit	-	Yes*****
Holy Word	Life	Attempts to banish *all* summoned and undead enemy figures from battle	-	Yes*****
Star Fires	Life	15 strength magic attack on target Chaos or Death unit	Yes	-
Cracks Call	Nature	25% chance of killing target unit outright	****	****
Ice Bolt	Nature	5 to 45 strength cold attack	Yes	-
Petrify	Nature	Tries to kill figures in target unit by stoning	-	Yes (none)
Web	Nature	Immobilizes target unit until it can free itself	****	****
Banish	Sorcery	Tries to banish all figures in target fantastic unit	-	Yes*****
Confusion	Sorcery	Disorients target unit which may fight for you during some turns	-	Yes (-4)
Creature Binding	Sorcery	Change allegiance of target fantastic unit which disappears after combat	-	Yes (-2)
Disenchant True	Sorcery	Tries to remove all enemy enchantments from battlefield	-	-
Dispel Magic True	Sorcery	Tries to remove enchantments from target unit	-	-
Mind Storm	Sorcery	Target unit loses 5 to all attacks, defense, and resistance	****	****
Psionic Blast	Sorcery	5 to 25 strength illusionary attack (ignores armor) on target unit	-	-
Vertigo	Sorcery	Tries to debilitate target unit, resulting in -2 To Hit and -1 shields	-	Yes (none)

This table indicates when spell effects are resisted (crosses) or defended (shields).

*The number in parentheses is the modifier to the target unit's or figure's resistance (i.e., saving roll). Note that if these spells are cast by a hero who has an artifact with *spell save modifiers*, then the target's ability to resist

Table 21.5 Cont. *Destructive Combat Spells*

will be lowered further by that number. So, if a hero has -2 spell saves and casts Creature Binding, the target unit's resistance will be lowered by 4 crosses (-2 for the spell and -2 for the hero's item).

**Whether a unit has to defend or resist the spell's effects depends on which effect (Chaos Channels, Disintegrate, Doom Bolt, Fire Bolt of strength 15, Warp Creature, or Warp Lightning) hits the unit.

***Any unit with a resistance less than 10 automatically dies. Be sure to cast spells that lower enemy resistances first, if necessary.

****Unless the target unit is immune to this spell, it has no ability to resist or defend the spell's effects.

*****Resistance modifiers vary as follows: Life Drain and Banish—target unit's resistance is lowered by one per extra five mana spent casting these spells, however, Banish *starts* with a resistance modifier of -3; Dispel Evil—Chaos and Death units have a -4 resistance modifier; undead units (those raised from the dead) have -9; Holy Word—Undeads must defend at -7 to resistance, other fantastic units defend at -2 to their resistance.

See Chapter 17 for a detailed breakdown of the attributes affected by each unit enchantment.

---

apply to units that must resist the effects of combat enchantments (like Wrack).

While some spells are clearly awesome (Flame Strike, Death Spell, Holy Word, etc.) because they target large numbers of opponents, other spells can also be quite useful. Taking over creatures with Possession, Creature Binding, or Animate Dead is a powerful way to shift the odds in any battle by taking your opponent's units away and adding them to your ranks. Animate Dead even lets you walk away from combat with the animated unit! Note that Confusion really falls into this combat spell class, as well, because there is a chance during every combat turn that the confused unit will fight for you.

Spells that decrease attack capabilities should not be underestimated either. In the absence of effective destructive spells (and better units have too many shields to really be hurt by most such spells), decreasing the enemy's To Hit or attack strength ratings will keep your units alive and fighting longer in battle.

Some combinations of spells can be particularly effective. For example, casting Web on a flying unit and then casting Cracks Call (both of these spells cannot be defended

against or resisted) is a good way to eliminate too-powerful flying enemy units (such as drakes). Other spells that automatically do damage, like Doom Bolt and Warp Wood are also particularly good to have in one's spell book or in a hero's artifact.

Many of the straightforward destructive spells (Ice Bolt, Fire Bolt, Psionic Bolt, Fireball, and others) are in many ways a waste of valuable mana unless you have no other options. To make these spells effective you generally have to pump huge quantities of mana into casting them. Even then, the results are frequently less than spectacular. Use these spells when you have nothing else that you think will work. Otherwise there are a wealth of other, better things, you can do when casting spells in combat.

Finally, you should be aware that many units are immune to various kinds of damage (see Chapter 20 for specifics). Many of the Chaos magic spells, for instance, inflict *fire* damage; any unit immune to fire will not be affected by such spells. Similarly, there are many creatures immune to Death spells, cold attacks (Ice Bolt), illusions (most Sorcery spells) and stoning (Petrify). Worse, there are units (sky drakes and paladins) almost com-

Table 21.6 *Friendly Combat Spells*

Spell	Magic Realm	Effects
Recall Hero	Arcane	Hero is immediately returned to caster's Summoning Circle
Eldritch Weapon	Chaos	Normal unit gets magic weapons that are hard to block
Flame Blade	Chaos	Normal unit gets magic weapons with +2 strength
Immolation	Chaos	Gives normal unit a 4 strength fiery touch attack
Berserk	Death	Doubles attack strength, removes all shields
Cloak of Fear	Death	Makes enemy figures "think" twice before attacking
Wraithform	Death	Makes unit non-corporeal and immune to weapons
Bless	Life	Increases resistance and defense to Chaos and Death
Healing	Life	Restores up to 5 hit points to target
Heroism	Life	Normal unit goes to the elite experience level
Holy Armor	Life	Normal unit gets 2 extra shields
Holy Weapon	Life	Normal unit gets magic weapons with +1 To Hit
Invulnerability	Life	Unit gets weapon immunity and is unaffected by weak attacks
Lion Heart	Life	Significantly increases unit's attributes
Mass Healing	Life	Restores up to 5 hit points to *all* friendly units
Raise Dead	Life	Raises normal unit from the dead during combat
Righteousness	Life	Grants immunity to Chaos and Death magic
True Sight	Life	Unit becomes immune to illusions
Elemental Armor	Nature	Unit gets +10 resistance and defense to Chaos and Nature spells and red and green magic ranged attacks
Giant Strength	Nature	Increases unit's attack strength by 1
Iron Skin	Nature	Unit gets +5 to defense
Regeneration	Nature	Unit restores 1 hit point per combat turn and will be fully healed, even if killed, if you win the battle
Resist Elements	Nature	Unit gets +3 resistance to Chaos and Nature magic spells and +3 defense to red and green magic ranged attacks and spells
Stone Skin	Nature	Increases unit's defense by 1
Flight	Sorcery	Unit can fly at 3 movement per turn
Guardian Wind	Sorcery	Unit is granted missile immunity
Haste	Sorcery	Unit gets to attack or counterattack twice during every melee round
Invisibility	Sorcery	Unit cannot be targeted at range and attackers get -1 To Hit
Magic Immunity	Sorcery	Unit gets immunity to most spells, breath, touch, magic ranged, and gaze attacks
Resist Magic	Sorcery	Unit gets +5 resistance
Spell Lock	Sorcery	Unit's other enchantments cannot be removed until Spell Lock is dispelled
Word of Recall	Sorcery	Unit is immediately returned to caster's Summoning Circle

The spells Dispel Magic, Disenchant Area, Dispel Magic True, and Disenchant True are not listed in this table because they do not provide specific positive effects. However, they can be cast to remove negative enchantments from friendly units.

See Chapter 17 for a detailed breakdown of the attributes affected by each unit enchantment.

Table 21.7 *Non-Combat Unit Enchantments Affecting Battles*

Spell	Magic Realm	Effect
Chaos Channels	Chaos	Permanent alteration of normal unit so as to give the unit flying ability, fiery breath, or +3 shields
Black Channels	Death	Permanent conversion of normal unit into an Undead with enhanced attributes
Lycanthropy	Death	Permanent conversion of normal unit into Werewolves
Endurance	Life	Unit acquires +1 movement point per turn
Water Walking	Nature	Unit acquires ability to walk on water
Wind Walking	Sorcery	Unit moves over all terrain at 3 movement per turn

Note that some of these enchantments (Water Walking and Wind Walking) have effects that allow a unit to fight over water, where it ordinarily could not. They do not otherwise alter the target's combat abilities.

pletely resistant to all spells because they have magic immunity.

Targeting Friendly Units

Another useful combat approach is to enhance your own units. Most unit enchantments of this type can be cast outside of combat and, as long as you pay the upkeep, these enchantments will permanently improve your units' attributes. However, keeping a lot of enchantments going can become a drain on your mana reserves. Wait until you *have* to cast such spells, then choose carefully.

In addition to enhancing a friendly unit's statistics, you can employ other friendly combat spells (such as Healing) that can make an enormous difference when cast at the right time. Table 21.6 summarizes the spells you can cast on friendly units to improve your odds in battle.

Most of these *friendly* combat spells improve a unit's attributes. Be aware that, generally, improvements are on a *per figure* basis. Units with many figures, therefore, reap the greatest rewards from attribute-raising enchantments.

In some cases (Bless, Resist Elements, Elemental Armor, and Righteousness) the at-

tribute gains only affect the unit under specific circumstances (and, hence, won't be seen as additional shields, crosses, or other icons on the unit's statistics). For example, Elemental Armor only confers its protection when the enchanted unit is hit by Chaos or Nature spells. Knowing when a spell is appropriate to cast can be half the battle. Similarly, you don't want to cast spells that serve no immediate purpose. For instance, if you are not fighting missile units, it is not worthwhile to cast Guardian Wind.

Other spells have obvious specific functions. For example, you might want to cast Flight on one of your units so that it can selectively attack flying opponents (possibly even capitalizing on any first strike attacks that it has). You may also want to cast Flight on a unit to protect it from non-flying opponents like great wyrms.

The final word is that you're looking to give yourself the best odds of winning the battle and walking away with as many units afterward as possible. Only your own experience and style of conducting battles will ultimately decide whether you will opt for positive or negative, unit or global combat spells. We can't teach you safe-cracking; in other words, try different combinations until something works for you.

Enchantments
Imported to a Battle

Some unit enchantments that can only be cast outside of combat exert significant effects on the target unit's ability to fight. These enchantments are listed in Table 21.7.

Unit enchantments that can only be cast outside of combat should be considered when appropriate. Units that move faster than normal (by having Endurance cast on them) will be able to reach enemy lines sooner in battle, and with fewer losses from enemy missile fire. They can also attack after a partial move during a combat turn. Other units stand to gain valuable permanent physical attributes from spells such as Chaos Channels, Black Channels, or Lycanthropy. Such spells will make the enchanted units subject to the benefits and penalties of other spells (Chaos Surge, Warp Reality, Darkness, True Light, etc.).

Deciding when to cast unit enchantments (both combat and non-combat) and on which units to cast them, is not always an easy matter. Much depends on who your enemies are and what kinds of troops you have to work with. Strong, multi-figure troops like the Dwarven hammerhands or Halfling slingers, stand to gain immensely from unit enchantments. Other units with supremely valuable single figures, such as a great drake, may benefit from permanent spells that protect them from specific attacks (Magic Immunity, Guardian Wind). Other spells that give valuable, single figure units enormous advantages (picture a flying great wyrm, for example) should also be considered seriously.

You may also want to enchant weak multi-figure units if they form the core of your invasion forces early in the game. This can be cheaper, ultimately, than continuing to recast such spells during combat. Besides, enchantment will free your combat mana for other uses. This leads us to the next section that answers the question: How do you assess all of your combat spell options, and what should you do when?

Putting It All together

So there your forces stand, on the battlefield, facing your enemies. Bleakly looking at your units, you realize that their physical state is inferior to that of their foe's. Or, maybe you just need more assurance that your units will succeed. This is the time to open your spell book and flip through the pages.

Hmm, what to cast? When to cast it? Do you use a hero to cast this spell, or do you use one of their items, or do you cast it?

Well, the hero part is pretty easy. Unless you need their offensive punch, always use your heroes or, preferably, their items to cast your spells. This avoids draining your mana reserves and leaves you with more options later in the battle. Further, you can divide casting responsibilities, using the heroes to cast the lesser spells that they can afford, such as unit enchantments, special cheap spells like Web, Earth to Mud, Phantom Warriors, etc., while you cast the big combat enchantments, such as Prayer or Darkness. This will get more spells into play sooner, and timing is crucial in combat.

But that still leaves the question of which spells to choose and when to cast them. Some general guidelines are:

🐚 Cast spells with widespread effects if you can afford to. Combat enchantments are often the best spells you can cast, and they generally exert the broadest range of effects. However, it doesn't make sense for you to cast a spell like Metal Fires, even though it is a combat enchantment, if you're fighting with tons of summoned creatures instead of mostly multi-figure normal units, since this spell only affects normal units.

🐸 Unit enchantments provide more bang for the buck when cast on units with many figures in them. A +1 attack strength, such as from Giant Strength, will translate to six extra attacks from your standard six-figure swordsman unit.

🐸 Cast spells that lower your enemies' resistances and defenses before casting other spells and before attacking. This will improve your odds of doing both successfully.

🐸 Cast spells that units can't resist or defend against: Warp Wood, Cracks Call, Web, Doom Bolt, and Disintegrate (when cast on a unit with fewer than 10 crosses). These are all good spells to cast under appropriate circumstances to get the most from your mana.

🐸 Don't waste mana trying to cast the wrong spells at magic nodes unless you have no other choice. If you do cast something, the more expensive spells have a better chance of not fizzling.

🐸 Some of the simplest spells are the best. Delaying tactics, such as casting Earth to Mud, Entangle, or Web, can buy you time to make extra ranged attacks or cast more spells. So can summoning other creatures to fight on your side. Confusion is another great, inexpensive spell that can stir up a pot of trouble in your opponent's ranks.

🐸 When all else fails, stepping out of enemy range or sight, by casting Flight or Invisibility, may help your units win the day by exhausting your enemies.

Poof!

While a beautiful sunset is often seen as a great ball of fire plunging into the ground, it is no less satisfying to see a fireball cast upon an enemy's ranks. Magic provides many tools for your battlefield toolbox, offering a wide range of options that cover a myriad of potential opportunities. While it is unwise to get zap happy and cast wasteful combat spells that are billed to your mana reserve, it is always better to have than to need at the decisive moment in combat.

With swords, shields, and wands at the ready, then, we will consider the broader picture of combat. That is, how to mix and match forces to make effective combinations to meet various potential combat needs. The next chapter, oh sage of pages, awaits you.

22

Putting It All Together: Forming Armies

As is the case with many things, so it is for armies: They are not created equal. Some armies are built to garrison cities, while others are formed to conquer them. Some armies are built to capture specific nodes, and others are merely suicide squads formed to reduce infestations in tough areas. Some are budget armies, others are floating or flying corps. When it comes to making the arrangements, how you combine your different troop types is an important strategic element in *Master of Magic*.

Combined Arms Armies

Constructing mobile armies that can handle all but the most extraordinary circumstances should be your basic goal. Solid, *combined arms* armies are composed of an alloy that blends slower, hard-hitting units with ranged attack units, fast units, heroes, some flying units, etc. In other words, a solid, combined arms force has a variety of tools; it is a toolbox that you can employ to meet most battlefield circumstances.

While the quality and size of your armies will depend on the current stage of your game, some basic points always apply:

🐸 Slightly less than half of a combined arms army should be composed of missile or magic ranged attack units. Whole armies comprised of such units tend to be too fragile and can too easily be opposed with enemy magic or missile units. Armies that lack this ranged firepower support can find themselves "taking it" from the enemy while unable to "dish it out" in return.

🐸 The rest of a combined arms army should be mostly the strongest forces that you have and can afford. These units are the ones that will get up close and duke it out with the enemy. The better they are, the better your army will be. At the earliest point in the game, these units will be swordsmen; later, such units

might be halberdiers or cavalry; towards the end of the game, your best end-stage units (dragon turtles, stag beetles, paladins, etc.) will be an army's backbone.

Don't neglect to include these beefy units in your armies. Most battles evolve into tests of physical strength and counting hit points—exactly what these units provide.

🐸 If possible, include at least one flying unit in a combined arms army. Many of the computer armies in garrisons, lairs, and nodes have no way to fight flying units. The presence of such a unit often lets you outlast your enemies. Flyers also give you a chance to cast combat spells (you just need one unit on the battlefield, after all, to do that) in an effort to either win the fight or whittle down your foes.

🐸 If possible, include units that can combat enemy flying units. For instance, units with gaze, breath, or thrown attacks can attack flyers. Being able to attack flyers selectively instead of being forced to deal damage only through counterattacking them gives you many more tactical options as well as strength on the battlefield.

🐸 Finally, if you can, put a unit or hero who has a special ability like holy bonus, leadership, resistance to all, prayer master, or arms master in your army. These abilities benefit most or all units in the stack and can go a long way toward improving your battlefield odds.

Garrisons

What do you leave or place in a city to protect it from rampaging monsters, raiders, and token enemy forces? That all depends on your means, the difficulty setting of the game, and the location of the city relative to potential or current threats. It also depends on your playing style, loose or conservative.

Our somewhat conservative recommendations are:

Recommended Minimum Garrison Size During Peacetime

Depending On Game Difficulty:

Intro, Easy, or Normal:	2 normal units
Hard:	4 normal units
Impossible:	6 normal units

The size of a city's garrison should increase if the city is near neutral cities or several unconquered nodes, lairs, or ruins. Rampaging monsters and raiders often emerge in stacks and will destroy inadequately garrisoned towns. Further, always increase the size of your garrisons, especially those of cities bordering other wizards' territories, during wartime.

Note that you can often cut back on the size of your garrisons in cities deep within your own territory if you have eliminated their nearby potential threats. Also, if your cities are connected by enchanted roads, garrison sizes may also be somewhat reduced because you can move armies from one city to another in no time at all. Beware, however, of reducing the local garrisons too much, because invading forces can use your enchanted roads just as easily as you can!

Finally, allow us to discuss garrison troop quality. Your Enchanted Fortress should always be protected by the best units you have, unless you have some special reason for wanting to be banished (such as the twisted motive, upon your return, of moving your fortress to a different city without having access to the Nature spell, Move Fortress). Garrisons deep within your territory can be protected by lesser and cheaper units. Simply defending in a town gives troops more shields to protect them against invaders, so garrisoned units do not have to be as good as your offensive, romping-stomping armies. Garrisons on the borders of your territory, especially those near

enemy wizards, should be comprised of the best or, at least, strong second-tier units.

A good ploy for building better garrisons is not to build them at the city requiring the garrison. Instead, build them at your army factory city (the one with the war college, if available) and move them to your new outpost and hamlets to serve as their garrisons. It won't cost you a single extra gold piece in upkeep to have these more experienced garrison troops on duty.

Heroes

There are many ways you can use heroes in *Master of Magic*. How to incorporate them into your armies or garrisons depends on how you wish to use your heroes. You may wish to leave some heroes in your Enchanted Fortress, or some other city, to provide it maximum protection. Alternately, you may send all of your heroes out to fight.

For the heroes sent out to do battle, you may wish to stack all of them together into an awesome fighting band or split them up so that they each lead their own armies. Much depends on the nature(s) of your hero(es) and on how you wish to exploit their abilities.

To Battle?

On the question of whether or not to send heroes out to battle, a number of factors may influence your choice:

For example, you may choose to leave spell-casting heroes in your Enchanted Fortress to help elevate your overland spell-casting skill (see Chapters 18 and 21) or send those heroes out with your armies to take advantage of their spell-casting abilities in combat. Both places are useful for such heroes.

Well-equipped heroes are, of course, far better than those with no items or only flimsy equipment. Storing heroes in your Enchanted Fortress until you can equip them properly is reasonable, especially since losing heroes during a battle or while fleeing decreases your fame.

🐢 You may also simply wish to leave your best heroes in your Enchanted Fortress on the theory that they are your best units and, therefore, it is logical to include them in your most important garrison.

🐢 You may find some heroes more useful for exploration than for combat because of their high scouting ranges. So sending some heroes away from your Enchanted Fortress for purposes other than combat is also a possibility.

Beyond whether or not to leave particular heroes at home, another big question remains: Do you stack your heroes into a single, formidable band or split them up over multiple armies? This decision depends upon your mix of heroes and the other units in your armies.

Breaking Up The Band

Actually, a better first question might be how many conquering armies (i.e., *offensive stacks*) you want to form (or, more practically, can reasonably afford). Splitting your heroes among those armies is certainly a logical thing to do. Here are our thoughts.

Splitting spell-casting heroes over several armies makes sense in that all of your major forces can have their combat chances enhanced by the extra casting power such a hero brings to battle. In particular, you'll be able to cast multiple spells per battle turn, which allows you to quickly get all the enchantments you need in place.

Heroes with leadership ability increase the melee attack strengths of all normal units in their armies. If you have several of these heroes, you may want to split them up so that more than one army can profit from this combat bonus.

Similarly, heroes with arms master increase the rate of experience gathered by normal units with which they're stacked. Splitting such heroes over several armies is the way to go. However, you may also wish to rotate arms master heroes through different stacks so that you can raise several armies to their elite unit status. Don't let an arms master hero linger with experienced troops—even if that means rotating through city garrisons to improve them. And remember, fantastic units can't gain experience, so create armies of normal units around arms masters.

Heroes with path finding or wind walking skills may be rotated among stacks so that your armies can get where they want to go quickly and efficiently. In other words, these heroes can carry otherwise slow-moving stacks and dump them where you want them. Think of path finders and wind walkers as ferries (note the spelling) and use them accordingly.

If you only have weak unit types, you may wish to band your heroes together in a single stack for their mutual protection. Conversely, if you have strong basic units in your armies (such as elven lords, minotaurs, and paladins), a single hero (or two, at the most) is sufficient to balance that army stack and give it a keen edge in battle.

Chapter 18 has more information on the specifics of heroes in *Master of Magic*.

Special Operations

You will probably find that you have to create special armies to meet various specific challenges in *Master of Magic*. Sometimes you will want to form a special army to combat a particularly tough node, lair, or tower. Occasionally, you will find neutral or enemy cities stocked to the rafters with units your current army couldn't beat on its best day. You may even get a little tired of enemy forces sailing on to your shores and massing near your cities, and decide that you want to send out a naval or flying force to sink those ships before they can dock.

In the sections that follow, we have compiled specific hints related to forming and using armies for special purposes.

Taking Out Enemy Fleets or Flying Units

Flying corps are particularly useful for taking out enemy fleets. Enemy ships tend to flee at the sight of armies composed entirely of flying creatures. While fleeing, half of them should die (complete with their cargo), giving you fame points in the process. Just in case, though, make sure your flying units have ranged attack capabilities.

Floating task forces can also deal with enemy fleets or flying units coming too close to your shores. Floating stacks are best rounded out with a few warships (for their strong, long range attacks and high survivability). A floating island or wind walking stack laden with tough fighting units is also an excellent option for guarding your coasts.

Kamikaze Corps for Tough Nodes and Lairs

Suicide squads are armies of units you send in to wear down huge armies defending nodes, lairs, towers, and cities. You want to form groups like this when you do not have the spell-casting capability or the units to destroy the occupying army in a single battle. In such cases, attritioning enemy units by one or two per battle eventually brings you victory after a few suicidal sorties.

In particular, multiple suicide squads are often necessary to conquer multi-drake or multi-wyrm nodes and lairs. Good suicide squads are made of heavy hitters; armies of Dwarven hammerhands, Beastmen minotaurs, Halfling slingers, High Elf elven lords, and High Men paladins are particularly good for wearing down major monster infestations. The better the basic unit you send in, the better

your results will be. Naturally, try to build your suicide units in cities with adamantium mines and alchemist's guilds—they'll need all the help they can get!

Note that many of the particularly nasty denizens of nodes are flying units. They can be Webbed if you have giant spiders along or if you can cast that Nature spell without it fizzling. Webbing such units lets you pick your targets during your battle turns. This allows you to gang up your units on one or two limping monsters and finish them off before you're wiped out. Alternatively, if you can cast Cracks Call, this works exceptionally well on great wyrms and Webbed drakes.

Speaking of drakes, another possibility is to make sure your units are enchanted with spells that confer protection against the drakes' deadly breath attacks. Bless, Righteousness, Elemental Armor, Resist Elements, and Magic Immunity will help in your battles against these monsters.

De-Wyrming Armies

One of the easiest and best approaches to dealing with lairs or Nature nodes full of great wyrms is to bring in flying, ranged attack

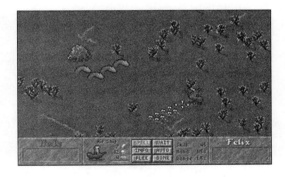

Figure 22-1. *Bring flying units with ranged attacks into great wyrm lairs, especially if you can cast Cracks Call.*

units. If you can take out one wyrm, or more, every time you go in, you can stage repeated assaults on the wyrm hole until you've gotten them all.

To do this, just bring in your flying army. The great wyrms will stay where they are (since they cannot attack flying units). Then close in and shoot at one wyrm repeatedly until it dies. When you've used up your ammo, keep hitting Done until the battle ends. Your troops will withdraw and you can send them in for an encore on the next game turn.

Alternatively, you can take down wyrms with one wimpy flying unit if you can cast Nature's Cracks Call. This spell has a straight 25 percent shot of killing a ground unit. The target unit gets no chance to defend or resist, either. Cracks Call works particularly well on grounded, tough units. Hint: You can even use this spell on deadly enemy heroes! To use this spell against great wyrms, fly into their lair, cast Cracks Call on the wyrms and wait out the end of combat. Repeat until all the wyrms are dead.

Note that none of these approaches yields you much in the way of fame points when you finally take the node or lair. However, you will earn the reward for conquering that site when it's all over.

Tackling Massive Sprite Formations

Perhaps the most annoying and devastating lair denizens are masses of sprites. While each sprite unit alone is fairly weak, large bands of them, particularly when their stats are pumped up around Nature nodes, can destroy early armies made of swordsmen, bowmen, or other simple normal units. There are several ways to deal with these flimsy creatures, short of casting mass destruction spells like Flame Strike.

First, you'll need units sturdy enough to survive the sprites' first wave of attacks. Be prepared to lose some of your weakest units before you get your chance to retaliate.

The Nature spell Web (or giant spiders casting Web) can be used to ground and tie up a sprite unit for several turns. Doing so should give your ground troops the time they need to get to the sprites and knock them out before they start shooting again.

Missile or magic ranged units that have been enchanted so that they either have increased defenses (by casting Stone Skin or Holy Armor, for example) or an increased ability to withstand sprite magic attacks (Resist Elements and Elemental Armor) are also extremely useful. If these units can survive the sprites' initial attack, they'll be able to kill sprites quickly and efficiently. Other ranged attack units with more staying power, such as heroes, catapults, and steam cannons, are also good spritebusters.

Fast moving units with missile, thrown, gaze, or breath attacks can usually reach sprites and kill them before they die. Useful units for this purpose include horsebowmen, centaurs, stag beetles, and dragon turtles.

Of course, any unit with magic immunity (such as paladins) has no trouble against sprites, nor does any really solid unit, no matter how slow or incapable of attacking flyers. All of the good, end-stage units, such as the aforementioned paladins, golems, hammerhands, and elven lords are usually capable of surviving long enough to kill sprites after their magic ranged attacks are exhausted.

One final spell deserves special mention here: Mana Leak. This spell will quickly exhaust the sprites' ammunition, decreasing the time during which your units are assaulted by their magic ranged attacks.

Shedding Some Light on Dark Lairs

Some of the worst lairs are those infested with Death units, especially shadow demons, death knights, and demon lords. Unless your armies are full of tough units, you will want to use a lot of magic in your battles against these creatures. The True Light spell and other global combat enchantments, such as Black Prayer, High Prayer, and Prayer, can help your units withstand these forces of evil.

Spells that protect against the shadow demons' and demon lords' ranged attacks (Bless, Righteousness, Magic Immunity, Invisibility) should be cast where possible. Mana Leak will decrease the number of magic ranged attacks these units have and can help your army survive until these monsters come closer to attack.

Web can ground demon lords and death knights, placing your army on more of an "even footing" for combat. Once you have webbed these units, you can try casting Cracks Call for a quick and dirty way to eliminate them.

The life-stealing attacks of demon lords and death knights can be circumvented if you only attack their lairs with units that are immune to Death magic (such as other Death creatures, golems, and Black Channeled units). Invading with such a force will at least destroy the healing benefit that demon lords and death knights get from their attacks. If you don't have access to such creatures, consider casting spells that raise the resistance of your units (Resist Magic, Lion Heart). Alternatively, go in with a stack that contains a unit with resistance to all (guardian spirits or unicorns) or prayer master. Higher resistance will improve the odds that your units survive the life-stealing attacks.

Other than the above suggestions, your best bet is to enter such lairs with strong missile units (heavily enchanted with defensive spells) and a few strong troops, preferably flying ones.

Armies on Six Mana a Month

Any army can get expensive. Besides the high inherent upkeep costs of certain units (heroes, rare and very rare creatures, high-end normal units, etc.), consider the cost of enchantments. For example, the cost of keeping water walking or flight on an entire stack of units is prohibitive, especially in the earlier stages of the game. Using wind walkers and ships to carry other units is a far more practical alternative.

Building and maintaining armies is mainly a matter of economics. Can you really afford the per-turn costs in mana and gold for that new unit or permanent enchantment? While it is natural to want to spare no expense for your "A-Team" stack of killer troops, keep an eye on your budget. Deficit spending *will* catch up with you!

Hey, Clean Up That Mess!

Those are our thoughts on forming effective armies. We hope the philosophies and specific tips offered here will help you get the right troops organized to succeed. Like everything in life, the secret is to have the right tool to do the job (or, failing that, to develop the skills to improvise with what you do have).

From here, we'll clean up the battlefield. Post-combat effects such as changing ownership of cities and assigning fame are discussed in the next chapter.

23

Post Combat

After every battle, the computer tidies up the pieces and conducts the aftermath. What are the consequences of winning and losing? We'll tell you.

Who Won and Who Lost?

The loser of a battle is the side that fled or was completely eliminated. If both sides lost their last unit simultaneously, the defender is deemed to have won. Also, if time expired, the defender is the winner.

Fleeing

An army that flees often suffers serious flight attrition. Each non-hero unit has a 50 percent chance of being killed (rather than retreating safely) after fleeing. Heroes automatically flee without risk when playing at the Intro and Easy levels and have a 25 percent chance of dying in flight at the other difficulty levels.

Regeneration and Raising the Dead

Surviving units that regenerate regain all of their hit points at the end of a battle. Furthermore, the winner's dead units that regen-

Figure 23-1. *Units fleeing from combat have a 50 percent chance of dying at most of the game difficulty levels.*

erate spring back to life, completely healed (unless they were killed by life-stealing attacks or destroyed by spells like Cracks Call and Disintegrate). Thus, it is important to victoriously hold the field of battle if you are to save all those precious dead troll units who fell.

Any of the loser's units that fell because they lost more than half of their hit points to life-stealing and ghoul attacks will rise as undead units belonging to the winner after the battle. The only exceptions are if stacking limits are exceeded. If the victorious player's stack is full (either with nine units or, if a lair or node garrison, it already possesses units of two different types, see Appendix C), no undead units will be created.

Animate Dead

Creatures under the influence of an Animate Dead spell (see Chapter 9) stay with the player who created them even after combat is over. Note that the animated unit will have an elevated upkeep cost (50 percent more than usual).

Creature Binding & Possession (Poof!)

Possessed units (see Chapter 9) commit suicide at the end of a battle. Units bound by Creature Binding (see Chapter 12) also disappear (should they survive) after a battle.

Wounded Units

Units that are not killed but that don't regenerate will retain their wounds after a battle. Note that creatures of Death (see Chapter 9) don't heal. Other units will, over time.

Changing City Ownership

When a city is conquered (or razed), several things occur. First, there is probably some fame won or lost (see Tables 4.4 and 4.5). Second, there may be damage to assess.

City Damage

After a battle is fought at a city, two values are generated. One is the percent chance of each population point (other than the first one) being destroyed, and the other is the percent chance of each building being destroyed.

At the end of each of the attacker's battle turns, the destroyed population point percentage goes up by +2 percent for *each* attacking unit that occupies a city square. If the attacker wins, another 10 percent is added to the total. The maximum value for this total is 50 percent. Note that rampaging monsters always kill everyone and turn the city into a ruin (i.e., a new monster lair). Each population point (other than the first one) rolls against this percentage to see if it was slain in battle.

The destroyed building percentage goes up by +1 percent at the end of each of the attacking player's battle turns for *each* attacking unit that occupies a city square. If the attacker wins, another 10 percent is added to the total if the city belonged to another wizard. If the conquered city belonged to a neutral player, another 50 percent is added, instead. The maximum value for this total is 75 percent. Each building rolls against this percentage to see if it was destroyed in battle.

Enchanted Fortress Capture

If you capture another player's Enchanted Fortress city, said fortress is automatically destroyed. If the defeated player has enough mana and a city to return to, that wizard is banished and begins to cast the Spell of Return. If the defeated wizard has neither the mana nor a city to return to, that wizard is destroyed.

Banishment

A banished wizard's armies do not cease movement. That wizard's empire ceases to produce mana, but its cities otherwise continue their production. Note that banished wizards can use alchemy to convert gold to mana, thus ex-

pediting the wizard's return. If all of a banished wizard's cities are captured, that wizard is destroyed by the player who conquers the last of the banished wizard's cities.

Destroying Another Wizard

When a wizard is destroyed, the player who put the last nail in the coffin receives the fame and victory point awards (see Chapters 3 and 4). Furthermore, the triumphant player will receive two random spells from the destroyed wizard's spell book from colors that both wizards share.

Setting Production

Finally, the conqueror of a city will have an opportunity to reset its production. The default setting is trade goods.

Loot

Of course, there are often spoils to divide after a battle. When a hero falls in battle (except through disintegration, petrification, stoning, banishment, or via Cracks Call), any items belonging to that hero become the property of the victorious wizard (or are lost if the winner was the garrison of a node, lair, or neutral city). All other types of loot are explained fully in Appendix C.

Fame

As fully explained in Chapter 4, a player's fame will rise and fall after certain battles. Refer to Tables 4.4 and 4.5 for details.

"Après moi, le deluge"

The Sun King, Louis XIV of France, saw it coming. As quoted in this section heading, he said "After me, the deluge." Now we have closed this grand section on combat with this *post bellum* chapter.

With the battles over and the fields of honor reset, we move onto a new section—the deluge, if you will. Our final series of chapters will cover the broader, global aspects of

Master of Magic, including random events, diplomacy, and the subject of our next chapter, game-altering global enchantments.

Section 7

Global Considerations

24

Large Scale Spell Casting

Many of the most devastating and powerful spells in *Master of Magic* are in the global enchantments. These spells are generally very rare, requiring much spell research to learn and considerable mana to cast. This chapter is about coping with these negative global enchantments when they are cast by other wizards and making the most of your own global enchantments.

Dispelling Myths

There are ways to deal directly with the global spells of enemies. There are also ways in which you can make your own global enchantments harder to eliminate. Consider the following:

Disjunction Junction

The most obvious thing to do when another wizard casts a damaging global enchantment is to try to shut if off. Two spells, Arcane's Disjunction and Sorcery's Disjunction True are the only spells that can eliminate global enchantments. (Page 107 in the game manual has the formula for dispelling spells.)

Except for the spell Suppress Magic, statistically, the best way to get rid of nasty global spells is to cast multiple Disjunctions on them. Strive to cast the strongest Disjunction spell you can in the fewest number of turns. For example, if your spell-casting skill is 80 and you wish to eliminate a global spell, you can cast the minimum Disjunction spell (with a 200 mana casting cost) in three turns. But in those same three turns you can actually spend 240 (80 mana per turn times 3) mana on casting this spell. So, for an additional 40 mana spent casting Disjunction, you get a stronger dispel in the same number of turns.

Better still, cheat. Pay attention to the number of turns that elapse. One or two turns before your Disjunction is finished, save the game and replay the next couple of turns over

and over again until your Disjunction succeeds (hehehe).

The exception to spending the minimum amount of mana on a Disjunction spell is trying to dispel a Suppress Magic enchantment. In this case, for the Disjunction to even get off the ground, it must first overcome the Suppress Magic's dispelling force of 500 mana! You want your Disjunction to be strong enough to overcome that dispelling force so that it has a chance of dispelling the global enchantment.

Disjunction True gives you three times the dispelling force of Disjunction for the same casting cost! This is why Sorcery magic is so valuable to have. Further, the wizard skill Runemaster gives all your dispels double strength. Combining Runemaster with a Ph.D. in Sorcery magic, therefore, gives your dispel strengths *six times* their normal force (when casting the Sorcery versions of these spells)! If you're playing a defensive game, then, one of the best things you can do is to guarantee yourself this special anti-magic combination.

Blast Away!

One of the best ways to deal with other wizards' damaging spells is to nuke them before they're cast. This is where the Sorcery Spell Blast comes in handy. Keep a Detect Magic spell going at all times, particularly if you are playing against Chaos or Death magic wielding wizards (Tauron, Sss'ra, Rjak, Sharee, etc.). When you see them trying to get a nasty global spell off the ground, start casting Spell Blast in an effort to preempt it. Just be sure you have enough mana in your reserves, since you have to match the mana the opposing wizard has already spent on the spell that you're trying to kill.

We Have Ways . . .

If you can cast Life Force or Tranquility (both are Life spells), you can create a 500-strength dispel against all new non-combat Death or

Chaos magic spells. This is one way to keep other wizards from launching their evil spells. This defensive ploy is a good insurance policy against the worst kinds of global spells.

The Sorcery spell Suppress Magic takes Life Force and Tranquility to their logical end point. This spell forces *all* other wizard's noncombat spells to resist a 500-strength dispel before they can be successfully cast. This is the ultimate insurance policy against the actions of your enemies.

The Nature spell Nature's Wrath pays back wizards who are casting evil overland Chaos or Death magic spells. Every time they cast one, all of their cities are hit by a mini-earthquake, destroying buildings and killing units there. This spell doesn't actually help you deal with their global enchantments, but it at least gives you the satisfaction of causing them some pain for their profit.

Evil Omens, a Death spell, increases the casting cost of all Nature and Life spells by 50 percent. While this won't stop other wizards from casting their global spells, it makes them pay a pricy premium for such spells.

Spell Sneak

Sorcery offers another wily way to deal with enemy spells. Spell Binding allows you to steal another wizard's global enchantment and make it your own! It is always better to steal an enemy's weapon for yourself than to merely disarm him.

Stop the Clock!

Sorcery is full of ways to stymie others' efforts. The spell Time Stop will give you a chance to deal with your enemies while everything they are trying to do is put on hold. You can cast this before they get a global enchantment cast or afterwards. Either way, it gives you time to amass troops and march on their Enchanted Fortress so that you can get rid of them and their wicked spells.

It's Huntin' Time!

Face it, the surest way to permanently eliminate a global enchantment is to destroy the wizard responsible for casting it. So, if you're out of other options, or you just think it's time, get your best army together and march to glory against that player's Enchanted Fortress.

Holding on to Your Enchantments

If you're the one casting global enchantments, you should know about the few wizard skills that will make your spells harder to dispel. Archmage will make all of your enchantments twice as difficult to destroy. Chaos, Nature, and Sorcery Mastery make all spells from the corresponding magic realm twice as difficult to remove. Combining, for example, Nature Mastery and Archmage will make all of your Nature enchantments *three times* as difficult to dispel! If global enchantments are your thing, pick up one or more of these wizard skills at the beginning of the game.

The Power of Random Events

One random event, Disjunction, eliminates all global enchantments. This is the event to hope for if you are out of other options, but as for all random things, you can't count on it happening. So, you must find other ways to deal with the nefarious designs of your enemies.

The Many Colors of Disaster

All magic realms offer at least a global spell or two that is designed to hurt or hinder other wizards. How you cope with these global disasters and how you make use of your own global enchantments can often spell the difference between winning and losing in *Master of Magic*.

The Storms of Chaos

Most of the Chaos global spells are vicious and damaging in nature. First, however, let's consider those Chaos enchantments that specifically help your cause when you cast them.

Doom Mastery turns all your new normal units into creatures of Chaos by transforming them with Chaos Channels. This will permanently endow your new units with any one of the following benefits: flying ability, extra defense, or fiery breath. In combination with Chaos Surge, which improves all the combat statistics of all Chaos units, Doom Mastery can be particularly helpful for you. When you have cast these enchantments, it is time for you to focus on building huge armies of normal units (although they won't be normal once they're made because Chaos Channels alters them into fantastic creatures). If you can, build new units at cities with war colleges or an Altar of Battle (the Life spell Crusade and Warlord wizard skill help too), since Chaos Channeled units don't gain experience levels or benefits.

Note that Chaos Surge can be a double-edged sword since it helps *all* Chaos creatures, not just yours. Just make sure that you aren't battling Tauron or some other practitioner of Chaos magic before you cast this spell or you'll help them as much as you help yourself.

Since Doom Mastery and Chaos Surge are not immediately damaging to you when cast by other wizards, there is no need for you to exert extraordinary efforts to get rid of these spells. Just cast the odd Disjunction and concentrate your efforts on building up your own armies.

Chaos magic also has some evil, nasty, horrible global spells: Armageddon raises volcanoes everywhere and increases unrest; Great Wasting corrupts land and increases unrest; and Meteor Storms can kill your wandering troops and destroys buildings in your cities. Clearly, these are spells that must be removed if possible. But how do you cope with their destructive effects in the interim?

Green and white magic are best suited for dealing with the evil Chaos enchantments. Table 24-1 lists specific ways (aside from dis-

pelling efforts or attempts to destroy the offending wizard) of dealing with each of these global enchantments and their effects:

If you are the caster of these destructive Chaos enchantments, you should view your frontiers as closed (since, before long, there won't be much left in your enemies' cities worth conquering). The best times to cast these spells are when you are trying to wear down a particularly difficult opponent or when you are holed up, casting the Spell of Mastery.

When Death and Darkness Fall Upon the Land

Death magic's global spells tend to be far less destructive than Chaos magic's spells. In general, Death magic's spells are more positive for the caster than they are negative for his opponents.

Eternal Night is a global Darkness spell. Since it benefits all creatures of Death, it is best to cast this when none of your opponents specialize in black magic. Eternal Night also weakens all creatures of Life, but there are so few of these (guardian spirits, unicorns, angels, and arch angels) that this particular aspect of Eternal Night is hardly a good reason to cast this spell.

If you are at war with an opponent who has cast this spell, concentrating on improving your armies should be a sufficient defense. Note that True Light and Heavenly Light are two Life spells that specifically counter the effects of Darkness and Eternal Night in cities or on battlefields. So if your armies are comprised of Life units, cast True Light in combat to even the odds.

Evil Omens increases the casting cost of all Nature and Life spells by 50 percent. While this is not pleasant if you happen to specialize in one or both of these magic colors, it is hardly crippling. Just make sure that you maximize the amount of mana going into your reserves

Table 24-1. *Coping with Chaos*

Spell or Strategy	Armageddon	Great Wasting	Meteor Storms
Change Terrain (Nature)	eliminates volcanoes		
Elemental Armor (Nature)			protects units from fire damage
Gaia's Blessing (Nature)	eliminates volcanoes; reduces unrest	eliminates corruption; reduces unrest	
Herb Mastery (Nature)			heals all units every turn
Iron Skin (Nature)			increases unit defenses
Nature's Cures (Nature)			lets you heal damaged stacks of units
Regeneration (Nature)			lets units heal from damage
Resist Elements (Nature)			protects units from fire damage
Stone Skin (Nature)			increases unit defenses
Bless (Life)			protects units from fire damage
Charm of Life (Life)			gives units extra hearts so they last longer
Consecration (Life)	protects against all effects	protects against all effects	protects against buildings' destruction
Crusade (Life)			can increase units' hearts, improving their longevity
Endurance (Life)			gets units to their destination faster; decreases amount of time exposed to attacks
Heroism (Life)			increases new units' defenses and hearts
Holy Armor (Life)			increased unit defenses
Just Cause (Life)	reduces unrest	reduces unrest	
Lion Heart (Life)			increases units' hearts so they last longer

Table 24-1. Cont. *Coping with Chaos*

Spell or Strategy	Armageddon	Great Wasting	Meteor Storms
Righteousness (Life)			protects units from fire damage
Stream of Life (Life)	eliminates unrest	eliminates unrest	
Chaos Channels (Chaos)			can increase a units' defenses
Chaos Surge (Chaos)			increases unit defenses
Doom Mastery (Chaos)			as for Chaos Channels
Enchant Road (Sorcery)			units can move faster over land, decreasing exposure time
Flight (Sorcery)			can increase units' speed, decreasing time exposed to attacks
Magic Immunity (Sorcery)			protects units from fire damage
Wind Walking (Sorcery)			can increase a stack's speed, decreasing time exposed to fire attacks
move units into cities			protects units from fire damage
purify land with priests/shamans		eliminates corruption	
increase cities' garrison sizes	reduces unrest	reduces unrest	
increase gold income in cities through trade goods	buy back important destroyed buildings		buy back important destroyed buildings

so that you can continue to cast the spells you need.

Zombie Mastery turns normal units that have died in battle into zombies controlled by the caster of this spell (if he won the battle). If your enemy has cast this spell, again, just concentrate on developing the strengths of your own armies. Zombies, while nice, are not so strong that you should quake in fear at their burgeoning numbers. If you have cast Zombie Mastery, consider casting Eternal Night, as well, to boost the combat statistics of your zombie armies.

Death Wish is a global spell that you can do nothing about (once it is successfully cast). This spell tries to kill all normal enemy units. If Death Wish is cast against you, just step up your unit building until your city and node garrisons have been replenished. You don't need to do anything else. Some good reasons for casting this spell, if you can, are to wear down garrisons in cities that you are trying to conquer and to decimate armies that are encroaching on your territory.

The Wellspring of Life

Most of Life's global spells are meant to enhance the casting wizard's armies: Crusade raises normal units' experience levels; Charm of Life gives all your units extra hearts; and Holy Arms gives all your normal units a Holy Weapon with which to fight. Since most of the improvements are primarily applicable to normal units, combine casting these spells with developing large armies of powerful normal units (like minotaurs, hammerhands, elven lords, or paladins).

When an opposing wizard casts one or more of these enchantments, there is no need to panic. Just improve your own armies and remember that you are superior to your computer opponents in terms of strategy and tactics (especially after reading this book).

None of the rest of Life's global spells are directly damaging, either. Life Force and

Figure 24-1. *Zombie Mastery can rapidly increase the size of the caster's armies.*

Tranquility make enemy Death and Chaos non-combat spells harder to cast successfully. As a wizard of Life magic, it is in your interest to cast these spells when you are warring with enemies adept in these magic colors. If you have these spells cast *against* you, there is little you can do except try to dispel the enchantments or destroy the casting wizard. Otherwise, your best strategy is to focus on building strong armies of normal units instead of summoning red or black creatures. Save your casting efforts for combat, rather than wasting them on overland spells.

Planar Seal can certainly make things more difficult for you. On the other hand, you generally do not *have* to get to the other world. If you already have a city on both Arcanus and Myrror, Planar Seal hardly presents a problem, since you can build units and summon creatures on both worlds (by moving your Summoning Circle). Enemy wizards are less adept, again, at handling unusual situations, so casting this spell to limit their transplanar migrations can be a good idea, especially if you are the sole player on Myrror. Just remember that your movements are as limited as your enemies', so if you want to move your killer stack to the other plane, unseal things first. Note, Word of Recall and Recall Hero are other ways of getting around a Planar Seal (see Chapter 8).

Say Hello to Mother Nature

Nature magic does not boast of many global spells, and only one of these spells is damaging: Nature's Wrath, which causes earthquakes in all cities owned by enemy wizards every time they cast Chaos or Death spells outside of combat. The reasons to cast this spell are obvious: Tauron, Rjak, Sharee, etc. (Bear in mind how frequently computer opponents cast summoning spells, and you will get a picture of how useful this spell can be for you.)

If Nature's Wrath has been cast against you, don't worry too much. First, you generally don't have to cast non-combat spells. You can construct perfectly good armies out of normal units, and your ability to cast devastating Chaos and Death spells in combat is unaffected by this spell. Since Chaos and Death magic have few superb positive city, unit, or global enchantments, you don't have to worry about casting those spells either. If you *really* want to cast a non-combat spell, go ahead and do it, just be cognizant of the risks.

The other two Nature global spells are wonderful for the caster and don't have that much impact on other wizards. Herb Mastery heals the caster's units completely at the end of every game turn. If you are at war with someone who has cast this, concentrate on spells and actions that eliminate whole units instead of just damaging them. Also, make sure that you have enough stacks of armies when you try to conquer your enemy's cities. You can't count on weakened defenders when you invade with a second stack, unless you do so during the same game turn.

Nature's Awareness is the last of green's global spells and does no harm to anyone, while being enormously beneficial to the (human) caster. This spell reveals all map squares, cities, wizards, and non-invisible units to the casting wizard. If you have the spell, there is no reason not to cast it, and if someone else casts it, there is no reason to remove it, short of spite.

Sorcery's Bewitching Spells

Blue's global spells are not much nicer than red's, even though they are less obviously destructive. Nonetheless, they generally do not present immediate or insurmountable obstacles to other wizards in the game.

Aura of Majesty improves the casting wizard's diplomatic relations with opponent computer wizards. There are obvious benefits to you when you cast it, but should you do something about another wizard who has cast the spell? The answer to this is, probably not.

Basically, the computer wizards tend to buddy up; you'll often have multiple wizards ganging up on you, particularly during the later stages of a game. Your best recourse in this situation, short of eliminating the spell, is to make friends with the casting wizard. Generally, there is little reason to change your play style when someone else casts Aura of Majesty.

Wind Mastery doubles the speed of the caster's ships and floating islands, something that can give the caster a clear strategic advantage. Unfortunately, everyone else's ships move at half speed! While this isn't a devastating spell, it can be annoying. If this spell is cast by one of your opponents, you can minimize the negative effects on your ships' speed (if ships are playing a big role in your game) by casting the Life spell Endurance or Sorcery's Flight on them. These spells will get your ships moving at a slightly better pace. You can also circumvent this problem by casting Earth Gate in several of your cities, which will let you teleport units between Earth Gates on the same plane. If none of these options is available to you, summoning or building flying units instead of land bound ones will decrease your need for ships.

Once Great Unsummoning has been cast, there is nothing you can do. Look around and see where you've lost fantastic units and replace them with new units. If you can cast Great Unsummoning, though, it is worth doing, particularly just before invading enemy cities. Your computer opponents are big on summoning spells and, generally, have large quantities of fantastic units around. It's safer and easier, after all, to get rid of these units *before* combat rather than during.

Casting Suppress Magic, when you can, is always helpful. Since computer opponents are obsessed with casting spells, this spell will really be a thorn in their sides. However, Suppress Magic will make your life difficult if someone else casts it against you. You have a few options when this happens: cast mega-

Figure 24-2. *Hold everything! Sorcery's Time Stop spell can be very useful indeed.*

The Ultimate Global Spell

Spell of Mastery is *the* global spell. Since successfully casting this spell will win the game for the caster, it behooves you to do something about it once someone else starts casting it. Get thee hither to the caster's Enchanted Fortress and conquer it. That's the best and simplest advice we have. If you are toying with the idea of casting this spell yourself, just be sure your cities are well garrisoned and that you have enough mana reserves to handle casting this spell and any combat spells you may need (for fending off irate enemies) for several turns into the future.

From Pain to Politics

After having looked at the painful global mischief that wizards can inflict on one another, we're off to the arena of politics. As you will see in our next chapter, there's more to *Master of Magic* than combat and casting. Beyond the staff and sword, there remains the dagger—poised at your back and ready to bring you down. Turn the page, wizard, and learn the diplomatic repercussions of your actions.

strength Disjunctions; kill the casting wizard; or concentrate your efforts on building strong armies of normal units and win at swordpoint without a heavy reliance on magic. Since you can continue to cast combat spells, Suppress Magic, as evil as it seems, should do no more than slow you down. It can't stop you.

Time Stop can, however, (stop you, that is). When this spell is cast against you, guess what? You get to sit there and twiddle your thumbs while the caster moves his units wherever he wants. Eventually, of course, time will return, but until then, there isn't a darn thing you can do about it. Your best defense is in preparation. If you are waging war against Jafar or some other Sorcery master, make sure your garrisons and mana reserves are in good shape. That way, if he invades your cities during a Time Stop, you will be well equipped to handle it. Cast this spell yourself if you are trying to delay another wizard's negative spells or when you want to launch a surprise attack (since your target will have no chance to prepare or recover from invasions).

25
Diplomacy or "Mirror, Mirror on the Wall . . ."

"Diplomacy is the art of letting

the other guy have your own way." Axiom

layers already familiar with strategy games including *Master of Orion* and *Civilization* will recognize that diplomacy in *Master of Magic*, while fairly rich in detail, seems a less vital concern than in those other games. This perception stems from the blurry distinctions between states of war and states of peace, with units maneuvering around other player's seemingly "rightful" territory with virtual impunity. This perception is further reinforced by the fact that, unlike in *Master of Orion*, the other players cannot conspire and vote that you lose the game. Clearly, in *Master of Magic* there is less risk in ignoring other players diplomatically than in other games of this genre.

Therefore, players tend to use diplomacy in *Master of Magic* as a way to trade spells. Threats, bribes, and other diplomatic chicanery are often relegated to the back of players' minds as they focus on empire building and conquest. However, diplomacy *can* be an effective tool in this game.

In this chapter, we shine some light on what is happening diplomatically in *Master of Magic*, helping you get more out of every parlay. It is a simple truth that one minute of diplomacy with other players can save you several minutes on the combat display with them.

Here we'll examine your diplomatic options. More importantly, we will give you insight into the logic underlying each leader's personality as well as her objective. Note that we refer to a typical computer player wizard as a female in this chapter, using the pronouns *she* and *her*.

This Land is My Land

Computer players have only a limited concept of *rightful territory*. The only real estate they care about includes areas within two squares of their cities, plus *every* land square on the continent where their Enchanted Fortress resides. This land mass, known as that wizard's Home Continent, consists of every contiguous land square connected to the fortress.

Although computer players will garrison their nodes and Towers of Wizardry to protect them, they don't perceive any diplomatic consequence in taking or losing such sites (unless they are on their Home Continent or within two squares of one of their cities, of course). Note that the size of the land masses you opt to play with when setting up the game can have a considerable effect on diplomacy. With small land masses, most of the islands in the world will be up for grabs without a lot of diplomatic penalties. On large land masses, computer players will stake out huge amounts of territory and consider them rightfully theirs, thus limiting all players' abilities to peacefully expand.

Contact: Establishing Diplomatic Relations

Diplomacy with another wizard begins in earnest after you make contact with one of her units or cities. At the end of the turn in which you first make contact with her, you will receive a carefully worded greeting. Its tone gives an indication of her current attitude toward you and, more importantly, her personality.

Make no mistake Felix, I absolutely will not tolerate any interference from your forces.

Figure 25-1. *A typical first contact greeting.*

You will only lose contact with another wizard when her Enchanted Fortress is captured. At this point she will be either destroyed or banished. The latter case means that she can come back if she has the mana to cast the Spell of Return and if she still owns a city to which she *can* return. When banished wizards return, they will announce their arrival, and diplomacy with them picks up where it left off.

The Levers of Diplomacy

When you wish to conduct diplomacy or receive an updated look at your opponents, use the Magic Summary screen. (It appears when you press the Magic button at the top of the Main Movement screen.) The gems along the top of the Magic Summary screen are used to communicate with the wizards pictured in them.

Right-clicking on one of these mirrors will produce a screen with a current profile on that wizard. Here, you can see your current relationship level with her, including any formal diplomatic status (i.e., *treaties*). Beneath that are her personality and objective. Next are her current gold and mana reserves, plus her spell books, fame, and skills. Finally, the heroes currently serving her are listed.

Note: Every wizard has the same full roster of heroes to choose from. Although other wizards always change the names of their heroes (presumably, to protect the innocent), their titles (such as "The Healer," "The Unknown," etc.) are the same. Therefore, a quick look down the roster of heroes (see Table 18.1) can quickly tell you exactly who these heroes are.

Left-clicking on a gem bearing a wizard's face means you want to engage in diplomacy with her. A Greeting screen will appear, similar to one from your first contact. From the text of the greeting, again, you can infer your current relations with that wizard, her personality, and objective.

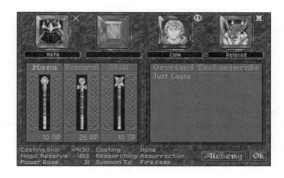

Figure 25-2. The gems at the top of the Magic Summary screen, the faces in them, and the symbols next to them are your conduit to diplomacy.

Note, however, the color of the eyes of the two gargoyles on either side of the magic mirror. They will glow in a color ranging from bright red, to dim yellow, to bright green. When their eyes are red, this indicates the wizard's dislike for you (the brighter the red, the greater the dislike). Conversely, green eyes symbolize that the wizard likes you. If the eyes are yellow, she feels neutral about you. Vet-

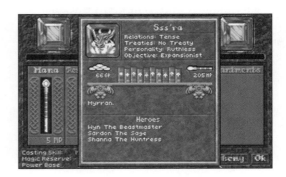

Figure 25-3. Right-clicking on a gem bearing a wizard's face will bring up his or her profile information.

Table 25.1 *The Diplomatic Relations Scale*

Relationship Level (Name)	Diplomacy Point (DP)	Spread
Harmony	+83 to +100	
Friendly	+65 to +82	
Peaceful	+47 to +64	The Green Eyes Zone
Calm	+29 to +46	
Relaxed	+11 to +28	
Neutral	-10 to +10	The Yellow Eyes Zone
Uneasy	-11 to -28	
Restless	-29 to -46	
Tense	-47 to -64	The Red Eyes Zone
Troubled	-65 to -82	
Hatred	-83 to -100	

Note that you will never see a graphic image of these scales, nor know the exact number of where any wizard's relations stand with another. Your only gauge is the single word describing your own relations levels found under each wizard's gem on the Magic Summary screen. (This information is also duplicated on the top line of her Information screen and in the color of the gargoyles' eyes next to the magic mirror you communicate through.)

eran *Master of Orion* players will remember this color scheme from the Relations Bars in that game.

Measuring a Diplomacy Point

Each computer opponent keeps track of each other player's current diplomatic standing with them as a single numerical value on a scale ranging from -100 to +100. This provides a 201 point spread (0 counts, too, you know!), similar to that used in *Master of Orion*. Each point on this scale is called a Diplomacy Point, or DP for short. When another wizard's actions please a computer player, the wizard earns positive DPs. DPs are lost when a computer player wizard is angered. The principle of Diplomacy Points, and the Diplomatic Relations Scale shown in Table 25.1, are important concepts to understand before proceeding.

Important Note: Although computer players use Diplomacy Points to keep track of other

players' actions (including yours), you (the human player) have no such tool. You must rely on your own memory and feelings about

Greetings, most powerful Felix.

Figure 25-4. *You rang? A Greeting screen reminds you of your relations with a wizard (check the color of the gargoyle's eyes).*

Table 25.2 *Permanent Diplomacy Point Modifiers* (not used for Temporary Modifiers)

If you please another wizard, thus increasing your DPs with her, and your current DP standing with her is between . . .

-100 and -1, you gain double the benefit (up to a maximum of +10 on the scale)

0 and +24, you gain the full benefit.

+25 and +49, you only gain 1/2 of its benefit.

+50 and +74, you only gain 1/3 of its benefit.

+75 and +99, you only gain 1/4 of its benefit.

If you anger another wizard, thus reducing your DPs with her, and your current DP standing with her is between . . .

-99 and -75, you only suffer 1/4 of the penalty.

-74 and -50, you only suffer 1/3 of the penalty.

-49 and -25, you only suffer 1/2 of the penalty.

-24 and 0, you suffer the full penalty.

+1 and +100, you suffer double the penalty.

Notes:

1. A Charismatic wizard *doubles* all positive DPs earned and *halves* all DPs lost.

2. All DP gains earned with a Maniacal leader are multiplied by 0.75.

3. All DP decreases with a Lawful leader are doubled. If your relations level with her are positive, the decreases are *quadrupled*.

4. All DP decreases with a Manical leader are multiplied by 1.5. If your relations level with her are positive, the decreases are *tripled*.

5. *All* computer players receive double the amount of any positive Diplomacy Points earned with another computer player after turn 100.

6. When playing at the Hard difficulty level, all negative DPs earned between computer players are reduced by 25 percent. In other words, computer players are more tolerant of each other's faux pas.

7. At the Impossible level, negative DPs earned between computer players are reduced by 50 percent.

8. Fractional DPs are always rounded down to the nearest whole number.

9. When at war, a player's relations can never improve beyond -25.

10. When at peace, a player's relations can never improve beyond +65 without an alliance.

each computer player and make your own decisions based on your best judgment. All the following information about Diplomacy Points is included to help *you* understand what *they* think, not to tell you how to feel toward them!

Permanent Diplomacy Point Modifiers

This chapter considers many events that add or subtract DPs. Before any DPs are added or subtracted to one player's Diplomacy Relations Scale, however, they are *always* modified as shown in Table 25.2.

Natural Relations Gravitation

On turns in which no Diplomacy Points are earned or lost between two wizards, their relations will automatically gravitate a single DP toward their *natural state*, as shown in Table 25.3. Two wizards have a natural state of relations that is determined by the colors of the

Table 25.3 *Starting (Base) Diplomacy Point Levels*

0 is the Base starting point

-2 per Red spell book owned

-3 per Black spell book owned*

+2 per White spell book owned*

+2 per White, Red, Green, and Blue spell book that both wizards have in common

*When one wizard has black magic and the other white, these values are superseded. Instead, substitute -5 per Life/Death spell book difference. (I.e., if one wizard has three Life spell books and another has five Black ones, this creates a -40 DP rift between them at the beginning and defines their poor natural relations level.)

Note: Each time two wizards change their status to "At War," the following occurs: 1) They each receive an immediate -5 DP penalty on each other's Diplomatic Relations Scale, and 2) they each receive a permanent -5 penalty on their above listed Starting (Base) Diplomacy Point Levels.

spell books they own. This natural drift in relations is not subject to the above permanent DP modifiers.

Diplomacy and Magic Spells

A wizard who casts Aura of Majesty receives +1 DP per turn with all computer player wizards. A wizard suffering the effects of another's Subversion spell instantly takes a -25 DP hit on her relations with all other computer player wizards.

Enchantments According to Hoyle

A treaty with another player (either a Wizard's Pact, Alliance, or Peace Treaty), obliges both parties to not throw further negative unit or city enchantments against each other. However, this does *not* preclude them from casting negative *global enchantments*. Chances are, though, that if a wizard gets cocky and casts (or continues to maintain) a nasty global spell, it will cause all of her treaties to break very quickly. She will be at fault for breaking those treaties, too, and will receive an Oath Breaker penalty for each one. Remember, this could happen to you!

Casting the Spell of Mastery

Although researching the Spell of Mastery has no consequences, casting it does. While it is being cast, all other wizards are supposed to go to and remain at war with the casting wizard. Furthermore, it is very likely that these wars will intensify into Jihad campaigns against any wizard casting the Spell of Mastery.

The Audience Menu: Important Background Information

Naturally, you can run into diplomatic snags. One concerns wizards who no longer want to speak with you. Another concerns wizards that speak to you but say "No" (or worse!). To understand why you are rejected and to help you get what you want from a diplomatic parlay, we must first explain what elements combine to affect computer players' feelings toward you and how they make their diplomatic decisions.

A Computer Player's Core Reaction

Core Reaction is another vital concept in this chapter. A computer player's Core Reaction is

Table 25.4 *Considering Wizard's Leader Personality Modifiers for Determining Core Reactions*

Personality Type:	Normal	Charismatic*
Pacifist	+20	+40
Lawful	+10	+20
Chaotic**	-40 to +40	-20 to +80
Aggressive	-10	-5
Ruthless	-30	-15
Maniacal	-50	-25

*Charismatic leaders have positive modifiers doubled and negative modifiers halved.

**A random value rolled once at the start of each turn.

her current general feeling about another player. It is kept track of separately for each wizard and is the key to most of their decisions. A computer player's Core Reaction is a number generated by a combination of the following five variables:

Variable 1. The Diplomacy Point value of her Base Relations with that wizard (see Table 25.3).

Variable 2. A permanent +5 modifier toward a wizard for each spell received from her as tribute, regardless of the spell. (Monetary tribute does not modify Core Reactions; it just creates a temporary positive DP bump to that player's Diplomatic Relations Scale.) This positive value earned from spell tribute is then combined with:

Variable 3. A permanent -5 penalty for each *Oath Breaker* action committed against this wizard by the wizard being considered. Every time a Wizard's Pact, Alliance, or Peace Treaty is broken, the breaking player has committed a heinous act we've dubbed an *Oath Breaker*. Note that this is separate from the permanent -5 penalty to one's Base Relations for each new war (see Table 25.3).

The combined values of Variables 2 and 3 cannot modify a Core Reaction by more than +30 to the good, but can modify it by an un-

limited negative amount. If a wizard proves treacherous enough, it is possible for another wizard to never want to speak to her again! Remember, each Oath Breaker penalty can be offset by a corresponding gift of a spell as tribute.

Variable 4. The Personality Modifier of the considering wizard also affects her Core Reaction toward all other wizards, as shown in Table 25.4.

Variable 5. Finally, their Core Reaction is modified by your current position on their Diplomatic Relations Scale. Thus, it's a modifier that can range from -100 to +100, depending on your present relations with that wizard. Note that the information in Table 25.1 can give you an idea of what this number might be.

A Computer Player's Reaction Modifier Temporary Variables

Besides a wizard's fairly stable Core Reaction, most of the diplomatic decisions she makes are also affected by more volatile temporary modifier variables. These apply in each of the following decision making areas and are kept track of separately:

🐍 Temporary Treaty Modifier (for Wizard's Pacts and Alliances)

🐚 Temporary Peace Modifier (for Peace Treaties)

🐚 Temporary Exchange Modifier (for spell exchanges)

🐚 Temporary Cold Shoulder Modifier (for their leader's patience)

"No" Really Means "Stop Asking"

Every parlay, no matter its outcome, inflicts a -10 point penalty to each of these four temporary modifiers. (In effect, you're wearing down that wizard's patience.) If your diplomatic offer is rejected, then the temporary modifier for the area you were specifically rejected in receives a -30 point penalty instead of the usual -10 point penalty that would have occurred had she agreed.

These temporary modifier penalties are cumulative. They are adjusted back toward zero at the rate of 10 points per turn per category.

The principle behind these temporary modifiers is quite simple. They're designed to prevent you from annoying computer players with incessant demands on their diplomatic time. They simulate that point where computer players simply get tired of dealing with you and, consequently, will be more likely to say "No" to any of your proposals. It might help to think of these temporary modifiers as "patience modifiers" instead.

The Cold Shoulder

A wizard won't always negotiate with you. Sometimes, she'll cut you off before you can ever access the Diplomacy menu and parlay. Specifically, this occurs when her Core Reaction toward you, plus her Temporary Cold Shoulder Modifier, falls below -100. In such cases, all you can do is let time pass to reduce her Temporary Cold Shoulder Modifier and let your relations gravitate (as previously explained) to a possibly better position on the Diplomatic Relations Scale.

Temporary Modifiers: Charismatic Advantages

In addition to doubling the effects of any positive DPs they earn, halving any negative DPs they're fined (see Table 25.2), and improving their Personality Modifiers (see Table 25.4), Charismatic gives yet another advantage to wizards. They receive a +60 bonus to all of their Treaty and Exchange Spell Temporary Modifiers when offering these deals to other wizards. This bonus does not affect the Temporary Cold Shoulder Modifier, however, nor does it lower the minimum current diplomatic level required with another wizard before she will accept certain agreements (see below).

Counter-Offers

Occasionally, you'll entreat another wizard who will say neither "Yes" nor "No" to your proposal. Instead, she will make you a counter-offer, as shown in Figure 25-5. When this happens, the first thing she'll do is look for a random spell you have that she doesn't, and she'll ask you for it. If you agree to share it with her, she'll accept your original offer; if not, she'll reject it.

Only if you don't have a spell that she can use (and acquire, because she has the neces-

If you also offer me Drain Power spell I would accept.

Agree
Forget It

Figure 25-5. *A counter-offer being made to your proposal.*

sary spell books) will a wizard consider taking a cash inducement instead. The amount she'll want is equal to the sum of two d8 rolls, times the game turn number (with the result rounded down to the nearest whole 25 gold). If you don't have that much money in your treasury, she will make no counter-offer and will simply reject your original proposal instead.

For example, on turn 33, another wizard decides that your latest proposal is almost, but not quite, acceptable. Therefore, she needs you to sweeten the deal. First, she'll peruse your researched spells. Upon discovering that she has everything that you do, she considers a cash bribe. In her mind, she rolls two eight-sided dice and adds the results together (the average result will be nine, so let's assume that is the outcome of the roll for this example), and multiplies that sum by the game turn number that, in this case, is 33. Well, 9 times 33 is 297, so the bribe amount she'll require is 275 gold (297 rounded down to the nearest 25 gold). If you have at least that amount in your treasury, she'll ask you for it. If not, she won't even bother and will simply reject your proposal out of hand.

The moral is: before entering into a parlay where you really want the other wizard to accept your offer, check to make sure that you have a spell she doesn't have and can use. Failing that, have plenty of gold on hand in case she demands a bribe to accept your offer. Money in the bank for these little diplomatic palm (and claw) greasing emergencies can make all the difference in the worlds.

The Oath Breaker Penalties

Every time one player breaks a treaty with another, whether a Peace Treaty, Wizard's Pact, or Alliance, they will be remembered by the aggrieved wizard as an *oath breaker* for doing so, thus suffering a double penalty. First, they must endure a permanent, cumulative -5 modifier to that player's Core Reaction

toward them. Second, they will suffer an immediate drop of about two levels (-40 DPs) on that player's Diplomatic Relations Scale. Think long and hard, therefore, before you go around breaking treaties, and be careful not to break any by accident.

You Can Say "No," Too

If you reject a computer player's offer or counter-offer, you receive no direct diplomatic penalty. All you really lose is the benefits you might have gained by accepting her proposal, so don't be shy about giving her the thumbs down when you want to.

The Diplomacy Menu: Decisions, Decisions

The way to formally initiate diplomacy with another wizard is to seek an audience with her. If she receives you and matters move to the Diplomacy menu, you'll have some options to consider. (By the way, there is no diplomatic penalty for failing to complete a parlay by escaping before one side either accepts or rejects a proposal.)

The Propose Treaty Option

The first of your diplomatic options, Propose Treaty, lets you ask for agreements that improve your relations with that wizard, or lets you pressure her into degrading her relations with another player. Here, we explain the subtleties of getting each proposal accepted, and the exact effect it will have.

Wizard's Pact

Another wizard will only accept a Wizard's Pact if your current relationship with her is at least +11 DPs on the Diplomatic Relations Scale (i.e., relaxed or better). Once a Wizard's Pact is in place, you have mutually agreed not to attack each other's garrisoned objectives (nodes and Towers of Wizardry) and cities, including attacking via negative unit and city enchantments. This does not prevent either side from moving forces to the other wizard's Home Continent, moving adjacent to garrisoned objectives, or attacking the other player's units located elsewhere.

A Wizard's Pact immediately increases your Diplomatic Relations Scale by +20 Diplomacy Points, plus a random +1 to +3 DPs per turn, subject to the permanent DP modifiers (see Table 25.2).

Alliance

Another wizard will only accept an Alliance if your current relationship with her is at least +51 DPs on the Diplomatic Relations Scale (i.e., peaceful or better). Once an Alliance is in effect, you have mutually agreed not to attack each other under any circumstances (except with global enchantments). An Alliance also halves all of the totals needed to succeed in your future proposal requests with that ally, making it only half as difficult to get what you want from them in future parlays. Furthermore, an ally will not send additional troops to your Home Continent.

Computer players always ask their allies to fulfill the *mutual defense clause* that is a *de facto* part of every Alliance. In other words, she *will* ask you to declare war on her enemies. You, too, may ask your allies to fulfill this obligation and declare war on third parties with whom you are at war.

While allied, a wizard will declare war on your behalf to fulfill this mutual defense clause without fail. However, there is a 75 percent chance that she will demand a random spell you've researched in exchange. If you have no such spell, or refuse to give it to her, then she will callously reject your pleas for assistance. (Hey, you can always ask again.)

When you become allies, your relations with that wizard will immediately increase by +20 Diplomacy Points, plus a random +1 to +6 DPs per turn, subject to the permanent DP modifiers (see Table 25.2).

Peace Treaty

If a war is really looking bad for you, or if you are persevering but want to end the wasteful destruction and concentrate on building up your economic and political position, then sue for peace. The Temporary Peace Variable, however, has two additional modifiers. Added to it is a positive number equal to the damage you inflicted upon that enemy wizard since the beginning of the current war between you. A negative number equal to the damage that she has inflicted upon your empire is also added to the Temporary Peace Variable. These damage modifiers are cumulative throughout the duration of war between you, and they are reset to zero once you establish a Peace Treaty.

These values are used during war in the opposite way that they would be during peace. In other words, while at peace, the damage you inflict on another wizard's empire is subtracted from her Diplomatic Relations Scale with you. During war, the damage you inflict is added to your chance to secure a Peace Treaty. Therefore, the best time to get a peace offer accepted is after time has removed any temporary negative modifiers from past rejections and other parlays (such as offering tribute) and, preferably, right after you've just conducted a particularly successful attack against that wizard (i.e., you are fairly sure that you're one up on her in the damage modifier department).

Note that all glory is fleeting. Because these damage modifiers (yours and the enemy's) are calculated into the Temporary Peace Variable, the changes in this variable due to success or failure in war will gradually be negated as the variable inexorably moves 10 points per turn back toward zero. Thus, a lull in the fighting allows the losing side to recover (politically, as well as economically and militarily) from a disastrous campaign, while the winning player's advantage slowly fades away.

Peace Treaty Effects

When a Peace Treaty is accepted, your Diplomatic Relations Scale with that player immediately shifts by +40 Diplomacy Points, subject to the permanent DP modifiers (see Table 25.2). Furthermore, both sides agree not to attack the other's forces anywhere in the worlds, including by casting adverse unit and city enchantments upon each other. They also agree not to send additional troops to the other's Home Continent for the duration of the peace agreement (they will not, however, withdraw the troops they already have there).

Naturally, a computer player expects reciprocating behavior from you. If your forces continue to arrive at her Home Continent during this period of enforced peace (even though you can't be certain exactly when it ends, see below), if you destroy the slightest thing of hers, or if you cast any kind of adverse enchantment her way, then you will instantly suffer an Oath Breaker penalty and end this era of enforced peace. Therefore, to keep the peace, don't attack that player for any reason until you no longer find the Peace Treaty convenient.

A peace agreement's duration of enforced peace is between 8 and 15 turns, determined randomly (i.e., it is not modified by game difficulty or leader personalities).

Declaration of War on Another Wizard

If you ask an ally to fulfill her treaty obligation to declare war on those with whom you're at war, she will automatically accept your proposal. However, 75 percent of the time, she will demand a bribe of one spell in exchange. If you have no such spell, she simply rejects your proposal. If you refuse to pay this bribe, you won't lose any Diplomacy Points with her, but she won't declare war on your behalf, either.

A wizard not allied with you will only declare war at your behest against a third party with whom you are at war if your current relationship with her is at least +19 DPs (i.e., relaxed or better). However, if she has a Wizard's Pact or Alliance with the third wizard, you're far more likely to be rejected. You will have more success at persuading a computer player to declare war if you get her to break her Wizard's Pact or Alliance with the third wizard as a separate action before asking her to declare war. We recommend this preliminary diplomatic maneuver as an attainable first step.

Just remember that you have to be very friendly with someone to get her to consider declaring war on another wizard. When that happens, of course, they will fight each other and, in turn, their attention will be attracted away from you (at least for their war's duration).

Break Alliance
(or Wizard's Pact) with Another Player

When this option is highlighted on the Propose Treaty menu, it means the wizard has either an Alliance or a Wizard's Pact with another player. Although the menu that appears after you choose this option lists all of the players she currently has either an Alliance or Wizard's Pact with, you can't tell which of these treaty types she has simply by looking at the list. Instead, you should look at that information on the Magic Summary screen before entering into diplomacy.

Next to each wizard's gemstone bearing their picture may be a column of icons indicating the wizard's diplomatic states with all the other players. The color of an icon corresponds to the player they share that state with, while the symbols indicate the exact nature of those diplomatic states. (Crossed swords indicate a state of war, a scroll symbolizes a Wizard's Pact, while a peace sign shows an Alliance—*not a Peace Treaty!*).

Another wizard will only break her Alliance/Wizard's Pact with another wizard at your behest if your current relationship with her is at least +19 DPs (i.e., relaxed or better). Note that it is harder to get a wizard to break an Alliance/Wizard's Pact with another wizard than it is to get her to declare war on that same wizard after she breaks the treaty. Once a treaty is broken, it is often a good idea to follow up your success by pressing the wizard to declare war on her former ally. With her treachery completed against your intended victim, you can bask in the glory of your duplicitous success, knowing that you got one wizard to be marked with Oath Breaker by another. Before you know it, they'll be busy fighting among themselves. You're a real Machiavellian Prince now.

The Threaten/Break Treaty Option

Next on the diplomatic list are the saber-rattling options through which you can break your current Wizard's Pact or Alliance with a wizard, and/or threaten to attack her. Any of these selections should be made with care after considering the consequences.

Break Wizard's Pact

Assuming you have a Wizard's Pact established with a wizard, this option will put the pact's effects to an immediate end. With the gloves off, you're free to attack the other wizard's units (particularly those at their nodes and Towers of Wizardry). Attacking their cities, however, remains an act of war.

You will immediately suffer a -12 DP penalty, subject to the permanent DP modifiers (see Table 25.2), and cease to get +1 to +3 DP bonus every turn for having a Wizard's Pact in effect. Furthermore, because you broke the treaty, that wizard will remember this as the act of an Oath Breaker, thus penalizing all your future diplomacy with that wizard.

Break Alliance

Similarly, if you have an Alliance to break, this option immediately ends its effects. A broken Alliance does not reduce to a Wizard's Pact. Once broken, all bets are off.

You will immediately suffer a -12 DP penalty, subject to the permanent DP modifiers (see Table 25.2), and cease to get the +1 to +6 DP bonus every turn for having an Alliance in place. Furthermore, an Oath Breaker penalty will permanently stain your future relations with your former ally.

Break Peace Treaty

Although it is not listed on the Diplomacy screen, you can break a Peace Treaty by committing any hostile actions while that Peace Treaty is in effect. A hostile action includes any violation of the peace, such as landing additional troops on the other player's Home Continent or attacking any of her units or cities. Additionally, any action that would brand you as an oath breaker (i.e., breaking an agreement) also breaks a Peace Treaty. This can quickly deteriorate your relations, often reverting them back to war. There is no immediate Diplomacy Point penalty for breaking the peace, per se (although the act used to break it probably has its own diplomatic consequences), but you will be remembered as a treacherous oath breaker by that player for doing so.

Since Peace Treaties last a random number of turns, between 8 and 15, if you want to start up a scrap with someone with whom you have a Peace Treaty, you might want to be patient and wait a few turns, so that you do not violate the treaty itself. This is because, when you break the peace, the other wizard will permanently brand you as an oath breaker.

Unfortunately, you will never know the exact duration of a Peace Treaty with another player, so you'll either have to wait the full 16 turns before attacking her again, or follow that wizard's lead if she attacks you first. Once a Peace Treaty is ended, either by a new war breaking out or simply by expiring over time, you may freely attack that other wizard to the point of starting a new war without the possibility of suffering an Oath Breaker penalty for doing so.

Threaten to Attack

Now, this is an interesting option. By rattling your saber, you are hoping to elicit one of two potentially favorable responses. One positive direction might be to get that wizard to cower before you and offer tribute in the face of your wrath. The other option you might be seeking is to provoke her into declaring war on you, thus saving you from an Oath Breaker penalty for declaring war yourself if you currently have a Peace Treaty, Wizard's Pact, or Alliance with her. The other player always has a third option, unsatisfactory to you, and that is to simply ignore your blustering threats.

Computer Player Considerations

Although we're not providing an exact formula here, we will describe the three variables that go into formulating a computer player's opinion of your strength relative to hers. Primarily, she will be most intimidated by the strength of your forces on her Home Continent. Her Personality Modifier (as found under the first column of Table 25.4) and the value of all the Oath Breaker penalties you have with her also enter the equation.

Appeasement

One result is that she will appease you with a bribe offer. First, she'll attempt to offer you a new spell that you can use. Basically, expect her to foist off a random spell of hers that a) you don't already have and b) is at least one rarity level below the highest she has researched in that color. Thus, you will never be bribed with a very rare spell.

If she doesn't have a spell for you that meets these criteria, you'll be offered a cash bribe instead. The amount is figured using the same formula that she would expect for a deal sweetener (i.e., the sum of two d8 dice, times the game turn number, rounded down to the nearest increment of 25 gold). If she just happens to have that amount in her reserve, she will offer it to you as a bribe. If she doesn't have that kind of money lying around, she automatically shrugs off bribing you and simply ignores you instead.

As you take a bribe, however, there is something important to keep in mind. Like being ignored, accepting a bribe still leaves a no war/no peace situation between you. She will still be free to declare war on you at any time (and may do so as early as the next turn) and vice versa. Nothing has really been resolved.

Cower

A second response to your threat might be that the computer player cowers. This establishes a *de facto* Peace Treaty between you, complete with the immediate +40 Diplomacy Point signing bonus. In other words, she will cease to attack your units throughout the worlds and will send no more troops to your Home continent for 6 to 20 turns. If you violate this new Peace Treaty, you will be considered an oath breaker. If a Peace Treaty is not what you wanted with that wizard, too bad. You're stuck with it now.

Ignore

There's also a chance that she'll figure (often correctly) that you are bluffing. In this case, she will ignore your threat to attack. (You *were* only bluffing, right?) When this occurs, nothing extraordinary happens except that the wizard will be upset that you even threatened to attack in the first place (see below).

Declare War

Finally, that wizard might decide not to take any more of your guff and will immediately declare war on you. Now, this may be part of a shrewd plan on your part to provoke *her* into declaring war, thus saving you from potential Oath Breaker penalties incurred by declaring war on her if you currently had a Peace Treaty, Wizard's Pact, or Alliance. On the other hand, this might just as easily be a bad case of *oops* on your part, with her taking your threat a bit harder than you'd hoped. Either way, brace yourself for a lot of fighting in the immediate future.

How Upset Do Computer Players Get When Threatened?

Whatever their reaction, threatening to attack a computer player will usually end your parlay with her and put you way up on her cold shoulder list for several turns. This is because if you threaten to attack another player, all of her temporary modifiers (as explained earlier) are adjusted by -50 points, including the Temporary Cold Shoulder Modifier. In other words, threatened wizards are not going to be available for extortion every turn. Threats readily cause these deep negative numbers.

Besides that potential Diplomacy Point penalty from excess negative temporary modifiers, a direct DP penalty is also immediately applied. Your threat will alter her Diplomatic Relations Scale with you by -30 DPs, *plus* it will change her Personality Modifier (see the first column of Table 25.4). For example, if you threaten a Maniacal leader (with her -50 point Personality Modifier), there will be an instant adjustment of -80 DPs on her Diplomatic Relations Scale! Therefore, threatening someone with whom your relations are already strained can greatly hasten a war between you, if it does not cause one outright as an immediate reaction to your threat.

The Offer Tribute Option

If you wish to immediately affect your relations in a positive way with another wizard, offer her a gift (known as tribute). Bribes to curry her favor in this manner come in two flavors: cash and spells. Each is discussed below.

Cash Bribes

When the wizard wants a cash bribe, several amounts will probably be presented for your consideration. The ones you can actually afford based upon your gold reserves are highlighted for your possible selection. What you will gain in positive DPs for your cash bribe depends on how far down on the list of options it is. The higher the value, the bigger the potential bump.

Spell Bribes

Giving spells as tribute has a double advantage. First, each spell you give another player as tribute adds a permanent +5 to her Core Reaction. The usefulness to the giftee of the particular spell doesn't matter when considering this bonus. Foisting off what you feel is your worst piece-of-junk spell that you think will do them the least amount of good awards you the same +5 modifier as a terrific spell. You also get an immediate Diplomacy Point gain on their Diplomatic Relations Scale.

The Exchange Spell Option

If you're not at war, another wizard will always be open to hear an offer for exchanging one of her spells for one of yours. Any trade you work out, however, must see her get a spell with a higher research cost than the one she gives. Note that they will never trade away their highest current spell item in any color of magic. (The world ain't a fair place, kid.)

An important note about exchanging spells is this: You can only trade spells in a shared color of magic. If all you have are Nature spells and the person you want to trade with has no green spell books, your trading options are

Chance of Declaration of War for Invading a Computer Player's Home Continent

Threat Value = Amount of invader's total unit upkeep costs (1 per gold + 1/2 per mana upkeep) on aggrieved player's Home Continent.

Paranoia = (Threat Value x 15) / threatened player's total unit upkeep costs (1 per gold + 2 per mana upkeep) on threatened player's Home Continent. If threatened player has no forces on her Home Continent, Paranoia = -50.

War Chance = Paranoia + Current Diplomatic Relations Scale value + threatened player's Personality Modifier (see the first column of table 25.4) + Oath Breaker penalties the threatened player has with the invading player.

If War Chance is less than -150, the threatened player declares war on the invader and the invader suffers an Oath Breaker penalty if a treaty was broken in the process.

Diplomacy Points Lost for Nearing Another Player's Cities

If the two players involved have a Wizard's Pact, Alliance, or Peace Treaty currently in effect:

First Turn of Violation = d10 in negative DPs/2 (round down)
Second Turn of Violation = No effect
Third Turn of Violation = -5 DPs and treaty broken with an Oath Breaker penalty assigned to the threatening player

If the two players involved have no treaty between them:

Any Turn of Violation = a 10% chance of a d10/2 (round down) in negative DPs

Note, these penalties are assessed *per turn of violation*, not per violation. In other words, being near ten enemy cities a given turn has no more diplomatic penalty than being near one.

limited to the common Arcane magic spells that every wizard always shares. Therefore, diplomatically speaking, it is often a good idea to have at least one spell book in a number of different colors (and better to have two spell books so that you can trade and receive rare spells).

Making Your Choices

If the above conditions are met, first she will let you select from a predetermined list of what she is willing to trade with you. Don't expect great things here, but you may find an important filler spell that isn't already in your spell book.

After selecting a single item from this list (which may only have one item), you must decide what you will give her in exchange. Brace yourself because your best spells are usually what she'll demand in trade. However, the better the items you can potentially offer her in exchange, the better your chances are that she'll accept the deal. Also, you'll gain +5 DPs in exchanges where the other wizard feels she really got a much better deal (when comparing spell research cost).

Table 25.5 *Diplomacy Point Penalties for Attacking Other Players*

Penalty in DPs	Action
-d10	for each engineer or settler unit you kill
-d20	for each other unit type you kill, except heroes
-20	for each enemy hero you kill
-20	if you attack a computer player's city (not outpost) and lose/retreat
-20	for banishing a wizard (applied to all other wizards)*
-40	if you attack the units or a city of someone with whom you have a treaty**
-40***	if you capture a computer player's city
-40	for killing a wizard (applied to all other wizards)
-60***	if you attack another player's Enchanted Fortress city and lose/retreat

All of the above penalties are cumulative, so capturing the city of someone with whom you have a treaty is a -80 DP penalty (and is an automatic declaration of war).

*If the enemy wizard was banished (not killed), the victorious wizard also gains five Fame points.
**The computer player stops you and reminds you that you're about to do this. Note that this action also breaks the treaty (duh).
***This is also a *casus belli*, changing the status of the two players involved to war.

Specific Actions That Affect Diplomacy Points

Some other specific actions will add or subtract points from your Diplomatic Relations Scale with another wizard. This section lists them all and explains their exact consequences.

Having Too Many Units on My Home Continent

As stated at the beginning of this chapter, computer players get a bit pushed when other players have troops on the land mass where their Enchanted Fortress is located (i.e., on their Home Continent). Computer players instantly determine the treat of such incursions and might opt to declare war if sufficiently threatened by a large scale invasion of their territory. The chance of such a declaration of war is given in the formula on page 373.

Massing Up Troops Against Another Player

If a player has any unit other than a settler or engineer within two squares of a computer player's city (of any size, except for outposts, which are completely ignored for this purpose), there may be some agitation. How many DPs the threatening player will lose on the city owner's Diplomatic Relations Scale is shown in the formula.

Attacking Another Player

Attacking another player is always considered a hostile act. Diplomacy Point penalties assessed against the aggressor by the aggrieved player are listed in Table 25.5.

Human Threat: Military Build Up

Every turn, each computer player separately rolls a d20. If she rolls a 1, she compares the

Table 25.6 Computer Player Paranoia About The Size of Your Empire

Land Mass Size Selection	Game Difficulty Level				
	Intro	Easy	Normal	Hard	Impossible
Small	9/15/21	8/13/18	7/11/15	6/9/12	5/7/9
Medium	13/20/27	12/18/24	11/16/21	10/14/18	9/12/15
Large	17/25/33	16/23/30	15/21/27	14/19/24	13/17/21

Numbers indicate the minimum number of cities that you must own to reach the computer players' Paranoia Tier. The first number (or tier) in each set of three begets a -2 DP penalty. Being found with at least as many cities at the middle number brings a -5 DP penalty. The largest number is the amount of cities you need to get socked with a -10 DP penalty.

For example, you're playing a Hard difficulty level game with the world set to large land masses. Computer players won't get paranoid about the size of your empire until you reach your 14th city. After reaching that tier, about every four turns, your relations with all other wizards will drop by -2 DPs due to their natural paranoia about the size of your empire. After you obtain your 19th city, the frequency of their paranoid outbursts won't change (it will still be about every four turns), but the degree increases to a -5 DP penalty. After reaching your 24th city and beyond, their paranoid outbursts bring with them a -10 DP penalty to your relations.

size of her military to yours. If your total army strength is double hers, you instantly take a -10 DP hit in your relations with her. If your forces are equal, there is a 50 percent chance of suffering this -10 DP penalty. When you have half her strength, there is only a 25 percent chance of this same negative reaction, etc.

Thus, the percentage chance of suffering this penalty with a particular wizard is based on a sliding scale depending on the strength ratio of your two armed forces. Note that you can easily compare gross military strengths by consulting your astrologer's Army Strength bar graph. (The value of each bar is the sum of the total gold upkeep for all of a player's normal units, plus double the mana upkeep cost of for *all* their units.)

The Human Threat: A Large Empire

Every turn, computer players share a d4 roll. If they roll a one, their mutual paranoia is checked against the size of your empire. (They want to see if you're becoming too powerful.) This is done by consulting Table 25.6.

Diplomagic Effects

So, you think you can cast horribly nasty magic spells and walk away unscathed diplomatically? Think again. Table 25.7 summarizes the diplomatic consequences for spell casting.

And when the going gets tough, the tough get going. When a player's DPs dip below -30 with a computer player, there is a per turn chance that a Declaration of War will ensue, as shown on Table 25.8.

Making the Enemies of Your Enemies Your Friends

When you attack another player and inflict damage upon her, any other player who is also at war with that player will be pleased with your actions. Thus, you can score bonus Diplomacy Points with these enemies of your enemies.

Computer Player Cheating

After turn 100, when dealing with each other, computer players receive *double* any net increase in Diplomacy Points due to positive

Table 25.7 *Computer Player Reactions to Various Spell Castings*

Spell Cast	Immediate DP Effect	Additional Per Turn DP Effect
City Spells:		
Call The Void	-20	0
Chaos Rift	-5	0
Corruption	-25	0
Cursed Lands	-5	0
Earthquake	-9	0
Evil Presence	-5	0
Famine	-5	0
Fire Storm	-3	0
Ice Storm	-3	0
Pestilence	-8	0
Raise Volcano	-50	0
Combat Spells:		
Any Damage Spell	-3	0
Black Wind	-3	0
Global Enchantments*:		
Armageddon	-25	-2
Aura of Majesty	+10	+1
Chaos Surge	-10	-1
Crusade	-10	-1
Doom Mastery	-8	0
Eternal Night	-12	-1
Evil Omens	-20	-2
Force of Nature	-20	-2
Great Wasting	-20	-2
Holy Arms	-5	0
Life Force	-20	-2
Meteor Storm	-15	-1
Suppress Magic	-25	-2
Tranquility	-20	-2
Wind Mastery	-4	0
Zombie Mastery	-14	-1
The Spell of Mastery*:		
Spell of Mastery**	-50	-25

Table 25.7 Cont. *Computer Player Reactions to Various Spell Castings*

*These spells affect that player's DPs with all computer players. Note that Herb Mastery, Just Cause, Nature's Awareness, and Time Stop have no diplomatic repercussions.

**Also, each computer player has a 10 percent chance per turn of declaring war on a player casting the Spell of Mastery.

For example, if you cast Armageddon, you'll earn -25 DPs with all the computer players; an additional -2 DPs per turn with all the computer players; plus another -50 DPs (for each particular computer player) per volcano that appears within the city limits of that player's cities. Yikes!

actions done for each other (i.e., bribes, trade, Peace Treaties, etc.). This makes it easier for computer players to avoid constant and futile bickering among themselves, allowing them to focus more of their attention and energy on dealing with you.

Also, when playing at the Hard difficulty level, all negative DPs earned by one computer player against another are reduced by 25 percent. In other words, computer players are more tolerant of each other's faux pas. At the Impossible level, this modifier is increased to 50 percent.

Note that *prior* to turn 100, computer players will not declare war on *you* through their own initiative. Unless you offer a *casus belli*

Figure 25-6. *A computer opponent gets fed up with your actions and declares war.*

by capturing on of their cities or attacking their Enchanted Fortress, the first 100 game turns are your diplomatic grace period.

Casting The Spell of Mastery: The End of Diplomacy

While *researching* the Spell of Mastery won't get you into trouble, *casting it* (in order to win the game) *will*. At the point that one player starts to cast the Spell of Mastery, all the other wizards will be notified, and each should declare war on the casting player. Diplomacy will cease to operate normally with wizards who are casting the Spell of Mastery.

Casus Belli: Why Wizards Declare War

Let us recap what provokes a computer player into declaring war on another wizard:

🦎 One of her cities was captured by that player

🦎 The other player is casting the Spell of Mastery

🦎 She has a Chaotic personality

🦎 She is responding strongly to a diplomatic threat

🦎 She is reacting to the other player having too much strength on her Home Continent

🦎 Her Enchanted Fortress was attacked (without success) by that player

🦎 Militarist and Expansionist (who are *not* also Lawful) consider breaking their treaties

Table 25.8 *Per Turn Declaration of War Chance for Current Bad Diplomatic Relations*

Relations Level	Per Turn Declaration of War Chance
-31 to -39	15%
-40 to -49	20%
-50 to -59	25%
-60 to -69	30%
-70 to -79	35%
-80 to -89	40%
-90 to -99	45%
-100	50%

and declaring twice as often as other computer players.

Diplomatic Strategy

Although winning a game of *Master of Magic* is seldom a diplomatic matter (it is more often a game of warfare, backed by magic and research), it is good to know who your friends are. To that end, pop open the Magic Summary screen every few turns. (As a suggestion, check this screen, say, every turn that a new building is completed somewhere in your empire or every time you discover a new spell. Pick some periodic occurrence like that to remind you to go in there and see who is doing what with whom.) Every time you open this screen, observe the treaty icons to the right of each opponent and right-click on all of the other wizards and keep an eye on their fame, mana, and gold reserves. Always make decisions of war and peace based on the most current information available.

Matters of War and Peace

Avoid wars with players whom you cannot beat relatively quickly. If your advantage is slight, a long and protracted war could leave you victorious but bled dry and well behind the other players who have been able to peacefully expand. It is better to cut your losses early

and prepare yourself for a swift, victorious campaign at a time of your choosing.

When you find yourself in a war without rosy prospects, don't be ashamed to kowtow and make peace if you can. Now, this might be difficult if the enemy is Ruthless or Maniacal. If that proves to be the case, try to form a coalition of wizards to join you in a crusade against your enemy (which shouldn't be too hard if she has an unsavory personality or objective). With enough of her empire under attack, your chances to get ahead in the war and either successfully sue for peace or eliminate that player go way up.

Skating Past Cold Shoulders

Whenever you can't deal with one wizard, deal with the others and try to set them against that wizard giving you grief. Basically, if one wizard won't talk to you face-to-face, get another wizard to stick a knife in her back. This should distract an obstinate leader's attention away from you, at least for a while.

Know How Heavy to Tread

Although wars can often begin by accident through uncontrolled circumstances, they, and the Peace Treaties that end them, are usually the products of skillful engineering on someone's part. You must learn to be that someone. Tread heavily around those whom you would provoke into declaring war on you. Kill their garrisons at nodes and Towers of Wizardry, move next to their cities, and threaten to attack them. It won't be long before you have provoked them into declaring war on you.

Always tread lightly, though, when you consider violating a treaty and breaking your oath. The negative modifiers the violation presents are permanent and can often leave you diplomatically crippled, perhaps even isolated during the later stages of a game. Do all you can to avoid upsetting someone whom you're trying to court into a treaty. Improving your relations with a wizard can be a slow process, but carefully nurtured good relations can all too easily drop like a stone if you tread heavily. When you need something from a computer player, approach her slowly and carefully, and walk on eggshells every step of the way.

Exchanging Spells

These deals must always be considered on the merits of the individual spells being exchanged. While you will always come out behind on these deals on a straight research cost basis, you might find a key piece of magic that you need among another wizard's offerings.

Note that if you have a wonderful new spell that every other player wants to trade for, you may want to trade it to them—*all of them!* In this way, you will get multiple spells back for trading away the same spell (to multiple players), whereas trading this spell with only one other player would leave you at a disadvantage. When you can trade that same spell two, three, or more times to different players, you come out way ahead on the deal! Usually, however, this can only be done if you're the first to discover a good Arcane spell such as

Awareness, Create Artifact, Disjunction, Summon Champion, or even the Spell of Mastery.

In fact, one good way to bring another wizard down is to give her the Spell of Mastery, if you have it. Naturally, she will cast it and earn every other player's enmity in the process. Not only should this help you get other computer players off your back while they gang up on the wizard you just traded the Spell of Mastery to, but you can even join in the crusade against her and pick up a few pieces of her besieged empire (hehehe).

Offering Tribute

When you want a treaty with another player badly enough, some major kissing up, by way of tribute, might be in order. Generally, you should always give another wizard a relatively harmless spell if you can, at least for the first six times you offer tribute. This will maximize your positive Core Reaction's permanent modifier with that wizard. After those first six spell tributes, you are still likely to earn more positive Diplomacy Points by offering spell bribes rather than cash, and spell tribute offsets accumulated Oath Breaker penalties, too. Remember, you cannot raise your DPs above -35 while at war with a player, no matter how frequent or generous your tribute!

Turning Our Backs On Diplomacy [Insert Knife Here]

By monitoring the computer networks, we've heard many players complain that they didn't understand why a computer player did this or that or reacted in some seemingly illogical way. If you have carefully examined all of the elements in this chapter, other wizard's actions should make a lot more sense now.

Also, we've noted those who've complained about Chaotic leaders. Chaotic leaders have their own problems, since they are seldom able to keep allies for long periods of time and often find themselves fighting in war after war. In other words, they have trouble sticking to a long-term strategy. If you don't like them, we urge you to mark them for extinction and take them out of the game first, or hit the [Alt]-[P] key until you have none left in the game. We think Chaotic leaders are quite realistic and have noted many diplomatic maneuvers on human players' parts that made Chaotic leaders look like Ghandi.

Finally, one diplomatic option that you might be looking for, but won't find, is excluded from the game. That would be the "Broker a Peace" option. You would want to use this between two other warring wizards so your ally (who is one of them) doesn't drag you into her stupid little private war that you don't want to fight.

All Politics Aside

And that, dear innocent gamer, is a concise look at the complex diplomatic web that is spun in every game of *Master of Magic*. Hopefully, you now appreciate the strengths and limitations of diplomacy, and recognize it as another tool for victory. By learning the dirty details of Diplomacy Points, oath breaking, and how various game play aspects affect diplomatic relations, you should be better able to deal with those artificial opponents who challenge you.

The diplomatic machinations in *Master of Magic* are meant to be easy for you to interact with; they were designed to be logical and challenging to compete against. They were *not* meant to be taught to you, as we have just done. This was a complicated subject, and we hope we explained it clearly, carefully, and thoroughly.

From here, our next global consideration is random events. While you do not have to suffer them, they make the game a bit more interesting, particularly with the occasional lasting events such as Good and Bad Moons, Population Booms, and Mana Shorts. For all the logic in what's random, turn the page.

26

Random Events

There are three categories of random events. The first is when opportunity knocks in the form of mercenaries, heroes, or merchants bearing items. These were all thoroughly covered in Chapter 4 and won't be discussed here.

The second type of random event is the creation of raiders from neutral cities, and rampaging monsters from unconquered nodes and lairs. Finally, of course, there are the game's actual random events. These latter two categories are the subject of this chapter. Excrement happens, and we're here to help you sort it all out.

Random Events

Although they can be switched off using the Game Settings menu, most people prefer to play with random events on. Brace yourself for a whirlwind explanation of everything there is to know about random events.

Frequency

When the event clock is set to zero (as it is at the start of the game) there is approximately a one percent chance that an event will occur that turn (actually this ranges from 0.6 percent at the Intro difficulty level to 1.2 percent at the Impossible level, but figure around one percent). Each turn, the percentage of a random event occurring increases between 0.1 percent to 0.2 percent (again, depending on the difficulty level). The median length of time between random events is shown in Table 26.1. (I.e., half of all random events will occur before that number of turns have passed, half will occur afterward. Most are likely to occur around that number of turns, however.)

After a random event occurs, the event clock shuts off for five turns. It starts up again, reset to zero, on the sixth turn after the last random event occurred.

Event Determination

Whenever a random event occurs, the computer selects from the entire list of events in the game. Thus, the same event can occur several times in a row.

Some events will be excluded due to a conflict, for example, if the event is already occurring. Also, certain ongoing events cannot occur simultaneously (Good Moon, Bad Moon, the Red, Green, and Blue Conjunctions, and Mana Short). Note that a Meteor Storm or Diplomatic Marriage cannot occur before turn 150 (i.e., June of 1412 on the game's calendar as found through the Historian).

Deciding On the Victim

The recipient of an event is based upon a proportionally weighted scale. This scale is the same one as shown by the Astrologer, combining magic power, spell research, and army strength.

To determine who is hit by a bad event, all players put a number of lotto balls in a fish bowl equal to the value shown by the Astrologer and one is pulled out. Thus, the mightier players have a proportionally greater chance of getting slapped. For a good event, an opposite procedure is used so that the weakest player is likely to be blessed by it.

When a city must be selected for a particular event (Plague, Earthquake, New Minerals, etc.), it is chosen randomly with one caveat: the computer must select a city whose racial unrest difference is no greater than one (see Table 15.2). Thus, only cities whose race "gets along" with your primary race are considered.

Random Event Listings

The following is our examination of what is *really* happening when a particular random event occurs. Brace yourself....

Table 26.1 *Median Time Between Random Events*

Difficulty Level	Median Number of Turns Between Random Event Occurrences
Intro	46
Easy	40
Normal	38
Hard	36
Impossible	33

Bad Moon

A Bad Moon doubles the mana produced from the shrines, temples, parthenons, and cathedrals of wizards with at least one Death spell book. This doubling occurs *after* the effects of Infernal Power and Dark Rituals have been applied. It also halves the mana produced (rounded up) from these same institutions belonging to wizards with at least one Life spell book.

This event lasts a minimum of five turns. On the sixth turn, there is a 10 percent chance it will end, increasing by +5 percent per turn thereafter. Thus, the minimum duration for this event is five turns, the maximum is 23 turns, and the average duration is nine turns.

Conjunction

Each of the Red, Green, or Blue Conjunctions doubles the mana produced from the appropriate colored nodes while halving the mana produced from the other two colors' nodes (each color is totaled and then rounded down). The duration of these events is the same as for a Bad Moon, above.

Depletion

This bad event will cause a random city within a player's empire to immediately lose one of its nearby mineral deposits. Note that quork and crysx crystals cannot be depleted by this event.

Diplomatic Marriage

Again, this good event can't occur before turn 150. One random neutral city, if one is available, will join the lucky player, provided the interracial tension between your primary race and the neutral city's race is less than one (see Table 15.2).

Disjunction

If there are any global enchantments currently in effect, this event immediately shuts them all off.

Donation

This good event immediately provides the giftee a random amount of gold between 105 and 600.

Figure 26-1. *The gods will smile on you on occasion.*

Earthquake

This bad event has the same effect on the victim's randomly selected city as an Earthquake spell. Each building stands a 15 percent chance of being destroyed, while all units, except those that are non-corporeal or flying, have a 25 percent chance of dying. Note that Earthquakes *can* hit your Enchanted Fortress city.

The Gift

This good event bestows a random item from the full list of all 250 items (with no limit to its value!) to the giftee.

Good Moon

This is the opposite of Bad Moon, above. Wizards with Life spell books receive the benefit, while wizards with Death spell books receive the penalty.

Great Meteor

This bit of bad news hits a random city in the victim's empire like a Call the Void spell. Every building in that city has a 50 percent chance of being destroyed and every unit immediately suffers 10 hits with no defense or resistance.

Mana Short

All sources of magical power cease to provide mana while this event is in effect. Note that you'll still receive research points from your libraries, etc. Also, heroes will still have their spell skills to support you in battle. A Mana Short lasts as long as Bad Moons do (see above).

This particular random event requires some strategy to cope with. When a Mana Short occurs, check your mana reserve. Remember, you're still obligated to complete any spells you're in the middle of casting and pay the upkeep on useful enchantments and fantastic creatures. Beyond this, you'll want mana in your reserve to support your troops in combat.

Remember, the average length of a Mana Short is nine turns. If it doesn't look like you have enough mana in your reserves to make it through at least a dozen turns, start shutting down various enchantments and dismissing fantastic units. You will simply have to keep your fixed mana expenses in line if you're to retain a proper reserve for battles during a Mana Short.

New Minerals

This bit of good news provides the recipient's city with a new mineral deposit. (A bug in some versions of the game mentions one city as receiving this event, when it has actually occurred at a different city belonging to that same player.) There is a 25 percent chance the city will receive a coal deposit and a 75 percent chance that one of the following deposits (selected at random) will be chosen instead: gold, gems, mithril, or (even if the city is on Arcanus!) adamantium.

Piracy

The bad news for the recipient is that a random amount between 30 percent and 50 per-

Figure 26-2. *A Mana Short always seems to happen at the worst possible time.*

Table 26.2 Raider Generation Table

Difficulty Level	Average Frequency	Raider Count*
Intro	30 turns	1
Easy	20 turns	1
Normal	15 turns	3
Hard	12.5 turns	4
Impossible	10 turns	6

*This value is halved, then rounded down for a raider force appearing on Myrror before turn 200.

cent of the recipient's gold is taken. Piracy won't happen to a player who has less than 100 gold in his or her reserve.

Plague

This is another bad event that will hit a player's city (exception: a city with a population boom is immune to plagues). It works like the black spell Pestilence (see Chapter 9).

A plague lasts a minimum of five turns. Beginning with the sixth turn, and each turn thereafter, there is a 5 percent chance of the plague ending (which means plagues can last a *long* time!). However, a plague ends automatically when a city's population reaches two population points. Note that a plague stops before it ever starts if it hits a city that has only one population point.

Population Boom

This happy event doubles the population growth in the city it affects each turn. Note that a city with plague will not be selected for a population boom.

Like a plague, a population boom lasts a minimum of five turns. Beginning with the sixth turn, and each turn thereafter, there is a 5 percent chance of it ending.

Rebellion

Only three types of cities can't rebel: those with an Enchanted Fortress, those where the fan-

tastic creatures outnumber the normal units at that city, and those where a hero is located. Otherwise, a city that rebels becomes neutral, its fantastic creatures disband, and all its normal units become its neutral garrison troops.

Raiders and Rampaging Monsters

When, where, and how many raiders and rampaging monsters appear is trickier to explain, but we'll give it a lash. Note that the game difficulty level affects both the frequency and strength of these roaming units.

Raiders

Raiders are generated by a neutral city on the same continent (group of contiguous land squares) as a non-neutral city. When a raider is generated, it appears at a randomly selected, qualifying neutral city. Table 26.2 provides more information about raiders.

Raider groups are formed primarily by the computer cloning units in the espousing neutral city, rather than stripping them from its garrison. Only one unit in three is actually removed from the garrison, thus reducing its size, when a raider force is formed. The experience level of these raiders is game-turn dependent and is shown in Table 26.3.

The Raider Count column from Table 26.2 refers to the maximum number of units that can appear in the raider's stack. If any player's

Table 26.3 *Raider Experience Levels*

Game Turn	Experience Level
1 to 40	recruits
41 to 120	regulars
121 to 250	veterans
251+	elite

Enchanted Fortress is on the same continent, the number of units in the raider force generates will be decreased by one-third.

The actual number of raider units created is:

Units in City x Game Difficulty / 6 (with a minimum of 1 unit)

Game Difficulty = 0 at the Intro level, 1 at the Easy level, 2 at Normal, 3 at Hard, and 4 at Impossible.

Rampaging Monsters

Rampaging monsters are generated by unconquered lairs and nodes on the same continent (group of contiguous land squares) as a non-neutral city. When a rampaging monster group is generated, it appears at a randomly selected, qualifying site. (Exception: a lair with Life creatures for its garrison *never* generates rampaging monsters!) Table 26.4 provides more information about rampaging monsters.

The earliest that rampaging monsters will appear is turn 50 (and a group of them is *always* generated on turn 50, guaranteed). The color of the creatures generated will be the same color as the garrison of that node or lair (again, Life creatures never rampage).

If the lair generating a group of rampaging monsters is on the same continent as any player's Enchanted Fortress, the strength of that group is halved. Note that if *your* Enchanted Fortress is on Myrror, rampaging

monsters will have a slightly greater tendency to appear on Myrror.

The actual strength of a group of rampaging monsters is based on the computer determining an amount of mana to spend on creatures of the appropriate color and then shopping for them (randomly, through the list of every monster in that color it can afford to purchase within its remaining budget, one unit at a time) until it has less than 25 mana to buy more (or until it has generated a full stack of nine rampaging monsters). The amount of mana spent on rampaging monsters is shown in Table 26.5.

Selected Advice

Although most of these events are of the pie-in-the-face variety (hitting you out of the blue while the computer, we suspect, laughs), they do provide a play balance element in *Master of Magic*. After all, the mighty tend to get the bad news while the weak tend to enjoy the occasional boost from good events. As for raiders and rampaging monsters, they're much less discriminating. Just be glad when they're your neighbor's problem and not your own.

Next, we take a relaxing step back to review a few early game strategies. These will refresh your memory of some of the important points for early game play and help you teach others how to get ramped up for a good game of *Master of Magic*.

Table 26.4 *Rampaging Monster Generation Table*

Difficulty Level	Average Frequency
Intro	50 turns
Easy	33 turns
Normal	25 turns
Hard	20 turns
Impossible	17 turns

Table 26.5 *Rampaging Monster Strength*

The formula used to create the amount of mana spent buying a group of rampaging monsters is:

Turn # x (Random Game Difficulty + 1) + (Random Game Difficulty + 1) / 5

Random Game Difficulty is a randomly generated number from zero to x, depending on the difficulty level of the game (x = zero for Intro, one for Easy, etc., through four for impossible).

In practical terms, this mana shopping budget can more easily be seen as a range of numbers based on the current game turn. Notice the pattern:

Turn	Difficulty Level: Intro	Easy	Normal	Hard	Impossible
50	20	20 to 40	20 to 60	20 to 80	20 to 100
100	40	40 to 80	40 to 120	40 to 160	40 to 200
150	60	60 to 120	60 to 180	60 to 240	60 to 300
200	80	80 to 160	80 to 240	80 to 320	80 to 400

27 Early Strategies

As stated in Chapter 1, the authors assume that the reader is already familiar with Master of Magic. It follows as a fair assumption on our part, therefore, that you've already developed some good opening strategies on your own. However, it is often helpful to compare notes and see what other players are doing. Also, when teaching *Master of Magic* to others, it is good to have a few organized thoughts on the subject of early empire building. To fulfill both of these needs, we present this chapter.

Pre-Game Spell Selections

Although we've already covered most aspects of pre-game decisions (Chapters 4 to 6), there is one area left unexamined. Before the game begins, you get to pick a certain number of spells that will be in your spell book (along with Magic Spirit and Spell of Return, which all players start with). Generally, these will be common spells. Here are our tips on good common spell picks to make at the beginning:

Life Magic

We would pick Healing first and Just Cause second. The former will keep your units alive during desperate battles, while the latter will

Figure 27-1. *Picking guaranteed spells at the beginning of the game.*

ease your gold worries and can bring you heroes and mercenaries more often during the crucial early game turns. Our third choice would be either Endurance or Holy Armor. The extra movement granted to a unit by the former or the +2 shields granted to a unit by the latter can greatly enhance the abilities of units commonly built during the early stages of a game.

Death Magic

Our first two choices would be Black Sleep and Skeletons. The former is useful for neutralizing enemy units in battle while the latter can be used to generate a fast, cheap, expendable army in no time flat — thus getting you off to a flying start (once you have some mana income to speak of). Our third choice would be Dark Rituals, although we're cautious about casting it until a city has grown quite a bit (since it slows population growth). Still, the double mana income from religious institutions, particularly early in the game, can significantly increase your mana income.

Chaos Magic

In red magic, we believe in getting the Fire Elemental and Eldritch Weapon spells out of the gate. The former is a pretty decent unit that can only be summoned on the battlefield, while the latter makes an enemy unit's defenses worse against friendly units enchanted by this spell. For our tertiary selection, we would opt for either Hell Hounds or Shatter. The former is a reasonably cheap unit to summon that can attack flying creatures (due to its fiery breath); the latter spell reduces an enemy unit's attack strength to one in combat.

Nature Magic

Our first two picks would be Web and Earth Lore. The former is a damn useful combat spell that holds weak units for a long period of time and grounds flying creatures for the duration of a battle, while the latter will help you discover the map in record time. After that, Alan and Petra opt for either Earth to Mud or Water Walking. The former creates an obstacle on the battlefield that a cunning warrior can exploit in combat, while the latter can enchant your key units (like heroes and settlers) and get them across the water to more easily expand your empire's reach (which is particularly useful before your ship building begins). Tom's favorites after Web are Stone Skin and Giant Strength because he enjoys having the best possible troops on the battlefield.

Sorcery Magic

Our first picks among the blue common spells would be Phantom Warriors and Confusion. The former is a cheap, hard-hitting (but quick dying) unit that you can summon in battle, while the latter spell can cause the enemy more than a little grief in combat. After those, Counter Magic, Floating Island, and Guardian Wind are all good selections. Counter Magic will squash an enemy's spells in combat before they're cast, while Guardian Wind will give a unit immunity from missile attacks. A Floating Island is useful for sending stacks of units across the oceans and is of particular value when massing up to attack an island node.

Developing Cities

You should try to develop at least one city per race to its limit. This way, you can select from all possible unit types to build there and receive the maximum benefits that the race has to offer. You must be more careful when developing other cities of that race. Not every city will show a profit in gold (see Chapter 15). Often, you'll have to either develop cities in a way that maximizes your gold income or assign cities that generate a lot of production points to the task of making trade goods just to keep a positive cash flow.

What Buildings to Construct First

There are many schools of thought on this subject and several variations among common themes. We prefer to maximize urban growth rates as our top priority, pausing only to make sure that a new city is adequately garrisoned (see below). Therefore, we opt for the builder's hall, granary, smithy, marketplace, farmer's market path at every new city. Once those buildings are in place, that city will have a healthy cash flow and a rapidly growing population. From there, examine your needs carefully before constructing the next building at that city.

Note, rather than constructing a new building at this point in a city's development, seriously consider switching that city's production to housing for a while. It can, at this point, add a new population point every four turns or so.

New City Garrisons

Whenever possible, we try to create new city garrisons at old, established cities and then march them over. That way, the troops are raised faster and may have a rank or two of experience when they are created, thus providing better quality units (and for the same cost as recruits, too!).

We also settle for spearmen as city garrisons during the early part of a game when upkeep costs are a major concern (they only eat food and require no gold for upkeep). After gold income ceases to be a problem, we upgrade our garrisons with better units (while still mindful of cash flow).

How many units should be in a city garrison? As a rule of thumb, keep at least two units when playing at the Intro, Easy, or Average difficulty levels, four units at Hard, and six at Impossible. Note that these are all pairs of normal units, since each pair provides the added advantage of suppressing one rioter.

Early Exploration

Actually, this subject was very thoroughly covered in Chapter 14. To recap: explore using Earth Lore whenever possible; send ships to outline the world's continents. Magic spirits make good exploration units early on because they are cheap and can cross water without ships. Be sure to quickly explore the continent that you start on!

Early Colonizing

Don't wait too long before creating your first colonist and founding a second city. Although they're none too bright about trans-oceanic and trans-planar colonizing, computer players will fill their starting continent with new cities in a flash. If you don't want to fall too far behind in the early empire building race, you'd better be colonizing aggressively, too.

Remember to escort your settlers with a pair of spearmen at least. This will help discourage raiders and rampaging monsters both before and after a settler converts to an outpost.

Tip: If another player's settler is found close to your (self-proclaimed) territory, shadow it closely with some of your troops. This will keep it from becoming an outpost and settling where you don't want it to.

Engineering

Build an engineer early, if you can. Use it to connect your empire's cities together by roads. This greatly facilitates the cities' mutual defense and even improves their gold production through increased trade.

Whatever Floats Your Boats

Overseas empires mandate a fleet. If you're playing with small land masses, an early ship or two is a necessity. A fleet can be used to deny the enemy easy access to your islands and will gain you an offensive posture plus superior exploration potential. Never underestimate the value of a good fleet.

Iron and Coal, You Dig?

Find a good city site that encompasses as many iron and coal resources as possible. This will be your soldier factory, so found a city on this site as early as you can and build up every unit type and experience improvement building (fighter's guild, war college) there that you can. After that, the new unit purchase discounts afforded that city by these iron and coal resources will keep you in armies for the rest of the game.

Your First "Killer" Army

Generally, you should build your first killer stack around the first hero(es) you can afford to hire. Back them up with a tall pile of whatever other units you can afford and use that stack to pry open whatever you can find. Just be sure to save the game before every battle so that, if things don't go the way you like, you can reload the game and not repeat your mistake the next time.

Early Targets of Opportunity

Poke your nose into every lair you discover (see figures 27-2 and 27-3). It might be unoccupied and provide you with some free gold or mana crystals (both of which are vitally

Figure 27-2. *Be sure to peek into every lair you can.*

important during the early stages of the game). You may even discover a weak neighboring city that you can easily pick off. Do so, particularly if the city is neutral. Rapidly adding another city to your empire (especially if it's of a different race) is a great boon to your early growth efforts.

Early Conquest Priorities

Because captured nodes are a constant, valuable source of mana, you should try to capture at least a few of them as an early priority. It's very important to establish as large of a mana income as possible early in the game. Most of what mana provides will come to you in the long term, so start planning your mana income future as early as possible.

Early Spell Research

When in doubt, always pick the fastest spell that you can research (i.e., the one in the upper-left hand corner of your research pages). Know that combat spells, however, are better to research early, as they'll help you conquer lairs, nodes, and towns sooner. Finally, remember that you can't research a higher level spell in any color until all lower level spells in that color have been either re-

search or exposed in your Research Book. (For example, you can't research an uncommon Life spell until all of the common Life spells have either been researched or are already listed in the Research pages of your Spell Book.)

The End of The Beginning and The Beginning of The End

Basically, the early stage of a game ends either when you have a Tower of Wizardry and are exploring the other world or when you have no real prospects for peaceful growth on the world where you started. At that point, batten down the hatches and move to your tough, game-winning play and strategies (like those we've taught you in previous chapters).

In the next chapter, we've put together the assorted items that were left on the cutting room floor. These are assembled in our traditional Odds & Ends chapter, which is always filled with interesting miscellany. Beyond that lie the appendices, stretching out before you like the showrooms of tabular information that they are.

Figure 27-3. You can sometimes even find spells in empty lairs!

Odds & Ends

After the banquet of information provided in this book, you certainly need a laxative. This chapter provides all of the little nuggets of information we found for this tome that did not fit neatly elsewhere. Rather than discard what was left on the print shop floor, we've swept them here for your final inspection.

Comprehensive Game Difficulty Analysis

When you choose a difficulty level to play, exactly what changes? In table 28-1, we have summarized the differences.

Computer Player Habits

The following sections offer a quick peek into the computer players' brains. Considering the lamentable state of the AI in *Master of Magic*'s early releases, we use the word "brains" loosely here.

Computer Players Spells

Have you ever wondered how computer players are paying for all of their enchantments and fantastic units? Especially when you take a look at their profiles and see their miniscule quantities of mana and gold? Well, computer players are big on using alchemy to convert gold into mana to pay their steep upkeep costs. This makes them easier to deal with in battles, since they often don't have enough mana to pay for brutal combat spells.

When computer players start running low on mana, they will disband fantastic units and enchantments. However, those nasty global enchantments are last on their list of things to eliminate. So don't expect those Meteor Storms or Great Wasting spells to disappear any time soon, even when you're putting the hurt on your enemies' mana supplies.

Note that computer players really like summoning spells. They like them so much, in fact, that it is futile for you to Spell Blast them. They'll just turn around and cast more. In addition, they place a high priority on researching Summon Hero and casting it repeatedly once learned. This is one reason why computer players always seem to have an early and full complement of heroes in the game.

Computer Players Cheat

There are several ways that computer players cheat. First, they always know the strength of lairs without entering them (Appendix C). This may be one reason you will see so many unexplored lairs within their territories. They do not seem to place a high priority on grabbing free loot from lairs (you can usually wander around and grab such loot before the computer players even consider doing so).

Computer players also have an advantage at the higher game settings, both economically and diplomatically. In general, computer players receive extra income of all types (mana, gold, production, etc.) and are far more forgiving of each other than they are of you. (See Chapter 25 for more information on diplomacy between your foes.)

Interestingly, there is a reverse cheat in *Master of Magic*, as well. Only you, the human player, get any fame bonuses from killing very rare fantastic creatures (Chapter 4). Since you also have the extra cheat of being able to save and reload games, you can moderate the number of fame points you earn or lose in battles. This is why, with cunning play, you will generally see your fame level far surpass that of computer opponents.

Computer Players in Combat

Compared to your intelligent strategies and tactics, computer players' forces rarely exhibit much in the way of combat intelligence (artificial or otherwise). First, they tend to be really reluctant to attack your weaker cities or units. And while they place a high priority on stealing your nodes, they seldom go after unconquered nodes on their own.

Table 28.1 *Game Difficulty Summary*

Area Affected	Difficulty Level				
	Intro.	Easy	Normal	Hard	Impossible
Initial spell/skill picks for CPs (Ch 25)	11	11	11	13	15
CPs must select from limited starting races?*	No	No	No	Yes	Yes
1 or 2 CPs must start on Myrror?	No	No	No	Yes	Yes
You can create a custom wizard?	No	Yes	Yes	Yes	Yes
CP Population/Outpost Growth Rate	100%	100%	150%	200%	300%
CP Production Points, Gold, Food, and Mana Producion	50%	100%	150%	200%	250%
CP Spell Research Multiple**	100%	100%	100%	110%	125%
CP Upkeep Discount Multiplier	100%	90%	75%	60%	50%
CP Negative Diplomacy Softener (Ch 25)	N/A	N/A	N/A	-25%	-50%
Your Hero's fleeing success	100%	100%	75%	75%	75%
Median Time between Random Event occurrences	46	40	38	36	33
Maximum number of CPs that will declare war against you concurrently (without a casus belli)	1	2	3	4	4
End Game Victory Point Multiplier	.5	.75	1.0	2.0	3.0

CP = Computer Player

*Only Halflings, High Elves, High Men, Klackons, or Nomads can be chosen when starting on Arcanus.

**Multiplies the adjusted total amount produced on a per city basis, rounded down.

Furthermore, if you attack one of their walled cities, they will rarely leave those walls, even when it's to their advantage to do so. As you know (or will find out), a big advantage to moving from city squares is that your buildings and citizens won't get squashed by the stomping boots of enemy units when a town's defenders are overrun.

The computer players, when controlling heroes in combat, tend to expend their mana on relatively useless spells instead of diverting it to launch lethal ranged attacks or to cast worthwhile combat spells.

Enemy units on the battlefield tend to target units they can kill in the shortest number of attacks (i.e., your least durable units). Furthermore, if they are attacking one of your cities and they can't target your units (if you have flying units and they don't, for instance), they will march straight for your city squares, to stomp on them mercilessly (thus increasing the post-combat damage assessment to the city) until combat ends.

When you're in battle against enemy units, you will find it almost hopelessly easy to confuse them. If you can move your units so that they equidistantly flank enemy troops, the enemy units will frequently not move at all.

Their indecisiveness can save your armies many times over when used properly. Additionly, spells like Earth to Mud frequently send enemy units scurrying to get out of mud patches or to move around them, when it would be more profitable for them to move directly toward your units.

Drawing Comparisons

The Astrologer and Historian functions both provide a measure of how your wizard compares to every other wizard that you've met. In the sections below, we take a look at how the game determines a wizard's power.

Astrologically Speaking

Have you ever wondered what exactly the Astrologer graphs are measuring? Table 28.2 answers that question.

Historian

The Historian shows a graph of total wizard power over game time. The value shown on the graph is the sum of Magic Power, Army Strength, and Spell Research for each wizard (Table 28.2).

Special Keys

There are a few keys that you might like know about if you play *Master of Magic* a lot (as we have):

🐾 Pressing [Alt]-P in the Main Movement screen scrambles computer player personalities. This is a good way for you to weed out wizards with Chaotic or Maniacal tendencies.

🐾 [F10] is an auto-save key. When you hit this button and leave the game, you can resume right where you left off by choosing the Continue option when you enter *Master of Magic*.

Figure 28-1. *How do you measure up to your opponents? Ask your Astrologer.*

Table 28.2 *The Astrologer*

The Astrologer's Scale has three components:

1) Spell Research = Sum of Spell Rankings for all learned spells / 8

Spell Rankings range from 1 to 40, from the spells with the lowest research costs (20 research points) to the highest (6,000 research points). Arcane spells only get ranked on a scale from 1 to 13, also in order of their research costs.

2) Army Strength = total gold maintenance costs for units + double the total mana maintenance costs for all fantastic units

3) Magic Power = total mana income - 10

Magic Power for the Computer Player = Magic Power x Game Difficulty Multiplier

Note that the magic power your opponents actually receive per game turn is what you see on this Astrologer's graph! The Game Difficulty Multiplier at the different difficulty settings is shown below.

Difficulty Setting	Game Difficulty Multiplier
Intro	.5
Easy	1.0
Normal	1.5
Hard	2.0
Impossible	2.5

Exterminator Specials

Below we've included some inconsistencies and other things that haven't been working correctly in earlier versions of *Master of Magic*. We can't promise that all of these will be fixed in version 1.3 (but we're hoping).

☙ Corruption does not seem to eliminate food production from affected terrain. This is why your enemies don't seem to suffer as much as they should when you corrupt all of the land around their cities.

☙ Volcanoes are supposed to revert to mountains with a 2 percent chance of doing so per game turn (and when they do, there is a 5 percent chance that they'll have some kind of minerals). So far they aren't doing this.

☙ When computer players are banished, even though they start casting the Spell of Return, they haven't been returning. We suspect this is due to their obstinate refusal to disband their expensive units and enchantments. This particular problem should be fixed in 1.3.

☙ Casting the Spell of Mastery doesn't actually seem to excite any of your enemies. At least they don't act aggressively to crush you into submission once you've cast this spell.

☙ An additional three shields are given to all units defending a city (on top of the bonus provided by city walls)! This problem should be crushed, but in case it isn't, the extra shields may explain why it is so difficult to kill enemy spearmen who garrison a city.

🐌 When you attack enemy or neutral cities, the units rarely leave the city. This should have been fixed. At least, the units should leave when you cast evil combat enchantments like Magic Vortex and Call Lightning.

🐌 Armageddon and Great Wasting were raising enormous quantities of rebels in the caster's cities! This should definitely be fixed in version 1.3.

🐌 In pre-1.3 versions of *Master of Magic*, a unit with an immunity to a special attack, was immune to all other attacks made by a unit that had that special attack. For example, ghouls have Death magic immunity. Ghouls could not be hit by death knights because they were immune to the death knights' life-stealing attacks. In later versions of the game, ghouls should be damaged by the death knights' normal melee attacks, although they will still be immune to the life-stealing attack.

🐌 In pre-1.3 versions of the game, magic immunity also protected units from all attacks by all fantastic creatures! That's what made paladins such awesome units.

🐌 Although we haven't gotten any confirmation on this, the spell Subversion does not seem to have the diplomatic repercussions it should. We never saw any effects from casting this spell, even when we cast it 10 or 15 times in a row on the same wizard.

🐌 Fleeing Trolls or other regenerating units do not get their full hit points back. Technically, this is because fleeing equals losing in the game's programming. And losing units don't get healed.

🐌 The Resource window in the City screen has a number of truncation errors. This window gives you a complete breakdown of what each building and terrain feature is doing for your city's resources. The good news is that this means you're usually earning a few more

mana, gold, and production points than you think you are.

🐌 The Surveyor button contains a certain amount of misinformation. To find out what terrain squares actually offer a new city in terms of food, gold, mana, production, etc., see Chapter 14.

🐌 Gaia's Blessing no longer raises the potential maximum city size above 25.

🐌 Units with Black Sleep occasionally move around in earlier versions of the game.

🐌 The guaranteed spell choices you get at the beginning of the game have not, in earlier versions, given you the same spells you asked for.

🐌 Djinns in earlier versions of the game don't have wind walking, although they're supposed to.

MOM

Finally, *Master of Magic* is frequently known by its loving acronym, "MOM."

Afterword

As we prepare to collapse in exhaustion after writing this 175,000 word tome (a word count equal to two or three normal computer game strategy guides), let us assess the damage to our lives with you. Petra put in roughly 715 hours writing this book, in addition to the 155 hours she spent writing the game's manual and spell book. Alan spent about 200 hours pounding keys for your reading pleasure, while Tom seems to have logged about 370 hours fact-finding and checking (source code in hand) and cranking out a few particularly juicy tables.

Beyond these hundreds of man hours spent composing the material for this book, hundreds more were spent playing MOM, notepads at the ready. Of course, SimTex suffered at least another couple of hundred hours of phone calls with niggling questions and suggestions for patches. All told, there are probably over 1,700 man hours invested in this book that you hold in your hands. It might not be perfect, but it's as close as we could get, and believe us, we tried.

As we put the last words in the processor, version 1.3 of the game has yet to be released. It is supposed to ratchet up the computer player's aggressiveness so that they present more of a challenge to beat. In that case, you should find this book that much more useful. Until the last spell is cast or the last Enchanted Fortress is captured, then, remember what we taught you.

Appendices

A
The Next Turn
Sequence of Play

After you hit the Next Turn button, the computer goes through a certain, pre set order of events. It might help you to know when these events occur in this, the *Sequence of Play*. They are listed in order below, with each computer player taking its turn in order, beginning with the one occupying the left-most gem on your Magic display screen.

I. Computer Players Prepare

A. Check to see if the player is under any *Peace Treaties* with any other players (see Chapter 25) and plan its turn accordingly if it is.

B. Assign a power value to each continent (contiguous land mass) for every player with units and cities on that continent.

C. Cast overland spells.

D. Consider troop values and make sure garrisons are either up to snuff or being improved.

F. Adjust mana ratios for wand, research, and skill level.

G. Eliminate any useless global spells.

H. Perform alchemy, if deemed necessary.

I. Adjust cities' production of resources, gold, and food.

J. Selects new buildings to build, if necessary.

K. Plan movement based on each player's need to expand or to press attacks against previously determined objectives, or react to defend from further attack by other players.

II. Neutral Players' Turns

A. Select Neutral Player new building construction, if any.

B. Adjust Neutral Player food production, if necessary.

C. Determine targets and head toward them.

D. Generate raiders and rampaging monsters.

E. Eliminate surplus neutral units (i.e., ones that can no longer be supported by the city that generated them).

F. Attempt to disband their units in stasis.

III. Computer Players Maneuver (in player turn order)

A. Consider hostility toward other players, states of war and peace, treaties; adjust all temporary Diplomacy Point modifiers by 10 points toward 0, etc. (see Chapter 25).

B. Disband unnecessary units.

C. Look for nearby Towers of Wizardry for inter-planar movement.

D. Interrupt previous orders if adjacent to an enemy force, city or node, and attack them if they are particularly weak.

E. Meld with nodes.

F. Attack cities.

G. Attack lairs.

H. Build new cities.

I. Garrison cities.

J. Node attacks.

K. Tower of Wizardry attacks.

L. Centralize armies, assembling efficient forces in a strategic position to react to danger.

M. Build roads.

N. Garrison nodes.

O. Garrison Towers of Wizardry.

P. Purify land.

Q. Explore new continents.

R. Move ships.

S. Pick up ships.

The Making of a Computer Player Wizard

ave you ever met a computer player wizard and wondered how he or she got that way? This appendix will tell you how. Note that the information provided here makes a lot more sense if you're familiar with Chapter 25 (diplomacy).

Wizard Personality Profiles

Each computer player has a distinct personality type. These personalities have a strong influence on most of a computer player's diplomatic decision-making (see Table 25.4), and some have additional quirks, as explained below:

Peaceful

Beyond their extremely high +20 Leader Personality Modifier, there is nothing particularly special about a peaceful leader.

Lawful

Lawful leaders have a mellow +10 Leader Personality Modifier — until you cross them. They take great umbrage at anyone breaking treaties with them, so all Oath Breaker penalties will be doubled when applied to relations with a Lawful leader. In other words, people who break their treaties with a Lawful leader will suffer an immediate -80 Diplomacy Point penalty (wow!) and have a permanent -10 modifier to that player's Core Reactions toward them.

Like Maniacal leaders, Lawful leaders also double all DP losses made on their Diplomatic Relations Scales. These are cumulative with the effects described in Table 25.2, so if you're ever above +50 on a Lawful leader's Diplomatic Relations Scale, any DP loss with that wizard will be quadrupled.

Lawful leaders will never attack someone with whom they currently have a treaty. Instead, they will take a turn to formally break the treaty first.

Chaotic

A Chaotic leader's Personality Modifier is rolled at the beginning of each turn and will be a random number between -40 and +40. Consequently, you never can predict what her mood might be on a given turn until you attempt to parlay with her.

A Chaotic leader has a straight two percent chance each turn that she will just up and declare war — completely out of the blue — on a single, random, contacted player with whom she is not currently at war.

Aggressive

Besides their -10 Leader Personality Modifier, aggressive leaders are twice as likely as other leaders to create settlers and peacefully expand.

Ruthless

Aside from their -30 Leader Personality Modifier, there is nothing special about a ruthless leader.

Maniacal

These wizards are mean. They hate everybody and have a -50 Leader Personality Modifier. Furthermore, they halve any Diplomacy Point gains and double all DP losses made with them. These are cumulative with the effects described in Table 25.2, so that if you're ever above +50 on a Maniacal wizard's Diplomatic Relations Scale, any DP loss will be quadrupled! (Don't ever expect to be popular with these guys.) Maniacal wizards also take almost every opportunity to attack (see below).

A Computer Player's Hostile Mentality

A computer player will randomly reevaluate her relations with all of the other players every 3 to 25 turns. She does so to consider how she will deal with each player until her next reevaluation. Computer players make these reevaluations separately, not necessarily all together on the same turn. Note that you will never see their attitude toward another player spelled out anywhere. This is all behind-the-scenes-programmer-stuff that you'll have to infer from actual game-playing experiences.

There are four increasing levels of aggression that a computer player can have toward another player: None, Annoyed, Warlike, and Jihad (explained below). When a computer player makes this random reevaluation of her hostility toward each player, she begins by resetting her status toward everyone to the lowest level, None.

Deciding Her Attitude

If that computer player is currently at war with another player (i.e., the crossed swords icon is in that player's color on the Magic Summary screen), the None status is immediately changed to Warlike. After this, a check is made to see if her new, Warlike level is increased to Jihad. Maniacal leaders have a 40 percent chance, Ruthless leaders have a 20 percent chance, and Chaotic leaders have a 10 percent chance of taking their formal wars extremely seriously at this time, thus upping their hostility against that player from Warlike to Jihad (at least until the next reevaluation in 3 to 25 turns). While another wizard is casting the Spell of Mastery, all computer players declare war, become Warlike, and have a 75 percent chance of going Jihad.

If that computer player currently has a Wizard's Pact, Alliance, or Peace Treaty in effect, her hostility rating stays at None with that particular wizard. Furthermore, she will conduct herself according to the rules of her agreement with that player.

However, if that computer player is neither in a formal war, nor bound by a formal agreement (Wizard's Pact, Alliance, or Peace Treaty), then things can get interesting. Under these circumstances, the reevaluating wizard receives a Hostility Chance value toward the wizard. This value is determined by one

Hostility Chance Formulae

If the present relations are less than zero between these two wizards:

The Hostility Chance = ([Negative DPs] / 2) + 25 + Leader Personality.

This means half of the absolute value of their negative DPs (rounded down) + 25. For example, if her relations were currently residing at -31 DPs, the absolute value of half of that would be 15.5, rounded down to 15. Adding 25 would give a total of 40. Thus, the Hostility Chance in this example would be 40, plus the evaluating Leader Personality modifier.

If the present relations are one or greater between these two wizards:

The Hostility Chance = ((100 - Positive DPs) / 4) + All Accumulated Oath Breaker Penalties (at +5 per) + Leader Personality

For example, if the relations level of the wizard being reevaluated was currently +73 DPs with the reevaluating wizard, the Hostility Chance would be 100 minus 73, which is 27. That 27 is then divided by 4, with a result of 6.75, which gets truncated to a 6. If the wizard being reevaluated had three outstanding Oath Breaker penalties against the reevaluating wizard, that would add another 15 to the 6, yielding a total Hostility Chance of 21 in this example, plus the evaluating Leader Personality modifier.

of the two formulae above:

Computer players who are neither at war with nor treaty bound to another wizard roll a d100 against their Hostility Chance toward the wizard being evaluated. If the die roll is less than or equal to their Hostility Chance,

Table B.1 *Leader Personality Modifiers for Evaluating Hostility Chances*

Personality Type	Modifier
Peaceful	-20
Lawful	-40*
Chaotic	-40 to +40**
Aggressive	+10
Ruthless	+30
Maniacal	+50

*This becomes a +40 modifier instead if the player being considered has any Oath Breaker penalties in effect with a reevaluating Lawful wizard. Yikes!

**Depending on their current turn's random Leader Personality rating.

her hostility is changed from None to Annoyed and she rolls again. If this second d100 roll also lands within the range of their Hostility Chance, forget Annoyed, the reevaluating wizard has increased her hostility to Warlike, and she rolls again! If this third d100 roll also succeeds, it's Jihad time. Once any of these d100 rolls fails to be less than or equal to her Hostility Chance, they stop rolling (until her next reevaluation period in 3 to 25 turns).

What Their Attitude Means

Of these four states of hostility, None means that the computer player will completely leave the other wizard alone. She won't cast any spells against nor attack that player's units or cities. However, she still considers ungarrisoned nodes and Towers of Wizardry fair game (so be sure to garrison these strategic locations).

A computer player can become Annoyed either as described above or automatically when anything short of taking one of their cities is done to them (i.e., casting a spell against her units or cities, attacking her troops, etc.). This is a sort of tit-for-tat state where she will start throwing spells back against the person she is Annoyed with. She will attack that player's units freely when she thinks she

has the advantage and even attack that player's cities when she figures that her attacking force is at least twice as strong as the city's garrison.

A computer player will adopt a Warlike state if one of her cities is taken or the evaluated wizard is casting the Spell of Mastery (these are both considered acts of war). The wizard committing these acts is considered an Oath Breaker against the player whose city fell (or all the other wizards, in the case of casting the Spell of Mastery) if there was a Wizard's Pact, Alliance, or Peace Treaty existing between them. A computer player's Warlike state is similar to Annoyed, except that she'll take more opportunities to throw hostile spells against her opponent's units and cities and will attack them wherever she can muster roughly even odds. Thus, computer players with a Warlike attitude no longer cautiously wait for an advantage before engaging in combat.

The Jihad state can only be reached in the circumstances described in the preceding section or when considering a player who is casting the Spell of Mastery. In addition to adopting a Warlike attitude against the player she has decided to launch a Jihad against, that computer player also ignores all previous and future wars and Jihads against other players until the current Jihad status changes. A computer player in a state of Jihad will relentlessly attack her enemy (although always looking for roughly equal odds before engaging in battle). She will attack even to the point of mobilizing all of her forces (including most of her garrison troops) to launch as many stacks against the targeted player as possible.

Note that computer players can, technically, cop a Warlike or Jihad attitude without actually being at war against that player. Adopting these attitudes does not cause wizard to declare war immediately. However, you can bet that a formal war will soon occur once troops start to mobilize and battles are fought.

Casus Belli: Why Wizards Declare War

Let us recap what provokes a computer player into declaring war on another wizard:

🐾 One of her cities was captured by that player

🐾 The other player is casting the Spell of Mastery

🐾 She has a Chaotic personality

🐾 She is responding strongly to a diplomatic threat

🐾 She is reacting to the other player having too much strength on her Home Continent

🐾 Her Enchanted Fortress was attacked (without success) by that player

Wizard Objectives

Besides a personality, each wizard has an objective. This determines her guidelines for certain decisions, such as where she focuses her efforts for expansion and research.

Expansionists

When not pressed for living space, expansionists will seize peaceful expansion opportunities twice as readily as most other wizards. They have twice the chance to make settlers and will try to build on every potential city site they can reach, regardless of how few people that city could support or how impoverished it will be.

Militarists

Since militarists tend to build so many troops (they have double the chance of building and summoning new units that other players do), their economy is often strained to support them. Economic warfare against militarists, therefore, is a key to their undoing. Taking their cities (and casting ruinous spells upon the ones you can't take) will often force a militarist to dismiss troops just to keep their economy balanced.

Perfectionist

Leaders with a perfectionist bent are far more likely to throw enchantments that improve their own cities than other types of enhancements. Also, they are only half as likely to develop a new troop unit as they are to construct a new building at a city.

Theurgist

A theurgist loves mana. Therefore, a theurgist will always race to build religious and learning institutes (shrines, libraries, etc.). She is also more likely to attack a node rather than a city objective (unless that city generates considerable amounts of mana/spell research). Interestingly, a wizard's objective is defined after races are selected while the game is being set up, so a theurgist is not more likely to start with a race that creates mana from its population.

Computer Player Preferences

Each computer player has a certain leaning as to her personality type and objective. These are generated after that wizard's spell picks and retorts are selected. Here is how your computer opposition is generated:

Table B.2 Computer Player Modifications

Step 1: Erasure Dice are rolled to determine the number of rolls on the Pick Erasure Table that will be made.

Game Difficulty Level	Erasure Dice Rolled	Notes
Introductory	*none*	*The number and colors of spell books and*
Easy	*none*	*retorts at these two levels never change.*
Normal	1 d3	1 to 3 rolls will be made below
Hard	2 d3	2 to 6 rolls will be made below
Impossible	2 d5	2 to 10 rolls will be made below

Step 2: The result is the number of times that wizard rolls on the table below. If a wizard does not have any spell books of that color or has already rolled All Wizard Skills, that roll is considered 'No Effect' and is not rerolled.

Pick Erasure Die Roll (d6)	Erased Spell Book or Retort
1	Life
2	Death
3	Chaos
4	Nature
5	Sorcery
6	All Wizard Skills

Step 3: After those items are removed, if any, that wizard determines how many total picks she receives according to the table below.

Game Difficulty Level	Total Picks Received
Introductory	11
Easy	11
Normal	11
Hard	13
Impossible	15

First, your opposing wizards are determined randomly. These wizards start out with the same spell books and wizard skills that they would have if you had picked them. If a wizard begins with two different colors of spell books (e.g., Merlin begins with green and white magic), she has a 20 percent chance of having her spell books converted entirely to one of those two colors (each color has an even chance of usurping the other's spell books).

That established, a certain number of spell books or all of that wizard's skills might be randomly erased and new spell books or wizard skills substituted. The number that many

Table B.2 Cont. *Computer Player Modifications*

Step 4: Any unfilled picks are filled by rolling on the table below. Between two and five pick's worth of that result will be added. Additional rolls are made until that wizard has the number of starting picks received, as shown above.

Pick Replacement Die Roll (d7)	2 to 5 Pick's Worth of:
1	Life spell books
2	Death spell books
3	Chaos spell books
4	Nature spell books
5	Sorcery spell books
6	Random Wizard Skills*
7	Random Wizard Skills*

*This could end up giving wizard skills that you would never be entitled to, such as Chaos Mastery when you have no red spell books, or Node Mastery when you don't have at least three different spell book colors. These wizard skills are taken completely at random!

might be lost or added is shown on Table B.2, below.

After their spell books and wizard skills are in place, each wizard's personality and objective is determined according to her primary magic color (i.e., the color she has the most spell books in, with ties resolved in the following preference order: green, blue, red, white, and black—which is how they are listed below). A wizard's personality and objective are also influenced by her starting wizard skills. All this is shown in Table B.3, below.

Think of the numbers in Table B.3 as a number of marked ping-pong balls thrown into a bowl. Each ping-pong ball has the name of its corresponding personality or objective on it. All of the personality ping-pong balls go into one bowl, are mixed together, and one is drawn to determine the wizard's personality. Objectives are handled similarly with their own ping-pong balls drawn from their own bowl. An N/A reference means that result will never happen, despite any wizard skill modifiers.

For example, a wizard has primarily white magic and the retorts of Divine Power and Conjurer. In the personality bowl will go a total of 14 ping-pong balls (one marked "Ruthless," two marked "Aggressive," two for "Lawful," and nine with "Peaceful"—five of these for that wizard's white magic and the other four for having Divine Power). Thus, this wizard's chances are 9 in 14 for being Peaceful, and only 1 in 14 for being Ruthless (and so forth).

In this wizard's objective bowl will go a total of 13 ping-pong balls (five marked "Militarist"—two for having primarily white magic and three more for being a Conjurer, three marked "Theurgist," four for "Perfectionist," and one for "Expansionist"). Consequently, this wizard is likely to be either a Militarist or a Perfectionist (with a 5 in 13 and 4 in 13 chance, respectively), and unlikely to be an Expansionist (with only a 1 in 13 chance).

Table B.3 *Wizard Starting Personality and Objective Probabilities*

Primary Spell Color	Personalities						Objectives			
	Mani	Ruth	Agg	Chao	Law	Peace	Milit	Theur	Perf	Expan
Green	0	1	1	1	5	2	2	2	4	2
Blue	1	2	3	1	2	1	1	4	2	3
Red	1	2	2	5	0	0	3	2	2	3
White	N/A	1	2	0	2	5	2	3	4	1
Black	3	3	2	1	1	N/A	4	1	1	4

Wizard Skills										
Warlord	-	+2	+3	-	-	-	+2	-	-	+3
Chaos Mastery	-	-	-	+3	-	-	-	+1	-	-
Nature Mastery	-	-	-	-	+3	-	-	+1	-	-
Infernal Power	+4	-	-	-	-	-	-	-	-	-
Divine Power	-	-	-	-	-	+4	-	-	-	-
Alchemy	-	-	-	-	-	-	-	-	+2	-
Myrran	-	-	-	-	-	-	-	-	-	+4
Conjurer	-	-	-	-	-	-	+3	-	-	-

Mani = Manicial

Ruth = Ruthless

Agg = Aggressive

Chao = Chaotic

Law = Lawful

Peace = Peaceful

Milit = Militarist

Theur = Theurgist

Perf = Perfectionist

Expan = Expansionist

Special Personality/ Objective scramble key

A special key has been provided in Master of *Magic* that allows you to randomly scramble all of the wizards' personalities and objectives. From the Main Movement screen, press [ALT]-P. The next time you check the other wizards, you'll find they have new personalities and objectives. If you don't like how things came out, exit back to the Main View screen and try it again until you get a group of opponents you can tolerate.

Note that this option is only available in version 1.2 and subsequent versions of *Master of Magic*.

Monsters & Treasure

For the terminally curious, here we explain how monsters and treasures are generated at your local node, lair, or tower. This can get tricky, so grab a caffeinated drink and try to relax while pondering this appendix.

Monsters!

Each lair, node, or Tower of Wizardry can hold a maximum of two different types of creatures and nine total units. When the worlds are created, 25 normal lairs (e.g., Ancient Temples, Ancient Ruins, Fallen Temples, Mysterious Caves, Dungeons, Abandoned Keeps, and Monster Lairs) and 32 weak lairs are randomly distributed between the two planes. There will also be 16 nodes on Arcanus, 14 on Myrror, plus six Towers of Wizardry on corresponding squares of both planes. Chapter 14 offers further details about specific terrain feature placements when the worlds are created.

Stocking Up

Each lair, node, and Tower of Wizardry is also stocked with monsters when the worlds are created. Treasure is generated after the guardian monsters' defeat. (Hint: save the game before conquering these sites and, if you don't like the treasure you receive, restart the game, refight the battle, and keep fishing until you get a satisfactory treasure at the end of it!) The values for these sites' garrisons and treasures are shown in Table C.1, below. Note that treasure ranges are constant except at the Impossible difficulty level.

Creature Budgets

The value range for creatures should be thought of as a mana budget. This is the maximum the computer will spend stocking that site with fantastic units to defend it.

After a random number within the range is determined, it is divided by the result of a d4 die roll. The result becomes that site's budget for buying big monsters.

For example, a Tower of Wizardry in a Hard difficulty level game has an initial creature budget range of 700 to 1,200 mana. The computer randomly picks a number in that range: say, 1,038 — that is the site's total budget for stocking itself with monsters.

The computer then divides 1,038 by the result of a d4 die roll. Rolling a '3,' the site's ceiling price (in mana) for buying its big monster type. This would be 1038 / 3, or 346 maximum, per big monster.

Creature Colors

After obtaining the creature budget, the color of the fantastic units that the computer will purchase to defend that site is determined according to Table C.2, below.

Continuing with our example, the computer rolls to determine the color of the monsters defending the Tower of Wizardry. The result is that Chaos (red) creatures will defend the tower.

Monster Shopping

The computer will buy the most expensive (in terms of casting cost) big monster type it can find within the constraints of its big monster budget and the color of magic it is shopping from. It will buy as many of this big monster type as it can afford within the site's total budget, but never more than eight. If it buys more than one of its big monster type, there is a 50 percent chance that it will throw one back.

Mana not spent on the big monster(s) is then allotted to shopping for secondary monsters. As with big monsters, a ceiling price is determined by taking the unspent mana budgeted for that site and dividing it by the result of a dx die roll (where x = 10 - the number of big monsters already purchased). It will then buy as many secondary monsters as it can afford with what's left of the site's budget,

Table C.1 *Site Budget Ranges*

Terrain Square	Plane	Value Row	Game Difficulty Level				
			Intro	Easy	Normal	Hard	Impossible
Tower of Wizardry	Both	Creatures	175-300	350-600	575-900	700-1200	875-1500
		Treasure	350-1500	350-1500	350-1500	350-1500	437-1875
Normal Lairs	Arcanus	Creatures	25-325	50-750	75-1075	100-1500	125-1825
		Treasure	50-1625	50-1875	50-1791	50-1875	62-2281
	Myrror	Creatures	50-625	100-1250	150-1875	200-2500	250-3125
		Treasure	150-4375	150-4375	150-4375	150-4375	187-5468
Weak Lairs	Arcanus	Creatures	2-25	5-50	7-75	10-100	12-125
		Treasure	50-125	50-125	50-125	50-125	50-156
	Myrror	Creatures	2-50	5-100	7-150	10-200	12-250
		Treasure	50-350	50-350	50-350	50-350	50-437
Nodes: Weak	Arcanus	Creatures	15-187	31-375	46-562	62-750	78-937
		Treasure	50-935	50-937	50-936	50-937	50-1171
	Myrror	Creatures	62-750	125-1500	187-2250	250-3000	312-3750
		Treasure	186-5250	187-5250	187-5250	187-5250	234-6562
Normal	Arcanus	Creatures	31-375	62-750	93-1125	125-1500	156-1875
		Treasure	62-1875	62-1875	62-1875	62-1875	78-2343
	Myrror	Creatures	125-1500	250-3000	375-4500	500-6000	625-7500
		Treasure	375-10500	375-10500	375-10500	375-10500	468-13125
Strong	Arcanus	Creatures	46-562	93-1125	140-1687	187-2250	234-2812
		Treasure	92-2810	93-2812	93-2811	93-2812	117-3515
	Myrror	Creatures	187-2250	375-4500	562-6750	750-9000	937-11250
		Treasure	561-15750	562-15750	562-15750	562-15750	702-19687

Table C.2 *Who's Home?*

Special Terrain Feature	Percent Chance of Fantastic Unit Color:				
	White	Black	Red	Green	Blue
Tower of Wizardry	16.7	33.2	16.7	16.7	16.7
Ancient Temple	25	75	0	0	0
Ancient Ruins	25	75	0	0	0
Fallen Temple	25	75	0	0	0
Mysterious Cave	0	33.3	33.3	33.3	0
Dungeon	0	33.3	33.3	33.3	0
Abandoned Keep	0	33.3	33.3	33.3	0
Monster Lair	0	33.3	33.3	33.3	0
Chaos Node	0	0	100	0	0
Nature Node	0	0	0	100	0
Sorcery Node	0	0	0	0	100

provided the total units in the square do not exceed nine.

Continuing with our example, the computer goes shopping. It looks on the Chaos creature menu and finds that the most expensive monster type it could cast within its 346 mana ceiling is doom bats (at 300 mana per unit). Within its total budget of 1,038 mana, it can afford three units of doom bats.

Since it has purchased more than one of its big monster unit type, there is a 50 percent chance of it throwing one back and spending that mana on secondary monsters. The die is cast, and the computer does throw a doom bat unit back. It has now allocated 600 of its 1,038 budget for two doom bats.

The remaining 438 mana points in the site's budget is then divided by the result of a d8 (8 = 10 - 2 for the two doom bats already purchased). The die roll is a "5." This makes the ceiling price on the secondary monster unit type 438 / 5, or 87.6. Checking the red roster, hell hounds are the most expensive unit type available for under 87.6 mana, at 40 mana each. Within its remaining budget of

438 mana, it can afford 10 hell hound units. However, since the stacking limit is nine units, and two doom bats have already been purchased, only seven hell hounds are acquired. Thus, this Tower of Wizardry is defended by two doom bats and seven hell hounds. The total value of these defenders, 880, then becomes the High/Low modifier for determining the treasure available upon conquest.

Lair Reinforcements

When the guardians of these sites can create undead units to serve them after they win a battle, the undeads will not appear if there are already two different unit types in its garrison. We're sure that breaks your heart.

Treasure!

The treasure rows in table C.1 give ranges for the raw value used to stock the site with treasure. The value selected within this range will roughly correspond with the value of the monsters guarding that site. In other words, if the monster value range was randomly deter-

Table C.3 *Raw Treasure Value to Loot Conversion Table*

Chance	Qualify	Spend*	Treasure	Limit
33.3%	300	400-3000	Artifact**	3
20.0%	50	50	Common spell	1 spell***
	200	200	Uncommon spell	
	450	450	Rare spell	
	800	800	Very Rare spell	
13.3%	50	200	10-200 Gold	
13.3%	50	200	10-200 Mana	
13.3%	1000	3000	1 Special****	1 Special
	2000	3000	2 Specials	2 Specials
6.7%	400	1000	Prisoner	1*****

*If remaining raw treasure is less than Spend value but greater than or equal to the qualify value, the resulting treasure is awarded but reduced to match the remaining raw treasure value, if possible.

Each artifact is chosen from the ITEMDAT.LBX file (that you can modify, using ITEMMAKE.EXE in your Master of Magic game directory). For purposes of its value as loot, an artifact's Spend cost can range anywhere from its actual gold value to half that amount. Note that any item above 3,000 can not be picked as a treasure in this manner, but can be picked as a gift from gods (see Chapter 26, Events), a consolation for an unawarded special treasure (see ** below), or an item from a merchant (if you have three times its value in gold in your treasury at the time).

***Spell rarity is determined randomly, when rolled on this table, by a d4 die roll (1 = common, 2 = uncommon, etc.). If spell loot is rolled twice, the rarity die roll values are added together and the Spend amount from the most recent d4 roll is deducted — the total rarity value can never exceed four (very rare), however. (Note that only one spell will ever be awarded as treasure per site no matter how many times it is rolled as loot.) If the lair is a Tower of Wizardry, the first roll is always a spell and it receives a 100 Spend value discount. Spell color is usually determined by the color of the creatures guarding the site.

****If the treasure is one or two specials, all other treasures are discarded. Specials are resolved as follows: There is a 74 percent chance of receiving spell books (a player's maximum spell books, by the way, is 13); the remaining 26 percent chance will generate wizard skills (wizards can have a maximum of six wizard skills). If you're full in the special area that you would have gotten loot in, you'll get an artifact of unlimited potential value instead.

*****If the victorious stack has nine units, no prisoner will be available. The prisoner hero is obtained in the same manner as a Summon Hero spell works (see Chapter 7).

Table C.4 *Spell Book Colors Awarded as Loot by Site*

Site Type	Spell Book Color
Chaos node	Red
Nature node	Green
Sorcery node	Blue
Ancient temple	White
Fallen temple	White
Dungeon	Black
Abandoned keep	Black
Ancient ruins	Black
Wizard tower	Random
Mysterious cave	Random
Monster lair	Random

mined to be on the high end, the site's treasure value will also be on its high end.

You can convert this raw treasure value into loot by checking on Table C.3 as many times as necessary. Whenever 50 or more raw treasure points remain to be converted to loot, a die is rolled on the Chance column to see what type of loot is added to the horde.

With each roll, the remaining raw treasure is compared against the minimum qualifying value and, if it meets or exceeds that minimum, that treasure type is added to the horde and an amount equal to the Spend column is deducted from the raw treasure. If it doesn't meet or exceed the minimum qualifying value, the treasure type is re-rolled.

For example, after you vanquish the two doom bats and seven hell hounds at the Tower of Wizardry, loot is awarded. The range of this site's raw treasure value is between 350 and 1,500, but since the monsters were a bit above average (at 880, see above) for their range, the treasure should be, too.

Let's say the computer generates a value of 1,050 for raw treasure.

Its first roll on Table C.3 is automatically a spell, since the site conquered was a neutral Tower of Wizardry (see note ***). A quick, subsequent die roll of '2' on a d4 determines that it will be an uncommon spell. Since the qualifying number is 200 (less 100 for this particular spell because it was found in a Tower of Wizardry) and there are 1,050 raw treasure points to be distributed, the net spend cost of 100 is deducted and an uncommon spell is the first loot to be added to the horde. There are still 950 raw treasure points unspent, which is equal to or greater than 50, so the computer checks again for more loot.

The second roll on Table C.3 is another spell. The d4 follow-up die roll is another '2', so 200 treasure points are deducted from the 950 remaining and the uncommon spell is raised two levels to a very rare spell. Great!

The third roll on Table C.3 comes up with specials, but since there is not at least 1,000 raw treasure remaining (there's only 750 at this point), that result is re-rolled. Now, mana crystals are found. Their qualifying number of 50 is well below 750, so the 200 Spend points are deducted from the remaining raw treasure, and a random 10 to 200 mana crystals are added to the horde. Let's say that 90 mana crystals were determined to be the exact amount. There are still 550 raw treasure points unspent, so another roll on Table C.3 ensues.

This time a prisoner is found. While the qualifying raw treasure required to get a prisoner is only 400, the Spend price is 1,000, meaning that the 550 remaining raw treasure points are exhausted and a prisoner hero will be added to the horde. Since less than 50 raw treasure remains, that's it for rolling on Table C.3 — the final yield of loot from this Tower of Wizardry will be: 1 very rare spell, 90 mana crystals, and a prisoner. Not bad, eh?

Additional Loot From Conquered Cities

When a city is conquered, some extra gold is awarded to the victor. If the city was neutral, each population point at that city (before any post-combat casualties are removed) generates a random 1 to 10 gold.

If the conquered city belonged to another player, a proportional amount of that player's gold reserve is awarded as booty. This proportion is equal to the conquered city's population points divided by defeated player's total population points (including those population points in the just conquered city).

If a city is razed, an additional amount of gold equal to 10 percent of the value of every building the city had is also awarded.

The Color of Treasure

The color of spell books awarded as special loot usually depends on the type of site conquered. These are listed in Table C.4.

New wizard skills are awarded completely randomly within the restrictions below:

🐸 Divine Power won't go to wizards with Death magic.

🐸 Infernal Power won't go to wizards with Life magic.

🐸 Myrran will not be awarded.

🐸 Warlord, Channeler, Famous, Divine, and Infernal Power all require two picks, so they can only be awarded when two specials are generated via Table C.3.

Translating the Runes

You may have noticed the strange runes that adorn your spell book before you complete researching a particular spell. Did you know that these runes can be decoded? If you want to cheat and see what spells are in your spell book before they appear on your research list, use the following key:

A	B	C	D	E	F	G	H	I	i
J	K	L	M	N	O	P	Q	R	S
T	U	V	W	X	Y	Z			
0	1	2	3	4	5	6	7	8	9
!	"	#	$	%	&	'	(	)	*
+	,	-	.	/	:	;	<	=	>
?	[	\	]	^	{	|	}		

Starting Neutral City Information

1t is interesting how neutral cities are built before the game begins. As you're wandering, you may be wondering why that neutral neighbor of yours has a certain population size and certain buildings. Allow us to explain how neutral cities are raised. (You already know how they are razed.)

Starting Population

At the Intro and Easy difficulty levels, neutral cities begin at a random population size of one to four. At the Normal difficulty level, this range increases to two to five. At the Hard and Impossible levels, the opening neutral city population range has an 80 percent chance of being from two to five and a 20 percent chance of ranging from two to eleven. Whenever you've found a neutral city with more than five population points early in the game, take note! Chances are that you're onto something good.

Starting Buildings

Depending on a neutral city's starting size, it will have a certain set of buildings at the beginning of the game. Table E.1 lists these buildings based on a neutral city's starting population points. Note that cities start with *all* of the buildings at and below their initial population point level.

Neutral City Growth

Neutral cities grow at half the normal rate. Furthermore, a population growth cap comes into play. While a neutral city will not grow beyond the capacity that its surrounding terrain and buildings will allow (i.e., by the same rules that govern your cities' growth), they are *further* restricted by a growth cap and will only grow to whichever maximum limit is *lower* in a particular city's case.

At the Intro level of difficulty, neutral cities can only grow by two population points beyond their starting size, maximum. At the Easy level they can grow by four population

Table E.1 *Neutral City Starting Buildings*

Minimum Pop. Pts	Starting Buildings
10	city walls
8	stables
7	granary
5	armory
4	builder's hall
3	smithy
2	barracks

points, and six, eight, and ten maximum growth from their starting population point levels for neutral cities are the caps at Normal, Hard, and Impossible levels, respectively.

Neutral City Soldiers

The maximum garrison size of a neutral city is equal to its current population points. Neutrals might build troops beyond that amount, but when they do, the *oldest* unit built is disbanded to make room for the new (and — hopefully for the neutral—improved) unit type.

Combat Tables

Here are a few useful tables to help you in combat. Pay close attention now, and memorize every number. There will be a quiz next week.

Unit Durability

Have you ever seen a full strength unit killed outright in one swipe? Do you know what it takes to do that? Table F.1 quantifies the answers and gives some insight into each unit's true durability on the battlefield. It is presented in two sections: the first listing every normal unit type, the second covering all of the fantastic units.

Following a unit's name are four major columns. The first column is informational and has three sub columns. Figs per Unit indicates the number of figures a full strength unit of that type has. The # of Shlds per Fig subcolumn lists the number of shields each figure possesses. Similarly, Hrts per Fig lists the number of hearts (hit points) each figure has.

The next column has two parts. Rcrt/Reg Dur means Recruit or Regular unit experience level Durability. The number that appears in this column is the average number of hits (not swings, but hits) it takes to kill that unit in one swipe. The Avg Shlds (Average Shields) subcolumn indicates the average number of hits that a single figure's shields will block per attack. This value is derived by multiplying the number of shields per figure by 0.3.

The third column is different for normal and fantastic unit types. For normal units, it shows the increase in average shields per figure at the Veteran experience level (due to receiving an extra shield per figure). Sharing that same number of average shields per figure, Elite units are shown with their increase in durability (due to receiving an extra heart per figure). The fourth column, similarly covers normal units that obtain Ultra Elite and Champion status.

For fantastic unit types, the third column indicates the changes in their statistics when fighting within the aura of their corresponding node type. Such fantastic units receive +2 to all of their attributes, including shields and hearts.

To modify Table F.1 for variations to a unit's statistics due to magical enchantments, use the following formulae:

- For each additional heart a unit receives per figure, add 1 point to its durability value per figure it has.

- For each additional shield a unit receives per figure, add .3 to its durability value per figure. Also, add +.3 (total, not per figure) to its Average Shields per Figure column. (Subtract these values if an enchantment reduces a unit's shields per figure.)

The Attack/Defense Matrix

Tom Hughes was in a nasty battle. All the opposing forces were great drakes. Unfortunately for Tom, his back line was heavily laden with ultra-elite human magicians. "Wonderful," he said, "no soft targets for my magical ranged artillery." (Can you tell Tom's a wargamer?)

What Tom meant was that these magicians, with their six, 7-strength fireball attacks, wouldn't put a dent in a Great Drake's 10 shield defense. They needed smaller fish to fry.

What was he to do? Not wanting to let those magicians just sit there and with no other targets to attack, Tom started lobbing off those magical ranged attacks against the impressively shielded great drakes.

Guess what? To his surprise, the first attack from a six-figure magician unit did 7 damage to a great drake. Interesting. . . However, the fact that these ultra-elite magicians

Table F.1 *Unit Durability Ratings*

SECTION 1 NORMAL UNITS	Figs per Unit	# of Shlds per Fig	Hrts per Fig	Rcrt /Reg Dur	Avg Shlds per Fig	Vet Dur +1 Def	Avg Shlds per Fig	Elite Dur +1 Heart	Ultra Elite Dur +1 Shld	Avg Shlds per Fig	Champion Durability +1 Heart
Trireme	1	4	10	12	1.2	12	1.5	13	13	1.8	14
Galley	1	4	20	22	1.2	22	1.5	23	23	1.8	24
Catapult	1	2	10	11	0.6	11	0.9	12	13	1.2	14
Warship	1	5	30	32	1.5	32	1.8	33	34	2.1	35
BARBARIANS											
Spearmen	8	2	1	13	0.6	16	0.9	24	26	1.2	34
Swordsmen	6	2	1	10	0.6	12	0.9	18	20	1.2	26
Bowmen	6	1	1	8	0.3	10	0.6	16	18	0.9	24
Cavalry	4	2	3	15	0.6	16	0.9	20	21	1.2	25
Shaman	4	3	1	8	0.9	9	1.2	13	15	1.5	19
Settlers	1	1	10	11	0.3	11	0.6	12	12	0.9	13
Berserkers	6	3	3	24	0.9	26	1.2	32	34	1.5	40
BEASTMEN											
Spearmen	8	2	2	21	0.6	24	0.9	32	34	1.2	42
Swordsmen	6	2	2	16	0.6	18	0.9	24	26	1.2	32
Halberdiers	6	3	2	18	0.9	20	1.2	26	28	1.5	34
Bowmen	6	1	2	14	0.3	16	0.6	22	24	0.9	30
Priests	4	4	2	13	1.2	15	1.5	19	20	1.8	24
Magicians	4	3	2	12	0.9	13	1.2	17	19	1.5	23
Engineers	6	1	2	14	0.3	16	0.6	22	24	0.9	30
Settlers	1	1	20	21	0.3	21	0.6	22	22	0.9	23
Centaurs	4	3	3	16	0.9	17	1.2	21	23	1.5	27
Manticores	2	3	7	16	0.9	17	1.2	19	20	1.5	22
Minotaurs	2	4	12	27	1.2	28	1.5	30	30	1.8	32
DARK ELVES											
Spearmen	8	2	1	13	0.6	16	0.9	24	26	1.2	34
Swordsmen	6	2	1	10	0.6	12	0.9	18	20	1.2	26
Halberdiers	6	3	1	12	0.9	14	1.2	20	22	1.5	28
Cavalry	4	2	3	15	0.6	16	0.9	20	21	1.2	25
Priests	4	4	1	9	1.2	11	1.5	15	16	1.8	20
Settlers	1	1	10	11	0.3	11	0.6	12	12	0.9	13
Nightblades	6	3	1	12	0.9	14	1.2	20	22	1.5	28
Warlocks	4	4	1	9	1.2	11	1.5	15	16	1.8	20
Nightmares	2	4	10	23	1.2	24	1.5	26	26	1.8	28

Table F.1 Cont. *Unit Durability Ratings*

SECTION 1 NORMAL UNITS	Figs per Unit	# of Shlds per Fig	Hrts per Fig	Rcrt /Reg Dur	Avg Shlds per Fig	Vet Dur +1 Def	Avg Shlds per Fig	Elite Dur +1 Heart	Ultra Elite Dur +1 Shld	Avg Shlds per Fig	Champion Durability +1 Heart
DRACONIANS											
Spearmen	8	3	1	16	0.9	18	1.2	26	29	1.5	37
Swordsmen	6	3	1	12	0.9	14	1.2	20	22	1.5	28
Halberdiers	6	4	1	14	1.2	16	1.5	22	23	1.8	29
Bowmen	6	2	1	10	0.6	12	0.9	18	20	1.2	26
Shaman	4	4	1	9	1.2	11	1.5	15	16	1.8	20
Magicians	4	4	1	9	1.2	11	1.5	15	16	1.8	20
Engineers	6	2	1	10	0.6	12	0.9	18	20	1.2	26
Settlers	1	2	10	11	0.6	11	0.9	12	13	1.2	14
Doom Drakes	2	3	10	22	0.9	23	1.2	25	26	1.5	28
Air Ship	1	5	20	22	1.5	22	1.8	23	24	2.1	25
DWARVEN											
Swordsmen	6	2	3	22	0.6	24	0.9	30	32	1.2	38
Halberdiers	6	3	3	24	0.9	26	1.2	32	34	1.5	40
Engineers	6	1	3	20	0.3	22	0.6	28	30	0.9	36
Hammerhands	6	4	4	32	1.2	34	1.5	40	41	1.8	47
Steam Cannon	1	2	12	13	0.6	13	0.9	14	15	1.2	16
Golem	1	8	20	23	2.4	23	2.7	24	25	3.0	26
Settlers	1	1	30	31	0.3	31	0.6	32	32	0.9	33
GNOLLS											
Spearmen	8	2	1	13	0.6	16	0.9	24	26	1.2	34
Swordsmen	6	2	1	10	0.6	12	0.9	18	20	1.2	26
Halberdiers	6	3	1	12	0.9	14	1.2	20	22	1.5	28
Bowmen	6	1	1	8	0.3	10	0.6	16	18	0.9	24
Settlers	1	1	10	11	0.3	11	0.6	12	12	0.9	13
Wolf Riders	4	3	5	24	0.9	25	1.2	29	31	1.5	35
HALFLINGS											
Spearmen	8	2	1	15	0.8	18	1.2	26	29	1.6	37
Swordsmen	8	2	1	15	0.8	18	1.2	26	29	1.6	37
Bowmen	6	1	1	9	0.4	11	0.8	17	20	1.2	26
Shaman	4	3	1	9	1.2	11	1.6	15	17	2.0	21
Settlers	1	1	10	11	0.4	11	0.8	12	13	1.2	14
Slingers	8	2	1	15	0.8	18	1.2	26	29	1.6	37

Table F.1 Cont. *Unit Durability Ratings*

SECTION 1 NORMAL UNITS	Figs per Unit	# of Shlds per Fig	Hrts per Fig	Rcrt /Reg Dur	Avg Shlds per Fig	Vet Dur +1 Def	Avg Shlds per Fig	Elite Dur +1 Heart	Ultra Elite Dur +1 Shld	Avg Shlds per Fig	Champion Durability +1 Heart
HIGH ELVES											
Spearmen	8	2	1	13	0.6	16	0.9	24	26	1.2	34
Swordsmen	6	2	1	10	0.6	12	0.9	18	20	1.2	26
Halberdiers	6	3	1	12	0.9	14	1.2	20	22	1.5	28
Cavalry	4	2	3	15	0.6	16	0.9	20	21	1.2	25
Magicians	4	3	1	8	0.9	9	1.2	13	15	1.5	19
Settlers	1	1	10	11	0.3	11	0.6	12	12	0.9	13
Longbowmen	6	2	1	10	0.6	12	0.9	18	20	1.2	26
Elven Lords	4	4	3	17	1.2	19	1.5	23	24	1.8	28
Pegasai	2	4	5	13	1.2	14	1.5	16	16	1.8	18
HIGH MEN											
Spearmen	8	2	1	13	0.6	16	0.9	24	26	1.2	34
Swordsmen	6	2	1	10	0.6	12	0.9	18	20	1.2	26
Bowmen	6	1	1	8	0.3	10	0.6	16	18	0.9	24
Cavalry	4	2	3	15	0.6	16	0.9	20	21	1.2	25
Priests	4	4	1	9	1.2	11	1.5	15	16	1.8	20
Magicians	6	3	1	12	0.9	14	1.2	20	22	1.5	28
Engineers	6	1	1	8	0.3	10	0.6	16	18	0.9	24
Settlers	1	1	10	11	0.3	11	0.6	12	12	0.9	13
Pikemen	8	3	1	16	0.9	18	1.2	26	29	1.5	37
Paladins	4	6	4	24	1.8	25	2.1	29	30	2.4	34
KLACKONS											
Spearmen	8	4	1	18	1.2	21	1.5	29	31	1.8	39
Swordsmen	6	4	1	14	1.2	16	1.5	22	23	1.8	29
Halberdiers	6	5	1	16	1.5	17	1.8	23	25	2.1	31
Engineers	6	1	1	8	0.3	10	0.6	16	18	0.9	24
Settlers	1	1	10	11	0.3	11	0.6	12	12	0.9	13
Stag Beetle	1	7	20	23	2.1	23	2.4	24	24	2.7	25
LIZARDMEN											
Spearmen	8	3	2	24	0.9	26	1.2	34	37	1.5	45
Swordsmen	6	3	2	18	0.9	20	1.2	26	28	1.5	34
Halberdiers	6	4	2	20	1.2	22	1.5	28	29	1.8	35
Javelineers	6	4	2	20	1.2	22	1.5	28	29	1.8	35
Shaman	4	3	2	12	0.9	13	1.2	17	19	1.5	23
Settlers	1	2	20	21	0.6	21	0.9	22	23	1.2	24
Dragon Turtle	1	8	15	18	2.4	18	2.7	19	20	3.0	21

Table F.1 Cont. *Unit Durability Ratings*

SECTION 1 NORMAL UNITS	Figs per Unit	# of Shlds per Fig	Hrts per Fig	Rcrt /Reg Dur	Avg Shlds per Fig	Vet Dur +1 Def	Avg Shlds per Fig	Elite Dur +1 Heart	Ultra Elite Dur +1 Shld	Avg Shlds per Fig	Champion Durability +1 Heart
NOMADS											
Spearmen	8	2	1	13	0.6	16	0.9	24	26	1.2	34
Swordsmen	6	2	1	10	0.6	12	0.9	18	20	1.2	26
Bowmen	6	1	1	8	0.3	10	0.6	16	18	0.9	24
Priests	4	4	1	9	1.2	11	1.5	15	16	1.8	20
Magicians	4	3	1	8	0.9	9	1.2	13	15	1.5	19
Settlers	1	1	10	11	0.3	11	0.6	12	12	0.9	13
Horsebowmen	4	2	3	15	0.6	16	0.9	20	21	1.2	25
Pikemen	8	3	1	16	0.9	18	1.2	26	29	1.5	37
Rangers	4	4	2	13	1.2	15	1.5	19	20	1.8	24
Griffins	2	5	10	24	1.5	24	1.8	26	27	2.1	29
ORCS											
Spearmen	8	2	1	13	0.6	16	0.9	24	26	1.2	34
Swordsmen	6	2	1	10	0.6	12	0.9	18	20	1.2	26
Halberdiers	6	3	1	12	0.9	14	1.2	20	22	1.5	28
Bowmen	6	1	1	8	0.3	10	0.6	16	18	0.9	24
Cavalry	4	2	3	15	0.6	16	0.9	20	21	1.2	25
Shaman	4	3	1	8	0.9	9	1.2	13	15	1.5	19
Magicians	4	3	1	8	0.9	9	1.2	13	15	1.5	19
Engineers	6	1	1	8	0.3	10	0.6	16	18	0.9	24
Settlers	1	1	10	11	0.3	11	0.6	12	12	0.9	13
Wyvern Riders	2	5	10	24	1.5	24	1.8	26	27	2.1	29
TROLLS											
Spearmen	4	2	4	19	0.6	20	0.9	24	25	1.2	29
Swordsmen	4	2	4	19	0.6	20	0.9	24	25	1.2	29
Halberdiers	4	3	4	20	0.9	21	1.2	25	27	1.5	31
Shaman	4	3	4	20	0.9	21	1.2	25	27	1.5	31
Settlers	1	1	40	41	0.3	41	0.6	42	42	0.9	43
War Trolls	4	4	5	25	1.2	27	1.5	31	32	1.8	36
War Mammoths	2	6	12	28	1.8	29	2.1	31	31	2.4	33

Table F.1 Cont. *Unit Durability Ratings*

SECTION 2 FANTASTIC UNITS	Figs per Unit	# of Shlds per Fig	Hrts per Fig	Rcrt /Reg Dur	Avg Shlds per Fig	At Node Dur	At Node Avg Shlds per Fig
ARCANE							
Magic Spirit	1	4	10	12	1.2		
CHAOS							
Hell Hounds	4	2	4	19	0.6	21	1.2
Gargoyles	4	8	4	26	2.4	29	3.0
Fire Giant	1	5	15	17	1.5	18	2.1
Fire Elemental	1	4	10	12	1.2	12	1.8
Chaos Spawn	1	6	15	17	1.8	18	2.4
Chimera	4	5	8	39	1.5	41	2.1
Doom Bat	1	5	20	22	1.5	23	2.1
Efreet	1	7	12	15	2.1	15	2.7
Hydra	9	4	10	101	1.2	107	1.8
Great Drake	1	10	30	34	3.0	34	3.6
DEATH							
Skeletons	6	4	1	14	1.2		
Ghouls	4	3	3	16	0.9		
Night Stalker	1	3	10	11	0.9		
Werewolves	6	1	5	32	0.3		
Demon	1	5	12	14	1.5		
Wraiths	4	6	8	40	1.8		
Shadow Demons	4	4	5	25	1.2		
Death Knights	4	8	8	42	2.4		
Demon Lord	1	10	20	24	3.0		
Zombies	6	3	3	24	0.9		
LIFE							
Unicorns	4	3	6	28	0.9		
Guardian Spirit	1	4	10	12	1.2		
Angel	1	8	15	18	2.4		
Arch Angel	1	12	18	22	3.6		
NATURE							
War Bears	2	3	8	18	0.9	20	1.5
Sprites	4	2	1	7	0.6	9	1.2
Cockatrices	4	3	3	16	0.9	19	1.5
Basilisk	1	4	30	32	1.2	32	1.8
Giant Spiders	2	3	10	22	0.9	24	1.5
Stone Giant	1	8	20	23	2.4	24	3.0

Table F.1 Cont. *Unit Durability Ratings*

SECTION 2 FANTASTIC UNITS	Figs per Unit	# of Shlds per Fig	Hrts per Fig	Rcrt /Reg Dur	Avg Shlds per Fig	At Node Dur	At Node Avg Shlds per Fig
NATURE (Cont.)							
Colossus	1	10	30	34	3.0	34	3.6
Gorgons	4	7	9	45	2.1	47	2.7
Earth Elemental	1	4	30	32	1.2	32	1.8
Behemoth	1	9	45	48	2.7	49	3.3
Great Wyrm	1	12	45	49	3.6	50	4.2
SORCERY							
Floating Island	1	0	45	45	0.0	46	0.6
Phantom Beast	1	0	20	20	0.0	21	0.6
Phantom Warriors	6	0	1	6	0.0	10	0.6
Storm Giant	1	7	20	23	2.1	23	2.7
Air Elemental	1	8	10	13	2.4	14	3.0
Djinn	1	8	20	23	2.4	24	3.0
Sky Drake	1	10	25	29	3.0	29	3.6
Nagas	2	3	6	14	0.9	16	1.5

damaged that great drake so effectively left him puzzled. How could it happen?

Maybe just a lucky shot. He then attacked with the rest of his magicians and found that 7 was the average damage that each six-figure magician unit inflicted.

Needless to say, Tom won the battle. However, he still didn't understand how those magicians did so well against a great drake's 10 shields. It was only after doing the probability calculations did he realized: a 7 strength +2 To Hit attack would do an average of 1.2 hits against a defense of 10 shields. Multiplying this by the six magician figures in a unit gave the 7 damage average he saw in battle. From this experience, he made these tables to help him decide who to attack, and how effective that attack would be.

Multi-Figure Unit Combat Revisited

Before going into this massive table, let's first describe the sequence of a multi-figured unit delivering an attack and inflicting damage against another multi-figured unit. This will highlight the usefulness and limitations of these tables.

The first attacking figure rolls a number of dice equal to its swords. The chance of each sword causing a hit is 0.3 (or 30 percent), plus or minus any To Hit modifiers it might have (at 0.1, or 10 percent, per point of modification). After any hits inflicted are counted (referred to here as *raw hits*), the first defending figure gets to try block some or all of those hits with its shields. The chance of each shield blocking a hit is 0.3 (or 30 percent), plus or minus any To Defend modifiers it might have (again, at 0.1, or 10 percent, per point of modification).

After any successful blocks are counted, their value is subtracted from the raw hits. The remaining hits, if any, actually damage the defending figure (and are referred to here as *penetrating hits*).

That ends the first figure's attack. Then the next attacking figure attacks and any raw hits it scores are defended by the shields of the same defending figure (assuming it survived the first attack, otherwise the next defender would be engaged), with any penetrating hits further damaging that figure.

If the defending figure dies before taking all the damage from an attack, the excess penetrating hits must the next defending figure and its shields attack (in essence, becoming raw hits again). Only the excess hits that aren't blocked by the second figures shields get to damage that defending figure. If the second defending figure dies before taking all the remaining damage, a third figure is engaged, and so on until all raw hits from the original attack have eventually been either blocked by defensive shields or damaged figures.

Eventually every attacking figure gets an *at bat* to generate raw hits that one or more defending figures will attempt to parry with their shields or, failing that, absorb with their flesh. Then the rolls could be reversed, with the defender counterattacking if the type of combat those two units are engaged in permits it (such as normal melee combat, see Chapter 20). If an attacking unit has six figures, then six attacks, each of which generates raw hits, will be made and individual defending figures must deal with them, one at a time, unto their death.

The Matrix

The matrix presented here assumes the defending unit's To Defend modifier is 0. (This might vary on rare occasions, but not enough for us to recreate this table multiple times.) It has, as its heart, the eighth column. This

eighth column represents the different average raw hits that attacks will generate.

Everything to the left of the eighth column is used to determine which row to use. This row is determined by finding which of the seven To Hit columns to use, then following that column down until arriving at the correct number of swords.

After finding the appropriate number of swords a figure is attacking with (at its current To Hit modifier), read the number in the eighth row. That is the average number of raw hits that figure's attack will generate. Remember, raw hits are the name of the game when it comes to attacking. It's not just the number of swords, but the number of swords times the total To Hit probability that gives average number of raw hits.

For example, look at the +3 To Hit column. Now, go down until you reach ten swords. Notice it is on the same row as twelve +2 To Hit swords, fifteen +1 To Hit swords, twenty +0 To Hit swords, and thirty -1 To Hit swords. That's because $10 \times 0.6 = 12 \times 0.5 = 15 \times 0.4 = 20 \times 0.3 = 30 \times 0.2 = 6.0$ average raw hits.

(Actually, you'll see 5.9 in the 0, or raw hits column, instead of 6.0. This is because these tables were generated by doing 1000 attacks at each defense—including 0 shields—and averaging the result. Unfortunately, the game's random number generator isn't perfect. However, the results on this matrix are exactly what you will get when playing *Master of Magic*.)

Now, everything to the right of the eighth column is used to determine how many raw hits won't be blocked by the defending figure's shields (i.e., won't become penetrating hits that inflict damage). Each column to the right represents the different shield strengths that a defending figure might have. Remember, column eight, which has a shield strength of 0, shows the raw hits.

Attack/Defense Matrix Use Example

Okay, let's use this table to check the magicians' attack against the sky drakes discussed earlier. First, find the +2 To Hit column on the left (because the magicians are ultra-elite). Now, go down to 7 swords (the strength of their magical ranged attacks).

By looking along that row to the eighth (0 shields) column, we see that each magician figure's attack will generate an average of 3.6 raw hits. Now, moving across the row to the 10 shield column, we see that an average of 1.2 hits will actually penetrate the sky drake's 10 shields and do damage. For example, its 10 shields block an average of 2.4 raw hits. Because there are 6 magician figures in the attacking unit, the math works out this way: 6 x 1.2 = 7.2, or about 7 hits of damage on average.

Thus, this table compares the relative strengths of different sword/To Hit combinations. For example, the seven +2 swords are equivalent to nine +1 swords. This means that, figure-for-figure, ultra-elite human mages do as much damage as elite dark elf mages. However, there are six human mages and only four dark elves mages in their respective units. So, except for the dark elf Doom Bolt advantage, the humans can have more powerful mages. This might persuade you to start a game with humans and the Warlord wizard skill (so you can obtain ultra-elite status for your units), instead of starting with the dark elves on Myrror.

Invulnerability

This table also shows when a unit's defenses are so good that it is, effectively, invulnerable to attacks from certain other units. For example, that great drake's ten +0 shields would provide be almost total protection against a unit with five or fewer +0 swords (i.e., that inflict 0.3 hits or less per attack). However, that great drake would be vulnerable (which we define as half or more of the raw hits inflicted actually penetrating) to a unit with twenty or more +0 swords per figure.

Multiple Defending Figures' Shields Effect

This table assumes that each figure's swords will have to attack only one defending figure's shields. This supposition is valid most of the time. However, when a defending figure is killed, the remaining penetrating hits must run the gauntlet again, this time of the next defending figure's shields.

Running the gauntlet of multiple figure's shields from a single figure's attack is not a problem when a low percentage of these attacks kill defending figures. After all, this matrix only gives estimates. Even when examining powerful single attacks that kill several figures per whack, this still is not a problem. That is because you either want to avoid that kind of combat (as defender) or don't care about these close estimates when so successfully hacking and slashing away (as the attacker).

However for those few math scientists out there that care to know how to compensate using this matrix in such cases, here's what to do: Follow the normal procedure, take the number of penetrating hits, and subtract the damage needed to kill that figure. Any remaining hits should be though of as a new attack (i.e., the remaining hits become the new raw hits value in column eight). Next, find the closest row in column eight that matches these remaining hits, and follow that row to the same shield column as before. The result is the average number of penetrating hits inflicted on the next figure.

For example, a colossus attacks elite elven lords that have Holy Armor. The colossus has a twenty strength +3 attack versus the eight strength shields (their basic six, plus two for having Holy Armor) per figure of the elven lords.

The Attack/Defense Matrix

To Hit Modifiers/ # of Swords per Figure | **Defender's Shields Per Figure**

+5	+4	+3	+2	+1	0	-1	0*	1	2	3	4	5	6	7	8	9	10	11	12	13	14	15	16	17	18	19	20	22	24	26	28	30	50**
						1	0.2	0.1	0.1	0.1	0.0	0.0	0.0	0.0	0.0	0.0	0.0	0.0	0.0	0.0	0.0	0.0	0.0	0.0	0.0	0.0	0.0	0.0	0.0	0.0	0.0	0.0	0.0
				1	1	2	0.4	0.3	0.2	0.1	0.1	0.1	0.1	0.0	0.0	0.0	0.0	0.0	0.0	0.0	0.0	0.0	0.0	0.0	0.0	0.0	0.0	0.0	0.0	0.0	0.0	0.0	0.0
		1	1		2	3	0.6	0.4	0.3	0.3	0.2	0.2	0.1	0.1	0.1	0.0	0.0	0.0	0.0	0.0	0.0	0.0	0.0	0.0	0.0	0.0	0.0	0.0	0.0	0.0	0.0	0.0	0.0
1	1			2		4	0.8	0.6	0.5	0.4	0.3	0.2	0.2	0.1	0.1	0.1	0.1	0.0	0.0	0.0	0.0	0.0	0.0	0.0	0.0	0.0	0.0	0.0	0.0	0.0	0.0	0.0	0.0
			2		3	5	1.0	0.9	0.6	0.5	0.4	0.3	0.2	0.2	0.1	0.1	0.1	0.1	0.1	0.0	0.0	0.0	0.0	0.0	0.0	0.0	0.0	0.0	0.0	0.0	0.0	0.0	0.0
		2		3	4	6	1.2	0.9	0.8	0.6	0.5	0.4	0.3	0.2	0.2	0.2	0.1	0.1	0.1	0.1	0.0	0.0	0.0	0.0	0.0	0.0	0.0	0.0	0.0	0.0	0.0	0.0	0.0
	2					7	1.4	1.2	1.0	0.8	0.7	0.5	0.4	0.4	0.3	0.2	0.2	0.2	0.1	0.1	0.1	0.1	0.0	0.0	0.0	0.0	0.0	0.0	0.0	0.0	0.0	0.0	0.0
2			3	4	5	8	1.7	1.3	1.1	0.9	0.7	0.7	0.5	0.5	0.3	0.3	0.3	0.2	0.2	0.1	0.1	0.1	0.1	0.0	0.0	0.0	0.0	0.0	0.0	0.0	0.0	0.0	0.0
		3			6	9	1.8	1.5	1.3	1.0	0.9	0.8	0.7	0.5	0.4	0.4	0.3	0.2	0.2	0.1	0.1	0.1	0.1	0.0	0.0	0.0	0.0	0.0	0.0	0.0	0.0	0.0	0.0
			4	5		10	1.9	1.7	1.5	1.3	1.0	0.9	0.7	0.7	0.5	0.4	0.4	0.3	0.2	0.2	0.2	0.1	0.1	0.1	0.1	0.0	0.0	0.0	0.0	0.0	0.0	0.0	0.0
	3				7	11	2.2	1.9	1.6	1.5	1.2	1.0	0.9	0.8	0.7	0.5	0.4	0.4	0.3	0.2	0.2	0.2	0.1	0.1	0.1	0.1	0.1	0.0	0.0	0.0	0.0	0.0	0.0
3		4		6	8	12	2.3	2.0	1.8	1.6	1.4	1.3	1.1	0.9	0.8	0.6	0.5	0.5	0.4	0.3	0.2	0.2	0.2	0.1	0.1	0.1	0.1	0.0	0.0	0.0	0.0	0.0	0.0
			5			13	2.6	2.4	2.0	1.8	1.6	1.4	1.2	0.9	0.9	0.7	0.6	0.5	0.4	0.4	0.3	0.2	0.2	0.2	0.1	0.1	0.1	0.1	0.0	0.0	0.0	0.0	0.0
	4			7	9	14	2.8	2.5	2.3	2.0	1.7	1.5	1.3	1.1	1.1	0.8	0.7	0.6	0.5	0.5	0.4	0.4	0.2	0.2	0.2	0.1	0.2	0.1	0.1	0.0	0.0	0.0	0.0
		5	6		10	15	3.1	2.7	2.4	2.2	1.9	1.6	1.4	1.2	1.1	1.0	0.8	0.7	0.6	0.5	0.4	0.4	0.3	0.2	0.2	0.2	0.2	0.1	0.1	0.0	0.0	0.0	0.0
4				8		16	3.2	2.9	2.6	2.4	2.1	1.9	1.6	1.5	1.2	1.1	0.9	0.8	0.7	0.6	0.5	0.4	0.3	0.3	0.3	0.2	0.2	0.2	0.1	0.1	0.0	0.0	0.0
					11	17	3.4	3.0	2.8	2.4	2.3	2.1	1.8	1.6	1.4	1.3	1.1	0.9	0.8	0.7	0.6	0.4	0.5	0.4	0.3	0.3	0.2	0.2	0.1	0.1	0.1	0.0	0.0
	5	6	7	9	12	18	3.6	3.3	3.1	2.8	2.4	2.3	2.0	1.8	1.6	1.3	1.2	1.0	0.9	0.9	0.7	0.6	0.5	0.4	0.4	0.3	0.3	0.2	0.1	0.1	0.1	0.0	0.0
						19	3.8	3.6	3.3	2.9	2.6	2.4	2.2	1.9	1.7	1.6	1.4	1.2	1.1	0.9	0.7	0.7	0.6	0.5	0.5	0.4	0.3	0.2	0.2	0.1	0.1	0.1	0.0
5			8	10	13	20	3.9	3.8	3.5	3.2	2.9	2.6	2.3	2.0	1.9	1.7	1.4	1.4	1.1	1.0	0.9	0.7	0.7	0.5	0.5	0.5	0.3	0.2	0.2	0.1	0.1	0.1	0.0
	6	7			14	21	4.1	4.1	3.6	3.3	3.1	2.8	2.5	2.3	2.1	1.9	1.7	1.4	1.3	1.2	1.0	0.8	0.8	0.6	0.6	0.5	0.4	0.3	0.2	0.2	0.1	0.1	0.0
				11		22	4.4	4.0	3.8	3.6	3.2	3.0	2.7	2.3	2.1	2.1	1.9	1.6	1.5	1.3	1.1	1.1	0.8	0.7	0.6	0.6	0.5	0.4	0.3	0.2	0.1	0.1	0.0
			9		15	23	4.6	4.3	4.0	3.8	3.4	3.1	2.9	2.7	2.3	2.2	2.0	1.8	1.5	1.3	1.3	1.1	1.1	0.8	0.7	0.7	0.6	0.4	0.3	0.2	0.2	0.1	0.0
6		8		12	16	24	4.8	4.4	4.3	3.9	3.5	3.3	3.2	2.9	2.6	2.3	2.1	1.8	1.7	1.6	1.4	1.1	1.1	1.0	0.8	0.7	0.6	0.5	0.4	0.2	0.2	0.1	0.0
	7		10			25	5.0	4.7	4.4	4.2	3.8	3.5	3.3	2.9	2.6	2.7	2.3	2.1	1.9	1.7	1.4	1.2	1.1	1.1	1.0	0.8	0.7	0.5	0.4	0.3	0.2	0.2	0.0
				13	17	26	5.1	4.9	4.6	4.4	3.8	3.8	3.6	3.2	3.0	2.6	2.5	2.2	2.1	1.8	1.7	1.5	1.3	1.1	1.1	0.9	0.8	0.6	0.5	0.3	0.2	0.2	0.0
		9			18	27	5.4	5.2	4.9	4.5	4.1	4.0	3.7	3.4	3.0	2.9	2.5	2.4	2.1	1.9	1.8	1.6	1.4	1.2	1.1	0.9	0.9	0.8	0.5	0.4	0.2	0.3	0.0
7	8		11	14		28	5.6	5.2	5.0	4.7	4.4	4.1	3.7	3.5	3.3	3.0	2.7	2.5	2.3	2.1	1.8	1.7	1.6	1.3	1.3	1.1	1.0	0.8	0.5	0.5	0.3	0.3	0.0
					19	29	5.8	5.4	5.2	4.9	4.5	4.3	4.0	3.7	3.5	3.2	2.9	2.7	2.5	2.2	2.2	1.9	1.8	1.4	1.3	1.2	1.1	0.8	0.6	0.5	0.4	0.3	0.0
		10	12	15	20	30	5.9	5.8	5.3	5.1	4.8	4.5	4.3	3.9	3.7	3.5	3.2	3.0	2.6	2.4	2.3	2.1	1.8	1.7	1.5	1.3	1.1	1.0	0.7	0.5	0.4	0.3	0.0
8	9			16	21		6.4	6.1	5.8	5.6	5.1	4.8	4.7	4.3	4.0	3.7	3.5	3.4	3.0	2.6	2.6	2.3	2.1	1.9	1.7	1.6	1.5	1.1	0.9	0.7	0.5	0.4	0.0
		11	13		22		6.5	6.3	6.0	5.6	5.3	5.1	4.9	4.5	4.3	3.9	3.7	3.4	3.3	2.9	2.7	2.5	2.2	2.1	1.9	1.7	1.5	1.2	1.0	0.8	0.6	0.5	0.0
				17			6.8	6.5	6.2	5.9	5.6	5.3	5.2	4.7	4.5	4.3	3.8	3.6	3.3	3.1	2.8	2.7	2.4	2.2	2.0	1.9	1.7	1.4	1.1	0.9	0.6	0.5	0.0
	10		14		23		6.9	6.6	6.6	6.1	5.8	5.4	5.2	4.8	4.7	4.4	4.0	3.8	3.5	3.2	3.0	2.8	2.7	2.4	2.1	2.0	1.8	1.5	1.1	0.9	0.7	0.6	0.0
9		12		18	24		7.3	6.9	6.6	6.1	5.9	5.6	5.5	5.0	4.9	4.5	4.3	4.1	3.7	3.5	3.2	2.9	2.9	2.7	2.2	2.0	1.9	1.6	1.4	1.1	0.8	0.7	0.0

The Attack/Defense Matrix Cont.

To Hit Modifiers / # of Swords per Figure and **Defender's Shields Per Figure**

+5	+4	+3	+2	+1	0	-1	0*	1	2	3	4	5	6	7	8	9	10	11	12	13	14	15	16	17	18	19	20	22	24	26	28	30	50**
			15	19	25		7.5	7.2	7.0	6.8	6.4	6.1	5.7	5.5	5.4	4.9	4.7	4.4	4.1	3.8	3.6	3.4	3.0	2.8	2.6	2.5	2.2	1.9	1.5	1.3	1.0	0.8	0.1
					26		7.9	7.4	7.2	6.9	6.7	6.3	6.0	5.5	5.4	5.3	4.8	4.5	4.3	4.0	3.7	3.4	3.4	3.0	2.7	2.6	2.4	1.9	1.5	1.3	1.1	0.8	0.1
10	11	13	16	20	27		7.9	7.7	7.6	7.0	6.7	6.5	6.1	6.0	5.6	5.4	5.1	4.8	4.4	4.2	3.9	3.8	3.5	3.2	3.0	2.8	2.6	2.1	1.7	1.6	1.3	0.9	0.1
					28		8.0	7.9	7.5	7.4	7.0	6.6	6.4	6.2	5.8	5.8	5.4	5.1	4.8	4.5	4.6	4.1	3.8	3.6	3.4	3.0	2.8	2.3	1.8	1.6	1.2	1.1	0.1
	12	14	17	21	28		8.4	8.1	7.8	7.5	7.1	6.8	6.4	6.4	5.8	5.4	5.1	5.2	5.0	4.6	4.3	4.1	3.8	3.6	3.3	2.9	2.7	2.5	2.0	1.6	1.4	1.3	0.2
					29		8.5	8.3	8.0	7.6	7.4	6.9	6.8	6.6	6.5	5.8	5.6	5.2	5.2	4.7	4.6	4.4	4.1	3.8	3.6	3.3	3.0	2.8	2.2	1.6	1.6	1.3	1.1	0.2
		15	18	22	30		8.7	8.4	8.3	7.7	7.6	7.2	7.1	6.5	6.3	5.9	5.7	5.5	5.3	5.1	4.7	4.7	4.4	4.1	3.9	3.5	3.3	3.0	2.4	2.0	1.6	1.4	1.3	0.2
							8.9	8.6	8.5	8.1	7.8	7.7	7.3	6.9	6.6	6.5	6.0	5.8	5.7	5.3	5.3	5.0	4.7	4.5	4.3	3.9	3.5	3.4	3.0	2.5	2.2	1.8	1.4	1.5	0.2
		16	19	24			9.0	8.9	8.6	8.2	8.0	7.8	7.3	7.1	7.0	6.5	6.2	6.3	5.9	5.7	5.3	5.2	5.0	4.7	4.3	4.1	3.8	3.4	3.0	2.6	2.2	1.8	1.4	0.2
12	14		20				9.5	9.5	9.1	8.6	8.3	8.2	7.8	7.4	7.0	6.6	6.8	6.4	6.3	5.9	5.7	5.4	5.0	5.1	4.6	4.4	4.1	3.9	3.0	2.5	2.2	1.9	1.5	0.2
		17		25			9.7	9.4	9.1	8.8	8.6	8.3	8.2	7.7	7.5	7.2	6.8	6.7	6.2	6.1	5.8	5.2	5.1	4.6	4.4	4.7	4.1	3.7	3.0	2.7	2.4	2.1	1.8	0.2
			21				9.9	9.6	9.4	9.0	8.7	8.5	8.2	7.7	7.6	7.4	7.1	6.7	6.2	6.2	5.7	5.4	5.3	5.0	5.1	4.7	4.4	4.1	3.4	3.0	2.4	2.4	2.1	0.3
13				26			9.9	10.0	9.4	9.1	8.7	8.7	8.3	8.0	7.6	7.4	7.1	7.0	6.6	6.4	6.1	5.9	5.6	5.3	5.1	4.7	4.2	4.1	3.4	3.1	2.5	2.2	2.2	0.4
	15		22				10.1	10.1	9.7	9.4	9.1	8.7	8.5	8.2	7.6	7.6	7.2	7.1	6.9	6.3	6.1	5.9	5.6	5.3	5.1	4.9	4.7	3.9	3.6	3.1	2.8	2.4	2.3	0.3
		18		27			10.5	10.2	9.9	9.5	9.1	8.9	8.6	8.3	8.2	7.8	7.5	7.3	6.7	6.6	6.3	6.1	6.0	5.6	5.3	4.9	4.7	4.7	3.9	3.3	2.8	2.5	2.5	0.4
							10.7	10.5	10.3	9.9	9.8	9.3	9.1	8.7	8.3	8.1	7.8	7.3	7.4	6.6	6.8	6.5	6.2	6.0	5.6	5.3	5.0	4.7	3.9	3.7	3.3	3.0	2.7	0.4
							10.8	10.5	10.2	9.7	9.7	9.5	9.1	8.9	8.8	8.3	8.1	7.8	7.4	7.5	7.0	6.6	6.6	6.2	5.9	5.6	5.3	5.2	4.6	3.9	3.4	3.1	2.7	0.4
14	16		23				11.3	10.9	10.4	10.1	9.8	9.3	9.4	9.1	8.3	8.1	8.2	7.9	7.3	7.3	7.0	6.8	6.7	6.3	5.9	5.6	5.3	4.3	3.9	3.5	3.3	2.9	0.6
						19	11.2	10.8	10.4	10.3	9.9	9.6	9.1	8.8	8.8	8.3	8.1	8.0	7.9	7.5	7.3	7.0	6.7	6.4	5.9	5.7	5.2	4.7	4.0	3.8	3.3	3.1	0.5
15	17	20		30			11.4	11.3	10.6	10.5	10.2	9.7	9.6	9.3	9.1	8.7	8.4	8.2	7.7	7.5	7.3	7.2	7.0	6.6	6.3	6.2	5.7	5.1	4.6	3.9	3.6	3.2	0.6
	18	21					11.8	11.6	11.0	10.6	10.3	10.2	9.9	9.6	9.0	8.7	8.6	8.2	8.5	7.9	7.8	7.5	7.3	6.6	6.2	6.0	5.5	4.9	4.3	3.8	3.6	0.8
16		22	25				12.4	12.3	11.7	11.0	11.3	11.3	10.8	10.1	9.7	9.3	9.0	8.7	8.8	8.7	8.4	8.1	7.7	7.5	6.8	6.7	6.1	5.6	4.9	4.3	4.1	0.9
			26				12.8	12.4	11.9	11.7	11.5	11.3	11.0	10.4	10.2	9.7	9.4	9.1	9.2	8.7	8.4	8.1	7.9	7.3	7.5	6.9	6.3	5.7	5.3	4.8	4.3	0.9
							12.9	12.8	12.3	11.9	11.6	11.2	11.2	10.9	10.5	10.4	10.1	9.7	9.4	9.1	8.8	8.4	8.6	8.2	7.9	7.5	7.3	7.0	6.3	5.7	5.4	4.7	4.3	1.1
	22						13.2	13.0	12.8	12.3	12.0	11.6	11.2	11.2	10.5	10.5	10.1	10.0	9.6	9.4	9.0	8.8	8.6	8.2	7.7	7.5	7.2	7.0	6.1	5.4	5.6	5.1	4.2	1.1
							13.4	13.0	12.8	12.4	12.2	11.8	11.6	11.4	10.8	10.6	10.4	10.0	10.0	9.4	9.1	8.7	8.6	8.3	7.9	7.6	7.4	6.3	5.8	5.6	5.2	4.6	4.3	1.2
17	20	23					13.6	13.2	12.6	12.6	12.3	11.8	11.8	11.3	11.2	10.6	10.1	10.5	9.9	9.6	9.3	9.0	8.8	8.4	8.3	7.8	7.7	7.0	6.3	6.0	5.2	5.0	4.6	1.2
			22				13.9	13.5	13.0	13.0	12.6	12.1	12.0	11.3	11.4	10.9	10.6	10.1	9.8	10.0	9.8	9.5	9.2	8.8	8.4	8.1	7.9	7.3	6.8	6.0	5.3	5.1	5.1	1.2
18	21	24					14.0	13.3	13.3	13.2	12.7	12.4	12.0	11.7	11.5	11.4	10.7	10.7	10.2	10.0	9.9	9.5	9.3	8.7	8.5	8.2	8.0	7.5	6.9	6.4	5.6	5.1	5.1	1.4
			23				14.2	13.9	13.5	13.2	12.8	12.6	12.4	11.7	11.5	11.5	11.2	10.7	10.5	10.3	9.9	9.7	9.3	9.4	9.0	8.3	7.9	7.5	7.1	6.6	6.0	5.6	5.5	1.4
							14.2	14.1	13.7	13.2	12.8	12.8	12.7	12.1	11.8	11.5	11.2	11.0	10.8	10.2	10.0	9.7	9.4	9.2	8.9	8.3	8.3	7.4	6.9	6.2	5.8	5.5	5.4	1.4
19		25					14.7	14.1	14.0	13.4	13.1	13.0	12.8	12.3	11.8	11.6	11.3	11.0	11.0	10.3	10.2	10.1	9.9	9.5	9.2	8.5	8.1	7.4	6.8	6.4	6.2	5.6	6.0	1.6
			29				14.7	14.2	14.2	13.6	13.5	13.4	12.9	12.5	12.0	11.8	11.7	11.3	10.9	10.5	10.9	10.1	9.9	9.5	9.2	8.9	8.5	8.1	7.5	7.0	6.8	6.1	6.0	1.6
	21		30				15.1	14.7	14.3	13.7	13.7	13.4	13.2	12.9	12.2	12.1	11.6	11.0	11.6	11.2	10.9	10.6	10.4	10.0	9.7	9.4	9.2	8.0	7.5	7.0	6.7	6.3	6.0	1.8
							15.1	14.8	14.6	14.4	13.9	13.7	13.4	13.1	12.8	12.4	12.1	11.7	11.9	11.7	11.3	11.0	10.8	10.3	9.8	9.7	9.4	9.1	8.6	8.1	7.3	6.7	6.4	1.8

The Attack/Defense Matrix Cont.

To Hit Modifiers/# of Swords per Figure / Defender's Shields Per Figure

+5	+4	+3	+2	+1	0	-1	0*	1	2	3	4	5	6	7	8	9	10	11	12	13	14	15	16	17	18	19	20	22	24	26	28	30	50**
	22						15.2	14.9	14.7	14.5	14.1	13.7	13.3	12.9	12.7	12.7	12.4	12.2	11.7	11.5	11.0	10.9	10.3	10.0	9.7	9.8	9.5	8.7	8.1	7.4	7.3	6.5	2.2
		26					15.4	15.2	14.8	14.9	14.4	14.1	13.6	13.2	13.3	12.9	12.5	12.3	11.8	11.5	11.5	10.9	10.8	10.3	9.9	10.0	9.5	9.0	8.5	7.5	7.2	6.9	2.2
20							15.6	15.7	15.3	15.1	14.7	14.5	14.0	13.8	13.4	13.1	13.0	12.7	12.4	11.9	11.6	11.4	11.1	10.8	10.7	10.2	9.8	9.5	8.8	8.1	7.7	7.1	2.5
	23	27					15.9	15.7	15.4	15.3	15.0	14.5	14.5	14.0	13.9	13.4	13.2	12.7	12.3	12.2	12.2	11.6	11.1	11.0	10.8	10.5	10.0	9.5	8.9	8.4	7.7	7.1	2.5
	24	28					16.2	16.2	16.1	15.7	15.5	15.3	15.0	14.5	14.2	13.9	13.6	13.4	12.9	12.9	12.5	12.1	11.9	11.6	11.2	11.0	10.6	10.3	9.4	9.1	8.3	7.8	3.0
		29					16.6	16.8	16.9	16.4	16.2	15.9	15.6	15.2	14.9	14.6	14.4	14.1	13.9	13.3	13.2	12.7	12.4	12.1	11.7	11.4	11.4	10.6	10.1	9.6	9.1	8.6	3.4
22	25						17.3	17.2	16.9	16.6	16.5	16.1	15.8	15.5	15.1	14.6	14.5	14.1	13.9	13.5	13.2	13.1	13.0	12.3	12.2	11.7	11.5	10.9	10.2	9.8	9.2	8.6	3.6
		30					17.5	17.6	17.2	17.2	16.6	16.7	16.2	15.6	15.7	15.2	15.0	14.5	14.5	14.1	13.6	13.4	13.1	12.9	12.4	12.1	11.7	11.4	10.8	10.1	9.3	8.7	3.8
	26						17.9	17.6	17.5	17.3	16.9	16.5	16.5	16.1	16.0	15.6	15.3	15.2	14.4	14.3	14.2	13.7	13.1	13.2	12.8	12.4	12.1	11.4	10.7	10.4	9.9	9.2	4.0
23							18.1	18.2	17.8	18.1	17.7	17.4	16.5	16.2	15.9	15.6	15.9	14.9	14.8	15.0	14.6	13.6	13.6	13.0	13.0	12.7	12.4	12.0	11.1	10.5	9.9	9.5	3.8
	27						18.3	18.7	18.3	18.1	17.7	17.5	17.1	16.8	16.7	16.3	15.9	15.5	15.3	15.0	14.8	14.4	14.1	13.8	13.7	13.5	12.9	12.5	11.6	10.8	10.5	9.5	3.8
24							18.6	18.7	18.6	18.2	17.9	18.0	17.6	17.0	16.8	16.5	16.2	15.9	15.4	15.2	15.1	14.4	14.3	14.2	13.8	13.3	13.2	12.7	12.2	11.3	10.7	10.1	4.6
	28						19.2	19.2	19.1	18.6	18.2	18.0	17.6	17.6	17.2	16.9	16.5	16.1	15.9	15.6	15.5	15.1	14.7	14.7	14.2	13.9	13.6	12.9	12.3	12.0	11.3	10.3	5.0
25							19.8	19.4	19.3	19.3	18.9	18.5	18.2	17.8	17.5	17.2	16.9	16.5	16.2	16.1	15.8	15.4	15.0	14.7	14.6	14.3	14.1	13.5	12.9	12.1	11.6	10.9	5.3
	29						20.0	19.9	19.7	19.5	19.0	18.9	18.6	18.2	17.9	17.7	17.3	16.5	16.7	16.4	16.0	15.7	15.5	15.2	15.0	14.7	14.5	14.1	13.5	12.9	12.5	11.9	10.9	5.9
26							20.4	19.9	20.1	19.8	19.7	19.4	18.9	18.7	18.2	17.7	17.3	17.1	16.7	16.8	16.5	16.0	16.0	15.5	15.5	15.0	14.7	14.5	13.9	13.1	12.5	11.9	10.9	5.9
	30						20.8	20.4	20.4	19.8	19.8	19.6	19.0	18.9	18.4	18.1	18.1	17.6	17.2	16.8	16.8	16.6	16.0	15.6	15.5	15.5	14.9	14.7	14.2	13.7	12.8	12.7	11.9	6.2
27							21.1	20.6	20.1	19.8	19.8	19.6	19.0	18.9	18.4	18.1	18.1	17.6	17.2	16.8	16.8	16.6	16.0	15.6	15.5	15.5	14.9	14.5	13.7	13.0	12.8	12.7	11.9	6.3
28							21.5	21.2	20.9	20.6	20.1	20.1	19.6	19.3	19.0	18.9	18.6	18.2	17.8	17.7	17.2	16.9	16.8	16.6	16.1	15.6	15.4	15.0	14.3	13.9	13.2	12.5	6.8
29							22.1	21.9	21.8	21.5	20.9	20.8	20.7	20.1	19.7	19.8	19.3	18.8	18.9	18.4	18.1	17.7	17.5	17.4	16.7	16.5	16.5	15.6	15.0	14.6	14.0	13.4	7.5
							23.4	22.6	22.5	22.2	21.8	21.7	21.4	21.0	20.7	20.6	20.4	19.5	19.4	19.3	18.5	18.7	18.5	18.1	18.1	17.4	17.0	16.4	16.1	15.2	14.7	13.9	8.5
30							23.7	23.7	23.3	23.2	22.8	22.5	22.1	21.7	21.7	21.4	20.6	20.5	20.3	20.0	19.7	19.5	19.3	18.7	18.4	18.2	17.8	17.5	16.7	16.1	15.7	15.2	9.1

* = The value here is the attacking figure's raw hits.

** = When a unit has a certain type of immunity (e.g., weapon's immunity), it really has 50 shields versus that type of attack.

The average penetrating damage would be 9.6, but the first elven lord only has four hearts. This leaves an average of 5.6 damage to attack the shields of the second elven lord. Okay, that 5.6 is then found on the eighth (0 shield) column (next to the 28 strength on the -1 to hit column) and cross-referenced against the elven lord's eight shields again. This results in 3.3 average hits, which the second elven lord can absorb. Therefore, after that attack, two or three elven lord figures, on average will remain standing in that unit.

Blur

The effect of the Sorcery spell Blur can be accounted for by finding the appropriate at-

tack strength and consulting the eighth (0 shield) column first to obtain average raw hits. Reduce this value by 10 percent (for the effect of Blur). Go up the column until you located the new, reduced number of average raw hits in the eighth (0 shield) column, and use that row versus the defending unit's shields column to arrive a the correct penetrating damage.

Life-Stealing Attacks

Did you know that it is much more beneficial to conduct life-stealing attacks against units with a lower resistance value? Table F.2 explains why.

Table F.2 Life Stealing Attack Damage

	Final Resistance Value of Target Unit*								
	-8	-7	-6	-5	-4	-3	-2	-1	0
Damage Range**	9-18	8-17	7-16	6-15	5-14	4-13	3-12	2-11	1-10
Avg. Damage**	13.5	12.5	11.5	10.5	9.5	8.5	7.5	6.5	5.5

	Final Resistance Value of Target Unit*									
	+1	+2	+3	+4	+5	+6	+7	+8	+9	+10
Damage Range**	0-9	0-8	0-7	0-6	0-5	0-4	0-3	0-2	0-1	0
Avg. Damage**	4.5	3.6	2.8	2.1	1.5	1.0	0.6	0.3	0.1	0

* = The Final Resistance Value is determined after applying all resistance modifiers to target, including any life-stealing attack modifiers.

** = Damage Range and Average Damage were calculated assuming the target unit can absorb the maximum possible damage which that resistance level could sustain. If the target unit has fewer hearts than the maximum that can be stolen, lower the Average Damage according to the following table:

Max Damage Reduction Amount									
1	2	3	4	5	6	7	8	9	10

Avg. Damage Reduction Amount	.1	.3	.6	1.0	1.5	2.1	2.8	3.6	4.5	5.5

The conclusion to draw here is that you should target your units with life-stealing ability (death knights, wraiths, and demon lords) against units with the lowest resistance first. This will reap them the fastest, largest reward from these attacks and leave them stronger when they must face other enemy units with higher resistance values.

Dispelling in Combat

Table G.1 is a quick reference for when you throw a dispel during combat. Often, in the heat of battle, it is good to know what percent chance you'll have of removing an enemy's Wrack or Call Lightning spell. These numbers are also handy when you want to place a strong Counter Magic spell over the battlefield.

Table G.1 *Dispel Chances in Combat*

Spell Strength	Amount of Mana Spent to Dispel														
	10	15	20	25	30	35	40	45	**50***	60	70	80	90	100	120
80	11.1	15.8	20.0	23.8	27.3	30.4	33.3	36.0	**38.5**	42.9	46.7	50.0	52.9	55.6	60.0
75	11.8	16.7	21.1	25.0	28.6	31.8	34.8	37.5	**40.0**	44.4	48.3	51.6	54.5	57.1	61.5
70	12.5	17.6	22.2	26.3	30.0	33.3	36.4	39.1	**41.7**	46.2	50.0	53.3	56.3	58.8	63.2
65	13.3	18.8	23.5	27.8	31.6	35.0	38.1	40.9	**43.5**	48.0	51.9	55.2	58.1	60.6	64.9
60	14.3	20.0	25.0	29.4	33.3	36.8	40.0	42.9	**45.5**	50.0	53.8	57.1	60.0	62.5	66.7
55	15.4	21.4	26.7	31.3	35.3	38.9	42.1	45.0	**47.6**	52.2	56.0	59.3	62.1	64.5	68.6
50	16.7	23.1	28.6	33.3	37.5	41.2	44.4	47.4	**50.0**	54.5	58.3	61.5	64.3	66.7	70.6
45	18.2	25.0	30.8	35.7	40.0	43.8	47.1	50.0	**52.6**	57.1	60.9	64.0	66.7	69.0	72.7
40	20.0	27.3	33.3	38.5	42.9	46.7	50.0	52.9	**55.6**	60.0	63.6	66.7	69.2	71.4	75.0
35	22.2	30.0	36.4	41.7	46.2	50.0	53.3	56.3	**58.8**	63.2	66.7	69.6	72.0	74.1	77.4
30	25.0	33.3	40.0	45.5	50.0	53.8	57.1	60.0	**62.5**	66.7	70.0	72.7	75.0	76.9	80.0
25	28.6	37.5	44.4	50.0	54.5	58.3	61.5	64.3	**66.7**	70.6	73.7	76.2	78.3	80.0	82.8
20	33.3	42.9	50.0	55.6	60.0	63.6	66.7	69.2	**71.4**	75.0	77.8	80.0	81.8	83.3	85.7
15	40.0	50.0	57.1	62.5	66.7	70.0	72.7	75.0	**76.9**	80.0	82.4	84.2	85.7	87.0	88.9
10	50.0	60.0	66.7	71.4	75.0	77.8	80.0	81.8	**83.3**	85.7	87.5	88.9	90.0	90.9	92.3

\# Percent chance of successfully dispelling.

* The 50 strength dispel column is highlighted because it represents the strength of the dispel that operates at nodes. During combat, if you cast spells of a different color than the node, and if you don't have the skill Node Mastery, this column shows you the chance that your spell *will* fizzle.

Babbage's
America's Software Headquarters
208-Glenbrook Square Mall
Space B-7
4201 Coldwater Road
Fort Wayne, Indiana 46805
(219)482-7272

04-23-1996 20:57 208-1960424-012 TSL

870659 PCHINT   1 @ 9.99 ea   9.99
Master of Magic: Off Strat Gde

870635 PCHINT   1 @ 13.99 ea   13.99
X-Com UFO Defense: Off Strat

    Merchandise $ 23.98
    Sales Tax @ 5% $ 1.20
    Total $ 25.18

Payments
    MasterCard $ 25.18

I agree to pay the above total amount
according to the card issuer agreement.

    Thank You for Shopping at Babbage's
        We Appreciate Your Business

Index

Index